CHALLENGE AND CONFORMITY

THE LITTMAN LIBRARY OF
JEWISH CIVILIZATION

Dedicated to the memory of
LOUIS THOMAS SIDNEY LITTMAN
*who founded the Littman Library for the love of God
and as an act of charity in memory of his father*
JOSEPH AARON LITTMAN
and to the memory of
ROBERT JOSEPH LITTMAN
who continued what his father Louis had begun
יהא זכרם ברוך

'*Get wisdom, get understanding:
Forsake her not and she shall preserve thee*'
PROV. 4:5

*The Littman Library of Jewish Civilization is a registered UK charity
Registered charity no.* 1000784

CHALLENGE AND CONFORMITY

*

The Religious Lives of Orthodox Jewish Women

*

LINDSEY TAYLOR-GUTHARTZ

London
The Littman Library of Jewish Civilization
in association with Liverpool University Press
2021

The Littman Library of Jewish Civilization
Registered office: 4th floor, 7–10 Chandos Street, London WIG 9DQ

in association with Liverpool University Press
4 Cambridge Street, Liverpool L69 7ZU, UK
www.liverpooluniversitypress.co.uk/littman

Managing Editor: Connie Webber

Distributed in North America by
Oxford University Press Inc., 198 Madison Avenue
New York, NY 10016, USA

Catalogue records for this book are available from the
British Library and the Library of Congress

ISBN 978–1–786941–71–8

Publishing co-ordinator: Janet Moth
Copy-editing: Agi Erdos
Proof-reading: Beth Dufour
Index: Sarah Ereira
Production, design and typesetting by
Pete Russell, Faringdon, Oxon.

Printed and bound in Great Britain by
TJ Books Ltd., Padstow, Cornwall

Great Nature clothes the soul, which is but thin,
With fleshly garments, which the Fates do spin;
And when these garments are grown old and bare,
With sickness torn, Death takes them off with care,
And folds them up in peace and quiet rest,
And lays them safe within an earthly chest:
Then scours them well and makes them sweet and clean,
Fit for the soul to wear those clothes again.

MARGARET CAVENDISH
Duchess of Newcastle, 1653

ACKNOWLEDGEMENTS

M Y HEARTFELT THANKS go to everyone who helped me, first and fore-most the supervisors of my Ph.D. thesis, Professor Ada Rapoport-Albert and Dr Allen Abramson. I would also like to express my profound gratitude to the Trustees of London School of Jewish Studies for the financial assistance that enabled me to obtain my Ph.D., the research for which served as the basis for this book. My friends and colleagues at the Littman Library have given me constant support and invaluable assistance in bringing the book to publication, including a salutary reminder of the view from the other side of the copy-editor's pen, and I am particularly grateful to Connie Webber, Janet Moth, and Agi Erdos for their superb work.

I should also like to record my thanks to all the people who supported me in different ways: Sally Berkovic, for accompanying me to *berakhah* parties. Jo Bruce, for information on Edgware Megillah readings. Warren Burstein, for sending material on *segulot* from Israel. Professor Joe Cain, for advice on interviewing. Dr Miri Freud-Kandel, for references, advice, and support. Ian Gamse, for assistance with rabbinic sources and theological issues. Professor Jonathan Gershuny, for discussing methodology. Dr Julian Gilbey, for help with questionnaire spreadsheets and computer issues. Norman Guthartz, for support, patience, and listening. Rachel Guthartz, for support, discussion, and technical help. Sarah Guthartz, for support and discussion, and the book's title. Aviva Kaufman, for information on Megillah readings. The late and sadly missed Maureen Kendler, for discussion and support. Sharon Lee, for information on Stanmore Women's Tefillah Group, and the loan of her archive. Dr Naftali Loewenthal, for information on Habad, and help in finding interviewees. Miriam Lorie, for information on partnership *minyanim*. Dr Raphael Mankin, for advice and comments. Harry Marin, for editorial assistance. Pauline New-man, for material on Stanmore Women's Tefillah Group, and the loan of archive material. Jaq Nicholls, for the perfect artwork for the book's cover. Laurie and Gaby Scher, for information on partnership *minyanim*. Dr Lynne Scholefield, for reading drafts and giving feedback. Dr Jeremy Schonfield, for reading drafts and giving feedback. Dr Lindsay Simmonds, for references, loan of books, and discussion. Rabbi Gideon Sylvester, for information on Radlett Megillah readings. Connie Webber, for contacts and reading early drafts. Professor Jonathan Webber, for discussion of first ideas. Dr Debbie Weisman, for information on the origins of women's *tefilah* groups in Israel. Dr Beruriah Wiegand, for help with Yiddish transliteration. Brigit Wilmers and David Chisholm, for hosting me while writing. Catherine Wilmers and Graham Kingsley, for hosting me while writing. Dr Abigail Wood, for reading drafts and giving sage advice. Dr Tamra Wright, for support and advice. Rabbi Dr Raphael Zarum, for suggesting I undertake a Ph.D., and for assistance with financing my studies. Erla Zimmels, for help in finding books; and to all the interviewees, for their time and willingness to talk to me.

CONTENTS

❁

LIST OF TABLES

NOTE ON TRANSLITERATION

❋

THE TRANSLITERATION of Hebrew in this book reflects consideration of the type of book it is, in terms of its content, purpose, and readership. The system adopted therefore reflects a broad approach to transcription, rather than the narrower approaches found in the *Encyclopaedia Judaica* or other systems developed for text-based or linguistic studies. The aim has been to reflect the pronunciation prescribed for modern Hebrew, rather than the spelling or Hebrew word structure, and to do so using conventions that are generally familiar to the English-speaking reader.

In accordance with this approach, no attempt is made to indicate the distinctions between *alef* and *ayin*, *tet* and *taf*, *kaf* and *kuf*, *sin* and *samekh*, since these are not relevant to pronunciation; likewise, the *dagesh* is not indicated except where it affects pronunciation. Following the principle of using conventions familiar to the majority of readers, however, transcriptions that are well established have been retained even when they are not fully consistent with the transliteration system adopted. On similar grounds, the *tsadi* is rendered by 'tz' in such familiar words as barmitzvah. Likewise, the distinction between *het* and *khaf* has been retained, using *h* for the former and *kh* for the latter; the associated forms are generally familiar to readers, even if the distinction is not actually borne out in pronunciation, and for the same reason the final *heh* is indicated too. As in Hebrew, no capital letters are used, except that an initial capital has been retained in transliterating titles of published works (for example, *Shulḥan arukh*).

Since no distinction is made between *alef* and *ayin*, they are indicated by an apostrophe only in intervocalic positions where a failure to do so could lead an English-speaking reader to pronounce the vowel cluster as a diphthong—as, for example, in *ha'ir*—or otherwise mispronounce the word.

The *sheva na* is indicated by an *e*—*perikat ol*, *reshut*—except, again, when established convention dictates otherwise.

The *yod* is represented by *i* when it occurs as a vowel (*bereshit*), by *y* when it occurs as a consonant (*yesodot*), and by *yi* when it occurs as both (*yisra'el*).

Names have generally been left in their familiar forms, even when this is inconsistent with the overall system.

INTRODUCTION

❁

THIS BOOK had its genesis in the sense of perplexity I felt in 1997 upon returning to the UK from seventeen years in Jerusalem to live in London, where I encountered the local Jewish community for the first time. Coming from a Jewishly non-observant family and growing up in Cornwall, which in the 1970s had no organized Jewish community and very few Jews, my principal experience of and socialization into Jewish life had been at university in Cambridge, where I was part of a small and atypical Jewish community composed largely of students and resident academics. When I knew it, in 1977–80, it had no rabbi and its members prided themselves on their Jewish knowledge, self-sufficiency, and independence.

So London Jewish life in 1997 challenged my assumptions. The conservative Anglo-Jewish Orthodox community there, in which most women play traditional roles and seem not to want to increase their participation in public religious contexts, stood in marked contrast to the Kehilat Yedidya community I came from in Jerusalem, which in the 1980s was one of the first synagogues to champion women's ritual participation within the limits of halakhah (Jewish law), and the spiritual home of several outstanding women teachers and leaders. I gradually realized that trends in Israel, as also in the United States, typically take many years to filter into the Anglo-Jewish world, and that change is often initiated or aided by individuals who have spent significant periods of time in the Israeli or American communities.

While Jewish anthropological research has tended to concentrate on these two communities—understandably, since it has been estimated that together they account for approximately 84% of the world's Jews—the British Jewish community is nevertheless the fifth largest in the world,[1] and looking at change and how it takes place in the British context can provide an informative and fascinating comparison and contrast to the two 'mega-communities' of modern Jews, particularly in issues involving women. In many respects the British Jewish community resembles those of smaller American cities outside the New York area, being slow to accept change and very concerned with survival. However, Jewish denominational affiliation differs sharply in the two countries: in Britain, Orthodoxy—even if of a nominal

---

[1] DellaPergola, 'World Jewish Population, 2016'. The estimated Jewish population of Britain stood at 290,000 in 2016. France (460,000 Jews) and Canada (388,000 Jews) constitute the third and fourth largest communities (ibid.).

kind—is still the default position of the majority of synagogue-affiliated Jews (69%), while in America Orthodox Jews are very much in the minority (10%).[2] British Orthodoxy—ranging from the traditionalist, minimally practising majority to a growing strictly Orthodox, or haredi, minority—differs considerably from American Orthodoxy, whose members tend to be more observant.[3] Britain also provides a unique example of a Jewish community that has very strong ties to both Israeli and American Jewish cultures, since, on the one hand, it shares a language with the Jews of the United States, and, on the other, it is close to Israel in both geographical and emotional terms.[4] Though there have been some outstanding anthropological studies of Jewish women in both America and Israel, little research of this sort has yet been undertaken in Britain. This book attempts to make a contribution to the understanding of current trends among Orthodox Jewish women worldwide by focusing on women in the unique context of British Jewry.

For a few years in the early 2000s I tried, with my husband, to introduce in London some of the practices we had followed in Jerusalem, such as prayer services that enlarged women's roles; but though these would attract fifty or so people, they remained very marginal and did not have much impact. In addition, they had to be conducted 'underground', since participants were fearful of condemnation by local rabbis. However, many women I met were not only uninterested in greater ritual and study participation but were actively hostile to the idea. As I learnt about similar attempts in the past, which had also lacked widespread support, I became aware of a wide range of attitudes, goals, and frustrations among Orthodox Jewish women. Then, in

---

[2] Mashiah and Boyd, *Synagogue Membership in the United Kingdom in 2016*; Pew Research Center, *A Portrait of Jewish Americans*.

[3] This terminology is thoroughly explored in Ch. 2, but a brief definition of these subtypes of Orthodoxy, as used in this study, may be given here. I have used the term 'traditionalist' to describe the ethnic and emotional—rather than religious or ideological—Orthodox identity that is prevalent among Britain's Orthodox Jews; 'Modern Orthodox' has been reserved for a more self-consciously religious and ideological identification with Orthodoxy that accepts many Western values; and 'haredi', or 'strictly Orthodox', refers to hasidic and 'Lithuanian' or 'yeshivish' groups, who maintain varying degrees of separateness from modern Western culture.

[4] A somewhat higher percentage of British Jews emigrate to Israel than do American Jews: 1.6% of the British Jewish community, compared to 0.4% of the American Jewish community in 2001–10 (Staetsky, Sheps, and Boyd, *Immigration*, 6), and 95% of British Jews surveyed in 2010 had visited Israel (Graham and Boyd, *Committed, Concerned, and Conciliatory*, 18), as opposed to 43% of American Jews surveyed in 2013 (Pew Reseach Center, *A Portrait of Jewish Americans*). In terms of emotional attachment, 93% of British Jews stated in a 2015 survey that Israel was important or central to their Jewish identity, while only 69% of American Jews in a 2013 survey felt 'very attached' or 'somewhat attached' to Israel; see Pew Research Center, *A Portrait of Jewish Americans*, and Miller, Harris, and Shindler, *The Attitudes of British Jews*, 15.

2002, an informal talk on 'Jewish superstitions'[5] alerted me to a variety of individual, generally family- or home-based, practices that were very much part of women's religious lives, even though they were often described by both women and men as 'superstitions'. Most of these were unfamiliar to me, though many were recognized, and also practised, by members of the all-female audience. They included practices related to marriage, childbirth, and death, as well as protective rituals in everyday life. When I came to conduct formal interviews for this study, many more activities were mentioned. The women I interviewed told me about the Rosh Hodesh movement and women's *tefilah* groups, and their part in these groups; they explained about *berakhah* parties and partnership *minyanim*, which have sprung up in the last two decades and are still not widely known, raising the question of how change and innovation take place in a conservative community, and what factors determine the acceptance or rejection of a new practice.[6] I participated in all these activities and more as I explored how they form part of women's religious identity and constitute an area in which Jewish women can exercise agency, acting independently and making their own choices.

The Theoretical Background

In the 1980s and 1990s critiques of anthropological and ethnographic methods highlighted the problematic nature of much classic fieldwork and writing, including the representation of societies as static, suppression of the multiple voices within social arenas, and the exoticization of attitudes to the 'other' being studied.[7] Concerns were also raised about the absence of any representation of the experience of fieldwork, and the silence surrounding the relationship between anthropologists and the people they studied, including its political and emotional aspects and the effect these had on the research itself, as summed up elegantly by the novelist Ursula Le Guin:

[5] The talk, by Yehudit Weil, was given at the London School of Jewish Studies in the framework of the Susi Bradfield Women Educators Fellowships.

[6] The Rosh Hodesh (New Moon) movement of the 1970s and 1980s, beginning in the USA, sought to empower women, partly by reviving traditional celebration of the New Moon by women; women's *tefilah* (prayer) groups, first developed in the 1970s in the USA, are women-only services; *berakhah* (blessing) parties developed in Israel in the 2000s as a way for women to access spiritual and physical benefits by reciting liturgical blessings; and partnership *minyanim* (prayer quorums) are a more egalitarian form of service, which originated in Israel in 2002. All are discussed in detail in Ch. 4.

[7] See e.g. Clifford and Marcus (eds.), *Writing Culture*; Ortner, 'Ethnography Among the Newark'; Okely and Callaway (eds.), *Anthropology and Autobiography*.

The idea that objective observation can be performed only by an observer totally free of subjectivity involves an ideal of inhuman purity which we now recognize as being, fortunately, unattainable. But the dilemma of the subjective practitioner of objectivity persists, and presents itself to anthropologists in its most acute and painful form: the relationship between observer and observed when both of them are human.[8]

Another aspect of the rethinking of fieldwork exposes the split between the anthropologist's 'work' and 'life', with the former usually constituting the accepted subject matter of anthropological texts. A recent anthropological exploration of the work–life boundary asks: 'Must we accept the dichotomy of "life" and "work" that constitutes, yet also confounds, the experience of fieldwork? [This split is where] public knowledge and private knowledge have been ripped apart.'[9]

The nature of my research, exploring the religious lives of women in my own community, necessitated a consideration of my relationship with the women among whom I live, the balance between life and work, and the nature of 'objectivity' and scientific rigour. It has been noted that the academic ideal of scientific rigour has two aspects: 'the claim to disinterested, neutral, objective social inquiry', which is illusory at best and misleading at worst, and 'methodological propriety: careful adherence to established rules for collecting and interpreting research data', which is essential.[10] Since I am part of the community that I am studying I did not have the option of regarding its women as 'others' whom I could investigate and then 'write up' at a safe distance; my social network and my field of study overlapped. Nor did I feel disinterested or neutral. My study of women's religious lives in the Anglo-Jewish Orthodox community was largely prompted by a desire to understand why restrictions on their participation in public worship are so embedded and often unquestioned and what Jewish women feel and do about them, and by my own dissatisfaction at the limited religious options for women in this community.

Much has been written on the advantages and disadvantages of studying one's own society,[11] with 'native' anthropologists agonizing over the difficulties of preserving distance from one's subjects and avoiding emotional entanglement. In contrast, my own location simultaneously within and yet,

---

[8] Le Guin, 'Indian Uncles', 12. [9] Goslinga and Frank, 'In the Shadows', p. xii.
[10] Hale, 'In Praise of "Reckless Minds"', 116.
[11] See Ohnuki-Tierney, '"Native" Anthropologists'; Soon Kim, 'Can an Anthropologist Go Home Again?' The latter notes: 'Perhaps our anthropological community has too much polarized the role of insider (native) versus outsider (non-native). I believe one can complement the weakness of being an insider or an outsider through awareness of the shortcomings of each vantage point and through conscientious effort' (p. 945).

as a relative newcomer, on the margins of the Jewish community of north-west London proved essential to my research, giving me both the detail and the understanding available to an 'insider' and the critical distance of an 'outsider'. One researcher recorded her fears over the 'loss of distance' between herself and her subjects in a small company, who became her work colleagues, but came to realize that it is 'a commitment to analysis that creates the sense of distance and not the degree of shared knowledge between a researcher and the subjects of her research'—a formulation that I have found useful.[12] In my case, the direction of travel was the exact opposite: instead of gradually becoming incorporated into the studied group, I found that the role of researcher sharpened my sense of being a critical outsider. In addition, as an Orthodox Jew I had a personal 'baseline' of religious experience and practice to which other women's experiences could be compared. A disadvantage of being a 'native' researcher was the fact that I teach in the community, and my advocacy of women's participation in religious life was thus already known. It was therefore important to assure the women I interviewed that my role was research, not the promotion of my own opinions. Some women nevertheless hesitated; conversely, in some interviews women with whom I had participated in *tefilah* groups or Megillah readings[13] would treat me as an ally, expressing their frustrations with restrictions on women's religious opportunities, and voicing pointed criticism of the religious authorities (particularly before the recording machine was switched on and after it was switched off).

In order to explore women's religious lives more fully I combined a number of methodological approaches to illuminate different aspects of their experience and to enable their voices, and their understanding of that experience, to be heard. Five principal techniques were used to gather information, which in practice often intersected and contributed to each other. The bedrock was classic participant observation, supported by semi-structured interviews, a survey of customs, and analysis of a community email list and of the local Jewish press.

In addition to involvement in the activities usually defined as characteristic of women's Jewish lives, such as synagogue attendance, preparation for and participation in festivals, and so on, I had actively participated in women's *tefilah* groups and Megillah readings, both in Israel and in London, for many years before starting to research them in a formal context. I encountered no barriers to attending the recently inaugurated *berakhah* parties, being welcomed

---

[12] Knox, 'Imitative Participation and the Politics of "Joining In"', 6.

[13] The Megillah (the biblical book of Esther) is read twice on the festival of Purim; all-women readings are a recent innovation, discussed at greater length in Ch. 4.

as a new participant. In most situations I was not regarded as an outsider; even in the exceptions (as when I interviewed two hasidic women), my degree of distance was less than and different from that which would have been experienced by a non-Jewish researcher. Women generally felt comfortable talking to me and answering questions in their own terms, with none of the 'translated expressions' used when speaking to non-Jews.[14] Of course not all the activities and practices I observed or took part in during my research reflected my own beliefs, and at certain times I was more of an 'outsider' than at others. However, my conviction that Judaism is not a monolithic faith itself entails a commitment to understand the full range of Jewish women's religious lives and the factors that shape them, and I have tried throughout to represent these without personal bias.[15]

My own participation in Jewish communal life also led to increased opportunities for finding women to interview, my second research tool. I conducted interviews with thirty-seven individuals, mostly women; twenty-four of these interviews were recorded, most of the others were over the telephone or by means of Skype.[16] Most interviewees have been given pseudonyms. In keeping with the qualitative nature of my research, I used a combination of purposive sampling strategies.[17] Interviews would also sometimes make me aware of events that I could attend, or open up possibilities of new contacts and interviewees. Most of my interviewees also participated in the survey of women's customs that I conducted (see Chapter 6), my third source of information.

My fourth channel was EdgwareK,[18] a community email list that serves the

---

[14] Anglo-Jews typically modify their speech when talking to non-Jews, substituting 'synagogue' for 'shul', 'Passover' for Pesach, and so on, as well as clarifying or omitting details or names of prayers, festivals, rituals, and practices, and avoiding Yiddish words. An excellent account of the same phenomenon of 'Orthodox style-shifting' in America appears in Benor, *Becoming Frum*, 46–8; the author notes, 'In the Orthodox community, people change their language significantly depending on who they are speaking to' (p. 46).

[15] For an interesting reflection on the transformative and spiritual aspects of researching women's religious lives from a different, Christian, perspective, see Slee, 'Feminist Qualitative Research as Spiritual Practice'.

[16] I interviewed three male rabbis in order to explore their understanding of and views on women's religious roles and some women's practices, as well as a male co-founder of a partnership *minyan*. See the list of interviewees and full details of the type of interview in Appendix I.

[17] Patton, *Qualitative Research*, 230–46. I used a combination of maximum variation sampling and expert sampling. The interviews were semi-structured and based on a 'responsive interviewing' model; see Rubin and Rubin, *Qualitative Interviewing*, 30. I also benefited from the advice of Professor Joe Cain, at University College London's Department of Science and Technology Studies, to whom I am very grateful.

[18] Renamed 'EverywhereK' in 2014 to increase its appeal outside the north-west London

north-west London Orthodox Jewish community. Some of the posts proved very useful in locating women's religious events (such as the *berakhah* parties). It also provided information on most of the local lectures and classes designed specifically for women, giving me an insight into the type of religious education available to adult women in addition to that provided (in both all-female and mixed classes) at the London School of Jewish Studies, where I teach. Posts on the list often requested prayer or ritual actions on behalf of individuals who were ill or had been injured, and occasionally someone would post a 'new' *segulah*[19] with recommendations to use it, or would enquire whether anyone knew of a *segulah* for a particular purpose.[20]

The last main source of information was community newspapers, principally the *Jewish Chronicle* (founded in 1841) and the *Jewish Tribune* (founded in 1962). They provided a rich source of information about women's activities, roles, and struggles in the community. The foundation of and controversy over Stanmore Women's Tefillah Group, for instance, was amply documented in the pages of the *Jewish Chronicle* in 1992 and 1993. Articles and letters discussing two major reports on Jewish women in Britain—known as the Preston Report (1994) and the follow-up Women's Review (2009)[21]—and descriptions of and reactions to women's religious activities provided insight into a wide range of community attitudes. In contrast to the *Jewish Chronicle*, which reports events across the denominational spectrum, the *Jewish Tribune* caters to the haredi community, though it is read more widely, and reflects the attitudes of this sector of the British Jewish community to the roles played by women. Photographs of women never appear, as this

suburb of Edgware. It was founded in 2002 by Lawrence and Debbie Davidson as a local list for announcements and advertisements, but has since expanded nationwide. Its 17,000 members include both mainstream Orthodox and haredim, and evidence of affiliation to an Orthodox synagogue is required in order to join. A haredi rabbi, R. Zvi Lieberman, is consulted on the suitability of postings, and more radical or 'Modern' Orthodox activities, such as partnership *minyanim* or the annual cross-communal Limmud conference, are not accepted for posting (telephone conversation with Lawrence Davidson, December 2018).

[19] The Hebrew word *segulah* has a wide semantic range. The Alkalai dictionary defines it as 'treasure; characteristic, trait, property, quality, virtue, attribute; idiosyncrasy, peculiarity; remedy', but in popular usage, especially among Sephardim, it refers to a practice or action that gives access to a spiritual remedy or confers a blessing. See Ch. 6 for examples.

[20] For instance, the following request appeared on 23 Aug. 2012: 'Do you know where I can get hold of one of these necklaces that are a segulah during pregnancy to prevent miscarriage as my wife is pregnant?' This refers to the use of red stones or rubies to facilitate birth, enhance fertility, or prevent miscarriage, a practice also documented in my research questionnaire (see Appendix III). See Klein, *A Time To Be Born*, 33–4.

[21] See, respectively, Preston, Goodkin, and Citron, *Women in the Jewish Community* (1994); Preston et al., *Connection, Continuity and Community* (2009).

would be considered immodest, and women are generally mentioned only in contexts of philanthropy and education. Analysis of their portrayal in articles, letters, and the 'Women's Page' provided material embodying the 'official' or public ideal of Jewish women in this part of the Jewish community; advertisements and local news sections provided details of haredi women's religious events and activities.

A Brief Outline

Chapter 1 explores the problems of studying Orthodox Jewish women, in particular the 'double invisibility' they experience, first from the perspective of male Orthodox Jews, and secondly in the lack of knowledge about them in the non-Jewish world. Chapter 2 examines the historical and sociological context of Orthodox Jewish women in London, and applies concepts of community to analyse the religious geography of Orthodox Jews in Britain. Chapters 3 to 6 illustrate the results of my research, describing women's activities and how they understand them.

I divided these activities into four categories, arranged on two intersecting axes. The first pair was public or communal activity as opposed to private or domestic activity, which corresponds to the Jewish concept of the twin poles of synagogue and home. The second was 'official', communally sanctioned and culturally prescribed activity, shading into 'unofficial' activity, which tends not to form part of the public production of 'Jewishness' and 'Judaism', and may or may not be regarded with approval by rabbis and communal leaders. The categories are illustrated in Table 1, with examples of activities in each.

Chapter 3 examines the official communal sphere; Chapter 4 deals with unofficial communal activity; Chapter 5 covers official domestic practices;

Table 1 Categories of women's religious activities, with examples

	Public/communal	Private/domestic
Official	Attending synagogue	Lighting sabbath candles
	Joining a ladies' guild	Going to the *mikveh* (ritual bath)
	Batmitzvah	Keeping a kosher kitchen
Unofficial	*Berakhah* parties	Tying red thread on baby clothes
	Women's *tefilah* groups	Wearing an amulet
	Partnership *minyanim*	Not mending clothes while they are being worn

and Chapter 6 explores unofficial domestic customs. After documenting these activities I consider the variations within Orthodox women's practices and beliefs, and explore the way in which, through them, women find opportunities for self-expression and agency in a patriarchal context. Throughout this study the themes that reappear are the constraints imposed by a male-dominated authority system; the creative ways in which women both work around and reinforce those constraints; the range of world-views found among haredi, Orthodox, and traditionalist women; and the shared goals of women who seek to become better Jews, even if the methods they envisage as appropriate to this task vary widely. Chapter 7 presents the conclusions of my research and its wider implications for the study of Orthodox Jewish women.

STUDYING JEWISH WOMEN

A BOUT FORTY WOMEN are sitting at long, plastic-covered tables in the women's section of a Sephardi synagogue in north-west London. We are a varied lot: on my left is a Tunisian divorcee in her sixties who has confided that she isn't religious but likes being around religious people and hopes that the prayers this evening will help her find a new husband; on my right is a young haredi woman,[1] wearing a wig to cover her hair as prescribed by Jewish law for married women, who pronounces each blessing loudly, with great emphasis on each word. Some women are in their late teens, a few are in their sixties; there are two Nigerian converts, with elaborately tied headscarves. Some women are chatting or texting, while others are intent on following the slow recital of blessings over food, as one by one each woman picks up a piece of carrot or celery from the plates in front of her, recites the Hebrew blessing prescribed for vegetables, and bites into it while everyone else responds with a loud 'Amen!' Occasionally a woman prefaces her blessing with a list of names of people who are ill and who, she hopes, will benefit from the merit that she will earn by saying the blessing, and that others will acquire by responding to her words. Sitting at a separate table at the head of the room is a grey-haired rabbi, invited along as honorary leader of this women's ritual; he is busy alternately texting and studying a religious text—Torah study takes precedence over everything—until he is asked to recite a prayer for all the sick mentioned, once the women have finished their blessings. Amid the murmurings of 'Amen!' that break out at the end of his prayer, the Israeli organizer stands up. 'Ladies!', she announces. 'I have incredible news! As you know, we've been davening [praying] for our dear Sarah Rivkah for a long time, and she hasn't been eating, and I just wanted to share with you that yesterday she had her first meal for two weeks, and is much better! *Barukh hashem* [Blessed be God]!' As a chorus of delighted gasps and '*barukh hashem*'s breaks out,

---

[1] 'Haredi' (lit. 'trembling', i.e. before God), a term that has come to be widely used in Israel in recent years, is used here in preference to the somewhat clumsy and judgemental labels of 'ultra-Orthodox' or 'strictly Orthodox', which imply that other forms of Orthodoxy are less 'authentic' or 'strict'.

Menucha Mizrahi, a middle-aged woman in a blonde wig, leaps to her feet and shouts, 'I went to the Shotser Rebbe's *kever* [grave] last week and davened and lit two candles for her there!' A younger, Israeli, woman stands up and proclaims, 'I held a challah party[2] in her *zekhut* [i.e. to accrue merit for her] last week in my house!' The women exclaim and call out praise to God, topped by the organizer shouting: 'May we merit to see many more *yeshuot* [miraculous deliverances] from our *berakhot* [blessings]!'

A few months later and a mile away, about eighty women and a few dozen children, squashed into a classroom at the London School of Jewish Studies, have just finished listening to the Megillah, the book of Esther, chanted from a handwritten scroll by a series of women. It's the morning of Purim, the most exuberant and fun-filled festival in the Jewish calendar, and many of the women are wearing fancy dress, as are the children; most are also carrying a copy of the Megillah and a *grager*, a rattle swung at every mention of the villain Haman during the reading, in order to blot out his name. Two women are putting money in the bowl set out for donations to charity. This is one of the commandments linked to the festival, as is the giving of presents of food to acquaintances; friends hand me decoratively wrapped cardboard plates filled with homemade biscuits, luridly coloured sweets, and tangerines, and I rummage around in a bag to extract my own gifts. This is the tenth year the women's reading has been held; though in a standard service the entire book is read by a single man, we encourage as many women as possible to learn the special chant, and have ten readers, one per chapter. I have just been reading chapter 9, and like everyone else am still riding high on the atmosphere of excitement and achievement. As everyone slowly files out of the overheated room, talking and laughing, an elderly woman, perhaps in her eighties, wearing a turban-like headdress, approaches me and lays her hand on my arm. 'I just wanted to say that I didn't really want to come today—my daughter insisted, though I wasn't sure that I approved of women reading the Megillah. But now that I've heard it, I can't see how I would ever want to go back to sitting in the gallery and trying to make out what the men are doing down below! Hearing the story read by women—it's amazing! Of course it's all about Esther—but I would never have believed the difference women's voices would make! I was so moved by the reading!'

---

[2] Gatherings at which women make challah, the plaited bread traditionally eaten on the sabbath, focusing on the commandment to take off part of the dough after making a blessing; the separated portion was originally given to the priests but nowadays is burnt.

The Double Invisibility of Orthodox Jewish Women

The lively, noisy, and above all very new religious activities documented in these two vignettes undermine common depictions of the religious lives of Orthodox Jewish women as limited, passive, and restricted to the domestic sphere. As an observant Jewish woman, I am taken aback by the frequent depiction of Jewish women as voiceless, marginalized figures deprived by an unchallenged patriarchal system of any agency or expression. One such depiction comes from the pen of feminist scholar Rachel Elior:

the overseers of these [social] arrangements intimidated women through a system that would brand anyone who dissented from the patriarchal order, or even criticized it, as a rebel, a whore, a harlot, a traitor, or a deviant. In this way, there emerged a situation in which women (impure, silent, and ignorant by reason of being removed from sanctity and knowledge) were subservient to men (pure and learned, near to holiness and study, publicly vocal) in many areas, both external and internal. They were denied access to many sorts of knowledge, their entry into the study hall was forbidden, their entry into the synagogue was limited, and they were required to maintain complete silence in the public domain.[3]

In fact, many of the Orthodox women among whom I live, though often painfully aware of restrictions and limitations on their religious expression, are engaged in Jewish study and teaching, sometimes challenge their role in ritual, and are far from silent in the public domain. But the standard apologetic of Orthodox Judaism justifying women's exclusion from the public arena is just as misleading, portraying them as powerful, central figures in a domestically focused Judaism:

Throughout the ages, Jewish women have imbued spirituality into the Jewish home. As such, certain mitzvot are set aside especially for women because of their special connection to the home . . . the Torah released women from the obligations of certain time-bound mitzvot. This is not because of any difference in the level of sanctity between men and women. Rather, these exemptions allow a woman the ability to be totally devoted to her family without the constraints of having to fulfill such mitzvot at the correct time. Of course, whenever a woman does not face conflicting family obligations, she may fulfill these mitzvot and receive eternal reward. Whatever the case, she is fulfilling God's will, who knows that her spiritual growth is intertwined with her primary mission as the family cultivator.[4]

---

[3] Elior, 'Like Sophia and Marcelle and Lizzie', 17.

[4] Lev, 'Women and Mitzvot'. Mitzvot (commandments) are divided into positive and negative categories (enjoining or prohibiting an activity respectively), as well as those which must be performed at a set time ('time-bound') and those which have no associated time. Women are halakhically exempt from performing positive time-bound commandments, with some rather

Nor does this sketch correspond to the lives of many Orthodox women I know: it ignores those who are single, widowed, divorced, who have no children or whose children have grown up, as well as all the many women whose lives and religious experience extend beyond the boundaries of their home, as employees, professionals, Jewish educators, synagogue presidents, and students of Torah. Both pictures are caricatures. As will be shown below, Orthodox women engage in a wide range of communal and domestic religious activities, in spite of their exclusion from an active role in worship in synagogue and from some areas of Torah study, both of which are central religious activities—as defined by men. Orthodox and non-Orthodox writers alike, backed by classical sources, assume that the 'core' of Jewish religious life is public worship and Torah study, but while this may be true for men it is a misrepresentation of women's experience. The 'invisibility' of women's lives and the difficulty of actually seeing them without the preconceptions of a male context were first discussed in 1975 by anthropologist Edwin Ardener in his seminal essay 'Belief and the Problem of Women': 'if the models of a society made by most ethnographers tend to be models derived from the male portion of that society, how does the symbolic weight of that other mass of persons—half or more of a human population, as we have accepted—express itself?'[5]

Ellen Umansky points out that

Early feminist studies of the religious lives of Jewish women . . . shared the assumption that the study of religious texts and participation in public worship constituted what [Paula] Hyman labeled the 'heart and soul of traditional Judaism'. Women's exclusion from these areas made them little more than 'peripheral' Jews (i.e. radically different from men, who do not take into account 'the objective reality of women's lives, self-concept and education'). Without denying these conclusions, more recent feminist studies have recognized that to view study and communal worship as the heart and soul of traditional Judaism and then to focus on how women were excluded from (or sought to gain acceptance in) these areas is to accept

---

arbitrary exceptions, such as the requirement to eat matzah on Passover. However, not all positive time-bound commandments are equal in gender-weighting; while women's performance of some of them is very common and even encouraged (e.g. saying the Shema twice daily or eating in a sukkah on Sukkot), others are controversial (e.g. wearing *tsitsit* (ritual fringes) or *tefilin* (phylacteries)). The author's statement that certain women 'may fulfil' these mitzvot is disingenuous given that the same web page classifies two of the mitzvot from which women are 'exempted' (*tsitsit* and *tefilin*) as totally forbidden to them. For a new analysis of the original rationale behind the exemption of women from observing positive time-bound commandments, and its implications for contemporary Jewish feminists, see Alexander, *Gender and Time-bound Commandments*, esp. the 'Epilogue' (pp. 235–50).

[5] Ardener, 'Belief and the Problem of Women', 4.

an essentially androcentric vision of Judaism. This vision, focusing on the activities of men, universalizes their experiences and assigns them primary importance and at the same time minimizes or ignores the reality of women's religious lives.[6]

While this is a vital point, it is essential not to fall into the trap of espousing a mirror image of this androcentrically based claim, in which the Jewish woman's mission of creating a truly Jewish home in which the next generation of Jews can flourish is defined as the real centre of Judaism, with men's activities in the synagogue and the *beit midrash* (study house) relegated to an insignificant periphery; this approach has indeed been taken by some recent Orthodox apologists.[7] Both the domestic and the public arenas are central to Judaism, necessitating investigation of the hitherto under-reported and often undervalued experience of women in the domestic context, but also of women's experience in the equally significant communal and public zone, and this is the rationale undergirding this study.[8] In recent years religious women's lives in Israel have received attention from scholars such as Susan Sered, Tamar El-Or, and Rivka Neriya-Ben Shahar, and women from the Orthodox sector in the USA have begun to be researched by Ayala Fader, Sarah Bunin Benor, and others,[9] but little or no attention has yet been given to the unique features of British Orthodox women's religious experience. The present study is intended as a starting point to provide a greater understanding of the British Jewish community, but also to throw light on the ways in which factors of change and conformity operate in different communities.

The largely separate nature of the religious lives of Orthodox men and women, and the invisibility of Orthodox women's experience to their male co-religionists (and thus to the non-Jewish world),[10] are illustrated in a recent popular introduction to Judaism, in which a Modern Orthodox rabbi gives a sketch of 'a day in the life of a practising Jew' in twenty-first-century Britain, starting in the evening, the beginning of the Jewish day:

[6]   Umansky, 'Spiritual Expressions', 265–6.

[7]   See for instance 'The Role of Women' on the Judaism 101 website, which criticizes 'the mistaken assumption that Jewish religious life revolves around the synagogue. It does not; it revolves around the home, where the woman's role is every bit as important as the man's.' Some of my 14-year-old pupils reported that they had been told by female Orthodox teachers that women's roles in Judaism were far more important than those of men.

[8]   Male roles in the domestic context should also be examined, though this lies beyond the scope of the present discussion. Even a brief consideration, however, reveals that men often dominate here too, though this is not acknowledged in Orthodox apologetics, where the woman is glorified as supreme in the domestic sphere. See Ch. 5 for further discussion.

[9]   See the Bibliography for their publications.

[10]   The majority of books about (Orthodox) Judaism intended for a Jewish but non-observant or a non-Jewish audience are written by men, who naturally draw on their own experience but do not realize that it is shaped by gender.

The first ritual of the day following nightfall is the recitation of *ma'ariv*, the evening prayers . . . In general, prayers ought to be recited in the presence of a *minyan*, a quorum of ten male Jews above the age of thirteen. It is for this purpose that many observant Jews will go to the synagogue each evening. If it is not possible to pray with a *minyan* one may recite the prayers alone, with certain omissions . . . Mealtime has its own set of rituals, consisting mainly of blessings of thanksgiving to God both before as well as after eating . . . even an act as mundane and material such as eating can be infused with holiness. This is especially so if one eats in a dignified manner cognizant of the fact that one is, through this act, keeping body and soul together . . . At some point in the evening an observant Jew will study some Torah. The mitzvah to study the Torah is one of the most important, and in an ideal world one should study it assiduously. For those who spend the bulk of their day working this is not possible, and so they set aside time each evening and/or morning for the purpose of study. A set of prayers is recited before going to bed . . . An abridged version of these bedtime prayers [is] recited by children, and most parents make a point of teaching it to them at an early age . . . The first words uttered upon waking are a short prayer of thanksgiving to God for restoring our soul . . . Morning prayers, known as *shaharit* in Hebrew, are the most lengthy of all the daily prayers, taking a little under an hour to recite . . . these should ideally be recited along with a quorum at the synagogue . . . One of the noticeable characteristics of morning prayer is that male worshippers over the age of thirteen are required to wear *tefillin* . . . Many will also be wrapped in a *tallit* prayer shawl . . . After morning prayers most people will rush off to work, while some may remain behind for a while studying some Torah before starting the day . . . Most challenging for those at work [is] the afternoon prayer, or *mincha* . . . Travelling presents its own challenges, as one must remember to factor in *mincha*.[11]

This is an exclusively androcentric account, with women and children only visible in a passing reference to parents teaching children bedtime prayers. Formal prayer with a *minyan*, Torah study, and the wearing of *tefilin* and *talit* are all examples of positive time-bound commandments, from which women are exempt (and which, in the case of *talit* and *tefilin*, they are strongly discouraged from performing); very few Orthodox women attend synagogue on weekdays. In spite of the fact that Orthodoxy elevates the religious significance of the home, it appears in this account as a place to eat and sleep in between the significant activities of prayer and Torah study, ideally located in the synagogue. Even those activities defined by Orthodoxy as the supreme religious privileges of women, such as childcare and the preparation of kosher food, remain invisible in this account, let alone women's experience

[11] To protect the author's and his wife's identities, I have omitted the reference for this passage.

of prayer and Torah study. In spite of Orthodox apologetics justifying women's exclusion from central rituals and asserting that they are 'equal but different',[12] women's religious experience is largely invisible to Orthodox men and only mentioned or given theological support when it needs to be defended to the external world.

This author's wife's day is quite different:

As soon as I feel the impetus to jump out of bed my lips mouth the words of 'Modeh Ani',[13] thanking G-d[14] for another day . . . I begin my morning with a shower, followed by ritual washing to purify my hands, symbolizing the transition from an unconscious state of sleep to a state of physical alertness and spiritual awakening. I get dressed, usually in a dress or skirt that is long enough to fall below my knees. On my way downstairs I wake my kids up and listen to my youngest child recite 'Modeh Ani'. I enter the kitchen and repeat the ritual washing, this time followed by several morning blessings . . . Breakfast is generally a multi-tasking affair, eating while glancing at headline news, getting food out of the freezer for dinner or preparing a batch of dough that I will later bake into Challah, the traditional loaves for the Sabbath. I try to carve out some time for the traditional morning prayers before I leave for work. If I am taking the train into town, I will take along a pocket size prayer book and recite the morning prayer during the journey . . . During my work day I often refer to Jewish values in conversation with colleagues and use Jewish ethics to guide me in making choices . . . When the evening meal is over, my children and husband clear up and I spend some time reading or studying in preparation for a Jewish class I teach. By the time I get to bed I am rather tired and my bedtime 'Shema' prayer is punctuated with several yawns.[15]

While prayer is centrally important in this account, it is not the structure around which the day is organized but, rather, is adapted to the demands of running a household, caring for a family, and working, and is intertwined with everyday activities such as showering and travelling. Torah study is linked to teaching, rather than presented as an end in itself, and activity is

[12] For a Modern Orthodox critique of the 'equal but different' apologetic, see Harris, *Faith without Fear*, 38–9.

[13] The prayer recited upon awakening in the morning, thanking God for protection during the night. Ironically, this is the masculine form of the prayer; the feminine form would be *modah ani*. Most Orthodox women (and men) are unaware of the existence of this feminine form, and routinely use masculine first-person pronouns when reciting this and other formal prayers.

[14] Many Orthodox Jews extend the prohibition on writing God's name in full in a non-sacred context, originally limited to names and epithets of God in Hebrew, to English names and epithets too, such as G-d, L-rd, or A-mighty. This was originally a haredi practice but is becoming increasingly common among non-haredim.

[15] Account supplied at my request by the wife of the author of the 'male' passage cited above.

located in the home and the workplace, with no mention of the synagogue or the (male) social group that inhabits it—it is as invisible in this account as women's daily experience is in the first.

It is in the context of this double invisibility of Orthodox Jewish women—invisible both to Jewish men and to the outside world—that I will explore their religious lives, focusing on three principal questions:

1. What do Orthodox women actually do, as opposed to descriptions of their activities in standard introductions to Jewish life and to what rabbis and members of the male elite prescribe for women? How do women understand their own practices?

2. Are the variations within contemporary British Orthodoxy paralleled by variations in the practices, beliefs, and world-views of Orthodox women, and if so, what factors shape these differences?

3. Is there any space for women's creativity and agency in Orthodox life, and if so, how do the constraints and opportunities inherent in a patriarchal religious system shape them?

The Scope of Women's Religious Lives

Though the personal and the everyday are the basis of the religious life, they do not exhaust it. Few Orthodox Jewish women's practices—whether communal rituals, such as those described in the two scenes above and examined in Chapters 3 and 4 below, or the many individual or domestic practices described in Chapters 5 and 6—appear in standard works on Judaism. Such works often focus on a restricted definition of the woman's role in the home, especially the 'three women's mitzvot' of separating the first portion of dough when baking bread,[16] observing the regulations of the ritual purity system,[17]

---

[16] [*Hafrashat*] *ḥalah* (lit. '[separating] dough'), prescribed in Num. 15: 19–21 (see above, n. 2). It is not actually a woman's commandment, but should be performed by any Jew who bakes bread using a certain minimum amount of flour; the association with women comes from the fact that, before the availability of mass-produced bread, it was baked at home, generally by women.

[17] *Taharat hamishpaḥah* (lit. 'family purity'). The ritual and sexual framework created by these laws constitutes a major dimension of an observant married woman's life. Jewish law mandates total abstinence from sex and physical separation for married couples during the woman's menstruation and for a week afterwards; this period of ritual impurity is concluded by the rite of passage of the woman's immersion in a *mikveh*, after which sexual relations may be resumed. Although men are obviously affected by this too (and may voluntarily visit the *mikveh* themselves before major festivals), the *mikveh* is mandatory for married women and has a greater impact on their lives.

and lighting sabbath (and festival) candles.[18] This set of commandments was associated with women as early as the second century CE, and by the medieval period had become the focus of rabbinic writings on women's religious duties: Chava Weissler notes that 'Ashkenazic sources sometimes conveyed the impression that these three duties were the only ones women had been commanded to perform'.[19] The three commandments still feature prominently in Orthodox accounts of Jewish women's role,[20] as do other domestic activities such as keeping a kosher kitchen, preparing food for sabbath and festivals, and nurturing and educating children, plus a somewhat nebulous role in maintaining the home's Jewish character.

Notwithstanding this valorization of the exclusively domestic role of women, and its characterization as 'the natural order of things', several new communal religious activities are being organized by Orthodox women in London, in addition to the high-profile women's *tefilah* groups which have been running since 1993: they include *berakhah* parties, challah parties, *tehilim* groups, Rosh Hodesh groups, *ahavat yisra'el* groups, and *gemaḥs*.[21] Almost all are completely undocumented, apart from an occasional feature in the American Jewish and Israeli press covering parallel phenomena in those countries, and a couple of academic articles published recently on Israeli examples.[22] Indeed, many members of the London Orthodox Jewish community, both male and female, are unaware of their existence.[23] There is also a wide variety of women's Jewish study classes.

[18] *Hadlakat ner* (lit. 'lighting the lamp'); the original practice used oil lamps rather than candles, which only came into common use in the medieval period. This rabbinic (rather than biblical) commandment is incumbent upon each household, not specifically on each woman; men must light sabbath and festival candles if they live on their own or if the household's women are not present. Mainstream practice is for the mother to light candles, though under the influence of hasidic ideas widely promoted by Lubavitch (Habad) hasidism, it is becoming more common for unmarried girls to light their own candles too—an example of the silent 'seepage' of haredi customs into the non-haredi community.

[19] *Voices of the Matriarchs*, 29; a detailed account of the development of the 'three women's mitzvot' may be found there.

[20] See Ch. 5 for a discussion of women's experience of these three commandments.

[21] For Rosh Hodesh, women's *tefilah* groups, and *berakhah* parties, see above, Introduction, n. 6. Challah groups promote the baking of challah for spiritual and physical benefit; *tehilim* (psalm) groups encourage the reciting of psalms for the same aim, and *ahavat yisra'el* (love of Israel) groups aim to inculcate a love of fellow Jews. *Gemaḥs* provide interest-free loans of money and various items. See Ch. 4 for a full discussion of these activities.

[22] See Neriya-Ben Shahar, '"At 'Amen Meals' It's Me and God"', on *berakhah* parties (known as *se'udot amen*, 'amen meals', in Israel), and El-Or, 'A Temple in Your Kitchen', on challah parties.

[23] For instance, neither the two hasidic women from Stamford Hill nor the retired United Synagogue rabbi whom I interviewed had heard of *berakhah* parties.

It is also clear that standard descriptions of women's practices in the domestic and individual spheres omit many widespread customs and practices, often characterized as 'superstitions' (even by those who practise them), although they form an integral and meaningful part of many women's religious lives. Responses from 100 women who completed a questionnaire on these practices revealed both ancient customs documented in talmudic sources and recent pietistic practices,[24] often imported by younger women after a study year at an Israeli seminary. Women understand these practices as embodying their role as protectors of the family and community, and often feel empowered by them, though some women make a sharp distinction between 'halakhic practices' and 'superstitions', regarding the latter as trivial and perhaps even harmful. Both these practices and communal expressions of Orthodox women's religiosity are frequently denigrated or discounted by Orthodox men, paralleling the lack of scholarly interest in women's religious activities and beliefs until recent years.[25]

As far as I am aware, hardly any studies of these phenomena have been carried out among British Jews, and very little academic material on women's religious lives exists. Important information on women's perceptions of their religious opportunities in the British Jewish community appears in two reports commissioned by the chief rabbi in 1994 and 2009: *Women in the Jewish Community* (the Preston Report) and the follow-up report, *Connection, Continuity, and Community* (the Women's Review), both produced by teams led by Rosalind Preston. Sally Berkovic's personal memoir *Under My Hat* provides a vivid and critical picture of the experience of being an Orthodox woman in Britain from a Modern Orthodox perspective, and Naomi Alderman's novel *Disobedience* (2006) provides a fictional account of female alienation in the London Orthodox community. However, the only academic study of any aspect of British Orthodox women's religious lives of which I am aware is Jennifer Cousineau's essay on the effects of the introduction of the London *eruv* on women's experience of the sabbath.[26]

---

[24] I class as 'pietistic' those practices that consist of culturally defined virtuous activity, such as prayer or the particularly stringent performance of commandments, designed to please God and accumulate merit; examples might include praying for forty days at the Western Wall, or refraining from gossip for a set number of hours. Non-pietistic practices tend to be more mechanical and often more prophylactic in character, e.g. not giving a knife as a present for fear it will 'cut' the friendship. See Ch. 6 for a full discussion of the survey.

[25] Though see Neriya-Ben Shahar, '"At 'Amen Meals' It's Me and God"', and El-Or, 'A Temple in Your Kitchen', as well as other works by these authors, and further discussion below of some recent studies on Jewish women's religious lives in Israel and America.

[26] Cousineau, 'The Domestication of Urban Jewish Space'. An *eruv* is a halakhically defined construction linking private and public areas that permits Jews to carry objects and children in

Though hitherto undocumented, the rich world of women's communal and individual practice provides a wealth of information that can be used to answer the questions presented above. Study of Orthodox women highlights crucial issues of women's agency, self-understanding, and creativity in a patriarchal society—issues that are far less prominent in other Jewish denominations, which promote egalitarianism in ritual and leadership (though they do not always achieve it in practice).[27]

My focus here is thus principally on Orthodox women, and the variations within that category. Although haredi and non-haredi women are usually lumped together as 'Orthodox', analysis of their different attitudes to and practice within religious life throws light on the nature of the Orthodox Jewish community in Britain (and elsewhere), the competing forces of polarization and rapprochement that are shaping it, and the range of responses to pressures from within and outside the community. I suggest that, rather than a simple haredi/non-haredi dichotomy, there are actually three principal groups of Orthodox women in the British Jewish community: haredi, Modern Orthodox, and traditionalist. These categories do not necessarily coincide with institutional boundaries such as the Orthodox synagogue organizations, and can be applied to Orthodox men as well, highlighting the unique nature of the British Jewish community.

The religious geography of the Israeli, American, and British Jewish populations varies considerably (see Table 2). In Israel, though the largest segment of the Jewish population is secular (45%), the religious segment is dominated by the categories of traditional (25%) and *dati le'umi* or 'religious Zionist' (16%), which is roughly equivalent to Modern Orthodox, with a rapidly growing haredi sector (14%). There are also non-Orthodox denominations, largely introduced by American immigrants, but these are very much in the minority (estimates vary from 5% to 13% for Masorti/Conservative and Reform combined). In recent years, this situation has been complicated by the growth of an intermediate group with some haredi and some *dati le'umi* characteristics, known by the hybrid term *ḥardal*, for which no statistics are yet available.

In the USA, the non-Orthodox dominate (41% Reform and 18% Conservative), with a small, though growing, Orthodox population made up of

public areas on the sabbath and Yom Kippur; in its absence such carrying is not permitted; see below, Ch. 3. In addition, an important research project on Orthodox Jewish women, completed in 2019, is a doctoral dissertation by Dr Lindsay Simmonds entitled 'Generating Piety: Agency and the Religious Subject'.

[27] For resistance both to women rabbis and to egalitarian liturgical language in the British Reform movement, see Sheridan (ed.), *Hear Our Voice*, esp. the chapters by Jacqueline Tabick, Julia Neuberger, and Rachel Montagu.

Table 2 Religious affiliation of Jews in Israel, the UK, and the USA (2013–2018)

Country	Haredi	Modern Orthodox/ Dati le'umi	Traditional/ other Orthodox	Conservative/ Masorti	Reform/ other non-Orthodox denominations	Secular
Israel	14	16	25	n/a[a]	n/a[a]	45
UK	7		32	2	15	44
USA	6	3	1	18	41	30

Sources: Israel: Malach, Cahaner, and Choshen, *Statistical Report on Ultra-Orthodox Society in Israel*; Fefferman, *Rising Streams*; UK: Mashiach and Boyd, *Synagogue Membership in the United Kingdom in 2016*; USA: Pew Research Center, *A Portrait of Jewish Americans*, id., 'Comparisons between Jews in Israel and the U.S.'.

Note: Figures are expressed as a percentage of the total Jewish population of each country and are approximate. For Israel and the USA, the figure for the total Jewish population is based on self-identification of respondents as Jewish. For the UK, the percentages for denominational affiliation given in Mashiach and Boyd refer to the percentage of Jewish households formally affiliated to synagogues; I have extrapolated the corresponding percentages for the total number of Jewish households in the UK in order to make the figures comparable to those given for Israel and the USA.

[a] Official figures for Masorti (Conservative) and Reform are not available for Israel since the Israel Central Bureau of Statistics (ICBS), the source of the other figures for Israel in this table, does not include these categories. See Fefferman, *Rising Streams*, 20, concerning estimates of this figure as 5–13%. Figures for the 'Traditional/Other Orthodox' and 'Secular' categories would need to be adjusted to reflect this.

haredim (6%), Modern Orthodox (3%), and 'other Orthodox' (1%, possibly Sephardim). Secular Jews are in the minority (30%), probably because many individuals of Jewish ancestry simply cease to think of themselves as Jewish and 'disappear' into the non-Jewish majority.

Overall, the profile of the British Jewish population is closer to that of the Israeli than the American one, though it should be borne in mind that the available figures for the UK are based on formal synagogue affiliation rather than on self-identification, as in the other two countries. While the growing haredi sector currently stands at 7.3% of the UK Jewish population, the rest of the Orthodox sector is far larger (31.5%): it undoubtedly includes both Modern Orthodox and traditional Jews, though in the surveys consulted the labels used are 'centrist Orthodox' (29.8%) and 'Sephardi' (1.7%)—but neither of these labels is reflected in formal denominational affiliation. The non-Orthodox sector includes 1.7% Masorti (a reflection of the relatively recent introduction of this movement to the UK), 15.2% Reform and Liberal com-

bined, and 44.3% non-affiliated Jews (who may or may not consider themselves secular).[28]

Overlapping Worlds I: The Intersection of Men's and Women's Religious Lives

A major problem in studying women's religious lives and the ways in which
they differ from and intersect with those of men is imagining how women fit
into one's overall picture of Jewish religious activity. This applies whether one
is talking about contemporary Judaism or a Jewish community at some point
in the past. Given the difficulties we face in documenting and even 'seeing'
women's activity in the present, can we hope to discover evidence of it in the
past, let alone form an idea of how it was related to men's religious activity?
Nevertheless, the attempt is necessary, since otherwise we run the risk of
regarding the distinctive quality of Jewish women's religious lives—partly
separate from and partly overlapping with those of men—as a modern phenomenon, which would in turn shape attempts to account for its development and characteristics. I will examine the historical aspect first, before
turning to possible models of how women's and men's religious lives intersect.

Much work has been done in recent years to retrieve Jewish women's history, voices, and experiences from the male-produced and male-dominated
texts and records of the past.[29] New analyses of both familiar and obscure
textual sources have thrown some light on Jewish women's lives, and glimpses of their religious practice, beliefs, and understanding of their roles can be
gleaned.[30] It is not possible to present this research adequately here, but as a
brief illustration I will outline two historical studies.

The first is Shaye Cohen's discussion of medieval women's purity practices in his essay 'Purity, Piety, and Polemic', where he uses four rabbinic
responsa to explore women's understanding of the laws and rituals relating to
menstrual impurity (*nidah*). Noting that the laws recorded in halakhic texts
were devised and formulated by men, thus hiding women's perspective from
our view, he suggests that 'When the rabbis tell us that women were not doing
what they were supposed to be doing, they give us a brief glimpse at the reli-

[28] The Liberal movement is unique to the UK, but closely parallels the American Reform
movement; the British Reform movement is less radical than the American one.

[29] See e.g. Baskin (ed.), *Jewish Women in Historical Perspective*; Goldin, *Jewish Women in
Europe in the Middle Ages*; Grossman, *Pious and Rebellious*; and Kaplan and Moore (eds.), *Gender
and Jewish History*.   [30] See e.g. Grossman, *Pious and Rebellious*, ch. 7.

gious lives . . . of Jewish women.'[31] The texts reveal that women took the purification process very seriously, but did not always follow the rabbinically prescribed procedure, maintaining their own rituals. Women in Ashkenaz (France and Germany) followed the custom of bathing at the end of their menstrual period, then waited for the rabbinically ordained seven 'white' days (*yemei libun*) before immersing themselves in a *mikveh*, a practice which, the rabbis felt, 'slighted' the bath that women are required to take immediately before this ritual immersion. Women in Spain and the Byzantine empire observed the seven 'white' days, but then simply washed in a bath rather than immersing themselves in a *mikveh*. Egyptian women disregarded the 'white' days altogether, and had themselves sprinkled with water at the end of their menstrual period instead of using a *mikveh*. These women's responses to rabbinic criticism, preserved in some of these texts, show that they 'thought of themselves as righteous and of their customs as legitimate. Their piety was no less sincere and real than that of their rabbinic opponents.'[32] Cohen identifies a tension between the rabbinic demand for authority over rituals on the one hand and women's mimetic practices on the other, and the women's subversion of that authority and assumption of agency:

On the rabbinic side, polemic against 'incorrect' or 'heretical' practices was a political statement, an assertion of power. Menstrual practices were the preserve of women, taught by mother to daughter and woman to woman and observed in privacy, but even here (male) rabbinic authority was to be supreme. Women's traditions were wrong if they conflicted with the norms established by the (male) rabbis. Women must consult rabbis if they are to know what to do . . . Knowledge was power; ignorant women were powerless to resist rabbinic authority. The women of Byzantium and Egypt, however, were neither ignorant nor powerless.[33]

I found similar instances among Orthodox women in London, in which women's Passover cleaning practices and *nidah* rituals, often learnt mimetically from their mothers, did not conform to rabbinically prescribed procedures. In a similar vein, some of the women I interviewed complained that certain aspects of meat preparation had been almost entirely removed from the women's domestic sphere and assigned to (male) butchers 'because the rabbis don't trust women'.[34] Some examples of divergences in interpretation and practice were less fraught, for instance the significance attributed to cemetery visits, where it is easier to assign meanings that differ from standard rabbinic ones.[35] Although the historical evidence for such divergences in

---

[31] Cohen, 'Purity, Piety, and Polemic', 417.   [32] Ibid. 433.   [33] Ibid. 433–4.
[34] Lesley Sandman, interview. For a list and brief characterization of the women in my survey, see Appendix I.   [35] These are discussed in Ch. 5 below.

practice and interpretation is scanty, I would suggest that it is sufficient to support the existence of such patterns, which have persisted alongside the well-documented and 'normative' elite male tradition—both drawing from it and occasionally resisting or ignoring it—throughout Jewish history.

The second study is Chava Weissler's ground-breaking work on *tkhines*, Ashkenazi women's Yiddish prayers from the sixteenth to the early nineteenth centuries, which opens a window onto women's perception of their central religious role in the domestic sphere and its importance. Weissler identified

five types of relations between women's religion and elite male religion: (1) a valorization of women's separate sphere; (2) rituals created by women expressing some sort of women's religious culture; (3) a distancing of women from supposedly 'desirable' male activities; (4) an appropriation and transformation of motifs from scholarly culture; and (5) a direct challenge to elite, male gender definitions.[36]

Although expressed in very different ways than in the *tkhines* investigated by Weissler, similar relationships can be seen between the religious lives of Orthodox women in London and the associated elite male religion. Like Weissler's women, the women who responded to my survey—haredi, Modern Orthodox, and traditionalist—placed great emphasis on the sanctity and importance of their role as nurturers and protectors of family and community life (Weissler's first type), often asserting that this was more important than men's normative role as performers of communal rituals and Torah study. Just as the female author of a *tkhine* could imagine herself as a counterpart of the high priest lighting the Temple menorah when she lit sabbath candles,[37] Shirley Daniels, a young Modern Orthodox mother, saw herself as linked to and reproducing the act of the biblical matriarch Sarah when she performed the same ritual, and Sarah Segal, a young hasidic mother, envisioned herself as the 'interior minister' of her home, complementing her husband's role as 'foreign minister' dealing with the world outside. In terms of Weissler's second type, the traces of women's rituals and religious culture visible in the *tkhines*, such as using wicks with which graves had been measured to make candles for the synagogue,[38] are amply paralleled by recently

---

[36] *Voices of the Matriarchs*, 177.   [37] Ibid. 96–103.
[38] During the High Holiday season (and also in times of illness or trouble) women went to the cemetery, where they walked around the circumference and measured the whole area or individual graves with candlewick, all the while reciting *tkhines*. 'Between Rosh Hashanah and Yom Kippur . . . they made the wicks into candles "for the living" and "for the dead", again, reciting *tkhines* as they did so. On Yom Kippur, according to some customs, the candles were burned at home, while according to others, one or both of them burned in the synagogue' (Weissler, *Voices of the Matriarchs*, 133).

developed women's communal rituals (particularly prominent in the haredi sector), such as *berakhah* parties, challah parties, and *tehilim* groups, which are increasingly creating a separate women's religious culture. Another aspect of this can be seen in the maintenance of women's traditional customs and the invention of new pietistic practices in the domestic sphere. Weissler's fifth type is 'a direct challenge to elite, male gender definitions' and is exemplified in a *tkhine* written by Leah Horowitz, an eighteenth-century author of *tkhines*, which asserts that women's prayer can bring redemption. This finds an echo not only in haredi women's claims of 'power' in new rituals such as *berakhah* parties, but also in Modern Orthodox women's group performance of traditionally male rituals such as formal prayer services and Megillah readings. The recent rise of partnership *minyanim* illustrates a different approach, which runs counter to the trend of creating a completely separate women's religious sphere by offering women a substantial (though not completely equal) role in a standard service mostly led by men, a subtle shift of power between the genders.[39]

Weissler's third and fourth categories of relationship are less applicable to the modern context. Weissler herself is ambivalent about her third type, 'distanced participation'. She notes that, in some instances, *tkhines* express a view 'that takes specifically male activities to be of supreme importance and places women at the margins of those activities'.[40] She discusses a *tkhine* that articulates a gender-based hierarchy between men, expert in kabbalah, and women, who cannot aspire to such knowledge and hence remain marginal. The *tkhine* begins by describing correct kabbalistic prayer as desirable but unattainable: 'we are only flesh and blood, and have not the power to combine your holy Names and [engage in] all the mystical intentions in all of the prayers'. But it goes on to ask: 'May my prayer ascend before you to make a crown on your holy head with the other prayers of Jews who do know how to engage in mystical intentions.' The woman reciting the *tkhine* knows that male kabbalists can engage in this superior type of prayer, which is beyond her capabilities. However, Weissler then observes that the *tkhine* is itself a Yiddish adaptation of a male-authored Hebrew prayer designed for unlearned men, who, in the contemporary Ashkenazi hierarchy, were below learned men, though above (largely unlearned) women, few of whom knew Hebrew. The *tkhine* embodies a male hierarchical attitude that places (male) kabbalistic knowledge at the apex of spirituality, with unlearned women at the bottom of the ladder.[41] Weissler wonders if asking whether women were excluded from such

---

[39] This challenge to traditional gender roles is precisely why these initiatives are not welcomed or encouraged by male religious authorities.

[40] *Voices of the Matriarchs*, 180.

[41] Ibid. 180–2.

knowledge simply perpetuates a male-based scale of religious value, a point raised at the beginning of this chapter, where it was argued that neither the 'normative' male (communal, public, Torah-based) perspective nor a 'mirror-image' female (individual, domestic, non-text-based) perspective provides an appropriate basis for analysis of women's (or indeed men's) religious lives.

Interestingly, I found little or no evidence of the fourth type identified by Weissler—the appropriation and transformation of motifs or concepts from elite male culture. Modern British Orthodox women have not written any religious material, apart from relatively recent educational programmes and resources for schools,[42] and very little on their own experience of religion, apart from (Australian-born) Sally Berkovic.[43] Such voices are rarely heard, and appear mainly in letters to the *Jewish Chronicle* and *Jewish Tribune*, and in material presented in the Preston Report and the Women's Review; in none of these, nor in the interviews I conducted, was there much evidence of transformation of elite concepts. The only exception was the prevalence of the basic kabbalistic concept that prayer and ritual action can be theurgically effective, slightly adapted to assert that women's prayer and action are particularly powerful and redemptive. Another contributing factor to the lack of appropriation of male-authored concepts by Orthodox British women is the relatively low level of their Jewish education: few have studied classical Jewish texts, even in translation, and very few speak Hebrew fluently. Here, too, their situation differs from that of women in Israel and America: most *dati le'umi* and many traditional Israeli women (whose native language is Hebrew) attend religious schools, while in the USA the excellent Orthodox day schools provide Modern Orthodox women with a far higher level of Jewish knowledge and Hebrew than in the UK. In all three countries, haredi women are likely to have a high level of Hebrew knowledge and education focused on the Bible and practical aspects of halakhah, but little or no access to the Oral Torah, or to theological, kabbalistic, and philosophical works, since most haredi religious authorities regard study of these subjects as forbidden to women.[44]

The existence of specific, sometimes contested, women's religious practices in the past, such as the purity practices documented by Cohen, and

---

[42] Some exceptional women wrote on Jewish subjects in the nineteenth century, such as Grace Aguilar (1816–47) and Flora Sassoon (1859–1936).

[43] Berkovic, *Under My Hat*. There are also a few personal memoirs or pamphlets, such as Hubert, *A Jewish Woman's Handbook*, a short and unique attempt by an older woman with no formal Jewish education to articulate the essence of her religious life, which focuses on the sabbath, festivals, and food preparation.

[44] For a detailed discussion of different haredi attitudes to women's religious studies, see Fuchs, *Jewish Women's Torah Study*, chs. 3, 5, and 6. See Ch. 3 below for a discussion of changes in Jewish education.

the similarity of modern women's strategies to some of those identified by Weissler suggest that the innovations in ritual and practice and the 'women's customs' that were so visible in my research do not represent a break with the past. Rather, they constitute an extension and adaptation of patterns that Jewish women have used for centuries, exercising agency in creative ways within the constraints of a male-dominated system and creating female patterns of religious self-expression.

Turning now to the issue of contextualizing women's religious lives in relation to those of men in contemporary contexts, it is clear that neither the 'separate but equal' apologetic frequently heard in Orthodoxy nor the simplistic identification of 'oppressed and oppressors' made by some feminists provides an adequate way of thinking about the relationship between male and female lived experience of Judaism. An early attempt to characterize this relationship appears in Barbara Myerhoff's classic study *Number Our Days* (1978), which explores the lives of elderly Jewish men and women of east European origin living in Venice, California. Myerhoff describes both their initial struggle upon immigration to the United States to create a meaningful Jewish culture, adapted from their lives as children and young adults in eastern Europe, and their present difficulties, such as being constrained by the physical, financial, and familial problems of old age. Chapter 7 of the book is a perceptive study of the women's attitude to religion. Rachel, one of the most articulate informants, comes up with the term 'domestic religion' to describe women's religious lives in contrast to those of men, noting that

the boys . . . knew what the sacred words meant so they could argue and doubt. But with us girls, we couldn't doubt because what we knew came without understanding. These things were injected into you in childhood and chained together with that beautiful grandmother, so ever since infancy you can't know life without it. The boys in cheder [religious school] could learn the words and forget them, but in this domestic religion, you could never get rid of it.[45]

Myerhoff identifies this idea of 'domestic religion', acquired through imitation of one's elders,[46] and still a powerful element in the lives of these people, with Robert Redfield's concept, in *Peasant Society and Culture* (1956), of the 'little tradition', which he contrasts with a 'great tradition'. Redfield saw the 'great tradition' of a culture or religion as the central, often urban-based and

---

[45] Myerhoff, *Number Our Days*, 235.

[46] See Soloveitchik, 'Rupture and Reconstruction', which identifies the loss of mimetic learning and socialization and their replacement by text-based learning as a major factor in changes in Orthodoxy in modern times, especially its 'swing to the right'. Though Soloveitchik does not note this, mimetic learning and socialization are still common among women, surviving alongside the rise of text-based learning.

written, tradition, formulated and replicated by elite men, while the 'little tradition' represented the 'village' version, adapted to and often influenced by pre-existing traditions at the local level. He regarded the two as inter-dependent, but characterized the 'great tradition' as central and hierarchically superior, with the 'little tradition' being marginal and lower. Although this model was developed for peasant societies, Myerhoff adapted it to her mate-rial, characterizing the 'little tradition' as 'a local, folk expression of a group's beliefs; unsystematized, not elaborately idealized, it is an oral tradition prac-ticed constantly and often unconsciously by ordinary people',[47] in contrast to the 'great tradition' represented by the text-based studies of the elite. She iden-tified the 'domestic religion' characteristic of her informants, especially the women, with the 'little tradition', while reserving a (low) level of participation in the 'great tradition' for the men, who had some degree of literacy in Hebrew and Torah study—an educational advantage denied to the women. However, while this distinction has some attractions, it raises several prob-lems, as did Redfield's original pair of concepts.[48] In particular, the hierarchi-cal nature of the relationship between the two 'traditions' seems unfounded: in what sense can a 'tradition' participated in by only a very small elite be understood as superior to and determinative of a 'tradition' shared by the majority of members of a culture or religion? This is very similar to the as-sumption, called into question above, that a male perspective on religion is normative, while a female one is marginal and derivative. In addition, men's participation in the 'little tradition' is ignored, as is the nature of the relation-ship between the two types.

Myerhoff's observation of two interrelated modalities of religious life is still useful, however, if we see them in a horizontally rather than vertically ordered relationship, as two complementary and overlapping halves of a whole religious culture, even if one of those halves is under-documented. This approach is suggested by Susan Sered in her 1992 book *Women as Ritual Experts*, a study of the religious lives of elderly Sephardi women in Jerusalem. Basing her model on those of Myerhoff and Redfield, Sered characterizes the two traditions as the halakhic system, identified with men, and the 'extra-halakhic' system, identified with women.[49] While this conceptualization is open to the same kinds of criticism as Myerhoff's,[50] Sered introduces the important observation that power relations between the 'two traditions' are

[47] *Number Our Days*, 256.

[48] See Obeyesekere, 'The Great Tradition and the Little', for a critique.

[49] Sered, *Women as Ritual Experts*, 90–2.

[50] For instance, it ignores women's compliance with and relationship to the halakhic system, which applies to all Jews, regardless of its formation and control by a male elite.

not symmetrical: even if we view the halakhic–extra-halakhic spectrum as horizontally rather than vertically arranged, we must still take account of the popular view, internal to Jewish culture, that there is nevertheless a hierarchy, and of the ways in which women negotiate with and work around this system of power relations:

Within a system that defines male as normative, women frequently deviate from the norm. Within a system that is sexually segregated and in which the male world is defined as the official world, the content of the women's world needs to be examined by a different set of tools. [The interesting question] is not whether a women's brand of Judaism exists . . . but how the two religious systems (the male and female, and great and little, the *halachic* and extra-*halachic*) interact . . . Within the context of male-oriented religion, women clearly find strategies for constructing a meaningful religious life. Women reinterpret, ignore, borrow, circumvent, and shift emphases. But perhaps the most effective strategy available to women is to use the forms of the great tradition to sacralize their own, female life experiences.[51]

I discovered ample evidence of all these techniques and more, including the creation of new rituals, among Orthodox women in London. Sered notes that when prohibitions on lighting candles at sacred tombs prevented her inform-ants from practising a beloved ritual, they improvised a new one by throwing unlit candles through the railings at the tomb. She describes this as 'a rather typical instance of people responding to a novel situation through creating a ritual that refers to old situations', which would apply equally to the new *berakhah* and challah parties described in Chapter 4, and to the women-only readings of the books of Esther, Ruth, and Lamentations that are becoming increasingly popular in the Modern Orthodox sector. Responding to chang-ing concepts of women's roles and potential in general, non-Jewish society, women in the Orthodox world work within the constraints of the male-dominated system to create spaces within which their voices can be heard and their spiritual self-development promoted, while avoiding head-on conflict (though not controversy) with the existing system.

Sered also emphasizes women's ability to sacralize the everyday and recast it as the most important sphere of Jewish activity:

Once we begin looking for religion within the profane world rather than outside of it, we begin to discover realms of religiosity that are not limited to those times, people, places, objects, and events that seem extraordinary; we begin to see religion as potentially interwoven with all other aspects of human existence . . . in societies in which women are excluded from significant public or formal religious activities, they may become experts at sacralizing the everyday female sphere.[52]

[51] Sered, *Women as Ritual Experts*, 87.   [52] Ibid. 140.

This too found an echo in my own research, and prompted me to listen carefully for women's own understanding of their actions. One mother told me of the sacred significance of making a glass of carrot juice for her child, while another described her food preparations for the sabbath when asked about the structure of her 'Jewish week'; other women spoke of the founding of *gemaḥs*—local associations which lend useful items such as baby equipment or sim cards to their members: these loans are seen as pious acts that honour the women's deceased parents. Several women, particularly but not exclusively from the haredi sector, found difficulty in separating out the 'Jewish' or 'religious' parts of their lives, or objected to the idea,[53] since they experienced their lives as holistic and sacred rather than compartmentalized into Jewish/non-Jewish or religious/secular components. Flora Rendberg observed that 'being Jewish is everywhere in my life. It's not something I only take out on Fridays and Saturdays.'

Overlapping Worlds II: Living in Jewish and Western Contexts

In addition to considering the relationship between men's and women's religious lives within the Jewish community, we need to take account of women's constant negotiation between two worlds with different social, cultural, and religious values: that of the Jewish community and that of the wider Western liberal society in which British Orthodox women live. While this obviously applies to Jewish men too, it is a particularly difficult balancing act for women, who must deal not only with changing and sometimes contested expectations of gender roles in the wider society, but also with a parallel but different set of expectations in Jewish society, in particular in the Orthodox community. Here, many of the battles fought over gender roles in British society are being replayed, though against a different backdrop, and with the added complications inherent in being a minority community deeply concerned about its own survival.

Here, too, Myerhoff's study of elderly Jews is suggestive, as she examines the tension between two world-views: as well as the childhood values and culture of their east European shtetl background, still of immense emotional and ethical significance, these men and women held strong secular and socialist principles, including liberal ideals of equality and progress, which sometimes proved incompatible with the first set. This type of attachment to two, often

---

[53] This was often in reaction to my standard question, 'How is your Jewish week structured?'

conflicting, sets of values and expectations was characteristic of the tradition-alist and Modern Orthodox women in my own study, though much less so of the haredi women, who tend to prioritize the more traditional Jewish world-view inculcated by family and education.[54] Non-haredi women are often acutely conscious of this tension, like Stella James, who straddles the tradi-tionalist and Modern Orthodox categories:

My education and my outlook have very much been determined by the Western tradition, by Enlightenment philosophy, by things like that, and all I know about the Jewish way of thinking, the Jewish tradition, is what I've learned [at the London School of Jewish Studies], so I'm *very* Westernized in my thinking, and it doesn't always sit easily with me, the combination of the two things. I find that quite difficult. But there's no doubt it [Jewish tradition] is who I am, and it's a huge part of who I am, and now I no longer have parents, and *that* links me to my past, and I am hanging on for dear life to it, so it's an emotional thing not an intellectual thing for me. Intellectually, I find it difficult, and a lot of what I've learned here I've struggled with and struggled against, because it's not in tune with the way I think intellec-tually; but emotionally I'll *never* lose it.[55]

In contrast, more traditionalist women tend to cope with the tension either by 'compartmentalizing' their religious lives and leaving their secular values outside, or by simply ignoring aspects of religious life that clash with their Western liberal world-view.[56] Modern Orthodox women often react to the tension by trying to change aspects of their religious lives, such as participa-tion in standard communal rituals, in order to accommodate both world-views, with varying degrees of success, as will be documented below. Much previous research has tended to focus on hasidic communities, with the result that the complexities of religious life for non-haredi Orthodox women, who consciously and deliberately live in two worlds, have been overlooked.[57]

[54] This by no means implies that they are untouched by trends in the wider society, such as feminism, though they are less likely to acknowledge this or view it as a positive phenomenon. I heard plenty of feminist statements from haredi and traditionalist women, often preceded by a disclaimer such as 'I'm not a feminist but . . .'. See Morris, 'Agents or Victims?', for an analysis of hasidic women's location in feminist studies. For a fascinating study of American haredi women's negotiation of their two worlds, see Fader, *Mitzvah Girls*.

[55] For a similar consciousness and an examination of the tension between Western feminist principles and Modern Orthodoxy, see Hartman, *Feminism Encounters Traditional Judaism*, ch. 1.

[56] Such as the 'family purity' regulations, ignored by many traditionalist women, who see them as primitive and misogynistic, in spite of their halakhic importance; see Ch. 5.

[57] An excellent study of how Salafi Muslim women negotiate their two worlds appears in Inge, *The Making of a Salafi Muslim Woman*, ch. 5.

Power and Patriarchy: Do Orthodox Women Have Agency?

Given that Orthodox Judaism is undeniably patriarchal, with men leading the community, serving as clergy, performing public rituals (including worship services), and administering and sitting on the rabbinical courts, it may reasonably be asked whether women have any access to power or agency within the religious life of the community, particularly in matters of ritual and correct practice. While progress towards power-sharing has been made in the purely managerial and administrative roles of non-haredi institutions, there are as yet almost no changes in the ritual and halakhic spheres: only men serve as rabbis,[58] lead services, read from the Torah in synagogue, give sermons, sit as religious judges (*dayanim*), and make halakhic decisions.[59]

Nonetheless, the women I met were not merely passive spectators of men's activities. As described above, many of them regarded the creation and nurture of their families as a supremely important Jewish religious value and were very active in shaping this aspect of their religious lives; others created or participated in women-only religious rituals; while still others sought to participate and share in rituals and activities hitherto reserved for men. Women's agency may differ from that of men, but it exists. The interplay of consent, empowerment, appropriation, negotiation, resistance, and coercion is clearly visible here: acting within the constraints of a male-dominated community, Orthodox women do not seek to overthrow or combat the system as a

[58] Apart from the thirty-three women ordained as Orthodox rabbis at Yeshivat Maharat in New York (as of June 2019); and two women ordained in June 2015 and another five in August 2019 at Beit Midrash Har'el, an Orthodox institution in Jerusalem that ordains both men and women. Their ordination is not recognized by most Orthodox institutions in the USA, and is not recognized by any at all in the UK. Rabbi Shlomo Riskin, founder of several Orthodox educational enterprises in Israel, has been ordaining women as religious decisors (*posekot*), qualified to make decisions about Jewish law, since 2012. His programme has encountered less opposition, partly because the formal title granted to the women is *morah hora'ah* (which R. Riskin translates as 'Jewish legal leader'), rather than rabbi, and partly because religious diversity in Israel creates a more favourable climate for such innovations. See Sales, 'Why It's Easier to Ordain Orthodox Women in Israel'.

[59] Traditionalist and Modern Orthodox women share similar attitudes to other problematic areas of Jewish tradition, such as the lack of redress for Jewish women who want a divorce but whose husbands refuse to grant them one (*agunot*). Since none of my interviewees brought this subject up, I do not discuss it in this book; in addition, it is essentially political in nature (though part of a religious legal system), and has been well documented elsewhere. See Aranoff and Haut, *The Wed-Locked Agunot*; Breitowitz, *Between Civil and Religious Law*; and the *agunah* issue of the *JOFA Journal* (Summer 2005), available on the JOFA website. Haredi women, while suffering as much from this problem as other Orthodox women, do not usually express their views on this subject publicly, since it would involve a major challenge to rabbinical power.

whole, but, rather, seek to negotiate an expanded role within it. Those who participate in women's *tefilah* groups, for instance, do not claim to constitute and thereby redefine a quorum for prayer (*minyan*); rather, they seek an opportunity to perform a central ritual in a way that does not directly confront the existing power relationships but instead creates a coexisting alternative.

In general, Orthodox women do not doubt their right to agency but voluntarily shape that agency in terms of the wider male-dominated system, consenting to its authority. Indeed, given the fact that they can leave the community (though admittedly at a high social and personal cost), such consent is itself an act of women's agency. Recent anthropological work has begun to examine ideas of agency among non-liberal women in more nuanced terms, throwing light on this vexed question.[60] Saba Mahmood, in her 2005 study of the Islamic revival in Egypt, makes an important point about understanding women's agency in male-dominated societies, and points out the pitfalls of reducing complex situations to a simple dichotomy:

What [earlier feminist studies] fail to problematize is the universality of the desire—central for progressive and liberal thought, and presupposed by the concept of resistance it authorizes—to be free from relations of subordination and, for women, from structures of male domination. The positing of women's agency as consubstantial with resistance to relations of domination, and the concomitant naturalization of freedom as a social ideal, are not simply analytical oversights on the part of feminist authors . . . their assumptions reflect a deeper tension within feminism attributable to its dual character as both an *analytical* and a *politically prescriptive* project . . . I question the overwhelming tendency within poststructuralist feminist scholarship to conceptualize agency in terms of subversion or resignification of social norms, to locate agency within those operations that resist the dominating and subjectivating modes of power . . . In doing so, this scholarship elides dimensions of human action whose ethical and political status does not map onto the logic of repression and resistance.[61]

Mahmood's analysis is based on her research on Egyptian Muslim women who seek to create 'a pious self' that does not conform to Western ideals, but much of her understanding of women's agency can be applied to Orthodox Jewish women's search for communal ritual expression and participation while accepting the patriarchal system within which they live. As she notes, 'the fact that discourses of piety and male superiority are ineluctably intertwined does not mean that we can assume that the women who inhabit this conjoined matrix are motivated by the desire to subvert or resist terms that

---

[60] See Fader, *Mitzvah Girls*, 3–7, for a brief overview.
[61] Mahmood, *Politics of Piety*, 10, 14.

secure male domination'.[62] Like the women Mahmood studied, the haredi and Modern Orthodox women I encountered have a strong sense of agency, and, like their Muslim counterparts, they work around or alongside dominant modes of power rather than against them; they do not oppose or resist the system but seek to express themselves and act within it.[63] This holds true in particular of haredi women, who share many similarities with the Muslim women discussed by Mahmood, especially in their acceptance of a divinely ordered system of ethical behaviour and commanded action that includes submission to men.

Mahmood's account is less helpful, however, in understanding agency (or lack of agency) among non-haredi women. Though accepting the Orthodox world-view on its own terms, as do haredi women, traditionalist women will sometimes respond to the conflicts it engenders with a secular or liberal world-view by simply ignoring religious demands and expectations when they prove inconvenient. Any change in ritual is deeply problematic for them, however, as it threatens their Jewish identity, which is more ethnic than religious in character. Indeed, traditionalist women often vocally resist the efforts of Modern Orthodox women to challenge limitations and take a more active part in ritual for precisely this reason. Unfortunately for Modern Orthodox women, who often seek new or expanded roles when faced with tensions between their two world-views, the community's male power-holders, no less than post-structuralist feminists, tend to react by reframing their actions as an expression of challenge to (male) authority, creating a dichotomy of submission (defined in terms of conformity to the idealized norm of female behaviour) and resistance (defined as any attempt to innovate in the field of ritual). Perhaps it would be more just to reposition 'resistance' as the stance adopted by *men* who seek to oppose and limit women's religious adaptation and creativity as they respond to changing circumstances.

Another factor of immense importance to Orthodox Jewish women in Britain is their position as members of a small minority. Issues of identity and community affiliation and dependence are of prime importance to them, and the very real risks associated with leaving the community, or losing its approval and recognition, shape women's religious choices in ways that would not be applicable to members of a majority religion or ethnic group, such as the Egyptian Muslim women studied by Mahmood. She does not discuss the pressure felt by members of a minority to conform to their com-

---

[62] Mahmood, *Politics of Piety*, 175.

[63] Of course, there are many women who do come to regard the Orthodox world as hopelessly repressive and misogynistic, but they usually react by either switching to another denomination or abandoning religious affiliation altogether. See Nishma Research, 'Starting a Conversation'.

munity's expectations in order to retain their membership and identity, and indeed to ensure the very survival of their community.[64] Nor does she fully examine the role of expectations, pressures, payoffs, and rewards imposed or offered by the familial, religious, and social contexts in which women's lives are embedded.[65] These factors were of huge significance to the Jewish women I interviewed, many of whose religious choices were shaped by their commitment to their families and communities; they were often acutely aware of the trade-off between community membership and individual spiritual satisfaction. One young Modern Orthodox mother, who found religious fulfilment and a sense of belonging in women-only Orthodox and egalitarian Masorti services, was prepared to sacrifice this for the sake of her children's education, identity, and sense of security:

What keeps me Orthodox? Largely the children, because we've chosen the school and I've got a responsibility to them, I want them to finish at this school, and we've made a decision how to bring them up and how to educate them. I want to be Orthodox so the children have a background, because if I were to dilute things now they wouldn't know where they were coming from.[66]

In addition, Mahmood does not address the issue of the source of the 'pious self' into which her informants wanted to shape themselves. If the modest, shy, and submissive ideal to which they aspired is based exclusively or principally on male-defined prescriptions of the ideal woman, then the agency that women display in choosing to 'perform' and thereby internalize this ideal is subtly undermined. This remains a problem when considering agency in relation to haredi women. Nevertheless, in spite of these reservations, Mahmood's work is vitally important in raising the question of the limitations of earlier feminist analysis of non-liberal women and their choices, and in broadening our conceptions of agency: 'By tracing the multiple modalities of agency . . . I hope to address the profound inability within current feminist political thought to envision valuable forms of human flourishing outside the bounds of a liberal progressive imaginary.'[67] In focusing on non-liberal women,

---

[64] A major contribution to the understanding of the importance of ethnic identity and minority status in analyses of Orthodox Jewish women has been made by Bonnie Morris in 'Agents or Victims?' She notes that 'The present-day Hasidic construction of the Gentile as opponent/opposite is most significant and illustrates the tension between ethnic and female identity for Jewish women', and that hasidic women 'are more concerned with ethnic survival than with liberating themselves from Hasidic men' (p. 174).

[65] She does discuss the case of a newly religious wife whose activities were opposed by her less religious husband, and the pressures that each brought to bear on the other, but this was primarily a conflict between individuals rather than between a woman or group of women and their community; see Mahmood, *Politics of Piety*, 176–80.

[66] Bernice Susser, interview.   [67] *Politics of Piety*, 155.

however, she ignores the very specific dilemma of those women who are shaped by, and feel allegiance to, two competing world-views, such as non-haredi Orthodox women.

In the chapters that follow I build on earlier research and models to explore the range of responses and forms of agency exhibited by women within the male-dominated realm of Orthodox Judaism as they pursue religious goals of different types, from non-liberal ideals of piety that accept women's submission to male religious authority to feminist-influenced ideals of fuller ritual participation and a more egalitarian distribution of knowledge, power, and status. Faced with multiple life-narratives—feminist, traditional-conservative, atheist, devotional—from which to choose, and living as members of a minority in a liberal Western society that partly defines itself by the ability of women to make autonomous choices, the majority of Orthodox Jewish women choose to remain within the Orthodox community and conform to its expectations and values.[68] However, they do not do so unthinkingly or blindly; Western notions of self-fulfilment, choice, and gender equality shape even haredi women's attempts to find new ways of living as Orthodox women within the constraints of a male-dominated and highly conservative community. Change, even if unacknowledged, does occur within the Orthodox community, and current attempts both to create new women-only religious rituals and to enable women to participate in existing, currently male, rituals will inevitably engender further change. Catherine Bell notes:

if the ritual construction of power on the higher levels of social organization builds on the microrelations of power that shape daily life on the lower levels of the society, changes in the latter level can precipitate a crisis in which the demands of ritual to conform to traditional models clash with the ability of these rites to resonate with the real experiences of the social body.[69]

It is these tensions, created by the conflicting demands of the larger, Western society and the smaller, traditional community, that inspire and shape Jewish women's explorations of new communal rituals in particular, with a concomitant shift in power relationships within the Orthodox community.

---

[68] Though, as noted above, the price of exit is very high, so their choice is not entirely free.
[69] *Ritual Theory, Ritual Practice*, 213.

SETTING THE SCENE: THE JEWISH LANDSCAPE

> We were very much encouraged to both stand out and be invisible, which was
> a very Anglo-Jewish message of the early 1960s. The shadows of the Shoah
> fell very long . . . you can hear by the way I speak that I was very much encour-
> aged to iron out any traces of an East End or Jewish accent; fortunately that
> came very naturally to me, and that was considered very important.
>
> KATHERINE MARKS, interview

To UNDERSTAND women's religious lives and their associated choices, the immediate communal context and the history that has shaped it need to be established. This chapter also examines the nature of the community's self-identification and the affiliation of its members, the character of contemporary Orthodoxy in the UK, with its differences from Orthodox groups in Israel and the USA, and the historical factors underlying the topography of the Anglo-Jewish denominational landscape. I pay special attention to the brief period of accelerated change in women's religious activities in the early 1990s.

Jews in Britain: Historical Background

Although British Jews are a mobile community, with members emigrating to Israel, the United States, and elsewhere, and with new members arriving from all over the world, most of Britain's Jewish families have been here for three generations or more, and feel very 'British'. The community dates from 1656, when the small number of Sephardi Jews living 'undercover' in London was tacitly permitted to remain, while 1690 saw the foundation of the first Ashkenazi synagogue.[1] The Jewish population of Britain grew throughout the eighteenth and nineteenth centuries, fuelled largely by Ashkenazi immigrants from Germany and Poland, and by 1851 it reached about 35,000, some 20,000 of whom lived in London, with other, smaller communities developing around the country, particularly in mercantile centres and ports,

---

[1] This brief historical sketch is based on Bermant, *Troubled Eden*; Brook, *The Club*; and Alderman, *Modern British Jewry*.

such as Manchester, Leeds, and Bristol. Many put down roots and prospered, with roughly 5,000 moving to the newly fashionable West End in London. With the gradual disappearance of restrictions on their political, social, and economic activities through the nineteenth century, synagogues, schools, and community institutions such as the Board of Deputies of British Jews (founded in 1760) flourished, and Jews became more middle class.

This established community—numbering about 60,000 by 1880—was radically changed by a flood of Jews from the Russian Empire and eastern Europe, sparked by pogroms beginning in April 1881. Between 1881 and 1905, over 100,000 Yiddish-speaking Jews arrived in Britain, before the Aliens Act reduced the mass migration to a trickle. By 1900 London was home to about 144,000 Jews, 83% of them living in crowded and squalid conditions in the East End.

The solidly middle-class Jewish establishment was horrified by the 'primitive' newcomers with their 'oriental' and exuberant religiosity;[2] indeed, 'there was only one thing the old community could do, and that was to Anglicise the new'.[3] The project was largely successful, using schools and youth clubs to influence immigrant children. After immigration practically ended in 1914, the process of Jewish embourgeoisement in London (and elsewhere) proceeded apace, with the East End gradually losing its Jews to the new middle-class suburbs. During the 1930s, with this process once again largely complete, another 50,000 immigrants arrived, this time from Nazi Germany and Austria; most of them were not particularly observant, or belonged to the German Reform movement. This proved to be the last mass Jewish migration to Britain, though smaller groups arrived after the Second World War, notably from Hungary after the failure of the 1956 revolution, as well as from Iran, Iraq, Aden, and other Middle Eastern countries. In recent years, several thousand Israelis have moved to Britain, mostly settling in London, but they have had a much smaller effect on the community. Many are secular; others only reside in Britain temporarily, maintaining Israeli social networks rather than integrating into the British Jewish community.[4] Those Israelis who do participate in the community tend to be the Orthodox, who need institutions such as synagogues and Jewish schools, and they have had some influence on religious life in London.[5]

[2] 50,000 Jewish immigrants were repatriated by the Jewish Board of Guardians.

[3] Bermant, *Troubled Eden*, 30.

[4] Rocker, 'Expat and Excluded'. The 2011 Census revealed that there were about 23,000 Israelis living in Britain, 65% of whom declared their religion as Jewish (though presumably some of the 23% who recorded 'no religion' or failed to declare their religion might be ethnically Jewish). Of that number, perhaps 16–19% were haredi; see Graham, *Britain's Israeli Diaspora*, 2 and 12.

[5] *Berakhah* parties, for example, were introduced to Britain by Israeli women; see Ch. 4.

Today, about 172,000 of Britain's approximately 290,000 Jews live in London,[6] clustered in specific neighbourhoods.[7] A 2003 report on London's Jews by the Institute for Jewish Policy Research summarizes:

[London's Jews are] a relatively affluent group of people with middle-class values and middle-class lifestyles. It is an ageing population . . . the Jewish population is far from uniform and . . . comprises a complex social and religious fabric . . . there is a far from simple situation with regard to the religious–secular continuum. Even indubitably secular Jews still observe many customs that are of a religious origin. Many prefer to have their parents cared for in Jewish care homes; their children attend Jewish youth organizations and they engage in Jewish-based leisure and cultural activities. Many of them have their children educated in Jewish schools and more would if Jewish schools with a more attractive Jewish ethos were available. What is absolutely apparent . . . is that London's Jews have long since ceased to comprise a religious group. They are truly an ethnie within British society, with shared historical memories, a myth of common ancestry, differentiating elements of common culture and an overall sense of solidarity . . . it would not be untruthful to state quite clearly that among Jews in London ethnicity overrides belief, except perhaps for the belief that being Jewish is important.[8]

Most London Jews live in the suburbs of north-west London, such as Hendon, Golders Green, and Finchley; many, especially younger families, have moved into the Greater London area to satellite towns such as Borehamwood and Radlett.[9] Other sizeable Jewish communities in Britain include Manchester, Liverpool, and Leeds, but in recent years most provincial communities have declined in numbers. Stamford Hill in east London has a large, densely concentrated haredi population; the other main area of haredi residence is Golders Green.[10] Outside London, there are significant concentrations of haredi Jews in Manchester and Gateshead.

Community, Communities, Networks, and Identity

The term 'community' is constantly used by British Jews, generally in one of two distinct senses. The first, more general sense, used in popular discourse, refers to all Jews who identify as Jews and participate to some extent in Jewish activities, whether cultural or religious. Thus a woman who regularly attends

---

[6] Graham, Boyd, and Vulkan, *2011 Census Results: Initial Insights*, 2–3.

[7] A quarter of London's Jews live in eight of the 624 wards in the Greater London area. See Graham, *2011 Census Results: Initial Insights*.

[8] Becher et al., *A Portrait of Jews*, 64–5.   [9] Housing costs are the main factor.

[10] North-west London, including Golders Green, is estimated to have between 4,500 and 7,600 haredim, about 18% of the UK haredi population; see Graham, *2011 Census Results: A Tale of Two Jewish Populations*, 7 n. 9.

synagogue, belongs to a religious Jewish women's organization, and raises money for Jewish causes might be described as 'very active in the community', but the same phrase could equally be applied to a man who does not belong to a synagogue or observe any religious practices, but who attends pro-Israel demonstrations, volunteers at a Jewish care home, and belongs to a Jewish bridge club. This broad sense of the term is apparent in institutional names such as Community Security Trust[11] or London Jewish Community Centre. 'Community' membership, however, is not coterminous with ethnic Jewish origin, but is understood to be conferred by active involvement and self-identification. A Modern Orthodox[12] woman in her sixties reminisced about her student days:

Had I not become involved in what was then called I[nter]-U[niversity] J[ewish] F[ederation] . . . I probably would have been very Jewishly lost, and may even have been lost to the Jewish community, because all my friends were not Jewish.[13]

The second, narrower sense of the term, indicating a particular subgroup, is apparent when people speak of 'my community', 'the Plymouth community', 'the *frum* community',[14] or 'the Sephardi community', by which they mean respectively: the members of a particular synagogue, the Jews of a particular city, Jews of a particular religious orientation, or Jews of a particular origin. While all the women with whom I interacted thought of themselves as members of the wider Jewish community, they often spoke of 'my community' in the sense of the synagogue (or occasionally subgroup) to which they belonged, and frequently expressed their identification with it with warmth and passion:

I'm incredibly wedded to my own community, because that's where the form my current Jewish life takes began, and I *love* my community, and I'm too old now nor do I wish to leave it.[15]

Most Jews who identify as belonging to the Jewish community also belong to several of these 'subcommunities', all of which overlap with family and social circles within the Jewish and wider communities, and most of which are not mutually exclusive.[16]

[11] The Community Security Trust is a charity that 'provides physical security, training and advice for the protection of British Jews' (see the Community Security Trust website).

[12] For a definition of this and other terms, see below in this chapter.

[13] Sheila Dorfman, interview.

[14] *Frum* (Yid. 'pious') is used by British Jews to refer to someone who is religiously observant in a visible way, for instance by keeping the rules of kashrut and the sabbath strictly. It does not entirely correspond to the term 'religious', as it need not imply a spiritually or theologically aware person.   [15] Stella James, interview, speaking of her synagogue.

[16] For Jewish concepts of community, see Webber, 'Introduction', 23–4.

As Anthony Cohen has noted,[17] much anthropological and sociological discussion has focused on the difficulty of defining and analysing the concept of 'community'.[18] I will adopt his practice of seeking 'use' rather than 'lexical definition' of the term, concentrating on the 'consciousness of community . . . encapsulated in perception of its boundaries . . . which are themselves largely constituted by people in interaction'.[19] As Cohen notes, groups mark their social boundaries by using and manipulating shared symbols, which are sufficiently ambivalent to allow them to be interpreted in different ways by members of the same community, thus constantly transforming 'the reality of difference into the appearance of similarity with such efficacy that people can still invest the "community" with ideological integrity'.[20] Though Cohen emphasizes the way in which people 'can "think" themselves into difference', there are practical and organizational correlates of these symbolic boundaries: for instance, the way in which some Orthodox rabbis' declarations that Reform Judaism is 'pseudo-Judaism' have led to Orthodox rejection of Reform converts as Jews and refusal to call up identifiably Reform Jews to the Torah in Orthodox synagogues. A major storm over the symbolic boundary between the Orthodox and non-Orthodox blew up in October-November 2013 over Limmud, the cross-communal study conference held annually over Christmas and attended by more than 2,500 Jews.[21] In contrast to his immediate predecessor, the new chief rabbi, Ephraim Mirvis, announced he would be attending Limmud, whereupon the former head of the London Beth Din, Dayan Chanoch Ehrentreu,[22] issued a public letter strongly discouraging Orthodox Jews from going. This was followed by a similar letter from seven other haredi rabbis, a four-page letter in the same vein issued to his congregants by the rabbi of Ner Yisrael, an independent non-haredi Orthodox synagogue (many of whose congregants attend Limmud), and countless heated responses in the Jewish media and online. At stake was the creation of a boundary between Orthodoxy and non-Orthodoxy, viewed as essential to survival by the haredim and right-wing traditionalists, and as immoral and divisive by the left-wing traditionalists, the Modern Orthodox, and the non-Orthodox.[23] As we will see below, women's religious activities are often co-opted as Orthodox/non-Orthodox boundary markers (as can be observed in Israel and the USA as well), and hence attract heightened attention and emotions.

[17] *The Symbolic Construction of Community*, introduction.
[18] For a critique of the over-simplistic nature of many 'community studies' in the early and mid-twentieth century, see Day, *Community and Everyday Life*, ch. 2.
[19] A. Cohen, *The Symbolic Construction of Community*, 12.   [20] Ibid. 21.
[21] See the Limmud website.   [22] A *dayan* is a judge in a rabbinic court.
[23] See Rocker, 'Limmud Row'.

Cohen's thesis of the symbolic construction of community accords well with the lived experience of participating in the London Jewish community, which is hard to define or delimit in terms of locality, institutional structures, or even ethnic origin, but is constituted by many partly overlapping symbolic boundaries, expressed in denominational affiliation, cultural activities, social and marriage patterns, educational choices, eating and visiting habits, and dress.

The concept of 'networks' also provides a useful way of thinking about Jewish social life. Graham Day has observed that 'focusing on networks takes away the holistic connotations of "community", making it a question instead of the quality and pattern of interpersonal relations',[24] starting from the individual—an emphasis particularly useful in looking at women's religious lives, which often cut across the denominational, sub-denominational, and institutional boundaries subdividing the Jewish community.[25] Several factors seem to underlie women's greater freedom in crossing denominational lines: first, they are less heavily invested in denominational leadership positions (especially Orthodox women, who cannot be rabbis); second, since they are often regarded, particularly in the Orthodox world, as having lower status than men, they are consequently 'invisible' to some extent and can cross boundaries with a certain degree of impunity; third, since women are less likely to reach high levels of Jewish education (again, particularly in the Orthodox sector), they are less likely to harbour theological and ideological ideas that classify other forms of Judaism as 'inauthentic'; and fourth, since they are assigned special responsibility for the domestic and familial sphere, they are more likely than men to maintain contact with family members who belong to different denominations.

Recent technological and social developments are bringing and will continue to bring change to traditional notions of community. Harvey Goldberg notes that today the notion of community 'cannot be separated from new forms of literacy and communication', such as the Internet.[26] Developing Arjun Appadurai's idea of viewing local social action against a range of '-scapes', such as 'mediascapes' and 'ethnoscapes', he points out that Jews' 'creation of com-

---

[24] Day, *Community and Everyday Life*, 217.

[25] For instance, *berakhah* parties are attended by women from across the Orthodox spectrum —haredi, traditionalist Orthodox, Sephardi—and women's *tefilah* groups and partnership *minyanim* include some Masorti women (see Ch. 4). Surprisingly little attention is paid to this by participants. David Golinkin has observed that 'when it comes to expanding the participation of Jewish women in public ritual life, Jewish women tend to ignore and cross denominational lines' ('Participation', 59).

[26] Goldberg, *Jewish Passages*, 25. See also Institute of Jewish Policy Research, *New Conceptions of Community*, on recent developments.

munity . . . places them within dynamic textscapes', now often digitally accessed, that 'define and express versions of Judaism and infuse social links to other Jews'. Hitherto accepted concepts of community are thus changing and shifting:

In an era when some Jewish groups ideologically place themselves in strict opposition to others, they also find themselves facing the unprecedented possibility of mutual or overlapping communities.[27]

This possibility may not actually be 'unprecedented'—mutual and overlapping communities already exist in the British Jewish world in contexts such as Limmud—but the possibilities of constructing new types of community by means of the new technologies are already being explored. The Grassroots Jews community in London, with a loose membership that spans the denominational range and beyond, is an example; it is organized, promoted, and shaped on social media sites such as Facebook, but it also possesses a real presence in the form of services, study sessions, retreats, and social events.[28] The presence of young women with high levels of secular education among its founders and most active members is very noticeable, contrasting strongly with traditional forms of community such as synagogues. These new modes of communication may prove an important factor both in the development of new forms of community and in the transformation of existing forms, as the latter adapt to these new possibilities and seek to take advantage of them.

Community affiliation thus exists at several levels and in several modes, with an individual's particular combination of networks and community memberships providing basic parameters of his or her individual Jewish identity. That identity itself is a complex and contentious issue; as Jonathan Webber has observed,

It is the subtlety of the coexistence of multiple components that constitutes the ethnographic complexity of modern Jewish life and thereby the construction of

---

[27] Goldberg, *Jewish Passages*, 25. The influence of the Internet on Jewish religious life is already palpable in many ways, for instance, access to classical Jewish texts and translations of them; use of Orthodox and non-Orthodox outreach sites for study and personal religious development (see the account of the Ahavas Yisrael group in Ch. 4); access to teachers and rabbis around the world, whose lectures appear on YouTube or at 'virtual yeshivas'; and access to blogs, which often give alternative views of events in the community. For further research on the role of the Internet in modern Jewish culture, see the collection of articles in Bronner and Battegay (eds.), *Connected Jews*, and also Baumel-Schwartz, '"It is our custom from *der alte Heim*"'.

[28] See the Grassroots Jews website, where the group describes itself as 'a London pop-up High Holy Days community'. Since it is not an Orthodox community, though it has many Orthodox members, I have not investigated it for the purposes of this study.

modern Jewish identities. Both religious and secular elements could be said to be involved in, say, a tea-party organized by a group of religious women for the purpose of fundraising.[29]

This complex, layered character of modern Jewish identity also underlies and complicates the definition of the term 'Orthodox', discussed below.

The Development of British Orthodoxy and the British Jewish Landscape

The Orthodox landscape of Anglo-Jewry is unique, incorporating a large number of Jews who would probably belong to the Conservative movement if they lived in the United States or would be classed 'traditional' if they lived in Israel. The peculiarly British version of Orthodoxy developed within and embodied by the United Synagogue plays a central role in the tensions currently polarizing Orthodoxy in Britain, and is vital to understanding Orthodox women's choices and the constraints shaping them. It is necessary, first, to examine the development of the term 'Orthodoxy'.

As noted by Webber, 'the category of "orthodoxy" is itself modern in origin',[30] and it has been characterized as 'more a mutation than a direct continuation of the traditional Judaism from which it emerged'.[31] The term can be traced back to the early nineteenth century, when traditionalists sought to define themselves in opposition to Jewish reformers, who 'began to advocate not merely changes in Jewish thought, but reform of Jewish practices'.[32] At this point the term 'Orthodox', which originally signified a Christian or Jewish opponent of Enlightenment principles, began to take on the meaning of a Jewish opponent of Jewish religious reform—a change completed by the 1830s. By the 1870s the term 'Orthodox' had become the accepted label for traditionalist Jews who opposed the Reform movement (though other terms, such as 'Torah-true', were generated within their ranks and continue to be used alongside 'Orthodox'). 'The Orthodox' had become an identifiable group, thanks to their vigorous opposition to the threat posed by modernity to traditional Judaism, and to most of the measures proposed by the Reformers to find a modus vivendi between these two world-views.

Moshe Samet points out that, from the first, there were different trends within Orthodoxy, in particular the German and Hungarian types, which underlie the divisions within Orthodoxy today (Modern/Centrist Orthodoxy

---

[29] Webber, 'Modern Jewish Identities', 261.
[30] Ibid. 264.   [31] Samet, 'The Beginnings of Orthodoxy', 249.
[32] Blutinger, '"So-Called Orthodoxy"', 320.

and haredi Orthodoxy respectively).[33] The German (neo-)Orthodox, led by Samson Raphael Hirsch (1808–88), adopted a positive attitude to the non-Jewish modern world, sanctioning a certain degree of secular study and participation in the cultural life of the surrounding society: their slogan was *torah im derekh erets* ('Torah with the way of the land', i.e. secular culture). Simultaneously, however, they rejected the Reformers, preferring to set up their own religious and educational institutions, and thus splitting the Jewish community, rather than be forced to recognize and contribute to Reform institutions and practices. In contrast, the extremist Orthodox of north-eastern Hungary rejected all accommodation with or knowledge of the non-Jewish world, and developed a novel ideology and method of manipulating halakhah in order to justify their position;[34] their slogan might be characterized as *ḥadash asur min hatorah* ('All that is new is forbidden by the Torah').[35] Although just as opposed to the Reform movement as the German Orthodox, the Hungarian extremists felt particular loathing for the latter, characterizing them as hypocritical 'Sadducees'.

Samet argues that the hasidim, adherents of a movement originating in eastern Europe in the eighteenth century, and their opponents, the *mitnagedim*, were not originally part of the Orthodox grouping. He describes hasidism as a 'fundamentalist movement whose aim was to restore the religion to its pristine splendour, and to revitalize religious values which had lost their potency', and the opposing *mitnagedim* as 'a movement of protest against those who would tamper with the integrity of the tradition'.[36] Later, however, both these groups allied themselves with Orthodoxy, and today are regarded as quintessentially haredi Orthodox.[37]

In Britain, things developed rather differently: a 'traditional' rather than a self-consciously 'Orthodox' outlook has persisted from the nineteenth century until the present. A survey commissioned by Chief Rabbi Nathan Marcus Adler (1803–90) in 1845 revealed 'a series of Anglo-Jewish communities in which observance of orthodox practice was lax, synagogue attendance poor, and educational facilities woefully deficient',[38] and little changed thereafter. The first Reform synagogue was founded in 1840, but the small Reform movement did not present a particular threat to the traditional community,

---

[33] Samet, 'The Beginnings of Orthodoxy', 249.

[34] See Silber, 'The Emergence of Ultra-Orthodoxy'.

[35] A novel interpretation by R. Moses Sofer (1753–1839) of a phrase that originally referred to the prohibition on consuming new grain before the Omer offering is made.

[36] Samet, 'The Beginnings of Orthodoxy', 251.

[37] The label *mitnagedim* is obsolete; this group is now described as 'Lithuanian' or 'yeshivish'.

[38] Alderman, *Modern British Jewry*, 41. The word 'orthodox' here corresponds to 'traditional' in terms of the definitions used in the present study and set out later in this chapter.

most of whom were comfortably anglicized by the late nineteenth century, and whose synagogues were amalgamated by Act of Parliament in 1870 to form the United Synagogue, an Orthodox institution led by a chief rabbi. Geoffrey Alderman observes that 'the political considerations that had led German Jews to embrace Reform never existed in England, with the result that it was possible for the unique form of "genteel orthodoxy of the United Synagogue" to flourish and grow, where in other circumstances it would almost certainly have been crushed'.[39] Religious fervour was unusual, and most United Synagogue members felt that 'belonging to a synagogue was . . . more important than attending it';[40] a census of religious worship carried out by the *British Weekly* in October 1886 revealed that only 10–15% of the total Jewish population of west and north-west London attended synagogue on a sabbath morning. Though Nathan Adler had fiercely opposed suggestions to reform the prayer book and shorten the liturgy, his son, Chief Rabbi Hermann Adler (1839–1911), was more accommodating and in 1889 accepted shortened services, the omission of the priestly benediction on festivals, and the introduction of verbal expressions of consent for both bride and bridegroom—innovations unthinkable in an Orthodox context in the rest of Europe.

All this changed with the mass immigration of thousands of east European Jews in the 1880s, many of whom were deeply traditional. The large 'cathedral' synagogues of Anglo-Jewry were completely alien to them, and they preferred to organize their own small *hevras*,[41] in which they maintained the unreformed, noisy, 'oriental' tradition of prayer that shocked the decorous Jews of the host community. They also preferred the leadership of traditionally educated east European rabbis to the English-speaking, university-trained rabbis of the United Synagogue, and set up their own communal organizations, such as Mahazikei Hadat, which authorized marriages, divorces, and kosher slaughter, and founded traditional religious schools for children, all in direct competition with existing Anglo-Jewish institutions. The establishment, in the person of the Liberal MP Samuel Montagu (1832–1911), responded by founding the Federation of Synagogues in 1887 as an umbrella organization for the hitherto unregulated synagogues of the East End, with the aim of bringing the immigrants 'within the discipline of the existing communal structures'[42] and preventing schism in the community. Eventually the Federation absorbed most members of Mahazikei Hadat and proved to be 'the largest single instrument of Anglicization, as well as of social control, that Anglo-Jewry possessed'.[43]

---

[39] Alderman, *Modern British Jewry*, 95.   [40] Ibid. 106.
[41] The *hevra* was a small association, part synagogue and part social centre; see Bermant, *Troubled Eden*, 213.   [42] Ibid. 165.   [43] Ibid.

By the mid-twentieth century it had lost its east European and more intensely religious character, and its members had become very similar in lifestyle, aspirations, and religious practice to those of the United Synagogue, but it continued to guard its independence jealously, maintaining a parallel burial scheme, rabbinic court, kashrut supervision, and—after a brief flirtation with the United Synagogue—declining to recognize the authority of the chief rabbi.[44]

Further to the right, dissatisfaction with the 'milk-and-water' Orthodoxy of the United Synagogue prompted others, mainly from Germany and Austria-Hungary, to found their own independent and strictly neo-Orthodox syna-gogue, the North London Beth Hamedrash, in 1886. In 1909 they invited the Hungarian neo-Orthodox Rabbi Dr Victor Schonfeld (1880–1930) to lead them. Several smaller synagogues joined them, founding the Union of Orthodox Hebrew Congregations (UOHC, popularly known as the Adas) in 1926, after a series of rows with Chief Rabbi Dr Joseph Hertz (1872–1946) over marriage certification and ritual slaughter (sheḥitah).[45] The Union sup-ported its own communal rabbinical court, kashrut authority (Kedassia), and burial society, but constituent synagogues were free to govern themselves. Although its 'core' synagogue, the Stamford Hill Adas Yisroel, originally closely followed the traditions of Hirsch's Frankfurt synagogue, the influx of hasidim in the 1930s fundamentally changed the Union's character—a trend intensified by the arrival of more hasidim after the 1956 Hungarian uprising. By this time the older, Hirschian members were moving out of Stamford Hill to Golders Green and Hendon in north-west London, transforming Stamford Hill into a largely hasidic enclave.

Tensions and resentments endure between what Chaim Bermant called the 'White Adath [= Adas]' of north-west London and the 'Black Adath' of Stamford Hill,[46] though the formerly Hirschian 'White' faction has moved perceptibly to the right in outlook and practice, and might better be described as 'Grey' nowadays. Unlike its American counterpart, Hirsch's confident neo-Orthodoxy has largely petered out in Britain, due in part to the influence of hasidic groups and in part to the 'slide to the right' observable throughout the Orthodox world in the last four decades, which has seen the non-haredi world adopt many haredi standards, customs, and ideologies.[47]

Liberal Judaism, a breakaway movement to the left, emerged from main-stream Orthodoxy at roughly the same time as the Union. Founded by in-dividuals dissatisfied with the lack of spirituality of the United Synagogue, it was led by the Bible scholar Claude Montefiore (1858–1938), who promoted a universalist, ethically focused version of Judaism, and Lily Montagu (1873–1963), the daughter of Samuel Montagu, who was active in battling unem-

[44] Ibid., ch. 16.   [45] Ibid., ch. 17.   [46] Ibid. 222–3.   [47] See Heilman, *Sliding to the Right*.

ployment, poor housing, and the exploitation of workers. They set up the Jewish Religious Union in 1902, which became an egalitarian denomination to the left of Reform, establishing its first synagogue in 1911.

The last major schism in Anglo-Jewry was triggered by the 'Jacobs affair' in the early 1960s.[48] The Orthodox rabbi Louis Jacobs (1920–2006), a brilliant scholar educated both at the haredi Gateshead Yeshiva and at University College, London, had been appointed as lecturer at Jews' College, the Anglo-Jewish Orthodox rabbinical seminary, with the expectation that he would become the next principal of the college when the incumbent, Dr Isidore Epstein, retired in 1961; he was also a favoured candidate for the position of next chief rabbi. In 1957 he had published a book, *We Have Reason to Believe*, which, although designed as a defence of Orthodox Judaism, contained ideas about the origin of the Torah that, while by no means novel, were unacceptable to right-wing Orthodoxy. After Epstein's retirement, no move was made to appoint Jacobs, who eventually resigned from his lectureship in protest. The chief rabbi, Israel Brodie (1895–1979), influenced by the haredi London Beth Din, announced that he could not accept Jacobs's appointment because of the latter's theological opinions, and when in 1964 Jacobs sought to return to his previous pastoral post at the New West End Synagogue, Brodie refused to agree to this appointment unless Jacobs recanted. Over 300 members of the New West End left the synagogue, and bought the old St John's Wood Synagogue building, where they opened the New London Synagogue, led by Rabbi Jacobs. Although Jacobs, who regarded his own views as well within Orthodoxy, had had no intention of founding a new denomination, his synagogue and other small communities inspired by it later affiliated themselves to the American Conservative movement, founding the Assembly of Masorti Synagogues in 1985. In spite of this ideological shift, many British Masorti synagogues still preserve the atmosphere and practices of the 'old' United Synagogue, before its university-educated rabbis were largely replaced by haredim and its haredi Beth Din gained unprecedented power. This makes it attractive to United Synagogue members who are unhappy with the 'haredization' of their synagogues; several have moved to a Masorti synagogue as a result.

This complex history of schism and denominational proliferation underlies and continues to shape the contemporary religious geography of Anglo-Jewry, which forms the backdrop for this study of women's religious lives.

---

[48] See Bermant, *Troubled Eden*, ch. 19; Alderman, *Modern British Jewry*, 361–4; and Louis Jacobs's autobiography, *Helping with Inquiries*.

Jewish Religious Topography Today

Moving from left to right, current denominations include Liberal Judaism and Reform Judaism (outside the scope of this study); Masorti Judaism (mentioned tangentially here); and Orthodox Judaism, itself subdivided at the institutional level into the United Synagogue, the Federation of Synagogues, and the Union of Orthodox Hebrew Congregations. Sephardi synagogues are Orthodox, but embrace a wide range of practice and belief, and in some ways parallel the 'broad church' character of the United Synagogue. There are also a few independent Orthodox synagogues, occupying various positions on the spectrum, from Yakar (1978–2010) on the left to Ner Yisrael (founded in 1984) to the right of the United Synagogue.

In terms of size, a 2016 survey of synagogue affiliation in Britain by the Institute for Jewish Policy Research (JPR) found that 53% of affiliated Jews belonged to 'Central Orthodox' synagogues (mainly United Synagogue and Federation), while 13% belonged to 'Strictly Orthodox' (mainly UOHC) and 3% to Sephardi synagogues.[49] Comparison with figures from 1990 shows a 37% decrease from the previous 'Central Orthodox' share and a 28.9% decrease in the Sephardi, while the 'Strictly Orthodox' has increased by 139% (thanks to a high birth rate) and the Masorti by 114%, largely at the United Synagogue's expense. If we combine the Orthodox denominations and compare them to the combined non-Orthodox ones, it emerges that about 70% of the affiliated Jewish population belongs to an Orthodox synagogue and about 30% to a non-Orthodox one. The religious landscape of Anglo-Jewry is changing fast, however, with a trend towards polarization to right and left and the decline of the centre—the territory of the United Synagogue, which used to be the largest sector.

The neatness of this arrangement of denominational institutions, however, conceals a much more complex set of intertwining axes of religious life, making the construction of a consistent and accurate set of descriptive labels and definitions a nearly impossible task—and one of limited utility. The authors of the JPR report noted that the nature of synagogue affiliation itself is changing, with some families joining two synagogues of different denominations, and many Jews attending synagogue without formal affiliation.[50] In addition, new or alternative prayer services, such as the partnership *minyanim* discussed in Chapter 4, usually take place in private homes or on rented premises. When other aspects of Jewish religious life, such as religious practice, belief, and outlook, and personal religiosity or spirituality, are

---

[49] Mashiah and Boyd, *Synagogue Membership in the United Kingdom in 2016*. Non-Orthodox figures were: Masorti 3%, Reform 19%, Liberal 8%.   [50] Ibid. 22.

examined in addition to the denominational spectrum just described, and when factors such as the high degree of religious mobility apparent in Anglo-Jewry and recent trends within the denominations themselves (for instance the increasing influence of haredi Orthodoxy on the United Synagogue) are added, a much more complex and dynamic picture emerges.

Orthodox Jews in London perceive a basic division between Orthodoxy and other denominations, but they also increasingly experience Orthodoxy itself as consisting of two separate, though occasionally overlapping, communities: the haredim, often described as 'the black hats' or 'the *frum* community', and the non-haredim, variously characterized as 'United Synagogue', 'mainstream Orthodox', 'Centrist Orthodox', or 'Modern Orthodox'—though, as we shall see, this last term is not really accurate. The Sephardim, while recognized as Orthodox in a general sense, are perceived (both by themselves and by Ashkenazim) as a special case, a parallel community based on origin rather than theological or practical differences. Sephardim often point out the traditional rather than denominational character of their community as a particular advantage since it encourages communal unity, though they too are beginning to feel the divisive effects of the 'slide to the right'.

The Ashkenazi Orthodox community, however, seems to be increasingly polarized, with a widening gap in the centre.[51] The non-haredi Orthodox often feel they have more in common with Jews to the left of Orthodoxy, especially Masorti, than with haredim (indeed, faced with haredi encroachment into the non-haredi Orthodox community, many have moved leftwards to Masorti). Analysis of census data from 2011 has revealed that two distinct Jewish populations can be identified in demographic terms within the UK Jewish community:[52] the fast-growing haredi population, with an average age of 27, and the non-haredi population (non-haredi Orthodox, Masorti, Reform, and Liberal), with an average age of 44. In 2015, about 51% of all Jewish births in the UK were in the haredi community, which constitutes about 7.5% of the total Jewish population.[53] Since three of the five haredi residential neighbourhoods in the UK are in London, the existence of these separate, though linked, Jewish populations is very evident there. The demographic differences between the haredi and non-haredi Orthodox populations are reinforced by differences in education, occupation, dress, gender roles, and religious practice,

---

[51] For polarization in American Orthodoxy, see Heilman, *Sliding to the Right*. Many factors and trends identified there also apply to British Orthodoxy, although the American situation is different in important respects. Miri Freud-Kandel, in *Orthodox Judaism*, offers an account of the British version of the 'slide to the right' in institutional rather than 'grassroots' terms. See also Endelman, *The Jews of Britain*, 250–1.

[52] Graham, *2011 Census Results: A Tale of Two Jewish Populations*, 9.

[53] Mashiah, *Vital Statistics of the UK Jewish Population*, 9, based on the 2011 census.

to the extent that one can speak of two Orthodox Jewish communities in London, roughly corresponding to the denominational groupings of the United Synagogue and the UOHC, with the Federation occupying a somewhat ambiguous position in the middle.[54]

However, these groups are not rigidly bounded or completely separate: a better image might be of a clustering of individuals at both ends of a graduated spectrum, with a number of people in the middle who bridge or move between the two. In addition, there is constant movement and interpenetration between the two extremes: for instance, most non-haredi Orthodox Jewish schools employ haredi teachers for Jewish studies; many haredim prefer to consult Jewish doctors and lawyers, most of whom are not haredi; a high proportion of rabbis employed by United synagogues are haredim;[55] and growing numbers of non-haredi Jews become haredi as a result of religious conviction.[56] Further complicating the picture, some members of United synagogues are haredi in lifestyle and self-identification, while others' observance resembles that of Reform and Liberal Jews.

Rather than examine each community separately, I studied women across both groups: partly to examine differences in the religious views and lives of haredi and non-haredi women and to investigate how women from different backgrounds influenced each other, and partly for practical reasons, since my central locus was Hendon, where haredim are a significant minority within the Jewish population.[57] There are considerable differences of outlook and self-understanding between women from the two communities, shaping their religious lives in different ways, but in conversation they rarely used the haredi/non-haredi divide as a marker of religious behaviour. Indeed, a few had difficulty in deciding whether they belonged to one group or the other,[58]

[54] Federation rabbis (and ideology) are haredi, while the laity differs little from that of the United Synagogue, though there is an increasing trend towards the religious right.

[55] This trend accelerated when Jews' College (since renamed London School of Jewish Studies) ceased to ordain rabbis in 1999, and candidates for the rabbinate were forced to train either in Israel or in the USA, often in haredi yeshivas.

[56] Some individuals leave the haredi community, though anecdotal evidence suggests that they often drop all Jewish religious observance rather than joining the non-haredi Orthodox. GesherEU, a charity for people leaving the haredi community, was founded in 2013. By 2019 it had been contacted by over 100 men and women in search of support (information from Robert Bernard of GesherEU via email, 25 Apr. 2019; see also Oliver, 'Ex-Charedi Women'). See also Winston, *Unchosen*, for a study of haredi leavers in the USA. The phenomenon is gathering pace in Israel too, with an estimated 1,300 haredim under the age of 25 leaving yearly; see Rotem, 'For Israelis Who Flee the Ultra-Orthodox Fold'.

[57] Apart from interviewing two hasidic women, I did not attempt to study the Stamford Hill community: it would have been very difficult to gain acceptance there. My focus here is on the hitherto under-researched community of non-haredi Orthodox women.

[58] A single woman in her twenties tried to define her family: 'People would look at our family

reinforcing the image of a graduated spectrum between two poles, rather than two homogenous and separate communities.

Religious mobility does not stop within the bounds of the Orthodox community. An under-researched aspect of the British Jewish community is the surprisingly high level of movement across denominational borders and in levels of personal religious observance in the course of an individual's life, or within a single family. While several studies of *ba'alei teshuvah* (newly observant Jews) have been carried out, particularly in America,[59] and some research exists on Jews who abandon religious practice altogether,[60] little attention has been paid to those who move from Orthodoxy to Masorti or to Reform, and to the factors underlying their decision to do so (except for the beginnings of the Masorti movement in Britain).

This was demonstrated in the small sample of the twenty-eight women I interviewed. They included three women who had left Orthodoxy (one had ceased to define herself as religious,[61] the other two had joined the Masorti movement[62]), one woman who had moved from the haredi community to Modern Orthodoxy, and two women who had become less observant while remaining within Orthodoxy. Moving in the opposite direction, one woman from a nominally Orthodox but non-observant family had joined Lubavitch hasidism, one woman had converted to Modern Orthodoxy, and three women had become more observant and religiously engaged while staying within the Orthodox subdenomination in which they had grown up.

When the lives of their parents, children, siblings, and spouses are examined,[63] this tendency to move between (and sometimes out of) denominations continues: one woman's parents had moved from Modern Orthodoxy to Satmar hasidism, and another woman's sister and daughter had become haredi; one woman's husband had moved from Reform to (Sephardi) Orthodoxy; two women had children who had become 'more religious'; one woman had a daughter who had left Orthodoxy for Masorti, another a son who had

and say haredi, but we're not really . . . people who are haredi might consider us a bit more Modern Orthodox.' Sheyna Marcus, interview.

[59] See Kaufman, *Rachel's Daughters*; Davidman, *Tradition in a Rootless World*; Benor, *Becoming Frum.*   [60] See Endelman, *Radical Assimilation*, and above, n. 56.

[61] Although defining herself as a humanist, after a brief period attending Masorti synagogues she continues to keep a kosher kitchen as well as the sabbath and festivals, since her husband has remained Orthodox and her social circle is largely Orthodox.

[62] One married a non-religious man, and Masorti provided a 'halfway house' with which they were both happy; the other left the United Synagogue after a row occasioned by a rabbi's insensitivity over a relation's death, joined a Reform synagogue, and eventually moved to the Masorti movement, where she felt more at home.

[63] This is an impressionistic sketch that is based on what I was told; interviewees were not specifically asked to list all family members who had changed denomination.

joined Reform, and another a husband who had joined Masorti after lacking any previous affiliation; and one woman had a son, and another woman a sibling, who had abandoned all religious practice. This pattern of constant movement seems common across the entire British Jewish community. No research exists on the effects of this denominational mobility on religious life and belief, though a clear social effect can be seen in the links these moves create between different subcommunities; most Jews in London have relatives who belong to a wide range of denominations and to none.

Another important aspect of the Anglo-Jewish religious scene is the hugely varied and somewhat amorphous nature of the United Synagogue. While the haredi community is a much more bounded enclave and has specific, detailed expectations regarding religious practice and belief, backed up by powerful social controls enforcing conformity, the non-haredi sector lacks a strong, unified ideology or code of practice, and is consequently far harder to define and delimit. Within the 'broad church' of the United Synagogue (and, to a lesser extent, in the Federation), members may or may not keep kosher, observe the sabbath as prescribed by halakhah, believe in God, or accept the divine origin of the Torah.[64] The official position, embodied in rabbis' sermons, synagogue practice, synagogue-based activities, and the ethos of Orthodox schools, is uncompromisingly Orthodox, but the actual practice and beliefs of United Synagogue members vary from haredi to non-observant and atheist, with every possible variation in between. It is by no means uncommon to encounter United Synagogue members who will admit to lacking any religious beliefs whatsoever, or who are agnostic or doubtful about traditional theological claims, but who still maintain a kosher home, observe the festivals, send their children to a Jewish school, and expect them to marry within the faith. They can best be characterized as a subset of non-haredi Orthodoxy, whose Jewish identity is based primarily on an ethnic, traditionalist attachment rather than a religious or spiritual one.[65] Though taking little active part in shaping religious life, members of this ethnic-based/identity-based group often oppose change vigorously, including change designed to increase women's participation or rights, since any alteration in the synagogue or ritual practice they associate with their childhood and their families is deeply threatening to their sense of identity. I will refer to this group as 'traditionalists'.

[64] A 1992 review of the United Synagogue revealed that 'only 10% classified themselves as "strictly Orthodox (Shomrei Shabbat)", whilst 67% identified as "Traditional (but not strictly Orthodox)"'. Given that sabbath observance is a central tenet of Orthodoxy, this is a remarkably low figure. Only 29% attended synagogue every week, though attendance rose to 53% on Yom Kippur. See Kalms, *United Synagogue Review*, 240.
[65] See Webber, 'Modern Jewish Identities', 250–1, 255, which speaks of religion becoming 'the facade of the community', and of the 'redefinition of religion as ethnicity'.

The greatest advantage of the United Synagogue is that it provides a comfortable home for all levels of Jewish practice and belief: 'The United Synagogue was intended to function as an umbrella organization in which all Jews who were prepared to identify as Orthodox, regardless of their practice, could be encompassed.'[66] However, this inclusive character has simultaneously proved to be its Achilles' heel, and the traditional, tolerant, 'light' version of Orthodoxy that characterized the United Synagogue has not been robust enough to withstand more modern pressures. A religious lifestyle that was good enough for many women's parents would seem inadequate now. Remembering her childhood in the 1960s, Katherine Marks, a religiously observant Jewish educator, describes her intensely Jewish but halakhically inconsistent family:

My parents ticked a lot of the boxes of the absolute typical Anglo-thing of the time. So my parents wouldn't, unless they absolutely had to—and I do remember these rules being broken occasionally—go shopping on a Shabat, [but] if they really had to then they would, and they would drive on Shabat but only to go to an aunt's house or something like that, and I stopped driving on Shabat when I was about 13, 14, and that caused a lot of difficulty . . . My parents kept kosher in the home, but ate out [i.e. in non-kosher restaurants], very occasionally would eat *treyf* out,[67] but be very upset to do it in front of me . . . We took the days off school for *ḥagim*,[68] my mum and dad didn't work on *ḥagim*, and Friday night was Friday night. Friday night we lit the candles, always on time, whenever that was. We didn't make Kiddush, we didn't *bentsh*,[69] but my mum would make chicken and also she would do *cholent* for Shabat lunch,[70] and there was no washing or ironing on Shabat; it was a different day for her.

The standards of religious observance preached by rabbis and assumed by Jewish schools are now considerably stricter, and today's United Synagogue members are often at a loss to position themselves in religious terms and lack religious confidence. Several lifelong members wondered whether they were 'Orthodox enough' when I asked to interview them for research on Orthodox women. A woman in her fifties, who grew up in an observant United Synagogue home but is now Masorti, told me, 'I really understood the haredi world, I really understood the Reform world, I couldn't place myself anywhere, I'm all along the line.' A common narrative among older United Synagogue members concerns the child who goes to a Modern Orthodox or haredi

[66] Freud-Kandel, *Orthodox Judaism*, 10.

[67] Yid. 'non-kosher food'. In this particular context it means eating non-kosher meat, a greater breach of halakhah.   [68] Heb. 'festivals'.

[69] Yid. 'bless', i.e. recite the long grace after meals prescribed by halakhah.

[70] Cooking on the sabbath is prohibited; *cholent* is a traditional dish designed to cook slowly from Friday afternoon to Saturday lunchtime.

yeshiva or seminary in Israel for a year or two, and, returning home, rejects the vague theology and 'half-hearted' observance of the parents and 'becomes *frum*', often moving to a more right-wing synagogue or becoming haredi; in some cases, the parents follow the child's lead and change their own religious practice and affiliation.[71] The other common story is that of the child who abandons Orthodoxy altogether. Both narratives, and the unease of those 'left in the middle', are described by Sheila Dorfman, a religiously observant United Synagogue educator in her sixties:

The younger generation are polarizing; they're either becoming very very *frum*, in which case ... they find their satisfaction in the minutiae of religion, or they give up on United Synagogue-type religion and move further to the left ... I think there is a typical United Synagogue woman who goes to shul [synagogue] every week and is on the ladies' guild, and will go to lectures and will do a certain amount ... and they're very comfortable thank you, and they don't want *anything* to change. And I think that group of women is getting smaller.

It is not only the religiously observant or the yeshiva- or seminary-educated young who are scathing about United Synagogue religiosity (or lack thereof). Historians of Anglo-Jewry have also denigrated its undemanding traditionalism:

The United Synagogue acquired—perhaps had been born with—a species of religious schizophrenia, and deliberately so. Within and through it, orthodoxy survived, but usually in a much diluted form, supported by businessmen and their wives who reached an accommodation with a religious creed they themselves no longer practised to the full, or even fully understood.[72]

Such criticism was echoed by several interviewees, most of them members of the United Synagogue. Sheila Dorfman complained:

The United Synagogue has lost its identity, it's fearful, it's introverted, it's reversionary. Haredim have haredi rabbis, Reform have Reform rabbis, Masorti have Masorti rabbis, Liberals have Liberal rabbis, and the United Synagogue has haredi rabbis and a haredi *beis din*.[73] And consequently the United Synagogue is frightened of its own shadow, it doesn't know who it is, it doesn't know who it wants to be, and even if it does it's not going to say so because it might be thrown out into the deep yonder of non-Orthodox organizations, and it's petrified of that.

The gap between religious leaders and the laity is growing wider: Geoffrey Alderman recently observed that 'The U[nited] S[ynagogue] is bipolar . . . Its lay membership is more radical (by which I mean more liberal) than its

---

[71] Several interviewees had experienced this.

[72] Alderman, *Modern British Jewry*, 216.   [73] Yiddish form of *beit din*, a religious court.

clerical leadership and whereas in times past this membership was more than happy to pay rabbis to be Orthodox on its behalf, this is no longer the case.'[74] Many United Synagogue women, particularly those engaged and active in religious life, are very conscious of the fact that the model of Orthodox practice and belief presented to them by their rabbis, and by the Orthodox schools attended by their children and grandchildren, is increasingly haredi. They often recalled United Synagogue events or practices from their childhood, such as the acceptance of unsupervised cheese as kosher, or mixed dances and concerts featuring female singers held on United Synagogue premises, usually commenting, 'But of course you couldn't do that now.' This trend increases their sense of alienation and confusion. Less active United Synagogue women tended not to remark on the 'slide to the right', and may not be aware of it; since they rarely attend synagogue and are not observant themselves, they do not differentiate between 'religious' people to their right.

In contrast, haredi women rarely raise issues of dissatisfaction and insecurity, and seem much more confident and content in their religious lives and identity. This may be due to the conformist nature of haredi society, in which open expression of doubt carries heavy social penalties; it is questionable whether haredi women feel comfortable discussing such subjects with an anthropologist from the non-haredi community. Alternatively (or simultaneously), the much more unified and inculcated haredi ideology, actively promoted by rabbis and teachers, may be responsible, since the intensive forms of conditioning, or 'techniques of subjectification',[75] to which women are exposed from their earliest years effectively mould their self-understanding and religiosity into a haredi pattern. Part of the haredi ideal is a rejection of modern, secular values; like the Muslim women observed by Saba Mahmood,[76] haredi women are engaged in constructing a pious self with different goals and methods from those of Western liberal culture. Consequently, they do not experience the tension between the demands of the surrounding secular culture and those of traditional Orthodoxy in the same way as women in the non-haredi community. A combination of these factors may account for the apparently greater stability in haredi religious life.[77]

These shifts in the nature of a traditional religious community seem to be part of the phenomenon examined by Olivier Roy in his book *Holy Ignorance*, which documents the recent and increasing split between 'religion' and 'culture':

---

[74] Alderman, '"Safe" Choice'.
[75] Mahmood, *Politics of Piety*, 17 and n. 30.   [76] Ibid.
[77] Though see n. 56 above for evidence of the growing numbers of haredim who leave their community, in America, Israel, and the UK.

[R]eligious 'comeback' is merely an optical illusion: it would be more appropriate to speak of transformation. Religion is both more visible and at the same time frequently in decline. We are witnessing a reformulation of religion rather than a return to ancestral practices . . . one thing is undeniable: in all cases it is the so-called 'fundamentalist' or 'charismatic' forms of religion that have seen the most spectacular growth . . . Fundamentalism is the religious form that is most suited to globalization, because it accepts its own deculturation and makes it the instrument of its claim to universality.[78]

Changing Moods among British Jewish Women

The level of dissatisfaction among many women in the non-haredi Orthodox community seems to have been on the rise since the 1980s,[79] and this phenomenon has undoubtedly been influenced by the wider feminist movement. Earlier tensions between traditional expectations for women and new ideas about their role in the wider society were reflected in developments within the British Jewish community: the foundation of (egalitarian) Liberal Judaism in 1911, the growth of synagogue ladies' guilds and Jewish women's organizations in the post-war period, and the move towards egalitarianism in the Reform and Masorti movements in the last few decades. Orthodoxy, conservative in its very essence, has been slow to respond. For decades the only way in which Orthodox women could apply feminist ideas was either to throw all their efforts into their professional life outside the Jewish sphere, creating a paradoxical lifestyle where a top barrister or doctor would sit silently in the women's gallery in the synagogue, or to leave the Orthodox world for another, more egalitarian denomination. The very word 'feminist' carries negative connotations in most Orthodox communities, even among women who profess strongly feminist views in economic and political matters.[80]

As late as 1989 an observer of the Jewish community could still remark, 'it is difficult to foresee any great changes in the status of women within Anglo-Jewry', noting that initiatives such as a short-lived feminist Jewish magazine, the academic Jewish Women's History Group,[81] and a radical Jewish publishing group had made 'virtually no impact on religious Anglo-Jewry'. He added that women with ambitions beyond running the ladies' guild had probably

[78] Roy, *Holy Ignorance*, 5.   [79] See the discussion of the Rosh Hodesh movement in Ch. 4.
[80] When the (Orthodox) London School of Jewish Studies ran a course entitled 'The Female Jew', covering topics such as women in the Bible, the halakhic status of women, and divorce, several men and women who attended (and enjoyed it) expressed discomfort with the title, as it sounded 'too feminist'. For an analysis of the 'counter-feminism' of Habad women and their relationship to Western feminism, see Morris, 'Agents or Victims?', and *Lubavitcher Women*.
[81] The group collected women's oral histories.

already deserted Orthodoxy for the Progressive movement, and saw nothing but stagnation ahead.[82] In the 1990s, however, earlier developments in Israel and the United States—the rise of Rosh Hodesh groups, women's sabbath services and Torah readings, and the increase in Jewish educational opportunities for women—finally found an echo in Britain. Inspired by a visit by Dr Alice Shalvi (b.1926), a British educator living in Israel who had set up the Pelech experimental school for religious girls and founded the Israel Women's Network, several London women started a Rosh Hodesh group, and later organized two *shabatonim* (weekend events) for women at a hotel in Bournemouth, the latter including women-only sabbath morning services. Katherine Marks, who participated in this first period of Orthodox Jewish women's innovation and growth, recalled the excitement:

Those services, women's services, were a complete revelation, never to be repeated actually, and we had a reunion recently, and a lot of the women were saying how it was a very very important experience. Now those [services] were cross-communal, so of course the Orthodox women were practically foaming at the mouth—in a good way—and couldn't believe what was going on, and Masorti didn't really exist then, but the Reform women were *very* moved, because they'd never had a women's thing, they were used to the egalitarian, but they loved the women's space. [They were] also moved at how moved *we* were.

The mood of excitement and the creative and purposeful activity by women continued with the establishment of the cross-communal Jewish Women's Network and the foundation of the first women's *tefilah* group at Stanmore in 1993. This proved too much for the London Beth Din, however; its leaders felt that the women had invaded the male territory of formal prayer services, and all the resources of the Orthodox religious establishment were employed to prevent them holding the services in the synagogue for the next eighteen years, and to brand them as rebels. The women were dismayed, since they had not regarded their activities as rebellious or subversive,[83] but as part of a quest for greater participation and spirituality. Most had no desire to confront rabbinic authority, and were anxious to remain members of the Orthodox community in good standing. Gradually the impetus slowed, and most of the groups dwindled; only two women's *tefilah* groups and a few Rosh Hodesh groups, largely monthly social meetings with entertainment or educational components, survived the general decline. Excitement and enthusiasm were replaced by frustration and resentment, or in some cases by withdrawal from Orthodoxy. Several felt that younger women did not share their aspirations: a teacher who had been a central figure in this wave noted:

[82] Brook, *The Club*, ch. 14.   [83] Their rabbi supported and encouraged the project.

The younger women see it as all a bit wacky, they're much more conventional, maybe Jewish schooling has made them less imaginative . . . you've got a few younger women here who are very energetic, but most of them enjoy Kinloss [United Synagogue] . . . We had a vision, we wanted something different for our daughters, but our daughters didn't want it.[84]

From 2005, however, a new wave of women's innovation, activity, and creativity has developed, including women's Megillah readings, some new Rosh Hodesh groups, and a revival of the Stanmore women's *tefilah* group, as well as a new range of pietistic activities, such as *berakhah* parties and challah parties, which are more typical of the haredi community. Institutional changes in the United Synagogue and the Federation, whereby women can serve as synagogue board members and (in the United Synagogue) synagogue presidents, point to a greater acceptance of a wider role for women in the non-haredi community.

In June 2013 two significant events occurred: a British branch of the American-based Jewish Orthodox Feminist Alliance (JOFA) was founded in London, led by Rebbetsin (now Rabba) Dina Brawer,[85] who organized regular seminars and events, and the first partnership *minyan* in Britain was held, with women leading parts of public worship. Both JOFA and the partnership *minyanim* are perceived as un-Orthodox and threatening by the Orthodox establishment in the UK; Rabba Brawer has been banned from speaking at Orthodox institutions, and some individuals associated with partnership *minyanim* have also been banned from speaking, leading prayers, or teaching in their own (United) synagogues.[86]

Less dramatic but equally revolutionary is the fact that an increasing number of younger married women are performing some of the domestic

---

[84]   Sharon Jastrow, interview.

[85]   She was given Orthodox ordination as a rabbi in May 2018. Her enrolment in the women's ordination programme (at Yeshivat Maharat in New York, founded in 2009), itself deeply controversial, sparked the ban on her speaking at any Orthodox synagogue or institution in the UK; shortly before her ordination she announced she would be moving to the USA to pursue her rabbinic career there.

[86]   For details of these bans, see Ch. 4 n. 166. Activities that might be considered to resemble those of partnership *minyanim* have also been discouraged in recent years. In late 2013 the head of the Federation *beit din*, Dayan Lichtenstein, prohibited women from dancing with a Torah scroll on Simhat Torah, and Maureen Kendler, a prominent educator, was barred from speaking in a series of lectures for women organized jointly by a United and an independent synagogue, on the grounds that she was 'associated with partnership *minyanim*'. In early 2014 the London Beth Din ordered the rabbi of Golders Green United Synagogue to discontinue the practice he had introduced of carrying the Torah scroll through the women's section before the Torah reading, claiming that this was an innovation and therefore forbidden. See also the section on partnership *minyanim* in Ch. 4 below.

sabbath rituals that used to be the exclusive preserve of men. The current developments are different in character from the 1990s 'movement', not least because non-haredi men are involved in some of the new activities, such as partnership *minyanim*, alongside women. Though haredi women create all their innovations in a women's space, both women and men from the left wing of non-haredi Orthodoxy are beginning to seek religious activities and rituals that are not framed by gender segregation, but that redefine gender roles in a shared space. British Orthodox women are currently experiencing far-reaching changes in the available options for religious participation and self-expression. It is too early to know how far the changes will go and how successful they will be, given the opposition from the Orthodox rabbinic establishment.

Defining Terms: Talking about the Anglo-Jewish Community

This complex and fluid situation makes it difficult to develop an adequate set of definitions for categorizing non-haredi Orthodox Jews in Britain. Should a non-practising United Synagogue member be described as Orthodox? How would one differentiate between United Synagogue women who cover their hair with a wig, keep a kosher household, observe the sabbath and all the festivals, and attend Talmud lessons and those who do not cover their hair, only attend synagogue on the High Holidays, cannot read Hebrew, and light sabbath candles on Friday night but shop on Saturday morning? The terms 'observant' and 'non-observant' seem appropriate here, but they only measure one axis of religious life, that of practice; what if the first group does not actually believe in God or the divine origin of the Torah, but the second does? Should we add terms such as 'non-believing' and 'believing' to measure the axis of religious belief? Personal religiosity or spirituality also varies: even if both groups of United Synagogue women believe in God and the divine origin of the Torah, what terms would mark the fact that the first group might have no interest in a personal relationship with the Divine, while members of the second might wish to develop their own spirituality and live in the presence of God? In addition to the fact that this deeply personal and private aspect of religious life is particularly hard to investigate, the terms 'devout', 'religious', or 'spiritual' and 'spiritually indifferent' are once again limited to this axis alone, and do not necessarily imply a particular level of practical observance, or a defined set of beliefs.[87]

[87] The interesting 'life-as-religion' and 'subjective-life spirituality' categories used in Heelas

Even if we adopt the binary definitions presented above, or revisualize each set as the poles of a continuum, they do not provide a satisfactory way of talking about variation over time in an individual's religious practice, belief, and inner life. As Sarah Benor has observed, 'trajectories of observance and identification are salient within Orthodox communities',[88] but are often difficult to identify and describe.

Many attempts have been made to define sets of terms with which to categorize Orthodoxy, but none adequately represents the experience of Jewish women in Britain, especially since most definitions focus on denominational affiliation to the exclusion of other axes of religious life, and very few are accompanied by an analysis of what the terms actually denote. Analysing the causes of the 'slide to the right' among American Orthodox Jews, Samuel Heilman uses the binary categories 'modern Orthodox' and 'haredi Orthodox' (also calling the latter 'contra-acculturative' and 'enclavist'), but provides no definitions or other categorizations.[89] Sarah Benor, looking at newly religious Jews in America, identifies several social axes, including Orthodox and non-Orthodox; 'trajectories of observance', for which she gives the categories '*frum* from birth, *gerim* [converts], *ba'alei teshuvah* [newly religious], and *hozrim beshe'alah* [newly secular]'; and 'Modern Orthodox and Black Hat', which she describes as 'a continuum between "Modern Orthodox" Jews at one end and "Black Hat" Jews at the other, based on observance, insularity, gender ideology, and, especially, cultural practices'.[90] The recognition of a continuum, rather than discrete categories, is helpful here and can be applied to the British Jewish community, as can the concept of 'trajectories of observance', attempting to describe the dynamic and sometimes changing nature of individuals' religious lives; the very notion of the multiplicity of axes along which 'religiousness' can be measured is of central importance, as noted above.

Earlier attempts to find useful categories for British Jews have struggled to create a satisfactory system. Examining the loss of the old United Synagogue version of Orthodoxy, Miri Freud-Kandel labels it 'spiritist Orthodoxy' and contrasts it with an undefined 'centrist Orthodoxy'.[91] She defines the former as

and Woodhead, *Spiritual Revolution*, which examines trends in a homogenous, largely Christian town, would not be as useful in an Orthodox Jewish context. The 'life-as-religion' component, in which 'conformity to external authority' is the key value, is a *sine qua non* of Orthodoxy, even though some individual Orthodox women may seek to increase the 'subjective-life spirituality' aspect, in which the key value is 'authentic connection with the inner depths of one's unique life-in-relation' (ch. 1).

[88] *Becoming Frum*, 9.   [89] Heilman, *Sliding to the Right*.
[90] *Becoming Frum*, 9. 'Black Hat' corresponds to the term 'haredi' used in this book.
[91] *Orthodox Judaism*, 84. The term 'spiritist' is intended to convey that adherents of this type

a distinct religious position in Anglo-Jewish Orthodoxy, [concentrating] on the importance of maintaining Jewish identity intact and preserving inherited traditions without directing too much attention to the minutiae of religious practices . . . It should not be viewed as a principled theological position on the left wing of Orthodox Judaism, which is demarcated by the Reform movement and Masorti Judaism.[92]

This seems to be less a definition of a movement within Orthodoxy and more of a description of the old-style United Synagogue; the traditionalist position she outlines is now disappearing with increasing rapidity, unable to withstand the more strident certainties of stricter versions of Orthodoxy.

A brief 1986 study of British Jewry simply used the terms 'Right-Wing Orthodox', 'Central Orthodox', and 'Sephardi' to cover the Orthodox sector.[93] A slightly more sophisticated survey of the social and political attitudes of British Jews carried out in 1995 used the following eclectic set of categories, with some minimal definitions:

Non-practising (i.e. secular) Jew; Just Jewish; Progressive Jew (e.g. Liberal, Reform); 'Traditional' (i.e. not strictly Orthodox); Strictly Orthodox (e.g. would *not* turn on a light on Shabbat).[94]

Tellingly, a 2011 study by JPR included a footnote:

In the past, it was easier to differentiate clearly between 'Central Orthodoxy' and 'Strict Orthodoxy' . . . Whilst the categories remain useful, the distinctions between them have become increasingly blurred in recent times.[95]

An earlier JPR study of 'the outlook of London's Jews' had critiqued this set of terms, noting that 'Previous labelling typologies . . . represented *nominal* scales, that is to say, they consisted of descriptive, categorical items only . . . being affiliation driven, this approach becomes rapidly dominated by the

---

of Orthodoxy were more interested in the 'spirit' than the practice of the religion, but given the widely documented lack of interest in theology and intellectual matters among British Jews, this seems wishful thinking rather than accurate description. See Endelman, *Jews of Britain*, 264–6.

[92] Freud-Kandel, *Orthodox Judaism*, 84. Interestingly, she makes no mention of Modern Orthodoxy, perhaps because few British Jews align themselves with this movement, although those who do so are often at the forefront of innovations. Many of those identifying themselves as Modern Orthodox have spent several years in Israel or the USA, where Modern Orthodoxy is far more common.

[93] Waterman and Kosmin, *British Jewry in the Eighties*, 28. The only other categories were 'Reform' and 'Liberal', with no mention of Masorti.

[94] Miller, Shmool, and Lerman, *Social and Political Attitudes of British Jews*. Once again, Masorti does not appear; in addition, the example given for 'Strictly Orthodox' of not using electricity on the sabbath would surprise many Masorti and United Synagogue Jews who observe this prohibition but would never dream of labelling themselves as 'Strictly Orthodox'!

[95] Abramson, Graham, and Boyd, *Key Trends*, 5 n. 1.

all-encompassing "Traditionals" and tends to miss the non-affiliated."[96] David Graham, the author of the study, observed that these nominal categories were usually treated as though they were ordinal, that is, ranked in a sequence from 'more' to 'less', and that they were imprecise:

What is the difference between the categories 'non-practising Jew' and 'Just Jewish', if any at all? Is 'Traditional' more religious than 'Progressive'? What indeed do we even mean by 'religious' in this instance: more observant, more affiliated or what?[97]

Graham proposed an ordinal scale based on 'outlook' (similar to the 'personal religiosity axis' mentioned above), with the categories 'religious', 'somewhat religious', 'somewhat secular', and 'secular', which had been used in JPR's 2002 survey of almost 3,000 London Jews. Acknowledging that these categories rested on self-definition by respondents, he argued that, since respondents 'placed themselves into categories rather than having (arbitrary) categories imposed upon them', empirical evidence of the 'Jewishness' of London's Jews was available for the first time. He noted:

The analysis . . . demonstrates that the cause-and-effect relationship between religiosity and Jewish practice is unclear, and that no single variable, or set of variables, can adequately describe the multifaceted nature of being a Jew in Greater London. Being thus self-defined, the concept of outlook takes on a complexity all of its own. If two Jews choose independently to define themselves as secular, they may in reality exhibit very different Jewish characteristics.[98]

It is doubtful whether (silently) self-defined categories that depend on the personal interpretations of questionnaire respondents are more likely to deliver 'empirical' findings than undefined categories imposed on respondents, though they are certainly very useful both in providing some qualitative sense of individuals' self-definition and personal religiosity and in problematizing the unexamined categories used by earlier studies. A table measuring these 'outlook'-based categories against the more traditional denominational ones indicates both the potential and the complexity of a multi-axial analysis (see Table 3).[99] For instance, of those Jews who defined themselves as being 'secular', 28% belonged to the United Synagogue or another 'mainstream' synagogue, very close to the 23% of the 'secular' who belong to the Reform movement; there was also a surprising 1% of the 'secular' who belonged to the haredi/independent Orthodox segment. The fact that 7% of those who defined themselves as 'religious' belonged to the Reform movement also highlights the problematic nature of the link between denomination and 'religiosity'. This begs the question of what people mean when they describe

[96] Graham, *Secular or Religious?*, 1.   [97] Ibid.   [98] Ibid. 2.   [99] Ibid. 15, table 9.

Table 3 Religious self-definition of UK Jews (2002, N = 2,820) by denominational affiliation (%)

Religious self-definition	Haredi / Independent Orthodox (UOHC) n = 83	Federation of Synagogues n = 138	Mainstream Orthodox / United Synagogue (US) n = 1,390	Masorti n = 116	Reform n = 567	Other n = 58	None n = 468
Secular	1	4	28	2	23	2	40
Somewhat secular	1	4	47	6	26	2	14
Somewhat religious	2	6	64	5	16	2	5
Religious	20	7	60	2	7	1	3

Source: Based on Graham, *Secular or Religious?*, table 9.

Note: Denominations are listed in declining order of orthodoxy. The data is from a survey and reflects self-identification (including denominational affiliation) by individuals, with no gender breakdown.

themselves as secular or religious, while simultaneously demonstrating that such categories do not necessarily correlate with formal denominational affiliation.

The equally problematic link between 'outlook'/personal religiosity and religious practice is illustrated by the survey's measurement of the observance of four religious 'markers' (lighting sabbath candles, attending a Passover Seder, fasting on Yom Kippur, and keeping kosher) against the four 'outlook' categories: 47% of the 'secular' attended a Seder every year, 30% of them fasted every Yom Kippur, and 22% kept a kosher home, while 11% of the 'religious' did not keep kosher at home and 16% ate non-kosher meat outside the home 'frequently' or 'occasionally'.[100]

Given this complex, shifting reality, I have not attempted to construct a rigid and all-encompassing system of precisely defined categories for this study, particularly since it has no pretensions to rigorous quantitative analysis. Wherever possible, the women's self-definitions are used, but where these were not forthcoming or obvious I have tried to use particular terms consistently, and to distinguish between different axes of religious life.

In order to provide a general set of terms with which to characterize different sectors of the Orthodox community, I will employ a representation of the spectrum of Anglo-Jewish Orthodoxy, ranging from an ethnically based iden-

---

[100] Graham, *Secular or Religious?*, 13–15. Unfortunately the full data on 'outlook' in relation to these four key practices were not published.

tification with traditional Anglo-Jewish ritual practice combined with acceptance of the wider society's Western-liberal ethos at one pole ('traditionalist'), to a religiously defined practice and an outlook that consciously rejects the Western-liberal ethos at the other pole ('haredi'), with the middle ground occupied by a religiously defined practice and an outlook that attempts to negotiate coexistence with the Western-liberal ethos ('Modern Orthodox'). In discussing other axes of religious life, I have used the following sets of terms:

- To denote denominational affiliation I have used the institutional labels of 'United Synagogue', 'Federation', and 'Union' or 'UOHC', as well as the non-institutional 'independent Orthodox' and 'haredi'.

- To describe religious practice and world-view (*hashkafah*), I have used 'haredi' again (since denomination, practice, and religious outlook are closely linked in this community), while reserving 'mainstream' or 'mainstream Orthodox' for non-haredi Orthodoxy. 'Observant' and 'non-observant' refer to observable religious practice, such as keeping kosher or fasting on Yom Kippur. Styles within 'mainstream Orthodoxy' are marked with the terms 'Modern Orthodox', implying a conscious choice to follow the aspiration of integrating Judaism and non-Jewish culture, and 'traditional', denoting a largely unconscious or unintellectualized acceptance of family and community practice and outlook, which, though ostensibly religious, is actually based on ethnic and identity-based considerations. I have avoided using the common term 'Centrist Orthodoxy' since it is unclear which 'centre' is meant here, nor is it obvious where the boundary between this and 'Modern Orthodox' lies.

- Beliefs and faith are discussed individually, rather than combining them with practice and outlook, to acknowledge that they do not always correlate with practice, as often assumed, let alone form coherent systems.[101] Not many women discussed this aspect of their religious lives, though sometimes remarkable divergences from classical Jewish beliefs became apparent, as in some of the opinions about angels expressed by women who engaged in *berakhah* parties and other quasi-magical practices.

- Personal religiosity—the degree of engagement with religion, including the relationship with the Divine—is discussed in terms of 'religious' or 'devout' versus 'religiously indifferent' tendencies; again, this was not always obvious.

---

[101] Luhrmann, *Persuasions of the Witch's Craft*, 308–9, notes: 'it is optimistic to think that people have an ordered set of beliefs about a particular endeavour which forms a consistent set with other beliefs which together describe the totality of thought and action. People are much fuzzier, and more complex, than that.'

Previous Research on British Orthodox Women

Unsurprisingly, given the general invisibility of women's religious lives described in Chapter 1, very little research has been done on this subject in Britain. Surveys of the British Jewish community, or of parts of it, occasionally devote a paragraph or two to women, though their practice of and attitudes to religion are rarely mentioned. A useful example is Geoffrey Alderman's *Modern British Jewry*, which devotes three pages to the subject, with another four pages on the problem of *agunot*.[102] Writing of the 1980s, he notes:

In the orthodox home the Jewish housewife reigns supreme. In the synagogue she is literally superfluous . . . in the world of centrist orthodoxy, as exemplified by the United Synagogue, the matter became contentious. Girls brought up within this centrist orthodoxy had taken full advantage of the educational opportunities open to women in British society after 1945. They obtained university education, and pursued professional careers whilst rearing children and maintaining orthodox homes. Jewish women whose career achievements had secured for them a status in wider society became resentful of their subordinate position within Anglo-Jewry. For some, younger, women, this resulted in defections to the progressive movement. But this solution, fraught with the obvious risk of future difficulties for their offspring in terms of Jewish identity, did not appeal to the majority.[103]

Alderman goes on to describe the 'women's renaissance' of the 1990s and the commissioning of the Preston Report. This document, published in 1994 and officially entitled *Women in the Jewish Community: Review and Recommendations*, remains 'the most exhaustive investigation ever undertaken into the feelings of Anglo-Jewish women about their spiritual needs and religious status'.[104] It was commissioned by Chief Rabbi Jonathan Sacks, and the research was led by Rosalind Preston, the first female vice president of the Board of Deputies of British Jews. The report presented information gathered across the denominational spectrum by 'taskforces' on education, synagogue and religious matters, social issues, the family, and Jewish divorce. More than 180 women, organized in groups across Britain, were involved in gathering and processing information. Over 100 recommendations were made, many on religious issues, for example requests for clarification on women's role in rituals such as saying Kaddish (the mourner's prayer), and that women be included in the planning and refurbishing of synagogues. The bulk of the report documented women's opinions, feelings, and desires on a wide range of issues, from celebrating the birth of a girl to the problems of being a single

[102] An *agunah* (lit. 'chained woman') is a woman whose husband refuses to grant her a Jewish divorce (*get*).   [103] Alderman, *Modern British Jewry*, 402–3.   [104] Ibid. 404.

Jewish woman, and a chapter was devoted to 'Spiritual Needs: The Orthodox Perspective'.[105] The authors reported:

While the majority of older women are content to preserve the status quo—with all its attendant features—the ladies' gallery, Mechitzah, ladies' guilds and catering duties, there is a creeping malaise among the next generation. A perception is growing, among younger Orthodox women, of the synagogue as a 'men's club', controlling, inhibiting and unfairly restricting the scope of women's involvement.[106]

Issues such as sadness at not being able to mark a *yahrzeit* (anniversary of a relative's death) in public, feelings of exclusion on Simhat Torah, and regret at not having had a good Jewish education gave support to this warning. Many of the problems and dissatisfactions recorded in the report appeared among my interviewees. After the report's publication, there were allegations that some of the requirements it had originally specified had been 'downgraded' to recommendations and that parts of the report had been rewritten to make it more acceptable.[107] Nevertheless it remains a unique record of Jewish women's opinions, and I have used it extensively.

Rewritten or not, few of the Preston Report's recommendations were implemented, and in 2008 Rosalind Preston asked the Board of Deputies to revisit the work carried out fifteen years earlier, to see what had changed and pursue the most relevant issues. The resulting report is generally known as the Women's Review, although officially it is entitled *Connection, Continuity and Community: British Jewish Women Speak Out*. On this occasion an online survey facilitated by SurveyMonkey was used, with over 700 respondents (7% of whom were men). 88% belonged to a synagogue, and of these, 57% were Orthodox. Once again, women from across the country and the denominational spectrum gave their opinions. After two pages providing a demographic overview, the remaining twenty-two pages of the report provide quotations from women's responses, identified by region, age, marital status, and denominational affiliation:

I think women need to be taught how to daven [pray]. Many of them never really learn, so in shul they talk, and then wonder why their kids wriggle around.
Outer NW London, married, 29, Orthodox, religious

If we understand what we are saying in shul, it would make it more meaningful.
North London, separated, 56, Orthodox, religious

---

[105] While no reason is given in the report for this focus on the Orthodox, I imagine that it is the same as my own in the present study: opportunities for religious expression in the Masorti, Reform, and Liberal movements, while these are not always completely egalitarian, are far greater than those available to Orthodox women.

[106] Preston, Goodkin, and Citron, *Women in the Jewish Community*, 29.

[107] Alderman, *Modern British Jewry*, 404–5.

Once again, though short, and largely an anthology of quotations, this report is invaluable for recording women's voices and concerns, and has been an important resource.

The only other published study of British Orthodox women's religious lives of which I am aware is a paper by Jennifer Cousineau that examines the far-reaching changes in experience of the sabbath occasioned by the construction of the North-West London Eruv.[108] Though dealing with both sexes, her paper focuses on women because the changes they describe are far more striking than those experienced by men. She notes that many women with small children had felt imprisoned on the sabbath, but now experienced a sense of release and joy, which enabled them to match religious expectations of the sabbath as holy and pleasurable. Although the study only covers one facet of women's religious lives, it provides a very valuable example of their opinions and understandings, and highlights how their perception of religious issues often differs fundamentally from that of Jewish men. Dr Lindsay Simmonds's doctoral thesis of 2019, entitled 'Generating Piety: Agency and the Religious Subject', will doubtless add much to our knowledge of Orthodox women in the British Jewish community.

[108] Cousineau, 'The Domestication of Urban Jewish Space'.

THREE

THE VIEW FROM THE LADIES' GALLERY: WOMEN'S 'OFFICIAL' LIFE IN THE COMMUNITY

When I was *very* little, I used to *love* sitting with my Dad; it was always prefer-able to sit downstairs with Dad in the main synagogue than be upstairs, and once you get to a certain age you can't do that anymore, and I really felt I was missing out. But I didn't know what I was missing out on, because it was just not in the spectrum of conversation.

BERNICE SUSSER, interview

ORTHODOX WOMEN participate in the formal religious life of the com-munity in the generally auxiliary role of an (optional) audience for the men at synagogue services, although many pray along quietly with the men. In contrast, they often play important roles in the management of synagogues and community welfare organizations that embody central religious values such as *ḥesed* (kindness, concern for others' welfare). Women are also over-represented in the Jewish education of children, particularly at preschool and primary school levels, but are under-represented as teachers in adult Jewish education, and are often barred from traditional Jewish study. In this chapter I document and analyse women's activity in and experience of formal public worship in the synagogue; occasions of particular tension for women, such as life-cycle celebrations and the festival of Simhat Torah; the changing nature of women's leadership roles in the synagogue; the restricted nature of women's Jewish education in the communal context; and (briefly) women's role in Jewish welfare organizations.

Women and the Synagogue

The central function of the synagogue is formal prayer. Three services every day, with additional services on sabbaths, New Moon (Rosh Hodesh), and fes-tivals, are obligatory for men; women's obligation to participate in these serv-ices is less clear, and most Orthodox women assume that they are exempt, at least to some degree.[1] In addition, men's formal prayer is ideally performed

[1] See Weiss, *Women at Prayer*, chs. 2 and 4, for a discussion of women's halakhic obligations

with a quorum of ten adult men, encouraging their presence at synagogue. Ritual Torah reading—a community obligation generally considered non-obligatory for women—also takes place in the synagogue, as does the reading of the Megillah on Purim (which women are obliged to hear). The synagogue is thus central to the performance of male religious obligations, but much less so to the performance of women's religious duties.

However, the synagogue has two additional and crucial communal functions for both men and women. As indicated by its Hebrew name, *beit keneset* (house of assembly), the synagogue is the locus for various activities, including formal and informal study, recreation, social gatherings, and life-cycle celebrations. Moreover, the synagogue embodies the community—a vital factor for women who attend sabbath and festival services regularly, particularly United Synagogue women (though many United Synagogue members attend rarely or only on the High Holidays). As noted earlier, the words 'shul' (Yiddish for synagogue) and 'community' are often used interchangeably, and women express deep attachment to their own synagogue. Flora Rendberg's synagogue is central to her identity:

My [relatives] in America attend a Conservative synagogue and I've felt absolutely at home in that environment but would not leave my own synagogue, maybe because it's my other family—I've been going there for over fifty years . . . I've never found a[nother] synagogue where I feel when I go in that I belong.

As noted in Chapter 2, a 2016 survey estimated that 52.8% of all British Jewish households affiliated to a synagogue belonged to 'Central Orthodox' synagogues, and 13.5% belonged to 'Strictly Orthodox' synagogues.[2] Many nominally Orthodox Jews primarily belong to a synagogue to obtain burial rights (included in synagogue membership), and secondarily to reserve a seat for the High Holidays, when attendance increases exponentially. Otherwise, they may attend very rarely, and are often colloquially described as 'three-times-a-year Jews'.[3] Synagogue attendance constitutes a major internal marker of level of observance: Belinda Cohen, a United Synagogue member, when asked to describe her Jewish upbringing, started by saying, 'As far as Jewish life's concerned, we always went to shul'. Her daughter, Beatrice Levi, in describing her own somewhat lower level of observance, pointed out in mitigation that 'we do regularly attend synagogue'.

with regard to prayer. When teaching on this subject, if I ask how many women think they are *not* obliged to pray daily, typically 70–80% of the women present raise their hands.

[2] Mashiah and Boyd, *Synagogue Membership in the United Kingdom in 2016*, 2. 56.3% of Jewish households were affiliated to a synagogue.

[3] Or 'twice-a-year Jews', referring either to the two festivals of Rosh Hashanah and Yom Kippur, or to the three days these involve.

North-west London, the most densely populated Jewish area in the UK, boasts a high number of synagogues of varying size and of all shades of Orthodoxy; an online directory lists sixty-six sabbath morning services in Hendon and Golders Green alone, in about fifty synagogues.[4] These include five United Synagogue (or affiliated) congregations, eight Sephardi services, and seventeen hasidic institutions. The larger synagogues generally offer an early service (*hashkamah*) and a later, more family-oriented one; they also offer youth and children's services. Other parts of London (with the exception of Stamford Hill) provide a smaller range.

(Not) Being There
Attendance

Many observant women rarely attend synagogue, even if their fathers, husbands, brothers, and sons go every week. This seems to have been the norm for most Jewish women at least until the 1970s;[5] some hasidic women still do not attend synagogue, or only rarely.[6] Many women and men born in the 1950s remembered their mothers never going to synagogue, or only attending on the High Holidays. One woman born in the 1970s noted that, in her childhood, 'women didn't go to Hagers', a hasidic synagogue in Golders Green. The most common reason was that their mothers 'came from a background in which Jewish women weren't obliged to attend services', though lack of knowledge of Hebrew, lack of interest, and distance from the synagogue were also cited. For the minority whose mothers did go more often, bad weather or 'a surfeit of guests' might prevent them. Women's attendance was (and still is) seen as optional, while that of men is compulsory: 'Orthodox synagogue attendance remains very much a men's thing.'[7]

Furthermore, some women who would have attended synagogue more regularly were prevented from going while their children were young by a halakhic factor: the absence of an *eruv*.[8] A woman born in the 1950s noted that 'When my siblings and I were small Mum didn't go as there was no *eruv*

---

[4] See 'This Week's Davening Times for London' on the Frum London website. Services are also held in private homes, which would not show up in this directory.

[5] In contrast, Cairo Genizah evidence suggests that medieval women in Egypt attended synagogue regularly, and Ashkenazi rabbinic literature from the thirteenth century onwards documents women's galleries or prayer rooms, women's prayers, and women prayer leaders, as well as regular attendance by women. See Reguer, 'Women and the Synagogue', and Taitz, 'Women's Voices, Women's Prayers'.

[6] Two hasidic women who filled in my questionnaire about customs (see Ch. 6) explained their lack of knowledge about synagogue customs associated with Yom Kippur by noting that they 'never' went to synagogue.

[7] Sztokman, *The Men's Section*, 12.   [8] See above, Ch. 2, n. 108.

and pushing a buggy was not an option as we were observant. After my sister could walk that far she would go as well. After we grew up she was always in shul on Shabat mornings.'[9]

In February 2003, after years of opposition from both Jews and non-Jews, north-west London acquired its first *eruv*, revolutionizing many women's experience of the sabbath and synagogue and enabling large numbers of younger women to attend.[10] Before this, observant women with babies or small children could not attend synagogue on the sabbath and Yom Kippur, though they could do so on other festivals, when carrying in public areas is permitted. Many women with large families did not attend sabbath services for years, a fact which may help explain many older women's difficulties in following the service. Disabled women and men were also affected, since they could not use wheelchairs. In 1994, the Preston Report singled out the absence of an *eruv* as 'essentially an Orthodox women's issue', and reported 'a firm belief that the Eruv represents a lifeline to young families, single parents, the disabled and the elderly'.[11]

In spite of dire warnings of the creation of ghettos and the potential hostility of the non-Jewish population, the *eruv* has proved to be such a success that three additional *eruvin* had been constructed in London (there are plans for several more), and one in Manchester, by 2016.[12] Not all rabbis accept the kosher status of the *eruv*, however; several haredi rabbis object to it and forbid their followers to use it, with the result that many haredi women with young families are still unable to attend synagogue on the sabbath, as well as some Sephardi women, since not all Sephardim accept the London *eruv* as kosher.[13] However, the *eruv*'s introduction has been the single most important factor in enabling women's synagogue attendance.

Even if an *eruv* is in place, women may decide not to attend synagogue if their children are very small, or unwell; since men have a greater halakhic obligation to attend synagogue, it is the mother who usually stays home. However, some large synagogues have early morning (*hashkamah*) services, partly designed to allow men to attend and then return home to enable their wives to go to the main service. Several of these were set up before the introduction of the *eruv*, so that mothers could attend synagogue.

[9] Email communication from a Modern Orthodox woman, 11 Apr. 2013.

[10] See Watson, 'Symbolic Spaces', for an analysis of the opposition and of the *eruv*'s importance for women (p. 508).

[11] Preston, Goodkin, and Citron, *Women in the Jewish Community*, 36.

[12] For a tenth-anniversary appraisal of the effect of the *eruv*, see Rocker, 'How the Eruv Liberated Families'. See also Cousineau, 'The Domestication of Urban Jewish Space', for an interesting study of women's perception of '*shabat* space' and the changes in their experience of the sabbath as a result of the *eruv*.

[13] Personal communication from Rabbi Dr Raphael Zarum, 12 July 2013.

Women's attendance on sabbath mornings follows much the same pattern across the spectrum of Orthodox synagogues. A few women arrive early, but most turn up halfway through the service, during the Torah reading, with some latecomers arriving just in time for the end of the service and, of course, for Kiddush, the social gathering after the service when the blessing over wine is made, usually accompanied by an array of drinks and snacks. Sheyna Marcus, a devout woman in her twenties, observed, 'The more religious the shul the later the women come . . . [T]here is a feeling that "I don't have a ḥiyuv [obligation] to be in shul and therefore I can come very late."'[14] In the large United synagogues, at the beginning of the service (8–9 a.m.) there are typically two dozen men and perhaps two or three women. Visits to six synagogues in 2013 yielded the data presented in Table 4.

The only synagogue I visited where unmarried women outnumbered married women was Alei Tzion, an independently founded synagogue now affiliated to the United Synagogue, which was set up in 2004 as a young, strongly Zionist, and more observant Modern Orthodox community. Most women there were young, ranging from late teens to 30-year-olds. There was a high number of very young children, and many married women remained outside the synagogue, either accompanying their children to one of the two age-based children's services or supervising their play. In this case, the very fact that the synagogue is a self-selecting community based on age and outlook differentiates it from both United Synagogue and haredi communities in terms of women's attendance.[15]

Even when attending, women find it hard to juggle children and synagogue prayer. Young mothers often accompany their offspring to children's services rather than participating in a standard service themselves; though many fathers organize and participate in children's services, others feel obliged to attend the main service, leaving childcare to their wives. Shirley Daniels, a young, university-educated mother of five who is married to a Sephardi rabbi, described her current synagogue experience:

Nowadays it's nothing, because the twins are 1 and we're coming up to starting being able to take them to shul, to participate in the children's service. So at the moment it's nothing other than a Kiddush and a celebration of other people's simḥahs [life-cycle celebrations] . . . There's definitely no service, so it's social and communal . . . on the occasion that I get to daven [pray] musaf [the additional service

---

[14] For her personal practice of arriving promptly, modified by her concepts of modesty, see Ch. 5.

[15] The differences between Alei Tzion, patronized by younger, more observant women, and the United synagogues attended by their traditionalist mothers reflect the contrast between 'text-based' and 'mimetic' communities analysed in Soloveitchik, 'Rupture and Reconstruction'.

Table 4 Women's synagogue attendance on sabbath morning in selected synagogues (spring–autumn 2013)

Synagogue	Denominational affiliation	Number of women attending (of whom unmarried[a])				Number of men
		Before Shema	Start of Torah reading	End of Torah reading	End of Service	
Alei Tzion	Affiliated to United Synagogue (US)	7 (7)	19 (14)	30 (18)	47 (31)	70
Hampstead Garden Suburb (Norrice Lea)	US	30	50	60 (10)	c.70	100–150
Heikhal Leah	Sephardi	1	2	7	11	70–80
Hendon Adas	Union of Orthodox Hebrew Congregations (UOHC)	11	17	27 (4)	25	40–50
Hendon (Raleigh Close)[b]	US	13	14	65 (5)	100	50–100+
North Hendon Adas	ex-UOHC, haredi	4 (1)	8 (2)	30 (9)	25 (8)	30–40

Note: The numbers in the women's gallery are best estimates as women and children were coming and going throughout the service, and, it being the sabbath, when writing is prohibited, I was unable to take notes. The numbers of men are similarly best estimates since it is impossible to count men accurately from a women's gallery or from behind a *meḥitsah*. The information in this table should therefore be treated as qualitative rather than quantitative and is meant to give an impression rather than full and precise documentation.

[a] It is possible to distinguish married from unmarried women in a synagogue context on the basis of the presence of head covering, as married women are required to cover their hair. Those who wore a hat or wig I identified as married, and those without any apparent head covering I identified as unmarried.

[b] Numbers at Hendon (Raleigh Close) were particularly high the week I visited because the sermon was given by the chief rabbi elect, attracting people who might have gone to other synagogues or not attended synagogue at all.

for the sabbath], because [my husband]'s gone to a *hashkamah* service, and then will take over with the children, I find myself desperate to try and pack it all in, and it's impossible to do.

Mothers who attend the main service may go in and out in response to children's needs; though in most synagogues it is acceptable for children to move around and play, other women may glare at mothers with crying or noisy children or request them to remove their children. Women often leave before the end of the service, particularly if they want to prepare for lunch guests, or if they are involved in setting out the communal Kiddush.

As a partial consequence of mothers' involvement in children's services and general childcare, most women who attend services are older, particularly in United synagogues, where most are in their sixties or above. The few younger women are often unmarried, and there is a scattering of girls, several only there briefly, 'visiting' their mothers. If a batmitzvah is being celebrated, there may be a score or so of 11- and 12-year-old girls sitting around the batmitzvah girl, who typically chat to each other throughout, sometimes provoking rebukes from the older women, and take no part in the service. Teenage girls attend youth services in smaller numbers than boys, and in United synagogues they often congregate in groups in quiet corners of the building, such as the ladies' toilets, getting on with their social life.

Attempts have been made at some synagogues to attract girls to some form of religious participation, often a discussion group. In 2013 Barnet United Synagogue offered 'Girls Talk' twice a month, described as 'a youth service just for the young ladies', but by 2016 this had been replaced by the 'T Party', a group aimed at helping pre-batmitzvah girls 'to learn to create a short one- or two-sentence explanation of what we read for each Aliyah (call-up[16]) and present it in the main shul service'. Boys were offered the 'AAA Team', which trained them to lead parts of the main service.[17] At Finchley United Synagogue (Kinloss), a 'Chat in a Flat' group for girls used to be run during the Torah reading: 'Chat' stands for 'Come Hear a Thought', and the aim was to hold a discussion on the weekly Torah portion, but apparently chat in the usual sense predominated, and the group was discontinued, partly because the youth leader wanted to encourage the girls to pray. Though there are youth services at most United synagogues, they offer little for the girls to do, and serve primarily as training and socializing groups for the boys. At Kinloss, girls may read the prayer for the queen and the prayer for the State of Israel,[18] and in 2013 a new slot was created, after the formal end of the service, in which a girl could give a short sermon. However, few girls are interested in praying, apart from 'a few sixth-form girls who sit at the back of the youth service and pray'; most come 'to see their friends and for the Kiddush'. Girls who would be more interested in getting involved if given the chance

---

[16] The sabbath morning Torah reading is divided into seven *aliyot* (lit. 'ascents'), with a man being called up to recite blessings before and after each *aliyah*.

[17] See the Barnet Synagogue website.

[18] The first of these (and sometimes the second) is read in English, so does not have the cachet of 'serious prayer'.

stay away from synagogue altogether, as there is next to nothing for them to do and little prospect of change.[19]

One pattern which has remained unchanged for several decades is that very few women—traditionalist, Modern Orthodox, or haredi—attend Friday night or festival eve services, sabbath afternoon services,[20] or weekday morning or evening prayers. The few women who do attend on Friday night are usually unmarried, often teenage girls (some possibly escaping the last-minute pre-sabbath rush at home). Some unmarried women see their presence at Friday night services as a marker of their single state, like Sheyna Marcus:

I've gone to shul on Friday night from quite a young age, so I'm not used to being at home when my mum lights candles, which in some ways is weird, because one day, hopefully, I will be at home lighting the candles, and it will be almost not like *shabes* [sabbath] for me because I'm so used to, you know, first thing go to shul on Friday night.

The Influence of Synagogue Layout on Women's Experience

In all Orthodox synagogues men and women sit separately,[21] but arrangements for this differ widely and play a major role in women's experience of communal prayer. Most large United synagogues have high, raked 'ladies' galleries' around three sides of the synagogue sanctuary, occasionally with a pierced screen from waist to head level above the parapet, though a few modern buildings have galleries of this type around the walls at ground level. Some synagogues have a 'mini-*meḥitsah*' (divider) to enable older or less mobile women to sit at the back of the main hall, behind the men, though many of these women dislike 'sitting with the men' and will struggle upstairs anyway. By 2017, fourteen United synagogues had constructed some type of ground-floor seating for women, with another three or so planning to do so; younger women and those more eager for change tend to prefer to sit downstairs, as they feel more integrated and less like spectators, but many older and more traditional women still prefer the galleries.

Haredi synagogues always have a screen above the gallery parapet, usually a wooden lattice or a metal grille; at the hasidic Hagers synagogue in Golders Green, the gallery parapet is topped with a thick, non-transparent curtain held

[19] Information on Kinloss from a phone conversation with a (male) teenage family friend, 11 Sept. 2013.

[20] Only two other women were present at the sabbath afternoon service I attended at Hampstead Garden Suburb United Synagogue on 18 May 2013, with forty to fifty men.

[21] For the origins and tenuous halakhic foundations of this practice, see Rothschild, 'Undermining the Pillars'.

in place by rods at top and bottom, which reaches above head height, blocking all sight of the men (though women occasionally push the curtain edge back to get a brief glimpse). Many women, particularly in the haredi community, accept and internalize the standard explanation for the separation of the sexes during prayer—that men will be distracted by the sight of women—and experience unease and shame if they pray where men can see them, though it is rare for men to express discomfort about arrangements for separate seating, even if they are makeshift.

Women are often unaware, or unconvinced, that there is no halakhic need for a *mehitsah* at all in a temporary place of prayer. For example, at an Orthodox service held at the Limmud conference, where the *mehitsah* was a chest-high net curtain, a young woman in her early twenties—who was moving from a traditionalist Orthodox background towards a more haredi outlook—attempted to pray behind a pillar, and, having subsequently complained about the lack of a proper *mehitsah*, attended no more services. None of the (mostly traditionalist Orthodox) men appeared to have any concerns about the *mehitsah*, and one even 'invaded' the women's side, looking for a book, much to the women's indignation.

Although the *mehitsah* is ostensibly there to 'protect' the men from seeing women, it is often women who express discomfort with inadequate or missing *mehitsot*. They may not subscribe to all the stringencies of modesty prescribed by haredi rabbis, but the sense that they should remain invisible to men in synagogue is deeply ingrained, especially in women from the traditionalist and haredi sectors.[22] Even Modern Orthodox women who identify as feminists enjoy having a 'women's space', and there has been little to no agitation within Orthodoxy to remove the *mehitsah* altogether, as opposed to making it less of an exclusionary feature.[23]

Alternative services, often held in smaller rooms within the synagogue complex, usually have a temporary curtain made of net fabric of varying degrees of transparency, about two metres high, with the men in front of the curtain and the women behind it, at the back of the room. At Hendon United Synagogue, before the alternative service moved location, the *mehitsah* ran down the middle, with men and women side by side, an arrangement that the women found preferable.[24]

At the Sephardi Heikhal Leah synagogue in Hendon, the women's section,

---

[22] For a discussion of modesty (*tseni'ut*), see Ch. 5.

[23] The political significance of the *mehitsah* as an Orthodox marker and one of the significant differences between Orthodox synagogues and those to the left of Orthodoxy has also tended to rule out opposition to the presence, as opposed to the type, of *mehitsah*.

[24] In a United synagogue that has recently undergone refurbishment, several members strongly urged the adoption of a 'side-by-side' *mehitsah*, but the rabbi refused.

on the ground floor, is separated by a wall with windows that are open during services. The opening is covered with net curtains, which are opened so that women can kiss the Torah scrolls as they are taken out (a practice that is controversial and often physically impossible in most Ashkenazi synagogues). However, the 'invisible' and auxiliary nature of women's attendance and of women's space was underlined by a couple of men who walked into the women's section well before the end of the service to set up long trestle tables for the Kiddush. They bustled about a couple of yards away from the praying women, with no attempt to minimize noise. At the Kiddush it became clear that seats at these tables were for the men only; the few women stood at a small table in the corridor outside the women's section, which was now occupied solely by men.

In haredi synagogues without galleries the curtain or wooden divider is often opaque, and continues to well above head height, so that women cannot see into the men's section. Sometimes the women are in a different room:

A friend of mine who's a lot more haredi, her father davens in Etz Hayim Yeshiva, and the women are upstairs in a different room and the men are downstairs, and [there's] this little hole in the floor through which women could peer down if they wanted to see what's going on. And she said that her father stopped going to the shul for a while and went to Hendon Adas because he was actually shocked to find that his daughter didn't know that the *sefer torah* [Torah scroll] was being held up at 'Vezot hatorah'.[25]

The height and degree of transparency of the *meḥitsah* is often the focus of intense disagreement, sometimes between congregants and rabbis, and sometimes between the congregants themselves. The Preston Report highlighted the dissatisfaction of many women: 'A restricted view often accompanied by worse acoustics has led many respondents in ladies' galleries throughout the country to feel estranged from the service . . . Young women commented that sitting "on the margins" they could not help but feel literally marginalized.'[26] One woman who had grown up in a UOHC (Adas) synagogue, where she had felt engaged even while praying 'by a wall', because she could hear everything going on, experienced a feeling of 'total disengagement' when she later joined a United Synagogue and had to sit in a ladies' gallery, where she felt 'that I'm in the cheap seats'.[27]

Synagogues with galleries accentuate the women's 'spectator' role. Apart

[25] Sheyna Marcus, interview. Note that the father decided which synagogue his daughter would attend. 'Vezot hatorah' ('And this is the Torah') is sung when the uncovered Torah scroll is raised after the Torah reading.

[26] Preston, Goodkin, and Citron, *Women in the Jewish Community*, 34–5.

[27] Katya Fuchs-Mendes, interview.

from joining in communally sung prayers, or silently following the prayers and listening to the Torah reading, they have no roles in the service. In the nineteenth and early twentieth centuries, United Synagogue women sang in synagogue choirs, but increasing rabbinic opposition led to their exclusion.[28] Men tend to sing loudly in synagogue, and some women join in the sung prayers, though too enthusiastic a contribution will earn a visitor disapproving looks. The women in Hagers synagogue, as in other haredi synagogues, do not sing at all but whisper the liturgical songs and the prayers, even though the uninhibited and noisy singing of the men below makes it impossible for them to be heard.[29] While in most synagogues, particularly haredi ones, many men *shokl* (rock back and forth) enthusiastically while praying, few, if any, women *shokl* in either United or haredi synagogues; a subdued, gentle swaying is occasionally seen, especially among younger women.

The ladies' gallery is not necessarily regarded as a place of prayer. At a sabbath morning service in Hendon United Synagogue, I counted fourteen 'chat groups', made up of between two and four women, during the Torah reading, when about sixty-five women were present. They kept up a steady conversation, with breaks to greet newcomers or to join other groups. One pair of women stood in the entrance aisle and continued to talk for half an hour. The talking almost stopped for the Prayer for the Royal Family (recited in English in United synagogues), the Prayer for the Welfare of the State of Israel, the sermon (in English), and the Amidah, the silent prayer of eighteen benedictions, which forms the core of the service. In contrast, women at the haredi Hendon Adas Yisroel tended to sit by themselves or in family groups and follow the service, and the only talking was by two elderly women, who only indulged themselves in the intervals between sections of the Torah reading; however, the men were less restrained, and there were several rounds of 'shushing' downstairs.

In all synagogues, women who want to pray tend to sit by themselves, following the service in the prayer book or *ḥumash*.[30] Those who only attend

---

[28] In 1892 Chief Rabbi Hermann Adler refused to allow a mixed choir at the foundation-stone ceremony of Hampstead United Synagogue: see Alderman, *Modern British Jewry*, 108. The last 'mixed' choir in Great Britain survives at the Princes Road Synagogue in Liverpool: see the Princes Road Synagogue website.

[29] The Talmud (*Ber.* 24a) records a debate about the permissibility or otherwise of men listening to women's voices (whether speaking or singing is unclear) while reciting the Shema. The major medieval authorities interpreted this in varying ways, but in the nineteenth century R. Moses Sofer, a conservative halakhist followed to this day by many haredi communities, ruled that men were forbidden to listen to women singing at any time, not just during prayers. For an introduction to this issue, see Golinkin, '"Kol B'ishah Ervah"', and for a survey of the historical reality of Jewish women singing, see Taitz, 'Kol Ishah: The Voice of Women'.

[30] A *ḥumash* is a printed edition of the Torah designed for use in synagogue; the text is divided

High Holiday services and life-cycle events such as barmitzvahs typically do not take a prayer book or *ḥumash* off the shelf, and talk throughout the service, often to the annoyance of more devout neighbours. Here again Alei Tzion was unusual; very few women talked and there was an atmosphere of concentration on prayer, with every woman following the service and singing along quietly.

Women's Experience of Synagogue

Women have mixed feelings about synagogue attendance. Some find it essential to their experience of the sabbath, like Kate Moskovitz, a haredi mother of eight, who replicated synagogue services at home when her children were small:

Shabes [sabbath] to me is going to shul *shabes* morning, and coming back from shul . . . when I couldn't go to shul because of the youngsters, I made a shul in the house, we all davened in the house, and we had a children's service when they were tiny.

Katherine Marks, a Jewish educator and mother of four, felt strongly enough about the local synagogues when she lived in a provincial town to set up her family's own services: 'Shul was terrible, so we started our own shul, which was run from our house in a college round the corner.' Like many others, she had happy memories of sitting in the men's section when young, only to be banished to the gallery when she reached the age of 12: 'When I was a little girl I remember sitting downstairs, and I *loved* that, just being part of that, and then of course when I got too big I had to go upstairs, and I didn't like that very much, but accepted it.'

In her teens, communal prayer during the summer school run by the Jewish Youth Study Group had left an indelible, enchanted memory of a deeply moving and spiritual experience:

On Friday, it was a ritual, we would all walk down to the beautiful shul by the river, and it was just the most incredibly spiritual experience to see. We'd all been scruffy and filthy all week, and the boys in suits and the girls in their long dresses—we'd all walk to shul, and it was very singy, and I *loved* the singing, and our boys were leading it, and there were enough there that had good voices, and that's where I learnt all the tunes, and we would sing for hours on Friday night. It was just amazing.

In contrast, her usual synagogue was 'meaningless':

into the weekly portions (*parashot*), accompanied by the weekly reading from the prophetic books (*haftarot*). Ḥumashim and prayer books in United synagogues always contain English translations and often include a commentary in English; further to the 'right' along the religious spectrum, more use is made of all-Hebrew *ḥumashim* and prayer books, reflecting the higher proportion of congregants who can at least read Hebrew (if not always understand it).

I did feel that it was all slow and long and boring, and I quite liked the singing, but I never knew what was going on. I was never able to follow the leyning;[31] even though I could read Hebrew *very* well and could translate most of it, it never *occurred* to me to follow the leyning because I couldn't really hear it, and it was so far away.

Memories of unusually spiritual moments during communal prayer are often accompanied by bitterness, resentment, and a sense that something is lacking. Some women are painfully aware of a mixed response, like Shirley Daniels:

I never really felt comfortable davening at home, because I was brought up in a davening-at-shul family. You know, there are other families where the women always davened at home and so it feels very natural, but I was brought up with davening at shul, and sitting next to my mum in shul always . . . but shul experience is so much bigger than the service of the *tefilah* [prayer], it's communal life . . . [there is] resentment connected to shul because [my husband] goes to it so much . . . so decided by men for men, to take them out of the house, and away from the children, and why are those my duties and not his duties or our duties—yeah, there's lots of conflicting emotions about it.

For Sharon Jastrow, an older woman brought up in a semi-observant Orthodox family, and whose 'religious direction had changed' when she married a non-observant man, her move to the Masorti movement was partly fuelled by intense dislike of the United Synagogue experience: 'I know I could never ever go to shul there, they are not interested in the fact that everybody talks, and nobody listens during Kaddish, and that the sermons are superficial junk . . . It doesn't bother them, there's a kind of separation between their intellectual and Jewish needs and shul.'

The Preston Report devoted three pages to 'Women in the Synagogue' in 1994, and many of the issues and complaints recorded were still being raised in the follow-up Women's Review of 2009,[32] as well as by the United Synagogue Orthodox women I talked to: the feeling that the rabbi's sermon was directed largely to the men; the loneliness and exclusion of single, divorced, or widowed women; the fact that 'in many mainstream Orthodox synagogues, catering continues to be the sum total of women's participation in synagogue life';[33] and 'the general disappointment of the dreariness and the boringness and the alienating experience of the United Synagogue'.[34] Many women, in

---

[31] The anglicized Yiddish word for the traditional chanting of the Torah.

[32] Preston et al., *Connection, Continuity and Community*, 12.

[33] Preston, Goodkin, and Citron, *Women in the Jewish Community*, 31; this refers to the traditional organization of the food and drinks for Kiddush after the service by the women of the community, often members of the ladies' guild, which I discuss below in this chapter.

[34] Katherine Marks, interview. These feelings are not limited to United Synagogue women;

particular the elderly, do not have sufficient knowledge of Hebrew to be able to follow the service, much less join in the prayers. It is not uncommon to hear traditionalist women dismiss the synagogue as 'just a boy's club', or to claim that they are glad that they do not have to attend services.

In contrast, haredi women express far fewer criticisms and complaints about their synagogue experience; often, they have a better Jewish education—enabling them to follow and recite the prayers—and they have accepted and internalized haredi expectations of women's roles. Sheyna Marcus, who described herself as being on the borderline between Modern Orthodox and haredi, valued the sincerity she sensed in her Edgware synagogue:

> It's not superficial, the rabbi there is not scared to say what he thinks or be blunt about what people should be doing, and, you know, whereas if you got up in the United Synagogue shul and you said, 'Oh, you have to stop talking in shul', or 'You have to cover your elbows when you come into shul', the community would get into an uproar, 'How could he say that in a pulpit'—no, the rabbi will quite happily get up and say 'You're not singing loud enough, I want to hear you', and people respect him for that, and the shul has become very close and real rather than superficial. So that's why I daven there during the year. But on Rosh Hashanah, Yom Kippur, and other times I prefer to be in a traditional United synagogue.

It is notable that, even though she appreciated the 'real' spiritual quality of her current synagogue, Sheyna preferred to return to the less spiritual but deeply traditional United synagogue in which she had been brought up for the most intense and significant festivals of the year; atmosphere and a sense of continuity are as important for many women as personal spiritual satisfaction. Women usually attend the synagogues to which their families belong, but frequently visit others for life-cycle events, such as bar- and batmitzvahs. However, they are unlikely to experiment with other denominations' synagogues, even if they are very unhappy with their own, as this potentially carries a high social cost, perhaps in difficulties for their children in finding marriage partners, or being asked to leave haredi schools.[35] One young mother with an excellent Jewish education and strongly held feminist principles who attends a haredi synagogue in Edgware is so alienated by her experience on Simhat Torah (see below) that she longs to try the local Masorti synagogue, but is aware that 'somebody is bound to see me going in'. A more conventional Sephardi mother in her thirties noted that because her daughter attends the haredi Beis Ya'akov school, she has to be very careful about which synagogues she goes to, or there will be problems with the school.

one of the hasidic women who told me she never went to synagogue (see above, n. 7) said that this was because it was 'boring'.

[35] Both possibilities were often cited by women as social sanctions for failure to fulfil

Flashpoints: Tension in the Synagogue

Although many Orthodox Jewish women are either content with or resigned to their synagogue experience, the tension between their assigned role as spectators and their desire to participate—or at least be acknowledged—sometimes reaches critical levels. Most of these occasions mark life-cycle events: birth, batmitzvahs and barmitzvahs, and the two key rituals that mark death—the recitation of Kaddish, the mourner's prayer, at set points in every service,[36] and the commemoration of a *yahrzeit*, the anniversary of a relative's death.[37] Another occasion on which such tension is palpable is the festival of Simhat Torah, the 'Rejoicing of the Law', during which men dance with the Torah scrolls, and every man is honoured with an *aliyah* to the Torah.

Women's Role in Life-Cycle Events

Women traditionally play no or very little role in life-cycle celebrations, as demonstrated by the following overview.

- Circumcision (*berit milah*), during which a boy is also named, is usually performed at home or in a hall; the mother usually sits in a different room and has no role.[38]

- A girl is usually named as part of the blessing following her father's *aliyah* in the synagogue on the sabbath following the birth; usually, especially if there is no *eruv*, the mother and the baby are not present in synagogue for the naming.[39]

- On the sabbath before a wedding, an Ashkenazi groom is given an *aliyah*,[40] and wedding songs are often sung after he completes the blessings; the bride-to-be may watch,[41] but has no parallel ceremony.[42]

communal expectations; nobody ever mentioned an actual example. It seems likely that such sanctions could only be applied in the haredi community.

[36] For a brief, harrowing account of an American Orthodox woman's difficulties in saying Kaddish, see Reguer, 'Kaddish from the "Wrong" Side of the Mechitzah'; for contrasting experiences, see Millen, 'The Female Voice of Kaddish', 181.

[37] A *yahrzeit* is marked publicly by the recitation of a memorial prayer during the Torah reading, usually after a (male) relation has been called up to the Torah.

[38] In Modern Orthodox circles, the mother may give a short Torah talk or explain the choice of the baby's name after the end of the actual ceremony.

[39] See Ch. 4 for *simhat bat* ceremonies for girls.

[40] The custom is known as an *aufruf* (Yid.-Ger. 'call-up').

[41] Many Ashkenazim follow the practice of the bride and groom not seeing each other for the week preceding the wedding, in which case the bride-to-be will attend a different synagogue. In my survey of customs (see Ch. 6), 41% of respondents had observed this practice, and another 42% were aware of it.

[42] The *shabat kalah* ('bride's sabbath') has developed more recently, partly in parallel to the

- Weddings are frequently celebrated in synagogues, though this is not mandatory. During the ceremony, unlike the groom, the bride says nothing, and her only active role is to walk around the groom seven times under the wedding canopy, before the ceremony begins.

- At barmitzvahs, a mother has no role to play, beyond watching from the gallery or the women's section.

- A girl's batmitzvah was not celebrated in synagogue until a few decades ago, but more recently group *bat ḥayil* and individual batmitzvah ceremonies have been introduced into United synagogues, though usually not in the context of sabbath communal prayer (see below).

- The recitation of Kaddish by women mourners is regarded in haredi and some traditionalist circles as an undesirable innovation,[43] though in recent years the United Synagogue has encouraged women to say it.

- Since women do not receive *aliyot* to the Torah, they cannot do this to mark the *yahrzeit* of relatives, as men customarily do.

However, change can be observed in some of these areas, particularly in United synagogues, sometimes as a result of women's desire for greater participation in public ritual. In order to elucidate the ways in which women negotiate and experience change in public communal rituals I shall examine three of these—baby blessings, batmitzvah, and the recitation of Kaddish and marking of a *yahrzeit*—and consider their implications for women's religious agency and experience.

Baby Blessings

Several United synagogues have, in recent decades, introduced group 'baby blessing' ceremonies. In the 1990s, Rabbi Jeffrey Cohen of Stanmore United Synagogue designed a brief ceremony, in which he read psalms and recited the priestly benediction over the babies at the end of the morning service on the second day of a festival, chosen to avoid the prohibition of carrying the baby to synagogue on the sabbath in the absence of an *eruv*.[44]

Other United synagogues followed suit. An early example was Woodside

---

increasingly popular non-Jewish 'hen party', but it is celebrated at home rather than in synagogue. So far it seems to be celebrated by younger, more observant women—the 'post-seminary' generation—from the haredi and Modern Orthodox sectors; it has not yet caught on in traditionalist circles.

[43] Historically, women have recited Kaddish, both for parents and for spouses, at least as far back as seventeenth-century Amsterdam; very few British Jewish women are aware of this. See Millen, 'The Female Voice of Kaddish'.

[44] Rabbi Cohen said he was unable to remember why he had introduced this innovation.

Park, where the ceremony was introduced at Passover in 2004,[45] despite initially strong opposition from the rabbi, who did not want women or babies on the *bimah*,[46] and was concerned that women might not dress modestly. The ceremony, held on the second day of Passover and Sukkot each year, takes place just before 'Adon olam', the concluding hymn. The families assemble in the centre of the prayer hall, the babies' names are read out, and the parents carry them onto the *bimah*. The mothers hold the babies while the fathers place their hands on the babies' heads and recite the traditional blessing for children.[47] The rabbi says a few words, and each baby is presented with a certificate, a teddy bear, and a Jewish children's book.

The lack of a speaking role for women is explained by the fact that the ceremony was largely introduced as a way of bringing in new, young families to the community, rather than enabling greater involvement of women.[48] Nevertheless, other synagogues have adapted the basic baby blessing ceremony to give women a more prominent role. Radlett United Synagogue, under the influence of a young rabbi and his wife, who arrived in 2011, has introduced a very popular baby blessing ceremony, which includes psalms and prayers read by the mothers, fathers, and grandparents.[49] A biblical text used to bless children is sung,[50] and the ceremony closes with the mothers holding the babies under a *talit* (prayer shawl) held aloft by all the fathers, while the rabbi reads the priestly blessing.[51] In order to avoid desecration of a festival by non-observant relatives driving to synagogue, the ceremony takes place on a Sunday, and is combined with a tea for all the families; this also means that photographs can be taken, which would be prohibited on festivals. Radlett is a young congregation in both senses: it was founded in 1981, and is one of the fastest-growing United synagogues, with many young families. The rebbetsin is employed alongside her husband (in older synagogues the rebbetsin was expected to work for free if she got involved in synagogue affairs), and is a

---

[45] Telephone conversation with Dr Hayden Kendler (a synagogue board member), 24 July 2013.

[46] The central podium from which prayers are led and the Torah is read. The rabbi had also objected to girls below the age of batmitzvah coming up to the podium for the traditional blessing given to children on Simhat Torah. The current, younger, rabbi supports the baby blessings enthusiastically.

[47] This blessing, which many parents recite on Friday nights, consists of a short introduction —'May God bless you like Sarah, Rebecca, Rachel, and Leah' for girls, and 'May God bless you like Ephraim and Manasseh' for boys, followed by the priestly blessing (Num. 6: 24–6). See *Authorised Daily Prayer Book*, 310–11.

[48] Dr Kendler made this point explicitly.

[49] These are read in English. Information about the Radlett baby blessings came from telephone interviews with Rabbi Leo Dee and Rebbetsin Lucy Dee, 24 July 2013.

[50] 'Hamalakh hago'el oti' (Gen. 48: 16); see *Authorised Daily Prayer Book*, 248–9.

[51] See above, n. 47.

major factor in the promotion of the baby blessings.[52] Similarly, a young rabbi appointed to Muswell Hill United Synagogue in September 2008 held a Sunday 'round-up' group baby blessing followed by lunch in June 2011 for all children born since his arrival, which was very popular, and he plans to hold more in future.[53]

Not every change that enables women to play a more participatory role in public rituals is inspired by a desire to empower them. The introduction of baby blessings is a case in point; rather than being designed to give women a role in birth rituals, they seem to have been developed and promoted by rabbis and (male) lay leaders as a way of attracting young, unaffiliated families into synagogues, with a view to encouraging their attendance or consumption of synagogue-based commercial services such as nurseries. Significantly, no rabbis reported any input or suggestions for the ceremony from participating parents, though all remarked that the ceremony had proved very popular. No objections to the ceremony, for instance on the grounds of its novelty and lack of any halakhic basis, were raised.[54] Parents with more radical views on the involvement and active participation of women tend to compose their own *simhat bat* or *zeved bat* ceremonies for daughters, held at home or in rented halls, and they often make creative use of biblical and midrashic texts. The social aspects of the baby blessing ceremony, rather than more narrowly defined religious values, are paramount.

Batmitzvah

Batmitzvah as a ceremony, rather than as the traditional Jewish legal concept of adulthood applied to a girl from the age of 12, is largely a twentieth-century development, though there were batmitzvah celebrations in nineteenth-century Egypt, Italy, Baghdad, Germany, and France.[55] Indeed, the elaborate celebrations now associated with the barmitzvah only began to develop in the fifteenth to sixteenth centuries.[56] In the twentieth century, it took some time for batmitzvah rituals to become accepted in Israel and the USA, and the first ceremonies took place outside the Orthodox sphere. The first modern batmitzvah ceremony, in 1922, was associated with Rabbi Mordecai Kaplan (1881–1983), who had Orthodox ordination but at the time was teaching at the

[52] She set up a mothers-and-toddlers group that forms the basic network for recruiting families to take part in the baby blessings, noting that 'if the rebbetsin is not engaged, the rabbi may not be aware of or have the necessary links with the mums' to get them to attend.

[53] Rabbi David Mason, telephone interview, 1 Aug. 2013.

[54] This serves as a further confirmation of the 'marketing' origin and nature of these ceremonies, since changes that allow women greater participation in ritual, such as women's *tefilah* groups, are routinely condemned by rabbinic authorities as innovations with no basis in tradition. See the section on women's *tefilah* groups in Ch. 4.

[55] Joseph, 'Bat Mitzvah', 4.   [56] Ibid.

Conservative Jewish Theological Seminary in New York. The first American Reform batmitzvah was held in 1931, and by the 1960s batmitzvah ceremonies were widely celebrated in the American Conservative movement, though it was only in the 1980s and 1990s that they reproduced the form of the barmitzvah.[57] British Jews were much slower to adopt the practice: the Liberal movement in the 1960s required any family whose sons had a barmitzvah to undertake to let their daughters have a batmitzvah;[58] the Reform movement introduced the practice in the 1970s,[59] and the Masorti movement followed suit in the 1980s.[60]

Things moved more slowly in the Orthodox world. Though Israeli rabbis generally took a positive view of modest celebrations, conducted outside synagogues, it took longer for the event to become naturalized in American Orthodox contexts, although an early example was a batmitzvah held in Brooklyn in 1944, at a Friday night celebration (*oneg shabat*). Orthodox rabbis in provincial American communities were under pressure from congregants, often less observant, who wanted rituals for girls that would match their brothers' barmitzvahs, and who often pioneered various types of batmitzvah. By the 1970s, batmitzvah celebrations were much more common, and by the end of the 1980s, they had become an unquestioned part of the American Orthodox landscape.[61]

In British Orthodox communities, the 'standard' for a barmitzvah boy is to start wearing *tefilin*, to be called up to the Torah on the sabbath after his birthday (during which he may read part or all of the weekly Torah portion and the accompanying reading from the Prophets), and to have a party. Some boys also begin wearing a *talit* (prayer shawl), though many Ashkenazi men do not wear a *talit* until they marry. The celebration of a girl reaching her religious majority thus presents Orthodox communities with a challenge: given that Orthodox women do not wear *tefilin*, read publicly from the Torah, or wear a *talit*,[62] how should a girl's batmitzvah be marked, if at all?

[57] Hyman, 'The Introduction of Bat Mitzvah'.

[58] Rigal and Rosenberg, *Liberal Judaism*, 255–6.

[59] Kershen and Romain, *Tradition and Change*, 336, mention that as late as the 1980s 'some synagogues did not encourage girls to have a *batmitzvah* in the same way the boys were expected to have a *barmitzvah*'.

[60] A Masorti interviewee remembered group batmitzvahs in the early 1980s held on Shavuot, very much like the Orthodox *bat ḥayil* (Cherie Jackson, interview), and noted that the girls did not stand on the *bimah*. Nobody I asked could remember when the present individual batmitzvah format was introduced. British Masorti communities differ widely in practice, but there are several egalitarian communities in which girls read the Torah and *haftarah* as the barmitzvah boys do.

[61] See Eleff and Butler, 'How Bat Mitzvah Became Orthodox', for a detailed account of developments in the USA.

[62] A small, though growing, number of Orthodox women in Israel and the USA wear *talit*

Like their colleagues in America, British Orthodox rabbis, aware only of non-Orthodox precedents for batmitzvah celebrations, did not favour their introduction.[63] In spite of this reluctance, popular demand for the recognition of girls' passage to religious adulthood led to a compromise in the 1960s, when a ceremony known as *bat ḥayil*[64] was instituted for groups of girls aged 12, sometimes after they had completed the synagogue cheder. It was usually held on a Sunday, sometimes in a synagogue,[65] with the girls reciting prayers or reading Proverbs 31: 1–31, a biblical description of the 'ideal woman'.[66] Many girls, however, felt the ceremony was impersonal and meaningless; a young woman remembers refusing to participate in one, though both her elder sisters had, as she felt it had no significance.[67] Katherine Marks participated in the second *bat ḥayil* held in Ilford United Synagogue, in 1967:

My *bat ḥayil* was a completely meaningless experience in that it was one of those things [like] when Napoleon baptized his soldiers by running a hose over all of them at once, it was quite similar to that, really, in that there were a group of twenty-five of us.

The girls read Proverbs 31, in Hebrew and English, and had tea afterwards in the Town Hall, where they were addressed by Lady Jakobovits, the wife of the chief rabbi. Katherine recalled being acutely aware that the ceremony was 'a very scaled-down version' of her brother's barmitzvah. Similar feelings were recorded by Sarah Ebner, a journalist, whose *bat ḥayil* at Kenton United Synagogue in the 1980s left her feeling 'that I was just a cog in the "I guess our girls should get to do something" machine'.[68] Reflecting on her *bat ḥayil* ceremony at Pinner United Synagogue in the 1980s, Jacqueline Nicholls, a Modern Orthodox artist, was struck by its lack of relevance:

and/or *tefilin*, but as far as I know there are only two Orthodox women in the UK who wear a *talit*, one of whom also wears *tefilin*. Neither woman uses these in public services.

[63] Joseph, 'Bat Mitzvah', notes that Orthodox rabbis today are completely unaware of nineteenth- and early twentieth-century Orthodox batmitzvah ceremonies. For a discussion of Orthodox rabbis' attitudes to batmitzvah and the halakhic considerations involved, see E. Brown, 'The Bat Mitzvah in Jewish Law and Contemporary Practice'; for a volume of articles by twenty-four Orthodox scholars (male and female) and rabbis who view batmitzvah ceremonies in a positive light, see Wiskind-Elper (ed.), *Traditions and Celebrations for the Bat Mitzvah*. None of the authors are British.

[64] 'Daughter of valour'; based on *eshet ḥayil*, 'woman of valour' (Prov. 31: 10).

[65] Hubert, *A Jewish Woman's Handbook*, 23, records a group batmitzvah in synagogue in 1975 as a novelty.

[66] Traditionally recited by a man in honour of his wife on Friday night, before Kiddush and the sabbath meal.   [67] Brenda Johns, interview.

[68] Ebner, 'Give Girls a Real Batmitzvah Experience'. Ebner chose to give her daughter a batmitzvah in a Masorti synagogue, since she felt that the options at an Orthodox (United) synagogue were unsatisfactory.

We had to say bits of random prayers in Hebrew and English . . . at the time I thought it was nonsense, and I was one of the good girls. I won lots of prizes in cheder, not least for the *bat ḥayil* project, 'a Jewish woman and her home' . . . None of it was about who we were as individuals; even being made to write some bland nonsense about our Hebrew name or favourite Jewish heroine would have been an improvement.[69]

The shortcomings of the *bat ḥayil* led to pressure for more individualized ceremonies, and today the individual batmitzvah is the norm in most United synagogues, with the group *bat ḥayil* being characteristic of more haredi synagogues.[70] The rabbi of Bushey United Synagogue thought that the decline of the *bat ḥayil* was linked to changes in Jewish education (possibly as better-educated girls are more capable of producing something for an individual batmitzvah?), but did not note the widespread resentment at having to share a generalized celebration with other girls.[71]

Individual synagogues develop their own guidelines, largely dependent on the rabbi's decision on what is permissible. At Yeshurun, a Federation synagogue in Edgware, the girl's father may be honoured with an *aliyah* on the occasion of her batmitzvah, and the girl is congratulated during the announcements, but anything else, such as the girl giving a short sermon, would happen at a private event. Batmitzvah innovations in the haredi sector include the girl organizing a fundraising project for a Jewish charity—a natural extension of the strong emphasis on women's welfare work (*ḥesed*) that would confirm rather than challenge gender roles in haredi society.

The nature of batmitzvah ceremonies is still fluid, with occasional examples of families trying to push for greater parity with barmitzvahs, though this is usually rejected by the rabbinic establishment. In late 2011 Dr Alexis Brassey, a member of Hampstead Garden Suburb United Synagogue, whose eldest daughter was approaching batmitzvah, asked the London Beth Din to find a way to allow her to have an *aliyah*.[72] The Beth Din turned down his request, on the grounds that 'Our mothers, grandmothers and great-grandmothers all loved the Torah no less than ourselves but were never called up

---

[69] Untitled document on *bat ḥayil*, originally available on the now defunct Jewish Community Centre for London website.

[70] The only example I could find of *bat ḥayil* being offered at a non-haredi synagogue was on the website of Bushey United Synagogue, 'Bar/Bat Mitzvah/Bat Chayil', though the synagogue's rabbi said they had only been held in the 1980s and 1990s, and had since been superseded by batmitzvahs (email from Rabbi Meir Salasnik, 28 Aug. 2013).   [71] Ibid.

[72] A copy of his (highly idiosyncratic) analysis of the relevant halakhic literature appears in Rocker, 'Should Batmitzvah Girls Be Called to the Torah?', published by the *Jewish Chronicle* and available on the Internet under the same title. See also Rocker, 'Why Can't My Girl Be Called to the Torah?' The *Chronicle* also ran a readers' poll on the question 'Should bat mitzvah girls be

to the Torah. That practice of "omission" hence dictates that it is forbidden to call women up.'[73]

The most usual format is for the girl to prepare a short sermon (*devar torah*), often related to the weekly Torah portion, which she delivers after the sabbath morning service. This is a deliberate policy, in order to avoid her participation in the service proper; in some cases, the message is underlined by having the girl speak outside the synagogue sanctuary, in a communal hall. Some families prefer to hold the ceremony on a Sunday, without the link to the communal service, enabling relatives who live further away to drive to the venue.

A typical example of a United Synagogue batmitzvah comes from the website of Borehamwood & Elstree United Synagogue:

The format of the Bat Mitzvah involves the girl delivering a D'var Torah (Torah discourse) in front of the entire congregation. She then follows this with the recital of a special Bat Mitzvah prayer. The parents are then invited to bless their daughter and offer thanks to the Almighty for this milestone in their lives. The rabbi then offers a Torah thought and some personal remarks, and the Bat Mitzvah girl is presented with a book and certificate.[74]

The girl usually studies with a tutor,[75] often the local rebbetsin; different tutors will have very different approaches to the subject matter, the level of study, and control over the final text of the girl's speech. In some synagogues, the rabbi or a warden will read the speech in advance, and may modify it to remove or tone down passages regarded as too controversial. In one instance in 2015, a girl wrote:

There are no female role models in this Parasha [weekly Torah portion] for me to learn from. However, I choose to see this in a different light; the Torah always has something to teach us, even if it is a warning of how not to live one's life as opposed to a positive role model. The lack of female voices can help me to learn about myself: the fact that this silence disturbs me so much helps me to realise that I will not fall into this trap . . . I refuse to be a silent character in my future as a member of the Jewish people. Women have come so far since the time of the events in my Parasha. Especially in the 21st century, I will not let my voice go unheard and I will acknow-

called to the Torah?', with 59% of the 735 respondents in favour. The page, accessed on 31 July 2013, is no longer available.

[73] The Beth Din did not address the halakhic arguments in Dr Brassey's request; see Rocker, 'Beth Din'.

[74] This would all happen after the end of the service. See <https://www.borehamwoodshul.org/lifecycle/bat-mitzvah>.

[75] I have tutored girls for batmitzvah for the last twelve years, and much of the information in this section is based on my experience.

ledge that I indeed have a voice and an important part to play in my Jewish community.

Ironically, the rabbi of her synagogue rewrote this, effectively erasing the girl's challenging voice:

On reflection though, the lack of audible female voices in this week's Parasha can help me to learn about myself: the fact that I have noted this silence has prompted me to realise the importance of not remaining silent . . . I would like my voice to be heard as a member of the Jewish people. Women have come so far since the time of the events in my Parasha. Especially in the 21st century, I think it is important that I acknowledge that I indeed have a voice and a vital part to play in Jewish life and in my Jewish community.

The limited and somewhat sidelined nature of this type of batmitzvah ceremony has led to variations, often urged by the girl's family. At Stanmore United Synagogue, in the early 2000s, one girl read the previous sabbath's *haftarah* in the traditional chant on a Sunday morning, as well as giving a *devar torah*.[76] At South Hampstead United Synagogue, with full support from the rabbi and rebbetsin (who participated in the service), a girl read the Torah portion from a *ḥumash* (rather than a scroll) at an all-women's Rosh Hodesh service on a Sunday in November 2007,[77] and later gave a *devar torah* during a party, held at the synagogue.

However, sometimes the girl and her family want more than the rabbi is willing to permit in synagogue, and in recent years batmitzvah celebrations have increasingly been held in private homes, sometimes in a marquee in the garden, or in rented halls; sometimes this is in addition to the 'standard' *devar torah* after the service in the synagogue. Often no mention is made publicly or on invitations of these more radical ceremonies, allowing the family to avoid a confrontation with their rabbi and to sidestep the objections of more traditional family members. At these alternative and semi-secret celebrations, the girl often chants the Torah portion from a Torah scroll, at an all-women service or a partnership *minyan*. In one case, a girl had a standard batmitzvah

[76] This seems to have been a one-off; the format does not appear on the synagogue's current list of options for batmitzvah, which include 'communal ceremony in shul at the Shabbat morning service; private ceremony in shul after the Shabbat morning service; private havdallah service in shul or at home; private afternoon ceremony on Sunday at shul or at home; private lunch at home with a special ceremony; private party with special ceremony; shul based Women's Learning Experience group ceremony' ('B'nei Mitzvah Preparation, Advice & Guidelines'). There are only two options (sabbath morning or midweek) for barmitzvah.

[77] This was actually a women's *tefilah* group, of the type described in Ch. 4, using a shortened form of the standard service and omitting the prayers that require a *minyan*. It proved very popular, and a few more were held on Sundays that coincided with Rosh Hodesh, including one service that was not part of a batmitzvah celebration.

at her local United Synagogue, and another, involving chanting from a Torah scroll, at a *havurah* to which her family belongs.[78] In June 2014 another girl read the book of Ruth on the second day of Shavuot at a private service held at her home.[79] Several girls have read the Torah portion or the *haftarah* from a *humash* at the Stanmore Women's Tefillah Group.[80] Another United synagogue followed suit in 2015, with the rabbi's daughter's batmitzvah serving as the focus for the first women-only service. Half a dozen girls read from the *parashah* or *haftarah* at similar services in the next two years.

Many United Synagogue girls and their families are searching for meaningful, personal ceremonies to celebrate a spiritual landmark, showing remarkable creativity: personal charity projects, study projects, and family history research projects have been designed, or traditional Jewish women's skills have been acquired and used in celebrations such as challah parties. The London School of Jewish Studies has been running a mother-and-daughter study course for batmitzvah girls (Kolot), designed and taught by women, since 2000; approximately thirty to forty mother–daughter pairs registered for it in 2013. The emphasis is on the study of texts relating to outstanding women in the Bible and in later Jewish tradition, rather than on socialization as future wife and mother. Some synagogues have taken up the idea: in 2016, Edgware United Synagogue advertised the Shoshanim (Roses) course, run by the rabbi and rebbetsin, which offered an exploration of 'Jewish heritage and values with fun hands-on activities, text-based learning and trips'.[81]

Older women who missed the opportunity of having a batmitzvah often regret this, and in 2013 the rebbetsin of Stanmore United Synagogue ran an eight-week 'adult batmitzvah' course for twenty-five women. The curriculum included learning to bake challah, a lecture on the importance of kashrut, a tour of a *mikveh*,[82] tea with the chief rabbi's wife, and the option of writing

---

[78] The *havurah* movement started in the USA in the 1960s, with small groups of Jews reacting to the over-institutionalized nature of religious life by getting together for sabbath and festival celebrations. There are a few *havurot* in the UK, whose members are mostly from Masorti or Reform backgrounds.

[79] She also prepared a *devar torah*, which she delivered after the service at her family's (United) synagogue three weeks later. The book of Ruth is traditionally read (by a man) on Shavuot, usually from a printed version; the batmitzvah girl read it from a handwritten scroll, a much more ambitious undertaking.

[80] Over 100 women usually attended these batmitzvah celebrations, held at a hall rented from a local (non-Jewish) school before the group was allowed to meet at the synagogue. The girls' immediate male relatives were allowed in to hear them read; they sat at the back, a somewhat ironic reversal of women's presence on the sidelines of standard synagogue events.

[81] EdgwareK email list, 25 July 2016.

[82] Ritual bath. Several of the women had never been to one before. See Ch. 5 for a discussion of women's experience of the *mikveh*.

and delivering a *devar torah*—an interesting combination of central elements of women's traditional role, such as running a kosher kitchen and observing the laws of 'family purity', and newer elements such as Torah study.[83] The women received a certificate and a joint blessing in synagogue at the end of the course.

Batmitzvah provides an example of a fairly new public ritual that is still in flux, largely because of the inherent tension involved in women's participation in synagogue ceremonies, even if they are barely teenagers. There is strong pressure from non-haredi parents, and sometimes from the girls themselves, on the synagogue authorities to provide a ceremony that parallels the barmitzvah, reflecting broader British social concerns about gender equality and the empowerment of girls. This has led to the abandonment of the group *bat ḥayil* ceremony in most United synagogues, and the introduction of a range of 'compromise' batmitzvah ceremonies focusing on individual girls.

The rabbis seem to be fighting a rear-guard action to dissociate these ceremonies from public worship, insisting that girls deliver their batmitzvah talks after the service, outside the synagogue sanctuary, or not on the sabbath. The dissatisfaction felt by many families with this type of 'second-best' ceremony is reflected both in the alternative batmitzvah ceremonies held outside the synagogue framework, and in the occasional challenge to the authorities to justify their refusal to allow girls to experience the same treatment as boys on reaching religious maturity. Alternative settings such as women's *tefilah* groups and Megillah readings, challah parties, and the new partnership *minyanim* have served as public but non-official arenas for the celebration of batmitzvahs, and this trend is on the rise in the Modern Orthodox and parts of the traditionalist sectors. The recent origin of batmitzvah ceremonies and their consequent lack of standardization or halakhic constraints serve as a spur to the quest for innovation and relevance, and enable a high degree of creativity, in contrast to the 'sausage factory' of United Synagogue barmitzvah celebrations, largely determined by precedent and social expectations. It seems likely that batmitzvah will continue to be a contested area in which non-haredi women seek to make their voices heard and their presence felt: in July 2016 JOFA held a 'webinar' led by Rebbetsin Dina Brawer on the theme of 'Bat Mitzvah Reimagined', which 'explore[d] practical ways in which we can create rites of passage for our daughters that are within the framework of *halakha*, educationally valuable, spiritually meaningful, and deeply relevant

---

[83] This element was optional; it was clearly felt that some women might be put off by this innovation.

to contemporary girls on the cusp of womanhood', and featured an account of a unique batmitzvah ceremony created by a mother and a daughter.[84]

In contrast, the *bat ḥayil* ceremony is still being held in some haredi contexts, where women are far less likely to challenge the status quo or seek participation in 'male' contexts such as the synagogue. The highly gender-segregated nature of haredi society means that any innovations in batmitzvah celebrations tend to occur invisibly within the 'women's world' of *ḥesed* activity rather than in the ritual sphere.

Funerals, Kaddish, and Yahrzeit

Jewish funerals are organized by burial societies attached to synagogue organizations; thus the United Synagogue, the Federation, and the Union (UOHC) all maintain their own cemeteries and burial societies. The Union's burial society (popularly known as the Adas[85]) maintains a policy of excluding women from attendance at funerals, while the other societies permit it.[86] One man remembered that '[T]he Adas used to have a small lean-to at the side of the cemetery hall for the women to huddle, at least at Cheshunt. My mother and aunts were herded there at my father's funeral in '84.' Some women find this policy upsetting, and refuse to comply. Leonie Adelman, a traditionalist woman in her fifties, whose parents had belonged to the Adas burial scheme, had to fight in order to attend her mother's funeral. She asked other women friends and relations to join her, since 'they couldn't throw them out', but was very conscious of official disapproval, as well as being shocked at the hastiness and lack of respect shown during the funeral itself. She has since left the Adas burial scheme and joined that of the United Synagogue. Nor is this an isolated example—the Preston Report noted that:

Overwhelmingly, women insisted that they should have the right to attend funerals if they felt inclined to do so. Considerable numbers felt that it was not only unjust but also extremely unfeeling to ban a woman from attending the funeral of someone with whom she was closely connected, purely on gender terms. Many of these women expressed their hurt and anger at having been prevented from doing so.[87]

---

[84] JOFA newsletter (21 July 2016).   [85] Its formal name is the Adath Yisroel Burial Society.

[86] The custom of women not attending funerals is kabbalistic in origin, based on a statement in the Zohar ('Vayakhel', 196) that 'Satan dances' at funerals; this was incorporated in Karo, *Shulḥan arukh*, 'Yoreh de'ah', 359, where paragraph 1 notes that women should follow the coffin rather than go before it, and paragraph 2 rules that women should not enter the cemetery for the actual burial. See the 2009 email exchange between Aryeh Frimer and Zev Sero on the Aishdas website, <http://www.aishdas.org/avodah/vol26/v26n058.shtml#08>. However, most non-haredi communities do not prohibit women's attendance, and Maurice Lamm's popular handbook, *The Jewish Way in Death and Mourning*, does not even mention this custom.

[87] Preston, Goodkin, and Citron, *Women in the Jewish Community*, 73.

The report also recorded instances of rabbis refusing to perform funerals when women insisted on being present.

Although allowed to attend funerals, United Synagogue women (and men) were not allowed to deliver eulogies (*hespedim*) at them until 2008, since previously only rabbis had the right to speak at funerals.[88] At this point too, women were allowed to take part in the ritual of filling the grave,[89] which had only been permitted to men until then. Women have taken advantage of these changes and now often deliver eulogies themselves, as well as helping to fill the grave. Saying Kaddish at the graveside may be more difficult, and depends on the attitude of the rabbi conducting the funeral.

Though the saying of Kaddish for a parent at the thrice-daily formal services for eleven months after the death is of late origin,[90] it has become central to Jewish mourning customs, and is particularly important in creating a sense of community among men. Katherine Marks, who observed her husband's performance of the ritual after losing his mother, felt a distinct sense of envy, knowing that she would not discover the same sense of consolation when she loses her own parents: 'I quite envied him, the complete naturalness of it, the support that he got, and also, which I'm *really* envious of, the immense comfort he got from saying it in the *minyan*, to be in shul when it's said.'

Some United synagogues welcome women saying Kaddish, but the majority of haredi synagogues do not permit the practice. A booklet recently issued by Borehamwood United Synagogue for the guidance of bereaved members rules: 'A woman mourner may recite the Kaddish at any service provided there is at least one man reciting Kaddish at the same time.'[91]

Many women have never even contemplated saying Kaddish for a relative; Leonie Adelman, though insisting on attending her mother's funeral, did not want to say Kaddish, either at the funeral or during the year of mourning, since she 'was not brought up with it'. Sheila Dorfman, following her first husband's death in the 1990s, felt very strongly that Kaddish should be said for him by somebody who had known him, but never considered herself in this role:

I can't bear the idea of paying someone to say Kaddish for you. I think if you've got a connection to the person, that is the whole point of saying Kaddish. When my first husband died, there was me and three daughters, and there was nobody—my brother doesn't go to shul every day, and he said he would say Kaddish on the days

[88] Alderman, 'Yes, Bury the Absurd Eulogy Rule'.
[89] As burial is regarded as a commandment and an act of charity towards the deceased, mourners are encouraged to assist by shovelling in a spadeful of earth. See Lamm, *The Jewish Way in Death and Mourning*, 65.   [90] See Wieseltier, *Kaddish*, for the history of this custom.
[91] See 'Basic Guide for the Bereaved' on the Borehamwood Synagogue website.

when he did go to shul, and I was *not* going to do anything about somebody else saying Kaddish, when a good friend of ours who does go to shul every day said, 'Can I please say Kaddish for him?' and I was so touched that he was prepared to do that.[92]

According to the Preston Report, 'Several women reported that although on becoming mourners they had instinctively wished to say Kaddish, they lacked the energy to fight for the right at such a vulnerable time and in an emotionally weakened state.'[93] Recently, however, there have been steps to encourage women to say Kaddish. In September 2011 Dayan Ivan Binstock of the London Beth Din and his wife Rachel Binstock gave a lecture on the practice:

Many women have grown up with the idea that it is not permissible for them to say Kaddish . . . Dayan Binstock emphasised that women mourners who wish to say Kaddish may join the men in doing so. Women who wish to do so are welcome in St. John's Wood synagogue throughout their year of mourning, both at the Shabbat morning service and at the daily minyan, and on the Shabbat preceding their yahrzeit.[94]

Some women do experience some degree of support when they decide to take on the recitation of Kaddish. Very unusually, Ariella Julian, a 40-year-old unmarried United Synagogue woman, recited Kaddish for her father in 1998 for the full eleven months, three times a day. Her local synagogue and rabbi supported her, and she encountered no problems even when she had to resort to the hasidic Hagers synagogue: 'Nobody turned me away, or ridiculed or questioned me', though elsewhere 'there was slight ridicule at times, but nothing hostile'. She felt very separate from 'the old boys' club' of men and said Kaddish very quietly. On hearing a female friend recite Kaddish loudly and confidently at her father's *shivah* in 2012,[95] she noted that 'it was quite a revelation, as women still say it apologetically', though she felt that the situation for women who want to say Kaddish has started to improve rapidly in the last few years: 'the huge widespread sense that women *can't* do things is changing'.

---

[92] It is interesting to contrast her feelings and assumptions with those of Henrietta Szold (1860–1945), an American Orthodox Zionist leader, who, as the eldest of eight daughters, insisted on saying Kaddish for her mother in 1916, politely declining an offer from a male family friend to say it on her behalf. See her letter to Hayim Peretz, quoted in Wieseltier, *Kaddish*, 189–90.   [93] Preston, Goodkin, and Citron, *Women in the Jewish Community*, 73.

[94] 'Kaddish Class for Women' on the United Synagogue website.

[95] The *shivah* (Heb. 'seven') is the seven-day period of intense mourning after a death, during which formal prayer services are held at the mourners' house. The close relatives of the deceased sit on low chairs and receive condolences from visitors.

Nevertheless, many women continue to feel that they have no support and may face opposition if they say Kaddish, and that they have no way of marking the *yahrzeit* of relatives. In addition, if a woman is saying Kaddish in the women's gallery, the men below may not realize that she is doing so, and may speed ahead while she is still reciting the prayer; several women told me of experiencing this when they had been saying Kaddish, and of how it made them feel slighted. A woman quoted in the Preston Report noted that every year, on her father's *yahrzeit*, she had to persuade her reluctant brother to go to synagogue, since there was no way in which she could perform this duty, and her loss would not even be recognized if he did not attend: 'If I go alone, no-one in shul knows that I have a Yahrzeit and as a result I have never been wished "long life".'[96] Her words were echoed by Nicola Perlman, a United Synagogue woman in her sixties, who explained why the commemoration of *yahrzeit* at the Stanmore Women's Tefillah Group was such an important feature for the women who attended:

If I have a *yahrzeit*, and I want the name to be mentioned in shul, so they will say, for my father, 'for [name]', nobody would know that that is my father. So no-one would wish me long life, or whatever ... it's just another name.[97]

When a man commemorates a dead relative, the connection is obvious, as he is given an *aliyah*; if a woman appoints a proxy to do this,[98] the community cannot identify her as the mourner. At the Tefillah Group, each bereaved woman read a prayer for her loved ones, and was the focus of the group's attention and support.

Due to the trauma and emotional turmoil of bereavement, public rituals surrounding death are an even more powerful source of tension than bat-mitzvah ceremonies. Although many women accept traditional limitations on women's participation in (or even presence at) these rituals, there seems to be an increasing number of non-haredi women who refuse to accept these barriers, to the point where they are willing to challenge them in public and even leave community institutions over them (unlike in the case of bat-mitzvah, individuals cannot organize alternative funerary rituals, so dissatisfaction is expressed differently). It is significant that disputes over funerals are frequently the occasion of individuals and families leaving a synagogue or even joining a different denominational movement altogether.[99] Though

[96]   Preston, Goodkin, and Citron, *Women in the Jewish Community*, 74. 'I wish you long life', or just 'Long life', is the standard Anglo-Jewish condolence offered to mourners.

[97]   See also the section on women's *tefilah* groups in Ch. 4.

[98]   The Preston Report records that many synagogues send a standard letter to women before a *yahrzeit*, offering them the option of 'nominating a man to mark the event by proxy': Preston, Goodkin, and Citron, *Women in the Jewish Community*, 74.

[99]   A member of the Masorti movement who had grown up in the United Synagogue noted

burial rights are the 'glue' of Anglo-Jewish synagogue affiliation,[100] funerals and the associated rituals can also serve as tinderboxes, setting off rupture with the community. Since synagogue membership funds the United Synagogue, the institution cannot afford to alienate its members; perhaps uniquely in the sphere of Jewish ritual, United Synagogue women do have some bargaining power in this area. Once again, haredi women are far more likely to conform to their community's expectations, and since they are not members of synagogues in their own right (see below), they cannot wield the same economic power as their United Synagogue sisters.

Simhat Torah

The festival of Simhat Torah (Rejoicing of the Torah) is a medieval innovation, originating in Babylon in the geonic period,[101] and is held on the second day of the biblical festival of Shemini Atseret, in the autumn. It celebrates the conclusion of the annual round of Torah reading and the commencement of the new cycle. At the morning service, two men are honoured by being called up to complete the reading and start the new cycle; they bear the titles *ḥatan torah* ('bridegroom of the Torah', who reads the end of Deuteronomy) and *ḥatan bereshit* ('bridegroom of Genesis', who reads the beginning of Genesis). The main rituals in the morning service are the seven circumambulations (*hakafot*) in the prayer hall, during which all the synagogue's Torah scrolls are carried in procession, often with energetic dancing, and the calling up of every man present to read from the Torah, ending with the readings by the two *ḥatanim*.[102] The *hakafot* can last for an hour or more, and the *aliyot* go on for even longer, even though large synagogues hold several simultaneous readings in order to speed things up. In most synagogues, women take no part in the *hakafot* or the *aliyot*, but only watch the men, who are often fuelled by alcohol. Where there are several Torah readings within the synagogue, the general hubbub often means that the women cannot hear any of them.[103]

    In 2013 I toured seven synagogues in Hendon on Simhat Torah morning; in all but two, the few women present chatted to each other continuously

that her final break with Orthodoxy was in reaction to her rabbi's 'shocking' lack of sensitivity when her brother-in-law died in a car crash (a member of a Reform community, he had left instructions that he should be cremated, a practice forbidden in Orthodoxy). Cherie Jackson, interview.

[100] 'It was reported that some women's sole reason for remaining affiliated to a synagogue was in order to safeguard their right to be buried in a Jewish cemetery': Preston, Goodkin, and Citron, *Women in the Jewish Community*, 75.   [101] Elbogen, *Jewish Liturgy*, 117.

[102] The *hakafot* are performed at the evening service too; many synagogues hold a Torah reading with five *aliyot* in the evening, but without the *ḥatanim* ceremony.

[103] Keturah Allweiss, interview; I observed this at Ner Yisrael, Hendon, in 2013, where none of the three simultaneous readings was audible from the women's section.

without lowering their voices, only breaking off to deal with overexcited children when they burst into the gallery clutching bags of sweets. They completely ignored the dancing below. Many more women stood outside the main hall or the synagogue building, chatting to friends of both sexes and supervising children. The exceptions were the haredi Hendon Adas, where about twenty women and some teenage girls silently followed the Torah reading, and the 'young' Modern Orthodox Alei Tzion, where about fifty women crammed into the women's section to hear the *hatanim* reading their *aliyot*, following attentively. Two of the women were wearing plastic 'golden' crowns, marking their role either as the wives of the *hatanim* or as women chosen as *eshet ḥayil*.[104] The practice of choosing two women to honour in this way, adopted by some United synagogues, is an attempt to include women in the festivities, but as there is usually no active role for the *eshet ḥayil*, it smacks of tokenism.

This festival points up women's spectator status particularly sharply, and most women I interviewed expressed emotions ranging from active dislike to indifferent disdain for the celebrations. A woman in her seventies from the United Synagogue said that she felt 'totally alienated' on Simhat Torah; another elderly United Synagogue member described it as 'a man's festival', and a third, younger woman with young children said that she insists on going to Israel every year for Simhat Torah as she 'can't bear the thought of Simhat Torah in England'. Keturah Allweiss, a young mother who had experienced Simhat Torah in America at synagogues that encouraged women's participation, was devastated when she returned to England:

I remember coming to Simhat Torah at Norrice Lea and crying, really crying and crying and crying. I remember being in the gallery and them [the men] saying, 'OK, has everyone had an *aliyah*?'. And I said to the rabbi, 'Not everyone has had an *aliyah*. *I* haven't had an *aliyah*.'

The atmosphere of exclusion is vividly described by Katherine Marks:

I don't think it's offensive, I just think it's thoughtless and exclusive, all that stuff around the *bimah*, all the men are patting each other's backs and having private jokes and drinking, and sort of that whole lovely 'You're a man' and 'You belong here and this is what it's all for', and you're standing there *watching* it, from a gallery . . . it's not again so much my thing, that I'm so desperate to dance with the *sefer torah*, but I do find the whole thing just utterly utterly depressing.

---

[104] A parallel to the titles given to the male honorees would logically be *kalat torah* and *kalat bereshit* ('bride of the Torah' and 'bride of Genesis'), which would imply equality as well as a link to the Torah.

Nothing has changed from the views recorded in 1994 in the Preston Report: 'The dissatisfaction expressed with mainstream Orthodox Simchat Torah services was overwhelming. More than at any other time of the year women felt marginalised, literally "spectators at a men-only sport" . . . both women and young girls reported feeling degraded, "like monkeys in a cage"'.[105]

Haredi women expressed less resentment, but had very low expectations of personal participation beyond watching the men. One young haredi mother, whose small daughters had been barred from dancing with their father in the men's section of a Golders Green synagogue, endured a cramped women's section in another synagogue so that her children would be able to dance with their father. She recalled having a very negative experience herself as a child, and was insistent that her daughters should not repeat this. When asked what she would regard as an ideal Simhat Torah experience for herself, she simply repeated that she wanted her daughters to enjoy it, and could not imagine that she might herself have an enjoyable or spiritually meaningful experience. Liora Lachsman, a single academic in her forties from a hasidic background, reflected on her changing feelings about Simhat Torah in a hasidic synagogue:

The younger girls, including me, would try to squeeze to the front of the ladies and push the curtain aside to get a good view of the leibedik [lively] dancing and singing . . . Eventually, when I hit my teens, it really became a non-event for me. I might have continued going out of habit, but really, apart from some half-hearted attempts by other teenage girls to do our own dancing in a separate room (the light was off), I just stopped going. I don't remember feeling angry; more like a bit bored—even though the singing and dancing were quite lively in the men's section—and I stayed at home to read. My mother also stopped going: again, not angry, but she admitted she'd gone more for the children and that she didn't really get much out of it.[106]

Many women, both haredi and United Synagogue, simply stay away from the synagogue on Simhat Torah. Belinda Cohen noted that after her children had grown up she had stopped going, because 'at Stanmore [United Synagogue] the men drink, you never know where anybody is, it's unseemly'. Others cited boredom as the main factor for their absence. Even where United Synagogue women have succeeded for a few years in their attempt to participate, their activities have recently been curtailed. Alei Tzion allowed women to dance with a Torah scroll for its first few years of existence, until a new rabbi from Israel decided that, although it was halakhically permissible, he was not going to allow it on the grounds that 'it was not the custom of the syna-

---

[105] Preston, Goodkin, and Citron, *Women in the Jewish Community*, 34.
[106] Liora Lachsman, email, 12 Sept. 2013.

gogue'.[107] Similarly at Edgware United Synagogue, a new rabbi recently over-turned a former rabbi's permission for women to dance with a scroll—to some women's resentment.[108] At St John's Wood United Synagogue, women were not able to dance from 2010 to 2013, as there were several simultaneous services which occupied all the available rooms. At Norrice Lea, the women do dance with a scroll, thanks to the intervention of a few men:

They split [the hall] down the middle, the women can dance on one side, the men can dance on the other side. So usually someone like my husband just gives a *sefer torah* to the women. And it's kind of a *fait accompli*, really, and there are people who are against it, but he usually gives it to me . . . and I dance with it.[109]

Sometimes the women themselves, though unenthusiastic about the lack of any role for them in the festival, cannot overcome the deeply ingrained belief that women are forbidden to touch a Torah scroll because of purity issues.[110] In an interview in 2010 Stella James, a very active member of her United Synagogue community and the founder of the women's Megillah reading there, recounted that in 2008 she had taken the initiative in getting the women to dance with a Torah scroll:

A couple of years ago, I just trotted up to one of our members who was holding a *sefer* [scroll], and I said, 'Give it to me', and he gave it to me, and I went to the back with the women, and I said, 'Come on, let's get going!' We did it again this year, and nobody made a sound or a whimper, so I'm going to keep doing it, but the women are quite tentative. I sort of say, 'Here you are, take it', [and they say] 'I don't feel quite right', 'Is it alright that we take it?'

In this case, the women seem to have 'got away with it' because of the lack of male opposition and the presence of a determined woman; it is hard to imagine this happening in a synagogue whose rabbi or members are opposed to women dancing with the scrolls. The absence of the Torah scroll from most women's sections is not solely due to obstacles raised by men, however; the

[107] Information from a former member. Women from this community to whom I spoke in Sept. 2013 were unaware that women had ever danced with a scroll there.

[108] Shirley Daniels, interview. The rabbi objects to anyone dancing with the scrolls, but cannot stop the men doing so.

[109] Keturah Allweiss, interview. For the first few years the women's dancing was not 'officially' recognized as part of the synagogue's celebrations. Even after it became a regular feature, however, Keturah observed that 'if one year there was not someone who was committed to ensuring the women had the Sefer Torah, I'm not sure the default would be to pass it to the women. Every year, more and more women are happy to dance with the Sefer, but it seems to require an instigator' (email, 28 Aug. 2019).

[110] There is no halakhic support for this (see Weiss, *Women at Prayer*, ch. 7), but the vast majority of British Orthodox women believe it. Shaye Cohen, 'Purity and Piety', examines the history of this belief, and characterizes it as 'an expression of folk piety' (p. 112).

women's desire to dance with a scroll is equally crucial. When I asked the rabbi of Stella's synagogue in 2013 about women's participation in Simhat Torah, he said that, although the women do dance behind a *meḥitsah*, they seem uninterested in having a scroll, even though he would not object. It seems that since Stella has not attended Simhat Torah for the last few years, other women were not confident enough, or did not want, to ask for a scroll. On attending Golders Green United Synagogue for Simhat Torah in 2011—where the women had a space and a scroll to dance with—I noted that most women refused to hold the scroll and declined to dance, preferring to stand around the walls and chat. Keturah Allweiss commented, 'I find it very hard to pass it to other women. I'd say 95% of the women won't take it, for various reasons—they're scared to drop it, they think they can't.'

At some synagogues, women's participation is actively discouraged. At Hendon United Synagogue, a middle-aged woman who has recently become more observant noted that the rabbi 'allows the women to look and to throw sweets as long as it's not too many', but 'doesn't see the need for women to dance', although they are allowed to do so in the community centre building next to the synagogue. She did not object to this, as she enjoys watching the men, but did note that Simhat Torah is 'a bit of a drag' for women, and that only about thirty women turn up for it, most of whom leave early.[111] After the women lost their dancing space at St John's Wood synagogue, a member in her seventies forwarded material on women and Torah scrolls that had been issued by the United Synagogue women's organization to the rabbi and asked for a meeting to discuss it, but he did not respond. The women were reduced to having coffee in the gallery on the festival. In 2013 they were allowed to dance during the time the three congregations in the building were dancing outside, but the rabbi stated that it was 'against halakhah' for them to have a Torah scroll. Pressed further, he explained that this meant that women had to be 'properly' dressed.[112] Twenty women participated in the dancing.

Some women have organized alternative activities within their synagogues to celebrate Simhat Torah, often in the form of a study session. Katherine Marks, a prominent Jewish educator, describes a very successful example:

About eight or nine years ago, I was invited to give a *shiur* for the women at Muswell Hill, in the morning so there would be something for them to do, so that they would feel an incentive to come; there would be a women's Kiddush while the *hakafot*, which are endless, were going on. Not that there would be *hakafot* for women, but there would be a women-only thing. Could men come? The rabbi said at that stage he didn't mind, he would rather the men enjoyed that than hung around outside,

[111]   Fiona Inman, interview.
[112]   Phone conversation with and email from Gill Armstrong, 24 July 2013 and 10 Sept. 2013.

and one or two used to come . . . So we had a women's Kiddush and a *shiur*, and that was hugely successful, and it was the event of the year for Muswell Hill for the next eight years, when I used to walk over there, and sixty or so women would come, it was completely packed, and I made sure we did some learning from Torah.

Other women's learning sessions have been organized on Simhat Torah; in the year Keturah Allweiss's husband was *ḥatan torah*, she 'made a little party for the women with a *devar torah*' in a room at the synagogue during the Torah reading, 'and that was very nice, except that it was advertised as "cocktails"'. In Finchley United Synagogue, there was a women's learning programme in 2012 (attended by a few men too), which a young woman appreciated: 'It felt like a reason to go to shul.'[113]

Occasionally even these activities have been opposed by rabbis. In Woodside Park in the early 2000s, a group of women decided to meet in a private house on Simhat Torah, invite a (female) teacher, and have a learning session accompanied by coffee. Unfortunately they decided to seek permission from the rabbi (since retired), who immediately refused to allow it. In other communities, small groups of women meet in each others' houses for coffee, chat, and perhaps a short sermon.[114] For the vast majority of women, however, the only activity offered is watching the men or accompanying children, and most do not go to synagogue: 'When you have young children you go to shul for Simhat Torah. When you don't, you can always stay home with a good book.'[115]

Some women choose to attend alternative celebrations outside the Orthodox establishment; though the numbers involved are small, these events have continued almost annually over the last fifteen years. One woman noted that 'my elder daughter . . . used to sneak off to a Reform shul on Simhat Torah so she could dance with a *sefer* [Torah scroll]'.[116] In the late 1990s my husband and I organized a Simhat Torah service in a scout hut in Stanmore, with separate dancing for men and women, followed by separate Torah readings, with Torah scrolls for both men and women;[117] about ten men and ten women attended. After moving to Hendon in 2002 I organized women's readings with a Torah scroll on Simhat Torah at Yakar, an independent synagogue; and, following Yakar's closure in 2003, at its successor congregation, Ohel Avraham, until its closure in 2009. About twenty to thirty women used to attend.[118] Two women would be chosen for the honour of *kalat torah* and *kalat bereshit* ('bride of the Torah' and 'bride of Genesis'), in parallel to the men's *ḥatan*

[113] Hannah Augsberger, phone conversation, 23 July 2013.
[114] Lesley Sandman, interview.   [115] Ibid.   [116] Katherine Marks, interview.
[117] The format was based on the practice of our synagogue in Jerusalem, Kehilat Yedidya.
[118] See Ch. 4 n. 39.

torah and *ḥatan bereshit*. The atmosphere was always very lively, with energetic singing and dancing, and those who attended found the services very satisfying and would return year after year. Several women expressed interest in attending but felt they should go to their usual synagogues when husbands or other relatives were given the honour of being a *ḥatan* there, or when a son received a similar honour in the children's service.

There have been continuing alternative Simhat Torah celebrations of this type, with twenty-five women attending women's Torah readings in a private house in Golders Green in 2011 and 2012,[119] and in 2012 the 'alternative' community Grassroots Jews held its first Simhat Torah event in the evening,[120] attended by about sixty people, with both sexes reading the Torah and being called up for *aliyot*. In 2013 about 100 men and women attended the second Grassroots Jews Simhat Torah.[121] About ten women chose to dance separately in their own circle alongside the larger, mixed circle, with the Torah scroll passed between the two circles. Twenty-five men and women received an *aliyah*, and some women noted that this was the first time they had ever done this.[122]

Simhat Torah brings the exclusion of women from central rituals and contact with the Torah scroll, the most sacred symbolic object, into sharp relief, creating considerable resentment and indignation among women who sit placidly in a gallery the rest of the year, watching men perform below with no desire to emulate them. Lesley Sandman noted:

This experience of not having the *sefer torah*, and women gathering together—it's not the same thing. Let's be quite honest that learning and discussion, and at its most basic level, words of Torah, are not the same experience as singing and dancing. And it's clear that letting go is not something women are allowed to do. They need to be in control in Judaism.

Not only do women need to be 'in control' of themselves—and perhaps under the control of men—but they are denied access to the Torah scroll itself. The Torah is the central symbol of Orthodox Judaism, but women experience it vicariously, both in its physical manifestation and in its study (see below). The Torah has often been eroticized in classical Jewish culture, as documented by Daniel Boyarin:

---

[119] I attended and helped to organize the first of these.

[120] For brief accounts of Grassroots Jews, a non-denominational group with several Orthodox attendees, see Chs. 2 and 4.   [121] I attended and helped to organize this.

[122] The '*aliyot* for all' are usually held in the morning, with only five *aliyot* in the evening, but since the evening reading is customary rather than obligatory, and no synagogue would be offering women *aliyot* in the morning, it was decided to transfer this morning practice to the evening to enable women who wanted an *aliyah* to have one.

The Torah-study situation was structured as a male homosocial community, the life of which was conducted around an erotic attachment to the female Torah. The Torah and the wife are structural allomorphs and separated realms in the culture —both normatively to be highly valued but also to be kept separate.[123]

On Simhat Torah, more than at any other time of the year, such metaphors are given concrete form. Men dance with the Torah scrolls, undress them, open them, and, as 'bridegrooms', consummate their relationship through the act of reading. In the face of such basic metaphors, it is scarcely surprising that women react emotionally and negatively to the presence of the 'other woman', as it is carried, danced with, fondled, celebrated, and 'married' by the men of the community. In terms of this metaphor, women's only role is as jealous onlookers—their relationship to the Torah scroll is deeply problematic, as demonstrated by most traditionalist women's reluctance to touch or carry the scroll, even where permitted and even though there is no halakhic impediment: it 'feels wrong'. As noted above, the recent United Synagogue custom of choosing two women to honour in parallel to the 'bridegrooms' stops short of giving them the title of 'bride'.

In haredi contexts, where the separation of men's and women's roles is a central feature of religious ideology, accepted and often justified by women, women are less troubled by being spectators of men's activities, or avoid the tension by absenting themselves from the synagogue. In non-haredi Orthodox communities, individuals' ideals, ethics, expectations, and behaviour are shaped as much by secular trends within wider, Western society as by Jewish influences; hence the tension is far more palpable. Consequently, both Modern Orthodox and traditionalist women are more likely to express anger, resentment, and a sense of frustration and exclusion on Simhat Torah.

The ambivalence about the relationship of women to the Torah, especially in its physical form, may explain why they have done little to create alternative ceremonies or events to mark Simhat Torah. Uncertainty about women's roles in a religious culture that defines Jewishness as involvement with Torah, but then blocks women's access to Torah, provides an opportunity for them to exercise agency in redefining their roles, but also creates a higher level of risk attached to such redefinitions.

Non-haredi women are experiencing a period of flux and tension, in which different individuals choose responses that range from traditionalist minimal participation and the 'compartmentalized' acceptance of a haredi ideology in a circumscribed area of life to the more Modern Orthodox quest to redefine gender roles in the religious sphere. Nowhere can this be seen more clearly

[123] Boyarin, *Carnal Israel*, 196; see also Rubenstein, *The Culture of the Babylonian Talmud*, ch. 6 and pp. 154–6; Weissler, *Voices of the Matriarchs*, 174.

than in women's responses to Simhat Torah—from a virtual boycott of the synagogue to acceptance of their status as spectators, to attempts to organize women's participation.

Women and Synagogue Leadership: From Auxiliaries to Presidents

Although some women held formal titles in the synagogues of ancient Rome, there are no further instances of this until the twentieth century.[124] Orthodox women in Britain had no representation on communal bodies until the Union of Jewish Women was allowed to send representatives to the Board of Deputies in 1919, and women's representation on synagogue boards only began in 1994.[125] However, women played a vital if secondary role in the running and expansion of synagogues by means of the ladies' guilds: local associations of women who cater sabbath Kiddushim and social functions held at the synagogue, fundraise for improvements to synagogue complexes, and support the community's welfare work. Significantly, most United Synagogue ladies' guilds have now vanished, while at the same time opportunities for women to take up formal positions in synagogue management have increased. Further to the right, however, the pace of change is slower or non-existent.

Ladies' Guilds

Until the later twentieth century, relatively few middle-class women had jobs. By mid-century many British Jews had joined the middle class, and therefore most Jewish women had considerable leisure time. Many threw themselves into synagogue-related and charitable organizations, as can been seen from the activities of the ladies' guild of Willesden and Brondesbury Synagogue, which apparently consisted of about twenty women:

[In 1946] the ladies made Social afternoons to raise money for various good causes. The Guild's main work was 'collecting food and clothing for our brethren in Europe'. They . . . had sent off 180 sacks of clothing, 150 food parcels, 20 cases of Hebrew books and parcels of tools.

[In 1953/4] The Guild also provided new curtains and lino for the synagogue hall . . . The Ladies' Guild that year, as it always does, provided a weekly Kiddush, looked after the Succah, and decorated the synagogue with flowers at Shavuot. That year the Guild provided a Chumash for each [of twelve] Bar Mitzvah boy[s], as well as defraying the cost of parties for the children at Chanukah and Purim.[126]

---

[124] See Brooten, *Women Leaders in the Ancient Synagogue*. There is no evidence of what the titles implied in terms of power or active roles.

[125] Alderman, *Modern British Jewry*, 177–8, and see below.

[126] Susser, *The History of the Willesden and Brondesbury Synagogue*.

Fully subscribing to the ideal of the modest Jewish woman who enables others while effacing herself, the historian who noted the guild's achievements also observed that

the Congregation has been underpinned and supported by its Ladies' Guild. They work quietly and efficiently, without bureaucracy (they keep no Minutes), replenishing the fabric of the synagogue and refreshing the inner man. Look at any Annual Report of the Congregation and you will see a tribute to the work of the Ladies' Guild, whose workers work so quietly that their names are hardly known outside their own ranks.[127]

The activities of the ladies' guild provided a degree of status for the synagogue's women and opportunities for socializing and networking. Moreover, they embodied religious and social ideals of Jewish womanhood: nurturing and feeding others, especially children; enabling the men to carry out their obligations of Torah study and prayer; and caring for the weak, elderly, and disadvantaged. Nowadays, however, the heyday of the heroic ladies' guilds is gone. Many more Jewish women now have full-time or part-time jobs, and fewer are prepared to devote their scarce leisure time to the self-effacing support of the community; as a United Synagogue woman remarked, 'Most ladies don't want to be seen as waitresses' any more.

At Belmont United Synagogue, there is now a rota of fifteen to twenty women and a handful of men, aged between 40 and 60, who set out Kiddushim, buying prepared food rather than making it themselves.[128] A synagogue group called Belmont Community Care has taken over the guild's welfare functions, and a Functions Committee organizes special lunches; both groups include men and women. Although some food for events is still cooked in the Belmont synagogue kitchen (equipped by the former ladies' guild), other United synagogues, such as Stanmore, now use caterers, reflecting women's lack of free time and interest in fulfilling that role.[129] The middle-aged and elderly women of the few remaining guilds and the Kiddush rotas that have replaced them find it very difficult to recruit younger women:

The women with young children don't want to be out at meetings during the week; they're working during the day. The pattern of their lives is very different. And their concerns are very different . . . A lot of the guilds are dying off . . . Younger women will come and put out a Kiddush, but they're not there to run social and welfare stuff for the shul.[130]

---

[127] Ibid.   [128] Gwen Fishman, phone interview, 23 July 2013.
[129] Another factor might be increasingly stringent kashrut standards, and rabbis' reluctance to 'trust' women; see Ch. 5.   [130] Lesley Sandman, interview.

Women's Role in Synagogue Leadership

Reflecting the decline of the guilds, the United Synagogue Association of Ladies' Guilds (USALG), an umbrella organization, later became the Association of United Synagogue Women (AUSW), though it did little beyond organizing an annual dinner and quiz. In 2009 it was 'rebranded' and revitalized as US Women, which now serves as a forum for women to engage with issues that affect their religious lives. Lesley Sandman, a former executive member of USALG, recalled that in the 1980s it actively promoted communal and educational projects:

The Ladies' Guilds Association was very instrumental in pushing for the kashrut guide.[131] They also helped support the United Synagogue *mikvehs* . . . they would organize things like a pre-Rosh Hashanah, pre-Yom Kippur programme, an educational programme . . . Now we have a situation where every shul of any stripe has its own educational programme. They didn't then. It was just barren. So we put on these programmes, a day, two days' seminar, or an evening and a day seminar, pre-Pesach, pre-Rosh Hashanah, sometimes at other times of the year too. It was very exciting.[132]

Thirty years later, the focus has shifted away from welfare and education to women's leadership roles and halakhic issues, though a 2012 report revealed that Jewish women, in particular Orthodox women, still face greater problems in attaining leadership positions of all types within the Jewish community than they do outside it:

In the more orthodox part of the community there is a view that halacha is being used by some inappropriately to keep women from leadership roles. Without an in-depth knowledge of Jewish legal practice, which can be both empowering and effective, women are unable to question its impact on the way some of our organisations are structured and operate.[133]

Building partly on the report's results, US Women organized a series of panel evenings in 2013 entitled 'Women, the Rabbi and the Law', with male and female speakers, to discuss issues such as women lay leaders, women's relationship with the Torah, and batmitzvah girls. A 2014 roadshow, or travelling educational programme, entitled 'The Female Jew: Options for the 21st Century' aimed to educate women on halakhic issues concerning participa-

---

[131] *The Really Jewish Food Guide*, published annually by the Kashrut Division of the London Beth Din, lists most food products, classifying them as kosher or non-kosher.

[132] Between 70 and 100 women used to attend the educational programmes. Another activity was lobbying for the admission of women to synagogue boards of management.

[133] Jewish Leadership Council, *Inspiring Women Leaders*.

tion in worship and ritual. The organization also held a liaison session for female board of management members and council members of the United Synagogue, a dinner honouring the wife of the retiring chief rabbi, and a liaison meeting for women representatives from different synagogues.

The transformation of an umbrella organization for ladies' guilds into a women's advocacy forum embodies the gradual change in non-haredi women's self-perception and ambitions. The move to being fully participating members of synagogues, rather than an auxiliary support force, is paralleled by major changes in women's status within synagogues. In 1994 they were allowed 'to be elected to the Council of the United Synagogue and to the boards of management of its constituent synagogues'.[134] In 2001 they were permitted to be financial representatives or vice chairs of boards, but not chairs, and in December 2012 they could finally serve as synagogue board chairs.[135]

The first female synagogue chair was elected in April 2013,[136] and within a few months nine women had been elected to this position, some of whom had been acting as chairs for years in the absence of any male candidate; nineteen women were elected as vice chairs at the same elections.[137] In spring 2014, the current management system of seven male trustees and four 'women representatives' of the United Synagogue was replaced by a president (male) and eight trustees, four of each gender; the presidency of the entire organization remains the last male bastion, but even this may change.[138] The general impression is of an avalanche rapidly gathering speed as social conventions and halakhic certainties crumble before it.

There are significant signs of change further to the right too. The first women on Federation synagogue boards were elected in May 2013 at Yeshurun Synagogue in Edgware.[139] The Union has not yet allowed women to be members in their own name, even if they are widowed or divorced and heads of households. But when North Hendon Synagogue left the Union,[140] the women of the synagogue met the rabbi, the chairman, and a board member in May 2013 to discuss women's role and representation in the synagogue:

---

[134] Alderman, *Modern British Jewry*, 404.

[135] Rocker, 'United Synagogue Says Yes'.   [136] Grenby, 'St Albans Woman'.

[137] The United Synagogue has sixty-two member synagogues; Dalia Cramer, interview.

[138] Rocker, 'After Chairing Shuls'.

[139] Rocker, 'Progress for Women'. Five women were elected to the twelve-member board. Dayan Lichtenstein, the senior Federation rabbi, had given his permission for this step five years previously, but no synagogue had acted on it.

[140] This was in the wake of a scandal involving a rabbi alleged to have sexually abused women from his synagogue. The Union authorities refused to expel him or support the victims, and North Hendon members voted to leave in protest. See Rocker, 'London Synagogue Quits'.

One of the main topics discussed concerned how the views of women can be heard, and be counted . . . A number of views were offered but one recurring theme was that the recent issues in the wider community have highlighted the importance of making sure that every voice is heard, and particularly those of women.[141] A further reason was suggested that the recent EGM had brought into focus the rules of voting set out in the shul's Constitution, and in particular the condition that only male members are eligible to vote. Many felt that there was a disjoint between our prevailing rules and longstanding developments in broader society, as well as changes to the voting rules in other institutions.[142] Finally, while in many cases it's possible for a married couple to cast a joint vote through the husband, this is not always practical, particularly in the cases of single women, divorcees and widows.[143]

At the rabbi's suggestion, a 'women's forum' of four was set up to discuss possibilities. The rabbi himself was in favour of a separate AGM for women at which they could vote, since he felt that there were 'issues that are specifically relevant to women on which it would be inappropriate for men to vote, and issues specific to men on which it would be inappropriate for women to vote'.[144] The synagogue's website now lists a board of management with ten male members, and, separately, a lone 'women's forum' representative.[145]

The decline of the Ladies' Guilds and the rise of women's synagogue leadership during the last two decades encapsulate fundamental changes in the way in which non-haredi Orthodox women, both Modern Orthodox and traditionalist, understand their roles and standing within their synagogues. Many have moved from being anonymous auxiliaries concerned with providing a safe and functioning environment for male performance to autonomous individuals who are, in many respects, equal members of the community and who have the right and the responsibility to participate in decision-making for the entire community. The trickle-down effect of feminism in non-Jewish British society is undoubtedly the major factor, reinforced by change in non-Orthodox Jewish denominations, and latterly by change on the left within Orthodoxy. However, greater equality for women remains more achievable outside the 'ritual arena' of synagogue prayer and ceremonies; the sacred remains the largely uncontested domain of men.[146]

---

[141] This refers to the sex scandal mentioned in the previous note.

[142] A reference to the United Synagogue and Federation.

[143] 'Women's Meeting with the Rov', report on the synagogue's website (no longer available). Women attended and voted at the March 2014 AGM.   [144] Ibid.

[145] The website recorded this in 2015, but in recent years password-guarded access has been introduced and the website is no longer accessible to non-members.

[146] See the discussion of women's *tefilah* groups in Ch. 4 for the disproportionate level of resistance to women 'invading' male rituals and male sacred space.

The Changing Place of Women in Other Communal Institutions

Women and Jewish Education

As Tamar El-Or has observed, 'Religious-halachic knowledge forms the primary power centre in the organization of the daily life of religious Jewish individuals and communities. It is the material from which the imperative conceptual, moral, political, and ideological fabric is woven. This knowledge lies in the hands of "knowing" men.'[147] In premodern Jewish communities, few women received a formal Jewish education, particularly in halakhic subjects; indeed, a much higher proportion of women than men were illiterate in Hebrew, the language of religious knowledge, throughout Jewish history.[148] 'Book learning', however, is not the only form of religious knowledge, and although women have rarely attained a high level of textual expertise,[149] they have always learnt from their mothers and other female relatives about the practical implementation of halakhic norms in kashrut, sabbath observance, and menstrual purity regulations, as well as a wide range of popular customs. Susan Sered's sensitive study of elderly Sephardi women in Jerusalem describes illiterate women who are confident in their mastery of these complex areas of halakhah.[150] However, since a traditional, mimetic mode of learning has given way to a more text-based mode, as observed by Haym Soloveitchik,[151] women's traditional spheres of knowledge and ways of transmitting that knowledge have become impoverished and undervalued. Some of the women I interviewed were acutely conscious of this process and resented it.[152]

Formal Education

Modern Jewish women in the UK have not fared better in formal Jewish education, even though the number of schools and of children attending them has increased enormously since the mid-twentieth century. In 1950 about 4,000 children attended Jewish day schools, while in 2005–6 the number had risen to 26,460, in spite of the Jewish community's decline in numbers. By 2011 over 50% of Jewish children aged 4–18 attended a Jewish school; 48% of these attended a haredi school.[153] Among non-haredi Jews, this does not

---

[147] El-Or, *Educated and Ignorant*, 29–30.

[148] Shaul Stampfer, in his excellent essay 'Gender Differentiation and the Education of Jewish Women', argues that women benefited from the less stressful informal educational frameworks in which they studied, and from the availability of a wide range of Yiddish literature, including translations and summaries of key religious texts.

[149] For exceptions, see Zolty, *'And All Your Children Shall Be Learned'*.

[150] *Women as Ritual Experts*, 88–90.   [151] 'Rupture and Reconstruction'.

[152] See the section on kashrut in Ch. 5 for an example.

[153] Abramson, Graham, and Boyd, *Key Trends*, 8.

seem to be primarily for religious reasons; as a United Synagogue woman in her forties remarked, 'Parents want their kids to go [to Jewish schools] as they think it will be a better education than state schools.'[154]

In spite of this, most Orthodox women (and, to a lesser extent, men) emerge from the Jewish educational systems, whether formal or informal, with little competence in reading Hebrew or in studying classical texts, particularly halakhic literature.[155] British Jewish education lags far behind that in both Israel and the USA. Haredi women are the exception here: haredi education promotes a solid level of Hebrew competence and the ability to read the Bible and some classic commentators, though girls are not taught Talmud or classic halakhic texts. Generational differences play a large role too: those who were children during the Second World War were often evacuated and had no Jewish education of any kind;[156] women born in the 1940s and 1950s often attended cheder[157] but generally went to non-Jewish schools; those born in the 1960s and later usually attended at least a Jewish primary school, and those born in the 1980s or later are more likely to have studied at a women's seminary in Israel for a year in addition to attending a Jewish school, at least to primary level. Today girls from haredi backgrounds attend only Jewish schools, while many non-haredi Orthodox girls attend a Jewish primary school and then transfer to a non-Jewish secondary school, especially if they or their parents are ambitious.

Predating the rise in Jewish schools, traditional cheders, attached to synagogues, provided (and continue to provide) basic Jewish education. The 1994 Preston Report highlighted Orthodox women's dissatisfaction with the standard of education provided by the cheder system: 'Both style and content were pilloried, the overriding message being one of deep regret at a lost learning opportunity. Lessons were held to be disorganised, boring and repetitious, offer-

[154] Caroline Deutsch, interview. This is supported by a preliminary reporting of unpublished data from the Redbridge Jewish community in Abramson, Graham, and Boyd, *Key Trends*, 29.

[155] This is not particularly surprising: when my daughters attended a United Synagogue primary school in the late 1990s and early 2000s, formal Jewish education was limited to four hours a week, one of which was 'Hebrew singing'.

[156] On the deficiencies of Jewish education during the war, see Steinberg, 'Jewish Education in Great Britain during World War II', who observes, 'Jewish education suffered disastrously as a result of wartime conditions, notably through the evacuation of children from the larger towns' (p. 31).

[157] Classes in religious instruction, usually provided by a synagogue. Before the rise of Jewish schools, many cheders held classes three times a week, but now classes are usually only on Sundays. Rabbis or their wives used to teach in the cheder; nowadays, most cheder teachers are unqualified, often young adults from the synagogue who want a weekend job, and the education provided tends to be low in quality. I have personally taught several children who had spent two or more years going to cheder without even having learnt all of the Hebrew alphabet, let alone anything else.

ing little or no scope for group discussion or the study of Modern Hebrew.'[158]
In spite of the report's fourteen recommendations concerning education,
the Women's Review recorded much the same state of affairs in cheders fifteen
years later.[159] In addition, the rise of Jewish schools has led to the decline of
cheders, as they are now only attended by children who go to non-Jewish schools.
Of course, many women never attended a cheder, either because of their gender or from lack of interest. Perle Taubman, a Lubavitch hasidic woman who
grew up in a non-haredi but traditional family, remembered:

I never even went to cheder, so by the time I graduated from university, I couldn't
read the alef-beis [the Hebrew alphabet]. I think that was probably because we were
two girls in the family, so there was no barmitzvah to prepare for, and I remember
distinctly my parents asking me if I would go to cheder, and I said, 'Oh no, I'm
much too busy!'

Attendance at a cheder, Jewish school, or women's seminary does not
necessarily provide girls and women with the learning skills and knowledge
base acquired by their brothers. In the haredi world this difference in study
content starts from the beginning of formal education, with boys learning
Mishnah from an early age,[160] and proceeding to Talmud in adolescence,
while girls learn 'ḥumash with Rashi',[161] graduate to other biblical books with
classic medieval commentaries, and never study primary halakhic texts.
Many haredi rabbis prohibit women from studying texts of the Oral Torah,
which includes all halakhic texts, while permitting them to study the Written
Torah, consisting of the Bible and associated exegetical literature.[162]

In the non-haredi Orthodox community, primary schoolchildren at Jewish schools generally learn the same subjects together (mainly Bible stories,
festival celebrations, and everyday rituals). Gender differentiation starts early,
with boys and girls being assigned different roles at weekly pre-sabbath

[158] Preston, Goodkin, and Citron, Women in the Jewish Community, 5–6. The poor level of
cheder education also affected boys. In contrast, Progressive women reported high levels of
satisfaction with their equivalent Hebrew classes (p. 7).

[159] Preston et al., Connection, Continuity and Community, 17.

[160] The Mishnah, c.200 CE, is the first document of the Oral Law (as opposed to the Torah, the
Written Law), and is the foundation of the Talmud.

[161] The Pentateuch, accompanied by the medieval commentary of Rashi (R. Solomon ben
Isaac, 1040–1105). Haredi boys learn ḥumash with Rashi at the start of their education but rarely
continue on to other biblical books as the girls do, since they move on to Talmud.

[162] For an account of the halakhic status of women in relation to Torah study, see Biale,
Women and Jewish Law, 29–41; for an example of a hasidic group (Habad-Lubavitch) that
permits women to study all Torah literature, see Handelman, 'Women and the Study of Torah';
and for a wide-ranging study of different Orthodox attitudes to women's Torah education from
the nineteenth to twentieth centuries, see Fuchs, Jewish Women's Torah Study.

assemblies, and boys being taught to say the blessings over *tsitsit* (ritual fringed garments) at daily morning prayers.[163] This intensifies around bar- and batmitzvah age, when boys often have access to Talmud study while girls have sessions on extracts from the Bible or Midrash,[164] or discussion groups about improving one's moral characteristics. Jewish education for girls at Jewish schools is frequently provided by young unmarried women who have spent a year at a seminary, often a haredi institution; they usually have no pedagogical training and the education they provide is often low in quality, and has a distinctly haredi character. One teenager was told by a seminary-educated teacher at her United Synagogue school that 'women are forbidden to learn Talmud'. The same type of endemic gender differentiation at Jewish schools has been observed in Israel and the USA, and was recently studied by Elana Sztokman and Chaya Gorsetman, using a survey of Orthodox day school educators and teaching materials from both primary and secondary schools in both countries.[165]

Even girls who spend a year studying at a 'sem' after finishing secondary education, whether in Israel (where seminaries range from Modern Orthodox to haredi) or at Gateshead (a haredi institution) in northern England, do not learn the same subjects or study in the same way as their brothers. At haredi seminaries, women study the Bible, classic biblical commentaries, moralistic texts, and character development, as well as minimal halakhic material designed to enable them to run a kosher kitchen and negotiate the difficulties of sabbath observance while caring for babies and small children; they do not usually use original halakhic texts but are taught orally or from modern, simplified halakhic manuals. Few British Jewish girls attend the Modern Orthodox seminaries in Israel where girls can study Talmud and halakhic literature;[166] most are guided in their choice of seminary by the school they attend, and these generally promote haredi seminaries. In contrast, male education at yeshiva is geared to the acquisition of Talmud-learning skills and halakhic competence. British women have no means of accessing classical text-based knowledge, and the recent leaps in opening up such knowledge to Orthodox women that have taken place in Israel and the USA are unknown to the majority of the British community. Those who attend Limmud catch brief glimpses of the possibilities from visiting speakers but have no way of engaging in such study in the UK (and usually lack the necessary linguistic training

---

[163] Some of my informants noted that the boys would stick out their tongues and sneer at the girls at this stage of the prayers! See also E. Sacks, '"Ima shel Shabbat"'.

[164] Early rabbinic commentary on the Bible.

[165] Gorsetman and Sztokman, *Educating in the Divine Image*.

[166] One barrier to this is the high level of Hebrew required. British Orthodox girls cannot match the excellent Hebrew and general Jewish knowledge of their American counterparts.

in any case).[167] The overall result is that women have little halakhic knowledge, no understanding of how the halakhic system works, and no resources that would enable them to acquire this knowledge. They thus have no way of making informed decisions independently, or of questioning or challenging rabbinic and male authority.[168]

Informal Education: A Case Study

Informal Jewish education for adults is available at a number of institutions, though in the haredi world, and in some non-haredi contexts, it is often gender-segregated, in terms of both content and attendance. To gain some idea of the character of classes (*shiurim*) available in London, I examined the advertisements on EdgwareK, a popular London-based Orthodox email list, between 1 September and 15 October 2010. In that period, forty-six classes were offered, which I analysed to discover differences between men's and women's classes, and between women's classes supplied by different subsets of the Orthodox community, as well as information about the teachers.[169] Of these classes, twenty-six were marked as being for 'women', 'ladies', or 'ladies and girls', six were marked as men only, eight were marked as 'men and women' or 'all', another two seemed likely to be intended for women, two were impossible to categorize, and two were Talmud lectures and therefore almost certainly exclusively for men.[170]

Of the eighteen classes held in private homes, all but one were for women (the exception was a Talmud lecture), and most were for haredi women. Of the ten women's classes given at synagogues or other institutions, seven were provided by outreach organizations, such as Aish and the Jewish Learning Exchange (JLE), which encourage less observant individuals to adopt a more haredi lifestyle. The three exceptions were a lecture that formed part of a series of women's classes at Belmont United Synagogue, another, text-based, session at Golders Green United Synagogue, and a talk that formed part of a fundraising event.

---

[167] See El-Or, *Next Year I Will Know More*, for a study of young Israeli Orthodox women's quest for such knowledge and the associated radical questioning of traditional gender roles.

[168] See El-Or, *Educated and Ignorant*, for an excellent analysis of the way in which haredi women's education (among Gur hasidim in Israel) is designed to preserve women's ignorance.

[169] Not all synagogues advertise their classes on this list, nor does the London School of Jewish Studies; in addition, not all private classes are advertised here, so this is by no means a complete list of all classes held in London in those six weeks.

[170] I know of only two regular Talmud classes (*shiurim*) in London that are open to both women and men, although most haredi synagogues and some United synagogues run at least one weekly Talmud *shiur*. Ironically, though many advertisements for Talmud classes listed on EdgwareK announce that 'Everyone is welcome!', a phone call to the organizers will generally reveal that the class does not welcome women.

Since the period chosen fell immediately before the High Holidays, many of the classes for both men and women focused on aspects of these festivals. Topics for women included the inspirational, such as 'The Meaning and Essence of Shofar', and the practical, such as 'A Mother's Survival Guide for the Yamim Nora'im [High Holidays]', as well as overviews of the halakhic aspects of the festivals—'The Halachos [Laws] of Yom Kippur'—most of which were provided by the outreach organizations. While men's talks also included inspirational and festival-linked topics, such as 'Preparing for Rosh Hashanah by Taking a Close Look at the Tefillos [Prayers]', there were several text-based halakhic sessions, such as 'Hair Covering for Married Women' and 'The Smallest Sukkah', the latter preceded by traditional *ḥavruta* (paired) learning to prepare the texts. This last class provides a good example of the difference in how halakhic subjects are taught to men and women. Men's classes often focus on theoretical matters of halakhah and halakhic problems in classic texts—in this case, the Talmud's discussion of the smallest dimensions possible for a kosher sukkah, a subject unlikely to be of immediate practical significance—while women's halakhic education focuses on the practical laws of which they need to be aware in running their households, such as how to heat food on festivals or look after babies on the sabbath. The class on married women's hair covering, an eminently practical subject which might have been expected to be aimed at women, involved analysis of primary halakhic texts and was therefore more 'appropriate' for men.

The only obviously text-based classes for women were all given by a Modern Orthodox rabbi who teaches in several places. Mixed classes were all of the inspirational type, e.g. 'The Road Back Home: Yom Kippur' and 'Bringing Hashem[171] Closer: The Sukkah'. Of the fifty-four teachers involved, only eight were women; two of these were rebbetsins and four were graduates of the Susi Bradfield Women Educators Programme run by the London School of Jewish Studies (LSJS), a Modern Orthodox institution. All the male teachers were rabbis.

The patterns visible in this sample—the predominance of inspirational and practical topics, generally taught without access to texts, in women's classes, as opposed to a high proportion of text-based, 'pure halakhah' classes for men; the location of haredi women's lectures largely in private homes; and the predominance of male teachers—are typical of the classes advertised on EdgwareK. United Synagogue educational programmes, under-represented on EdgwareK, often include historical and cultural topics, such as 'The Jews of Afghanistan', which are generally mixed events held at the synagogue. The only Modern Orthodox institution offering classes, most of which are mixed,

---

[171] Heb. 'the name', used particularly by Orthodox Jews as a name for God.

is the London School of Jewish Studies, which provides a wide range of text-based, inspirational, historical, philosophical, and issue-based classes, taught by a mix of male and female teachers, including both rabbis and university-trained laypeople.[172] The classes are attended by men and women, ranging from young adults to the elderly, and by non-Orthodox individuals (and some non-Jews) as well as the entire spectrum of the Orthodox community, including some haredi women (though no men) from the hasidic enclave of Stamford Hill. Even here, however, it is noticeable that some women do not want to attend the text-based classes; they are often fearful of revealing their 'ignorance' of classic texts or of Hebrew, even though this is often a problem for men too. LSJS runs some women-only classes, in part to provide a 'safe space' for them to tackle texts and subjects with which they are unfamiliar. In fifteen years of teaching there, I have noticed that many women lack confidence and often basic knowledge on Jewish topics; they are apologetic when asking questions and usually preface them with the phrase 'I expect this is a stupid question, but . . .'. They also find it much harder to ask questions of a male teacher. I once substituted for a rabbi who had been teaching a class for women in their sixties and seventies at a central London synagogue, on the topic of 'Moral Issues in the Talmud', for some weeks. After ten minutes I noticed a rather glazed look on several faces, and asked, 'Are you all familiar with what the Talmud actually is?' It turned out that none of them had any idea of the nature or structure of the Talmud, but nobody had wanted to 'bother the rabbi' by asking him to explain.

Women find it hard to place acquired knowledge in a wider context, and tend to describe themselves as 'not very learned', ignoring their often immense expertise in areas of domestic knowledge, such as the running of a Jewish household. In many cases these women have very high levels of secular education and work as expert professionals; it is not uncommon for Orthodox women to experience a sense of complete disconnection between their secular and Jewish educations. Many women regard the opportunity to study in an open and intellectually stimulating environment as vital to their religious lives:

I think LSJS is my lifeline to sanity. I think without LSJS I would have given up on Modern Orthodox Judaism a long time ago, but knowing that there are people here who believe what I believe, and who can encourage me and support me and move me on to new places, and can be a hub for people who think like this, it's just amazing.[173]

Another opportunity for traditionalist and Modern Orthodox women to

---

[172] See the London School of Jewish Studies website.   [173] Sheila Dorfman, interview.

attend innovative and high-quality educational sessions exists in Limmud, the grassroots-organized conference held over Christmas every year, where internationally renowned educators can be heard.[174] Haredi women do not attend, as the conference is viewed as suspect in the haredi sector because of the presence of non-Orthodox rabbis and teachers. Few British Orthodox rabbis attend, due to disapproval from haredi and even some Modern Orthodox quarters, even though many Orthodox rabbis from Israel and the USA teach at Limmud.[175]

Women's lack of confidence, text-based knowledge, and training has prevented them from becoming Jewish educators until recently, unless they were rebbetsins, whose duties often include teaching batmitzvah girls or cheder classes (often without any qualifications or training). Today, in addition to the 'sem girls' who have been providing informal Jewish education in Jewish schools since the 1990s, there are growing numbers of women trained in programmes specially designed for Jewish studies teachers in schools. A particularly important example of new roles for women in Jewish education, initiated and shaped by women in accordance with changing conceptions of their role in religious life, is the Susi Bradfield Women Educators Programme, founded by Dr Tamra Wright at the London School of Jewish Studies in 2000. Its significance lies in its foundation and continuous adaptation as a course designed by and for women, rather than as a copy or imitation of a previously existing male-designed model, and in its novel relationship with the male-dominated worlds of Jewish education and community philanthropy.

In the late 1990s Dr Wright noticed that less than 1% of the classes advertised in the *Jewish Chronicle* were taught by women;[176] simultaneously, she realized that she was constantly being invited to speak at synagogues and educational events, where her lecture would often be labelled as 'women's issues', even though her expertise is in modern Jewish philosophy. Charitably interpreting this as the Jewish community's desire for more women edu-

[174] Limmud is non-denominational, so presenters range across the denominational spectrum, which is the main reason for haredi and right-wing traditionalist opposition to the conference. It thus represents both an opportunity and a (potentially stimulating) challenge for Orthodox participants.

[175] See Rocker, 'Where Have All the (US) Rabbis Gone?' For a condemnation of Limmud by an Orthodox rabbi that sparked huge controversy, see Kimche, 'Let's Be Honest about Limmud', quoted in full in Gilbey, 'A Response'.

[176] Information on the programme comes from an interview with Dr Wright. Imbalance in male/female teacher ratios is not a thing of the past: in 2019, there were no women at all among the seventeen speakers invited to a United Synagogue in London between January and September.

cators rather than tokenism, Dr Wright approached a community philanthropist who wanted to set up a project in honour of his mother's seventieth birthday, specifically in the sphere of women's education.[177] The response was enthusiastic, initiating an unusually close and personal relationship between the sponsoring family and the programme's graduates. The year-long programme was intended to provide women with the requisite skills and self-confidence necessary to become good educators; Dr Wright notes that most of the first students were either foreign-born or had spent significant periods of time in America or Israel, and that British Jewish women were particularly lacking in self-confidence. The programme is designed to respond to women's needs and family obligations,[178] and consists of an intensive two-week summer school, followed by weekly day-long sessions, carefully co-ordinated with school calendars and timetables to enable women with children to attend. About fifteen women take part each year, listening to leading Jewish educators and analysing their teaching techniques, participating in a week of training in informal education, and developing their own sessions to be given and critiqued within the group.[179] Priority is given to rebbetsins, since they are often already involved in teaching with no training or support.

Some graduates go on to teach privately or in small classes, while others teach regularly at LSJS[180] and around the synagogue and community circuit. About forty-five graduates have taught at women's Rosh Hodesh groups,[181] and Kolot, the batmitzvah course described above, was developed and is run by graduates. Most students are Modern Orthodox or traditionalist, though some haredi women have taken part. The programme's impact has been predominantly in the non-haredi community: Dr Wright notes that it has 'normalized the idea of female educators' and that it is the only programme in the Orthodox community that provides training and feedback for informal educators, raising overall standards of Jewish education. Sharon Jastrow, a leading educator from the first wave of women's activity in the 1990s, observed of her own involvement as a teacher:

That was before you had LSJS; I never ever teach now—now everyone will know I don't know anything, then they all thought I knew something! If we didn't have all

[177] The approach was made as part of a set of proposals from the London School of Jewish Studies; Dr Wright was told not to present her project unless the philanthropist declined the earlier, 'mainstream' proposals, illustrating the marginality of women's education, even in Modern Orthodox institutions, at the time.

[178] See Belenky et al., *Women's Ways of Knowing*, for a discussion of the ways in which women learn.

[179] There were about 175 graduates by July 2016, not all of whom were active in education.

[180] About a third of the London School of Jewish Studies faculty are graduates of the programme.   [181] See Ch. 4 for a discussion of Rosh Hodesh groups.

of you, I'm serious, there's no-one [else] doing anything . . . [What I taught] was acceptable as knowledge [then] but it wouldn't be today.

The programme has adapted over the decade of its existence: in some years a 'leadership' track has been run in addition to the 'educators' track, training women to design and run educational programmes, and a track adapted to meet the needs of rebbetsins ran in 2014–15. Dr Wright speaks of the need for constant evaluation to make sure the programme remains relevant. This and its adaptivity are integral elements of women's agency and activity within the Orthodox world, where women have to negotiate with male institutions and establishments in order to create spaces in which they can flourish and their voices can be heard.

In 2016 Chief Rabbi Ephraim Mirvis founded Ma'ayan, an eighteen-month educational programme which trained ten women, mostly rabbis' wives, to be community educators and advisers on issues of women's health and *taharat hamishpahah*. It is still too early to assess the graduates' impact, and as of mid-2019 the course has not been repeated.[182]

Women and Welfare (Ḥesed)

A thorough description and analysis of women's roles in the remarkably active Jewish welfare organizations lies beyond the parameters of this study, but it is essential to understand the deeply religious nature of such activity, which forms part of the central value of *ḥesed*. It has been suggested that women were particularly active in this sphere because they were excluded from others:

because women were traditionally closed out of much of public religious life, community involvement through philanthropy became an alternative route to participation and empowerment . . . Jewish women's organizations have been, in the past, the shul for women.[183]

While this may contain some truth, it ignores the fact that providing assistance to the poor and disadvantaged of the community is a central religious duty, and is understood by many women in this way; a quick perusal of the pages of the haredi *Jewish Tribune* reveals a huge amount of charitable activity, mainly conducted by women. *Ḥesed* is one of the principal attributes of God, and for women (and men) across the denominational spectrum, care and nurturing of those who need help is a type of *imitatio Dei*. The analysis of

---

[182]   See the description of the programme on the website of the Office of the Chief Rabbi, and Rocker, 'Chief Rabbi Mirvis Launches New Qualification'.

[183]   Schneider, 'Jewish Women's Philanthropy', 9.

women's involvement in the foundation and running of *gemaḥs* (small lending societies) in Chapter 4 below will return to this theme.

This survey of women's activity and experience in the 'official' communal sphere clearly illustrates the different attitudes and strategies of the three groups identifiable in the London Jewish community: haredi, Modern Orthodox, and traditionalist.

Haredi women, who do not subscribe to a Western-liberal ethos, but seek to fashion themselves into pious Jews as defined by their community's ideals, find it easy to accept their position as spectators and enablers in the public arena, since they view the home and the family as their central sphere of action. They have little interest in change or amelioration of their position because they do not experience it as deficient or out of kilter with the rest of their lives.

At the other end of the spectrum, traditionalist women often feel threatened by change, particularly by innovations in the role of women in ritual and communal worship. Rather than serving as a vehicle for religious expression and work on the self, conventional practices serve as a guarantee of their Jewishness, which they define through existing and unchanging custom. Change in such practices thus challenges their core identity, which is constituted by conformity to accepted communal ideals and behaviours.

In contrast, their Modern Orthodox sisters, who struggle to reconcile feminist ideals prevalent in the wider society with a deep commitment to living according to a divinely ordained system of ritual and worship, experience a painful degree of tension as they are caught between the ideals and imperatives of two very different world-views. This is why the impetus for change and greater participation for women in communal ritual and leadership comes from this sector of the Jewish community. However, given that the established patterns of synagogue ritual are the core expression and performance of the traditional gender regime of Orthodoxy, they are very difficult to change, and the least gesture in the direction of increasing women's participation becomes loaded with symbolic meaning. Rather than being interpreted as the involvement of hitherto disaffected or excluded members of the community, such changes are regarded as women's aggressive 'invasion' of male territory, and as a threat to the essence of male Orthodox gender identity. Rabbis and congregants alike consent to maintain the defining patterns of male domination, centrality, and action, and female submission, marginality, and passivity. Those women who would like to see change often react with withdrawal and overstated indifference to what goes on in 'the boys' club', or, as described in the next chapter, seek alternative types of ritual, or duplicate existing rituals outside the synagogue. In terms of change in Orthodoxy, communal ritual as performed in synagogues is the final fortress, the last citadel.

CONTESTED PRAYERS AND POWERFUL BLESSINGS: WOMEN'S 'UNOFFICIAL' LIFE IN THE COMMUNITY

I want to strike a blow for women in Orthodoxy. I wanted Orthodoxy to open up a little to women. For me, to go and do it under our own steam wasn't what I wanted . . . there *are* places we can go and do this type of thing and have an egalitarian service or whatever we want to do, but that wasn't the aim of the game.

NICOLA PERLMAN, interview

ALONGSIDE women's participation in the 'official' life of the community, examined in the last chapter, a wide range of informal communal activities provides women with opportunities for religious or spiritual self-expression and for creating ritual contexts that function as substitutes for the communal rituals closed to them. It is here that they show most creativity and originality, often adapting or even inventing rituals. The absence (in most cases) of men means that women can explore new modes of religious action. Rather than a deliberate ruse to evade male supervision, an attempt to challenge religious norms, or conscious resistance to male domination of ritual, this is the result either of women's perception of core rituals as open to all Jews regardless of gender, or of their lack of theological or halakhic knowledge and consequent failure to realize some of the implications of their actions, in combination with their desire to express themselves as religious women and take an active part in central Jewish rituals and activities. In some cases, their attempts to introduce new practices, even if compliant with halakhic norms, can be blocked or delegitimized by the community's male-led institutions. These contested activities should be regarded as the sites of male resistance in the face of female agency, rather than of female resistance to the existing system, and they contrast sharply with the uncontroversial nature of women's rituals that are initiated, designed, or approved of by male rabbinic authority.

Such 'unofficial' activities, by no means always controversial, include women's *tefilah* groups, Megillah readings, Rosh Hodesh groups, *berakhah* parties, also known as amen parties or amen meals, *tehilim* groups, challah parties, certain welfare activities and groups, *gemaḥs*, various types of bat-mitzvah celebration, and *simḥat bat* celebrations.[1] This chapter surveys some of these, focusing on the nature of each, its origins and development, those who attend, their understanding of the activity, its function and theological underpinnings, and its visibility and level of approval within the wider Jewish community. The activities can be divided into three types: those designed to provide women with a sacred space in which they can pursue spiritual goals (*tefilah* groups, Megillah readings, and Rosh Hodesh groups); those designed to aid and protect others in the community (*berakhah* parties, challah parties, and *tehilim* groups); and life-cycle events (*simḥat bat* ceremonies and batmitz-vah celebrations). I also briefly survey the newest development, partnership *minyanim*, adopted by some Modern Orthodox, which offer an unprecedented and controversial opportunity for both men and women to share in the performance of rituals.

As discussed in Chapter 1, Orthodox women's efforts to create, appropriate, and modify rituals embody and illuminate the multiple choices, narratives, and influences that form part of the complex social and religious landscape they navigate daily. Their strategies for avoiding direct confrontation with the male establishment, and for remaining within the Orthodox community, can also be seen in the partnership *minyanim*, in which halakhic and rabbinic support (from abroad) plays an essential role in participants' attempts to normalize the practice, with its challenge to existing gender norms, and promote its acceptance in the Anglo-Jewish community. Haredi women, in contrast, rarely challenge existing gender norms openly; though they too display considerable creativity in devising new communal rituals and practices, they generally obtain rabbinic approval or active involvement at an early stage, as in the case of *berakhah* parties, and constantly refer to it when promoting new practices.

Creating Sacred Spaces

Women's *Tefilah* Groups

The first documented formal prayer service held by a group of Orthodox women was in April 1972, in Atlantic City, New Jersey.[2] On Simhat Torah of that year, a women's *tefilah* group was held at Lincoln Square Synagogue,

---

[1] *Simḥat bat*, lit. 'rejoicing in a daughter', is one of several names for ceremonies celebrating the birth of a girl.

[2] Email message from Dr Deborah Weissman, posted on the Women's Tefilla Network (now defunct), 19 Jan. 2000. Although there is evidence for women prayer leaders in medieval and early modern times (see Weissler, *Voices of the Matriarchs*, 9, and Taitz, 'Women's Voices,

New York, supported by the synagogue's rabbi, Shlomo Riskin, and women's *tefilah* groups have been held there regularly until the present.[3] Other American groups were set up, often in synagogues, in the late 1970s and early 1980s. In Israel, an occasional group met in a private home from 1972 until about 1979, and by Simhat Torah 1978 the group that later evolved into the Kehilat Yedidya congregation (established in 1980) was holding women's Torah readings.[4] Since then groups have been founded throughout the USA and in Israel, Australia, France, and Canada.[5] Britain has two surviving *tefilah* groups from this period, one (founded in 1992) associated with Stanmore United Synagogue in north-west London and the other (since 1994) with Yeshurun Synagogue in Manchester; in 2015, another one was founded in London.[6] Most groups meet every few weeks, typically on a sabbath morning, though one-off services are also very occasionally organized for special occasions, such as a batmitzvah, or for a bride on the sabbath preceding her wedding.[7] They have also been held on Rosh Hodesh; since that minor festival is traditionally associated with women, this underlines the 'female' nature of the group and provides a link to more traditional women's practices.[8]

Most groups follow the standard sabbath morning service, omitting prayers that require the presence of a *minyan* (a quorum of ten adult males).[9] The weekly Torah portion (*parashah*) is sometimes read from a scroll, as in a standard service, but more usually from a printed Pentateuch, which does not possess the sanctity associated with scrolls. Other elements, varying from

Women's Prayers'), and in many haredi schools girls pray together, forming a de facto '*tefilah* group', the social context and significance of modern *tefilah* groups is completely different (as shown by the fact that communal prayer in girls' schools is unremarked and uncontroversial).

[3] For more on *tefilah* groups, see Becher and Marcus, 'Women's Tefillah Movement'; Nusbacher, 'Efforts at Change'; ead., 'Orthodox Jewish Women's Prayer Groups'.

[4] Email from Dr Deborah Weissman, a participant in both groups, 19 July 2011.

[5] A list of 56 groups appears on the Edah website; of these, 44 are in the USA, 7 in Israel, 3 in Canada, 1 in Australia, and 1 in the UK. Another list, on the JOFA website, lists 53 groups worldwide, with 41 in the USA, 5 in Israel, 3 in Australia, 2 in the UK, 1 in France, and 1 in Canada. Neither list is complete, so the total number of groups is probably more in the region of 60 to 65.

[6] The rabbi involved in its foundation asked me not to name the synagogue; see below.

[7] As noted in Ch. 3 above, several one-off services have been held for batmitzvah celebrations in the UK, usually in private homes.

[8] Observation of the new moon is biblically prescribed (Exod. 12: 2). The first traditions linking the day of Rosh Hodesh to women appear in the Jerusalem Talmud (*Ta'an.* 1: 6), which records that women customarily abstained from work then. See Berrin (ed.), *Celebrating the New Moon*.

[9] These are 'Barekhu' (the 'call to prayer'), the Kedushah (an antiphonal doxology recited during the repetition of the Amidah prayer), and Kaddish (an Aramaic doxology recited at various points during the service and also as a mourner's prayer). Interestingly, the early groups in Israel did recite these prayers (Dr Deborah Weissman, email, 19 July 2011).

group to group, include a text-based sermon (*devar torah*), prayers for the sick, memorialization of dead relatives, and a special prayer for *agunot*, women unable to obtain a Jewish divorce. Most groups use a standard Orthodox prayer book, sometimes supplemented by a photocopied sheet that lists the prayers with their page numbers and the names of the women leading the service.

In Israel in particular, the related practice of women praying in the standard synagogue service but then conducting a separate women-only Torah reading has taken root in several places, notably at Kehilat Yedidya, a synagogue founded in 1980 by a group of English-speaking immigrants in Jerusalem.[10] This format has not caught on in Britain, in spite of efforts to introduce it in the early 2000s; too radical to be countenanced by United synagogues, it is not as radical as the partnership *minyanim* that began in 2013, and fell between two stools.

Though there has been rabbinic opposition (notably an 1984 responsum issued by five rabbis from Yeshiva University in New York),[11] several rabbis have written in support of women's *tefilah* groups, such as Rabbi Avi Weiss of the Hebrew Institute of Riverdale, who published a halakhic justification of the initiative in 1990.[12] At present, such groups are clearly disapproved of in the haredi sector, and are viewed with varying degrees of approval in the Modern Orthodox and traditionalist sectors.[13]

History

In Britain, women's *tefilah* groups have been far less popular and have met with greater opposition than in the USA and Israel. The 1994 Preston Report, issued shortly after the controversy that surrounded the foundation of the Stanmore Women's Tefillah Group, showed a wide range of women's views about such groups, from a majority in provincial communities such as Edinburgh, Newcastle, and Leeds who favoured the status quo to others, especially younger women, who were more favourably inclined to the introduction of prayer services for women.[14] Only 4% of the women who responded to the survey had actually attended a *tefilah* group.[15]

The Stanmore group was not the first in the UK, however. In February 1986 a one-off women's service had been held in Oxford as part of the 'Kol

[10]   For a reflection on the significance of a women's group practising this ritual in Yeruham, Israel, see El-Or, *Next Year I Will Know More*, 263–6.

[11]   Haut, 'Women's Prayer Groups and the Orthodox Synagogue', 146–7.

[12]   Weiss, *Women at Prayer*.

[13]   For a list of articles opposing women's *tefilah* groups (nine articles) and supporting them (seven articles), see Haut, 'Women's Prayer Groups and the Orthodox Synagogue', 151–2, n. 1.

[14]   Preston, Goodkin, and Citron, *Women in the Jewish Community*, 29–41, esp. pp. 32–4. At this time *tefilah* groups were a controversial novelty.   [15]   Ibid. 33.

Isha' (Woman's Voice) weekend conference, and after a women's Torah reading for Simhat Torah in 1987, a regular group was established in 1988, which usually holds one service per academic term and continues to this day.[16] Another early example is the two Rosh Hodesh services held in Cambridge in 1988, organized by Alexa Neville.[17] A male student concerned about their halakhic status wrote to Chief Rabbi Immanuel Jakobovits to ask if they were permitted. Jakobovits replied that they were and published his responsum,[18] but they seem to have been one-off events with no follow-up, and, like the Oxford group, went unreported in the Jewish press.

Until recently, the only regular prayer service for women in London was in Stanmore, in north-west London, under the auspices of Stanmore and Canons Park United Synagogue. Though founded in 1992, until September 2011 it was excluded from the synagogue premises.[19] Interviews with three founder members produced somewhat conflicting versions of the group's origins: in one, the local rabbi, Dr Jeffrey Cohen, learnt about the existence of *tefilah* groups on a visit to America and promoted the idea on his return, directly approaching the women. The second account credited one of the founders of the group, Linda Stone, with asking Rabbi Cohen whether he would support such a group after hearing him talk about the American groups at a private dinner; and the third account, by Linda Stone, records that she wrote to the rabbi to propose the foundation of such a group, and received a positive reply.[20] Rabbi Cohen himself remembered giving a sermon on the topic shortly after his return from the USA, after which he was approached by women who were interested in the idea. The disparate accounts seem to reflect a concern with the origin of the enterprise: the more conventional women preferred to attribute it to the rabbi, while those less concerned with social approval claimed that the impetus came from the women.

They found a male teacher to instruct them in the traditional chanting of the Torah (leyning, usually only taught to men) and prepared for their first service in late 1992. The original intention was to hold the service in Stanmore Synagogue's library, but when a formal request for permission, sup-

[16] I am grateful to Sarah Montagu for this information (personal email, 14 Nov. 2017); see also 'Women's Services' on the Oxford Jewish Congregation's website. Members of the London *tefilah* groups are completely unaware of this group, which does not appear on either the JOFA or the Edah list and seems to have escaped the attention of the British Jewish press.

[17] Alexa Neville, interview; she also participated in the first two Stanmore services in 1993.

[18] Interestingly, he allowed the women to use a Torah scroll (after the event had happened): see Jakobovits, 'From the Chief Rabbi's Correspondence'. See also 'Politics and Halacha', leader, *Jewish Chronicle* (18 Feb. 1994), and Lee, 'Women Await Halachic Ruling on Torah Use'.

[19] Rocker, 'Stanmore Women Meet in Shul at Last'.

[20] Interviews with Nicola Perlman, Sheila Dorfman, and Linda Stone.

ported by Rabbi Cohen,[21] was presented at a board meeting a week before the event, 'all hell broke loose'.[22] A vote approved the service by a majority of two, but that Friday an article about the proposal appeared in the *Jewish Chronicle*,[23] after details were leaked by a Stanmore community member who objected to the idea, and plans were halted. After initial support from the chief rabbi, the official position changed, and the following week Rabbi Cohen was informed that the London Beth Din objected to the plans.[24] A storm of readers' letters to the *Jewish Chronicle*, both supportive and opposing, followed in short order, transforming a small-scale enterprise at a single synagogue into a community-wide debate that was covered in the national press.[25] Accompanied and supported by Rabbi Cohen, the women's representatives visited both the chief rabbi and the London Beth Din,[26] and the chief rabbi subsequently issued the following conditions:

1. The women were 'advised' that no Torah scroll should be used.

2. No prayers requiring the presence of a male quorum could be said.

3. The service could not take place on synagogue premises.

The women did not mind the second condition, since they had never intended to recite the quorum-dependent prayers, and only some were troubled by the first condition,[27] but they were all upset by the ban on using synagogue premises. The London Beth Din did not provide any halakhic rationale beyond expressing a concern over 'how it would appear' were women to pray as a group in a synagogue, and that such a group would be 'divisive'.[28]

[21] Interviews with Nicola Perlman, Sheila Dorfman, and Linda Stone.

[22] Nicola Perlman, interview; her husband, a member of the board, was present at the meeting.

[23] Bass, 'Women-Only Services Planned'.   [24] Rabbi Dr Jeffrey Cohen, interview.

[25] Wachmann, 'Why Are Men So Scared?'; Bermant, 'Time for Chief to be a Man about Women'; Hinds, 'Women-Only Worship Splits Orthodox Jews'. See also the highly emotional letters to the editor, *Jewish Chronicle*, 27 Nov. 1992.

[26] According to a woman who attended these meetings, the chief rabbi originally promised that they could use a Torah scroll and meet in the synagogue, before changing his mind: 'He promised us the earth and delivered pizza' (Sheila Dorfman, interview).

[27] Nicola Perlman claimed that they had never wanted to use a Torah scroll as it is much more difficult to read from one than from a printed book (it is necessary to memorize the vowels and the musical notes since these do not appear in the scroll). But see Lee, 'Women Await Halachic Ruling on Torah Use', who quotes Doreen Fine, a member of the group, as saying, 'We sincerely believe that the use of a Sefer Torah will enhance and intensify our commitment to Torah, tefilah and mitzvot, as well as providing the spiritual uplift that is so lacking in the society in which we are living.' Linda Stone insisted the original plan had been to use a scroll, and Rabbi Cohen said he would have had no halakhic objection to this, though he did not remember the women asking for one.

[28] Nicola Perlman, interview. Rabbi Cohen recalled that about seven minor halakhic objec-

The first service was held on 27 February 1993, at the house of Celia and Elkan Levy (then president of the United Synagogue). About sixty women attended,[29] of all ages, and the founders were encouraged to continue. The lead-up to the service and the event itself were extensively reported in the *Jewish Chronicle* and other Jewish newspapers,[30] and for the first year or so the group was eagerly followed and commented on. The women were chosen as 'JC Newsmaker of the Year' by the *Jewish Chronicle*, displacing Israeli foreign minister Shimon Peres.[31] The correspondence pages of the *Chronicle* provide a vivid picture of the heat and controversy generated across the Jewish community.[32] The issue was further complicated when another group of women, led by Linda Stone, held a Rosh Hodesh service on a Sunday morning in March 1994 at Yakar, an independent Orthodox study centre and synagogue in Hendon. They used a Torah scroll, without seeking the approval of the chief rabbi, and in fact against his express wish.[33] Even though the service was not publicized by the organizers, the *Jewish Chronicle* reported it,[34] setting off yet another storm of correspondence.[35] Although the Yakar group did not continue on a regular basis,[36] the increased opposition it inspired seems to have influenced attitudes to the Stanmore group. In February 1994, a *tefilah* group began at Pinner, and it was reported that plans 'were afoot to create other women-only *tefilah* groups in Edgware, Kenton, Manchester, Birmingham, Leeds and Bristol';[37] of these, only those in Manchester and Leeds[38] actually materialized. Services were held on an occasional basis in north-west London in later years, but the only groups that lasted were those in Stanmore, Oxford, and Manchester.[39]

tions were presented to him by a panel of rabbis, including three *dayanim* (religious judges), the week after the *Jewish Chronicle* report appeared, but characterized them as 'petty little points'.

[29] Rocker, 'Women at Prayer Await Crowning Prize'.

[30] See e.g. Monchi and Maxted, 'Women Make History'; Rayner, 'Women and Worship'; 'Unanswered Question', leader, *Jewish Chronicle* (11 Feb. 1993); 'Ben Yitzchok' (pseud.), 'A Courageous Stand'; 'Women's Day', leader, *Jewish Chronicle* (5 Mar. 1993); Rothenberg, 'Stanmore Women Plan May Service'; Wolfson, 'Fringe Festival'; Sacks, 'Women and Prayer'.

[31] '"Ordinary" Women with an Extraordinary Effect', *Jewish Chronicle* (10 Sept. 1993).

[32] See e.g. letters to the editor, *Jewish Chronicle* (12 and 19 Feb. 1993, 18 Feb. 1994).

[33] Monchi, 'Rebuke from Chief Rabbi', which reported that the rabbi of Yakar, Michael (Mickey) Rosen, had supported the women in a public statement.

[34] Monchi, 'Women to Hold Second Service with Sefer Torah'.

[35] Letters to the editor, *Jewish Chronicle* (18 Feb. 1994, 22 and 29 July 1994); see also the leader 'Politics and Halacha' (18 Feb. 1994).

[36] Occasional women's services continued to be held at Yakar, including two in early May 1995 in conjunction with a women's study day; see Monchi, 'Jerusalem Trio's Provocative Boost'.   [37] Monchi, '"Overwhelming" Turnout at Pinner Women's Service'.

[38] 'Yorkshire's First Women Only Shabbat Service Held', *Jewish Chronicle* (16 June 1995).

[39] Between 1998 and 2002 my husband, Norm Guthartz, and I organized occasional services

Description

In Stanmore, two more services were held in private homes, with about a hundred women attending the second,[40] and the women then began to rent a room in a local sheltered housing complex, Oakmead Court, about ten minutes' walk from the synagogue. Services were limited to a maximum of six a year by the housing complex management; the women themselves clubbed together to raise the rental fee. In July 2011, after repeated requests over a decade and considerable pressure from the wardens of Stanmore Synagogue, the London Beth Din agreed that the service might take place on synagogue premises, on condition that its name be changed to 'The Women's Learning Experience' and that it be held no more than four times a year. By August 2013 the group felt confident enough to announce that 'we plan to increase to 6 services each year from 2014', as well as organizing a celebration for the group's twentieth anniversary.[41] As of July 2018, however, the number of annual services remains at four.

In their heyday, these services attracted forty to fifty women, with considerably more when a batmitzvah was celebrated. Because of health and safety regulations, on these occasions they had to rent space at Aylward School nearby, since about a hundred women might turn up. By the time the group was allowed to use the synagogue, however, numbers had declined considerably: some members had moved to Israel; others were prevented by their health from attending (the founders were mostly in their fifties in 1992, and now had less energy to spare). At a service I attended in March 2011 only twenty-one women were present. However, once the group was permitted to meet in the synagogue, attendance more than doubled, with over sixty women attending the first service held in the synagogue in September 2011, in a palpable atmosphere of rejuvenation. After this high point, however, numbers declined again, reaching an average of about twenty-five in 2018.

Here I describe a typical service from the Oakmead Court period, when the group met in the day room of the complex, a large, low-ceilinged room adorned by a portrait of the queen, containing several dozen low, padded

in the Stanmore/Edgware area, every two months or so, modelled on Kehilat Yedidya in Jerusalem, with separate Torah readings, with scrolls, for men and women. Because of their controversial nature they were only advertised by word of mouth. Typical attendance was about 30–50 people, mostly from a United Synagogue background. After moving to Hendon in 2002, I helped to organize occasional women's *tefilah* groups in this format at Yakar and its successor congregation, Ohel Avraham, until 2009; they took place on Simhat Torah and a few sabbaths each year, with about 20–30 women attending.

[40]   Maxted, 'Sacks Lends Support'.

[41]   'The Women's Learning Experience at Stanmore'. In July 2018 a twenty-fifth anniversary celebration was held, with sixty attendees.

chairs. These were arranged in lines facing the large picture window at the back of the room, which looks onto a pretty garden. A traditional prayer stand faced the chairs, and was used by the woman leading the prayers or reading the Torah portion. At the other side of the room, behind the chairs, stood long tables with plates of food and small plastic cups containing wine or whisky for Kiddush.[42]

Each chair bore a photocopied sheet listing the prayers to be recited, with the relevant page numbers.[43] The women picked up prayer books and photocopies of the week's *parashah* and *haftarah* (prophetic portion) as they entered. Very few wore wigs;[44] most displayed the elegant hats commonly seen in the United Synagogue, and wore elaborate outfits. Most were in their sixties or seventies, with no young girls in recent years, though earlier there were a few teenagers, always daughters of attendees.

There was usually some chatting and greeting before the service got under way. The women did not read all the traditional prayers, largely because of time constraints (they read them much more slowly than would be usual in a standard service), but also because many of them found it difficult to read Hebrew.[45] They included the most important prayers, such as the Shema and Amidah,[46] and those that can be sung, such as 'Mah tovu' and 'Yigdal' at the beginning of the service and 'Adon olam' at the end. The tunes they used were often those sung in Jewish schools rather than those used in the synagogue, and may have been learnt from children or grandchildren.[47] One woman stood at the front, facing the others, and led the prayers.[48] The atmosphere was very quiet and focused (the women pride themselves on their 'decorum'), in contrast to the often noisy and busy atmosphere of most Orthodox syna-gogues, in which both men and women go in and out, chat, and move around the synagogue. Nor was there the usual buzz of rapidly recited prayer as a

[42] One consequence of gaining access to the synagogue was the loss of the 'social space' of the group's Kiddush, an element that had undoubtedly promoted its members' sense of identity and cohesion.

[43] The prayers to be included were originally decided in consultation with Rabbi Cohen.

[44] These are characteristic of haredi women, though they are sometimes worn by Modern Orthodox and, very rarely, by traditionalist women. See Carrel, 'Hasidic Women's Head Coverings'.

[45] Many of the older women confided, 'Of course I'm not learned', describing their lack of any formal Jewish education; see the section on women and education in Ch. 3.

[46] Since the recitation of the Kedushah in the repetition of the Amidah requires the presence of a male quorum, the entire repetition was omitted, and the silent Amidah was concluded by singing 'Oseh shalom' ('The One who creates peace'), the last line of the Amidah—a practice not found in standard services.

[47] Women (and indeed most men) do not learn the traditional and complex musical tradition (*nusah*) used in the synagogue. Jewish schools use bouncy, easily learnt tunes for daily prayers, which are a much-reduced version of the daily liturgy.

[48] In a standard service the prayer leader faces the ark, with his back to the congregation.

constant undertone, characteristic of Orthodox men at prayer—the women read the prayers that are not sung, such as the Shema, in silence.

The ritual surrounding the taking out of the Torah scrolls was omitted, since no scrolls were used, so the Torah reading took place immediately after the sermon, which usually focused on the weekly Torah portion. Even though no scroll was used, the portion was always divided into its usual seven *aliyot* and seven women were 'called up' using their Hebrew names. No blessings were said before and after each *aliyah*, as would be done in a standard service, but the appropriate blessings were recited before and after the reading of the *haftarah*, perhaps because even in a standard service this is read from a printed copy.

After the *haftarah* reading, there were prayers for the sick, when women were invited to come to the reading desk and recite prayers in either Hebrew or English for named individuals, followed by the *hazkarah* prayer, in either Hebrew or English, for deceased relatives whose *yahrzeit* fell close to the date. In the standard service, both prayers are recited by the prayer leader or the *gabai* (service 'stage manager'); they are exclusively in Hebrew, are recited very quickly, and generally consist of a list of several names (for the sick). *Hazkarot* are usually recited individually after the *aliyah* given to the deceased person's relative. At the women's group, participants valued the opportunity to pray for sick friends and, especially, to commemorate family members, and saw this as one of the high points of the service.[49] It was always an emotional moment, often accompanied by tears. Next came the standard prayers for the queen and for the State of Israel, augmented by two non-standard prayers in English, one for the welfare of women and one for *agunot*;[50] these provided another opportunity to participate for women who do not feel confident reading Hebrew.

Instead of the ritual of replacing the Torah scrolls in the ark, the passage 'Ets ḥayim' from the prayer accompanying the standard ritual was sung, and the service continued with the *musaf* service, in which the repetition of the Amidah was replaced with singing its closing passage, 'Oseh shalom'. The liturgical poem 'Anim zemirot' was led by a young girl,[51] and the service concluded with announcements and thanks to the organizers, followed by Kiddush, the blessing over wine accompanied by snacks after the service. Husbands usually turned up at this point and one of them usually recited

---

[49] See also the section on funerals, Kaddish, and *yahrzeit* in Ch. 3.

[50] The prayer for *agunot* was composed by Shelly Frier List in English and is widely used by women's *tefilah* groups in English-speaking communities. See Sylberberg, 'International Coalition for Agunah Rights'.

[51] In the standard service boys under 13 lead the community in the recitation of this poem as part of their education in leading prayers and their socialization into the (male) congregation.

Kiddush for all present.[52] On special occasions, such as batmitzvahs, Rabbi Cohen or Elkan Levy would deliver a speech to the batmitzvah girl at the end of the service, which was much appreciated by the women as a sign of support.

The basic format of the service has not changed as a consequence of the move into the synagogue, in spite of the change of name (viewed by all participants as the Beth Din's attempt at saving face). In December 2012 the group held its first *shabaton* (sabbath programme with special events), with a service including a sermon by Maureen Kendler, a leading educator, a talk after the service by a group member, and a lunch for members and their families. Since this period of revival, however, numbers have again declined to about twenty-five, as noted above, unless a batmitzvah is being celebrated, when forty to fifty women may attend. Many of the founders are now elderly or have moved to Israel, and the group is experiencing some difficulty in attracting younger women, probably because most of the congregation's members are staunchly traditionalist, with few who could be identified as Modern Orthodox.[53]

Significance for the Women

Many women feel that these services constitute the high point of their religious lives, offering an opportunity for quiet reflection and participation:

Attending the Women's Tefilah Service has given me a great sense of fulfilment. We are there because we want to be there. In a peaceful and spiritual atmosphere we are able to follow the excellent guide through the Service, which is a joy.

I feel much more involved spiritually and practically in the Women's Tefilah Service than when I'm in the Ladies' gallery in shul.[54]

Other important features mentioned by the women include the opportunity for learning more about the service and individual prayers, the sense of active participation, and the opportunity for celebrating such events as births of daughters or granddaughters, batmitzvahs, and special birthdays. Both the educational value of the *tefilah* group and the fact that it had a special significance for single women were noted by Sheila Dorfman, one of the founders:

I think it has an *enormous* place for encouraging young girls to take on *tefilah*, for women who are not comfortable with *tefilah* to understand how to do it properly, because it was an amazing learning experience, both for those of us who were very

---

[52] Strangely, the women never seemed to have considered the possibility of a woman reciting Kiddush, even though this would be halakhically acceptable.

[53] Information from a telephone interview with Nicola Perlman, 24 July 2018.

[54] Participants' comments, Lee and Fine, *Women's Tefilah Services*.

active in taking the *tefilah*, and also for those people who just came along and for the first time in their life could understand what was going on, and in an atmosphere of hush and reverence that you never get in shul. And I think it was amazing for the older women in the community and other women who were on their own, and always feel like a spare part in shul because they don't have a man to be called up [to the Torah] for them, to daven [lead services] for them, to say the special prayers for them, and they could come to this service and do it for themselves, and not feel that they were alien.[55]

The 1994 Preston Report noted that 'a perception is growing among younger Orthodox women of the synagogue as a "men's club", controlling, inhibiting and unfairly restricting the scope of women's involvement'.[56] In this atmosphere, the Stanmore group was perceived by those who attended it as a spiritual beacon. Several Orthodox women in London expressed even more resentment about their lack of participation in synagogue in the follow-up survey of 2009: 'I no longer want to be a spectator at shul. I would like to be called up [for the Torah reading] when I have yahrzeit and to be able to say kaddish and *bensch gomel*[57] and to make a third at grace after meals.'[58]

In spite of these comments, however, not only had the Stanmore group declined by 2009, but none of the other attempts at setting up a similar group had survived (except in Manchester), and few women seemed interested in trying to start a new group. This lack of interest seemed to be associated with the Stanmore group's marginal position and original lack of endorsement by the United Synagogue establishment. As Sheila Dorfman noted at the time, 'I think sadly it's *because* it's been banned from the shul, and because of all the other restrictions placed on it, it's fading away.' The group's move to the synagogue did indeed confer a degree of official approval: there was a threefold rise in attendance (to sixty-three women) at the first service held on the synagogue premises, and numbers stayed in the thirties and

---

[55] Sheila Dorfman, interview.

[56] Preston, Goodkin, and Citron, *Women in the Jewish Community*, 29.

[57] Yiddish form of *birkat hagomel*, the blessing recited in public after a person survives illness, a dangerous journey, childbirth, or another potentially life-threatening situation. Men typically recite the blessing in synagogue after being called up to the Torah. Sephardi synagogues encourage women to recite it, but they do not always have an opportunity to do so in Ashkenazi synagogues, where a husband will sometimes recite it on his wife's behalf.

[58] Preston et al., *Connection, Continuity and Community*, 12. If three adult males or three adult females have eaten a meal including bread together, the Grace after Meals (*birkat hamazon*) is augmented by an introductory paragraph. Most halakhic authorities would not permit a mixed-gender group of three to recite this introduction, and although three women may (indeed, according to some authorities, must) do so, few women are aware of this. See Maimonides, *Mishneh torah*, 'Hilkhot berakhot', 5: 7; Joseph Karo, *Shulḥan arukh*, 'Oraḥ ḥayim', 199: 7. For a modern discussion of the issue, see Wolowelsky, 'Women and *Zimmun*'.

forties for a while, before falling again. Far from being ideologically driven feminists determined to shake off the shackles of patriarchy, the Stanmore women desperately wanted to keep the group under the auspices of the synagogue and to have the wholehearted approval of the community, especially its male religious leadership. I asked Nicola Perlman whether it had ever occurred to them to strike out on their own and abandon the attempt to run the service as part of the synagogue. She answered:

I want to stay in Orthodoxy but just be recognized. Otherwise there are places we can go and do this type of thing and have an egalitarian service, whatever we want to do. But that wasn't the aim of the game . . . We were very careful to follow strictly the guidelines they gave.

The desire to remain within the mainstream Orthodox community was stronger than the yearning for personal spiritual fulfilment and participation in ritual, and points up the existence of strong traditionalist as well as Modern Orthodox motivations among the members of the group. Nicola emphasized the fact that the rabbi continued to support them (if in a necessarily passive way) and that the group had accepted all the restrictions imposed upon them by the Beth Din, thus distancing itself from accusations of rebelliousness. Another interviewee spoke bitterly of the fear of change within the United Synagogue, but could not envision abandoning the institution in order to conduct women's religious activities without external constraints:

It's just fear, it's just status quo . . . the United Synagogue has no identity . . . It's fearful, it's introverted, it's reversionary . . . It's lost its way . . . We women have to take the initiative now, on the cusp of a new president and a new [chief] rabbi, and create facts on the ground, so that we are not just put back into our box and the lid put firmly down when the new president and the new chief rabbi are in place.[59]

For these women, who are on the boundary between Modern Orthodox and traditionalist, to be Orthodox and Jewish means to belong to an established community; they cannot envisage Orthodoxy or Judaism outside recognized communal institutions. They are very aware of the high cost of leaving or seeming to leave the Orthodox community.[60] This also seems to have been the

[59] Sheila Dorfman, interview. Lord Jonathan Sacks retired as chief rabbi in September 2013, and was succeeded by Rabbi Ephraim Mirvis. Elections for United Synagogue president and trustees took place in July 2011. The board at this time consisted of the president, three vice presidents, three treasurers (all male), and four 'women representatives'. For recent developments in women's leadership opportunities, see Ch. 3.

[60] For a discussion of the material and socio-psychological costs of leaving a minority community, see Reitman, 'On Exit', esp. pp. 194–5. I am indebted to Dr Lindsay Simmonds for this reference.

reason that the Stanmore women avoided every association with the women's services held at Yakar, an independent Orthodox institution that had no links to the United Synagogue or any other Orthodox association of synagogues.[61] The Yakar group did use a Torah scroll and was harshly criticized for this not only by those who opposed women's services in general, but also by many 'moderates' who supported the Stanmore group.[62] It appears that many Orthodox women, in particular those in the United Synagogue, resent their exclusion from public ritual, but are not prepared to pay the heavy price of leaving the Orthodox community, though they are well aware that many women have already made that choice, or are seeking the certainties of haredi ideology.[63]

Thus a major factor inhibiting women's willingness to demand increased participation in ritual or new forms of ritual is the risk this entails of exclusion from the community, or at least of strong disapproval from the Orthodox establishment, and the consequent impact on their own self-identification as Orthodox women. This was reinforced by the religious authorities' eighteen-year refusal to allow women's prayer on synagogue premises, and the existence of competing models of 'approved' women's activities that function within the synagogue, such as ladies' guilds.[64] Much of the antagonistic reaction to the Stanmore initiative, expressed by both men and women in the *Jewish Chronicle*'s correspondence pages, sought to delegitimize the group by asserting that other female activities exemplified true Orthodoxy, and by associating the women of the *tefilah* group with the external, non-Jewish (and thus alien) feminist movement:

It is high time that the women's lobby within the US [United Synagogue] took as its role models our great biblical matriarchs, as well as the many contemporary strictly Orthodox women who find spiritual and intellectual fulfilment in their duties and responsibilities as *n'shei chayil* [women of worth] . . . Torah Judaism . . . transcends secular values, and modern-day feminism has no place in it.[65]

[61] They refused to distribute flyers advertising the Yakar service; Linda Stone, interview.

[62] In a phone call to Linda Stone, Rabbi Cohen attempted to persuade the Yakar group organizers not to use a Torah scroll, adding that 'his goodwill would be dependent on the degree to which they accepted his authority' and that he 'strongly cautioned them not to do anything that would make him disassociate himself from the women's movement' since 'he had to satisfy halakhic authorities to the right of him'. Linda Stone, interview, during which she showed me notes she had made during the call.

[63] See Sheila Dorfman's remarks on polarization quoted in Ch. 2. For the attraction of haredi certainties in an era of rapidly changing and frequently questioned gender roles, see Davidman, *Tradition in a Rootless World*, 194–5.

[64] The Stanmore synagogue website's 'Living and Learning Programme' revealed that activities for women held on the synagogue premises in 2011 included the ladies' guild, a ladies' *shiur*, a *simḥah* dancing class, and a Rosh Hodesh group. Forbidding the *tefilah* group to use the synagogue sent a clear message that this was not an approved activity.

[65] Brian Gordon, letter to the editor, *Jewish Chronicle* (18 Feb. 1994).

A truly observant Jewish woman does not need to seek emancipation through women-only services. She *is* emancipated and, indeed, exerts a decisive influence on the whole of public life. It is she who is entrusted with the building of our homes, with kashrut and *taharah* (purity), and thereby, with the future of our children.[66]

Interestingly, the first women's group to appear since the Stanmore controversy was founded in June 2015, at a United synagogue.[67] Tanya Roth, a professional woman in her sixties from the community, made contact with the Stanmore group's leaders, and approached her rabbi; two Stanmore activists were later invited to discuss the services with her, the rabbi, and the rabbi's wife. The first service was attended by about seventy women, of whom about ten to fifteen (including the rebbetsin) formed a 'core' of organizers, and those with the skills needed to run the service. A group of about six women, mostly between 40 and 70, learned to chant the Torah in 2016, again from a *ḥumash*, not a Torah scroll. Services have continued fairly regularly since then and are held in the synagogue hall, often but not exclusively when a batmitzvah is being celebrated, and numbers remain stable. Tanya Roth was particularly interested in educating women to be more active and comfortable in formal prayer, and in encouraging them to engage more with both Torah and liturgical texts. While the rabbi's motivation was primarily 'to allow women to be skilled in an inclusive manner within halakhah', he also supported the group as an alternative to the newly founded partnership *minyanim* and a nearby Masorti congregation, both of which, he felt, might attract some of his congregants unless he 'did something for the women'. In this instance, fear of an even more radical and undesirable practice, of a much more autonomous nature, trumped lingering unease about women's independent ritual activity—a perfect example of a shift in the patterns of power leading to changes in ritual practice.[68] The rebbetsin noted that, in addition to providing a forum 'where women's voices could be heard', the service offered girls a chance to lead the liturgical poem 'Anim zemirot'—often the first portion of the liturgy that a boy learns to lead in synagogue—thus giving them a prominent and approved communal role parallel to that of boys.

The actual service is somewhat more limited than that at the Stanmore group, with fewer prayers recited and no blessings recited over the *haftarah*.[69] The women return to the main synagogue for the *musaf* service. It is proving

---

[66] S. M. Rubin, letter to the editor, *Jewish Chronicle* (27 Nov. 1992).

[67] The rabbi asked me not to identify the synagogue, and I have used pseudonyms here.

[68] See the discussion of Catherine Bell's observations on the link between power and ritual below.

[69] The rabbi emphasized that this was a policy decision rather than a halakhic one, designed to deflect criticism; he was nervous that higher rabbinic authorities might find out about the service and ban it.

very popular for batmitzvah celebrations, and the rabbi's wife and daughter participate regularly, which enhances its respectability. The community reacted favourably to the foundation of the group; women's Megillah readings (see below) had already been taking place in the synagogue for some years, and there were opportunities for women to dance with Torah scrolls on Simhat Torah (see below), so the new group did not seem particularly radical. In addition, the fact that the congregation is quite small (unlike Stanmore, which is the biggest Orthodox community in Europe) meant that the rabbi felt that innovations would be less likely to be remarked upon and condemned by higher rabbinic authorities.

The fate of women's prayer services in Britain sheds considerable light on the communal factors that determine the shape of women's religious lives: even with male and rabbinic support, certain activities, in themselves normative, become controversial and marginal when performed by women—though they may become considerably less controversial in the face of new and more radical practices, which may eventually render the older rituals acceptable to the same authorities who originally condemned them. I consider why this is so, and which activities are vulnerable to community pressures, at the end of this chapter.

Women's Megillah Readings

Somewhat less controversial are women's group readings of the Megillah, the biblical book of Esther, that form the central ritual of the minor festival of Purim. The Megillah is read both in the evening and in the morning of the festival, and both men and women have a halakhic obligation to hear it. In a standard service, the book is read from a handwritten parchment scroll by a man, and men, women, and children listen, waving rattles and booing to 'erase' the name of the villain, Haman. Purim is a light-hearted, carnival-like occasion, with adults and children dressing up, wearing masks, and engaging in parodies and joking about central rituals and practices. Role reversal is a central theme, which may contribute to the much lower level of controversy associated with women's Megillah readings.

Reading the Megillah demands a high level of skill and considerable investment in practice, since, like the Torah scroll, the Megillah scroll contains neither vowels nor musical notation, which must be memorized. There is no question here of women using a printed version, since the commandment to read the book includes the requirement that it be read from a handwritten scroll. The book is ten chapters long, takes up to forty-five minutes to read, and is recited in a unique musical mode. The question of whether women may read the Megillah, either for other women or for both men and women, has been discussed in both classical and modern halakhic works.[70] Several authorities permit this practice (including most of the medieval rabbis), while others limit it to women reading for other women, or even to individual women reading it for themselves.

History

The first women's Megillah readings took place in the USA[71] and Israel in the 1970s, roughly at the same time as the first women's *tefilah* services and in the same circles.[72] The first in the UK was held in Cambridge around 1991;[73] most regular readings were founded in the first decade of the twenty-first century, with the pace increasing from 2010 onwards.[74]

About thirteen women's Megillah readings now take place in the London area every year,[75] some associated with synagogues,[76] and others in private houses or rented premises.[77] All are in non-haredi contexts. Some take place in the evening and others in the morning. In all of them, several women share the reading, in contrast to standard readings, in which one man reads the entire book. The primary reason is practical: the reading must be done using a special musical mode, and many people find this hard to learn. The book is therefore divided into its constituent chapters, or smaller units, and women

[70] Frimer, 'Women's *Megilla* Reading'; a list of modern studies of this question appears in the first footnote. See also Landes, 'Are Women Obligated in Reading Megilla on Purim?'

[71] Email message from Freda Birnbaum, 24 July 2011: 'I remember women's megillah readings at Lincoln Square Synagogue in the early or mid-1970s.'

[72] According to Aryeh Frimer, the earliest modern responsum permitting women's Megillah readings dates from 1976, and was written by the chief rabbi of Beersheba, Elijah Katz; see Katz, *Ha'eshel (Bite'on hamo'atsah hadatit shel be'er-sheva)*, 13 (2003), 41–4, 48. See also Schmidt, letter to the editor, *Tradition*, 33/2 (1999), 80–2. I am indebted to Professor Frimer for these references.

[73] Email from Aviva Kaufmann, 27 July 2011.

[74] Women's readings include: London School of Jewish Studies (Hendon, begun in 2000); Hampstead Garden Suburb (2001/2 in a private house; moved to synagogue in 2013); Edgware (2006); Alei Tzion (Hendon, no date available); Borehamwood (2011); Muswell Hill (2012); Mill Hill (2013); South Hampstead (2013). I participated in several women's Megillah readings (and one highly controversial mixed reading) at Yakar before it closed in 2002, and organized women's readings for Yakar's successor congregation, Yakar Kehilla/Ohel Avraham, which closed in 2010.

[75] The only evidence of women's Megillah readings outside London, except for Cambridge, came from an interview in 2011 with Rabbi Mordechai Locardo, a Sephardi rabbi, who had permitted one for students in Leeds several years previously.

[76] The readings at Radlett, Hampstead Garden Suburb, Borehamwood, Muswell Hill, Finchley, Mill Hill, and Brondesbury Park take place in local synagogues; those in Edgware and Hendon are held at non-synagogal Jewish institutions. Several started in private homes.

[77] These do not include the 'women's readings' at which a man reads for a group of women; these are usually held to enable women with young children to fulfil their obligation of hearing the Megillah once their husbands have heard it and can therefore look after the children.

typically memorize the individual passages from recordings. Another reason for dividing the book up is to give more women a chance to participate.

The first women's Megillah reading in London was held at Yakar in 1995, on the initiative of the rabbi, Simon Harris; over seventy women attended.[78] However, the earliest readings to have continued annually to the present are those at London School of Jewish Studies and at Radlett United Synagogue. Stella James started the latter group in 2001:

I wanted something that we could do, that we could participate in. I hate just being an observer; if I could daven and leyn [read the Torah] I would, I'd *love* to . . . now having learnt to leyn Megillah I absolutely *love* doing it, it just means *so* much more if I can participate rather than just stand and watch.

An American woman recorded the reading on tapes so that women could learn,[79] and helped to organize the reading, which was shared between twenty women. The rabbi was very supportive,[80] and there was no opposition from the community, though the London Beth Din was not enthusiastic.[81] Over a hundred women attended the first reading, and about eighty turn up nowadays.[82]

In 2006 another reading was started in Edgware, largely on the initiative of two women who regularly attended morning readings by women in Hendon and Radlett, but had had 'awful experiences' at evening readings in their own synagogues.[83] Jewish law prescribes that every word of the Megillah should be heard, and if this is impossible, one should attend another reading in order to fulfil one's halakhic obligation. One woman spoke of the standard reading in Edgware United Synagogue as largely inaudible for both men and women, and felt compelled to seek out another reading afterwards to fulfil her obligation.[84] Before the first women's reading, the organizers were summoned by two local haredi rabbis and told to cancel the event, on the grounds that 'it would open a Pandora's box' and that they would 'destroy the unity of Edgware'. The rabbis acknowledged that they could find no halakhic objec-

[78] 'Women Read Megilah'.

[79] Significantly, she had grown up in a Conservative family and trained as a *ḥazanit* (female cantor), a role not available in the Orthodox world.

[80] Rabbi Gideon Sylvester, telephone conversation, 24 Aug. 2011. He felt that the popularity of the reading showed how positive it was; at the first reading, over 100 women came, in contrast to the two or three women who had attended the standard morning reading in previous years.

[81] 'There was a difficulty with the Beth Din, because they weren't that keen on it happening in the shul' (Stella James, interview).   [82] Ibid.

[83] Edgware: email (28 July 2011) and telephone (1 Aug. 2011) communications with Brenda Johns.

[84] The second reading was very fast, taking about twenty minutes, and was not a pleasant or meaningful experience for her (Brenda Johns, interview).

tions. Nevertheless, the reading went ahead, with about twenty women attending, five of whom served as readers. In 2011 about twenty-five women attended, with seven reading. Most were in their thirties. One organizer spoke of the reading as 'the highlight' of Purim, and noted that women tend to return year after year.

Another recent women's Megillah reading started in 2011 at Borehamwood,[85] initiated by a woman who put a notice in the synagogue newsletter asking if any other women were interested. The rabbi gave his permission and support, and taught the women the relevant halakhic rules. The reading took place at the synagogue, in a hall used as a nursery; the organizers had expected about thirty women to turn up, and were delighted when about sixty-five arrived, of varying ages. Eleven women read, and the event was very successful. There was little opposition within the community; some women were against the idea, while a few men were annoyed that they had to take their children to the special children's reading scheduled at the same time, and there were some concerns about 'splitting the community'.

In almost all cases, readings were initiated by a woman or a small group of women, with or without rabbinic support; actual opposition was only encountered from haredi rabbis, which the Modern Orthodox women to whom they spoke chose to ignore. It is significant that no haredi women have set up Megillah groups.

Description

The reading at the London School of Jewish Studies takes place in the morning, and is attended by sixty to eighty women and children.[86] Many women, and all the children, wear Purim costumes, and bring the traditional rattles. A tall reading table, draped in a red-and-gold sari, with a *talit* spread on top, holds the Megillah, which is unwound and folded 'like a letter', according to tradition, before the reading begins. The atmosphere is full of excitement, and the room is packed to overflowing. There is usually a different reader for each chapter; the woman who reads the first chapter also reads the opening and concluding blessings. A few announcements are made, silence falls, and the opening blessing is made, for which everyone stands. There is a brief pause as people sit down, and the reading begins, with two women flanking the reader at the table, correcting or prompting her if necessary. The speed and fluency of reading vary from reader to reader, but are generally slower than at a standard reading. Because of this, and because the listening women

---

[85] Email from Miriam Lorie, one of the organizers, 4 Aug. 2011.

[86] At first this was unaffiliated, but it became an official LSJS activity in 2012. I have attended and read at this reading since its inception; see also the vignette at the beginning of Ch. 1.

are completely focused and silent, it is a remarkably clear and distinct reading, with every word audible—something that can be difficult to achieve in large synagogues, where not everyone is aware of the halakhic necessity of hearing every word. This is one reason that many women cite for their preference for a women's reading. The noise made 'to blot out Haman's name' is more subdued than at a standard reading, and stops rapidly in order to allow the reader to continue (something that is by no means standard in United Synagogue readings). After the final blessing, for which everyone stands, some traditional songs are sung, and one of the organizers thanks the readers, and reminds the women that if anyone would like to learn how to read for the next year, they can do so. The gathering ends in a cheerful and excited atmosphere of greetings, general conversation, and the traditional exchange of Purim gifts of food (*mishlo'aḥ manot*) between acquaintances.

Significance for the Women

Several women reported their frustration at standard readings, which were often noisy and crowded, making it difficult if not impossible to hear the Megillah. They found the women's reading far more meaningful, noting that as it was slower, there was no sense 'of arrogance, of "look how fast I can do this"'.[87] Brenda Johns, a young Modern Orthodox mother of three, found the reading 'transformative' because every word was meaningful and the women read 'with lots of expression': 'It's wonderful to hear the women's voices reading the women's story . . . I feel really connected to "my" chapter.'

Stella James emphasized not only the personal but also the communal joy and empowerment women feel:

It's also a *wonderful* experience for the women, you know, a lot of women don't like doing things publicly . . . don't like saying things in public, speaking in public, let alone singing in public. Some of them have been very tentative about it, but it's been a huge leap for them . . . to learn how to do it [...] their Hebrew's not been that good, let alone learn how to leyn it, sing a *trop* [traditional chant], all that sort of thing . . . and then to have to get up in front of a load of other women and do it, and when they do, there is such a sort of sisterhood . . . there's just such a spirit among everyone, and the women in the congregation *love* it, they think that it has a very different *quality* to it, the nature of the reading's very different, it's very quiet, and they can hear every word. It's very beautiful, and that's not necessarily because of the singing, because some people have got lovely voices, others have kind of got Rex Harrison *My Fair Lady*-type growly voices, and they say it, growl it rather than singing it, it's all part of the rich tapestry, it's lovely.

The satisfaction and sense of achievement gained from mastering a hith-

---

[87] Brenda Johns, interview.

erto unfamiliar traditional technique and the consequent sense of ownership and connection are very important to the women. Opposition on the part of other women seems to be the result of a fear of changing tradition: 'There are still some women who are against it on [the] principle that they don't see that women should be doing such things.'[88] A few haredi women attend women's Megillah readings. Those who do not may be unaware of the existence of such readings, or may have asked the opinion of their rabbis, who tell them that such readings are forbidden; or they may fear that the quality of reading will be too low for them to fulfil their halakhic obligation of hearing each word properly pronounced.[89]

As with *tefilah* groups, Megillah readings answer women's desire to participate, to 'own' or 'perform' the tradition rather than always being spectators. They also allow women to act together as a religious community. In contrast to *tefilah* groups, however, more groups of this type exist, with less opposition to them. A number of factors explain this:

- Megillah readings occur once a year, so they are both less prominent and involve less organization.

- Women have a halakhic obligation to hear the Megillah, so there is less halakhic basis for opposition, and more support in halakhic literature.

- The Megillah story focuses on Esther, and the presence of a female heroine makes this a text with particular resonance for women.

All the London groups except one were initiated by women, often in response to a sense that they could not fulfil their halakhic obligation in a standard service; several enjoy strong support from their community rabbi.[90] Because there are two Megillah readings on Purim, women can schedule their attendance at a women's reading either in the evening or in the morning, at a time when their husbands are not attending the standard reading and can look after the children. Several girls have celebrated their batmitzvah by participating in a women's Megillah reading, thus creating an approximate parallel to the traditional Torah or *haftarah* reading by barmitzvah boys.

Although it takes time and effort to learn to chant the Megillah, it demands less investment than does preparing the Torah reading for a sabbath service, in which the text will be different each time. Since the Megillah text does not vary, one factor in its somewhat wider popularity seems to be the greater 'return' on the initial learning investment.

Given the existence not only of specific references to women reading the

---

[88] Stella James, interview.   [89] Brenda Johns, interview.

[90] The rabbis involved are young and Modern Orthodox rather than haredi.

Megillah in early halakhic literature but of approval of this by several early authorities,[91] it is much more difficult for those who object to find halakhic grounds to ban the practice. When rabbis do voice objections, it is usually on 'community' or 'policy' grounds, as in the case of the Edgware reading. However, the London Beth Din has not acted to discourage the readings in the same way as it did with the Stanmore *tefilah* group, so there is less overt disapproval on the part of the establishment, which allows women to feel that they can participate in these events without risking their position or status in the community. Perhaps partly as a result of the success of the women's Megillah groups, the other biblical books linked to festivals are becoming the focus of similar groups. Four batmitzvah girls have recently read the book of Ruth on Shavuot;[92] in summer 2014, a group of women organized a reading of Eikhah (book of Lamentations) on the fast of Tishah Be'av; and on Shavuot 2017 women from Woodside Park United Synagogue organized a group that read the book of Ruth at the rabbi's house, supervised by the rebbetsin. There are even fewer possible halakhic objections to women reading these scrolls, so it seems likely that this practice will spread.

Rosh Hodesh Groups

As described in Chapter 2, the introduction of Rosh Hodesh groups to Britain set off a wave of women's activity in the early 1990s. Though Rosh Hodesh had been associated with women from the rabbinic period onwards, it gained a new lease of life in the 1970s and 1980s, when American Jewish women inspired by feminist ideals sought to reclaim and reconstruct it as a monthly women's space for ritual activity and discussion, often with a radical agenda of general and Jewish social change.[93]

Rosh Hodesh groups were brought to Britain by the Israeli educator Alice Shalvi (b.1926). In the early 1980s a young teacher, Sharon Jastrow, had been invited to a fundraising event intended to raise money for Shalvi's new Jerusalem girls' school, Pelech, at which a letter from Shalvi to British Jewish women in advance of a planned visit was read out. Jastrow remembers:

[The letter] said, 'Now when I come to London it will be Rosh Hodesh, and there is a custom for women to celebrate Rosh Hodesh, and there are a number of things you

---

[91] This is in contrast to women's *tefilah* groups and the practice of women reading from the Torah, which are barely mentioned in premodern halakhic literature, though the latter was a feature of Shabateanism that outraged contemporaries. See Rapoport-Albert, *Women and the Messianic Heresy of Sabbatai Zevi*, 137–8, 140, 259.

[92] See Ch. 3 for a discussion of this ritual in the context of batmitzvah.

[93] See Berrin (ed.), *Celebrating the New Moon*, esp. the introduction by Blu Greenberg, and Adelman, *Miriam's Well*.

can do.' And she gave a list of what one does, and so one [thing] is light a candle, another give *tsedakah* [charity], wear a new outfit, [eat a new] fruit, study, meditate, yoga, she gave a list, eat, whatever. So everyone said, 'We don't do that, we're British!', you know, yoga and meditation, and then I said, 'I'll organize something.' And that was quite significant because I felt I had nothing to offer this group, I wasn't a fundraiser, I wasn't smart like one of them, but here I knew I could do something. I'd never ever met Alice, so the first evening I just invited whomever I knew.

Rosh Hodesh groups offered empowerment for Jewish women, who could finally 'do something'. Jastrow organized a Rosh Hodesh evening in Finchley at which Shalvi spoke, inspiring the women to set up regular Rosh Hodesh meetings in private homes: 'This was before Limmud was really established in Anglo-Jewry, and it was the first time women could meet cross-communally.'[94] The first group met in Finchley, but before long groups started in Pinner and Edgware, and outside London. There was a palpable sense of excitement, and the first members were passionately committed. Linda Stone started the Edgware group after attending the original Finchley one:

The Rosh Hodesh movement is definitely a spinoff of the second wave of women's liberation, those [Rosh Hodesh] groups that were set up in America and in Israel came out of that feeling of women meeting together, the consciousness-raising groups that I wasn't a part of. And it took a while for it to filter to the [other] Jewish communities. And by the [late] eighties, this consciousness of women and Rosh Hodesh [as] significant for women, and having a space for women, all really kind of exploded . . . I was someone with a very small child who was isolated, wondering why I didn't fit into the shul that was an old boys' network, and there wasn't a place for me . . . So I started to get involved in the Rosh Hodesh movement, and got very involved.

The creation of a women's space where issues central to them and sometimes controversial could be discussed galvanized many women into action: Linda Stone was later involved in both the Stanmore and the more controversial Yakar women's *tefilah* groups, was active in the campaign for *agunot*, co-founded the cross-communal Jewish Women's Network in 1993,[95] and established a fund to buy a Torah scroll for the Jewish women of Britain.[96]

[94] Sharon Jastrow, interview.
[95] The Jewish Women's Network produced a newsletter and held several debates, study sessions, and workshops, attracting hundreds of women, and produced a booklet on women and bereavement, but seems to have run out of steam after a triple event in 2006, the last advertised on its website.
[96] It amassed about £800 (Torah scrolls cost several thousand pounds), but was eventually

The activities pursued by the groups varied widely; Sally Berkovic, reviewing the Rosh Hodesh movement in 1997, recorded:

each group is free to develop its own ceremonies and set of rituals as there are no prescribed formulas. I have attended groups which start with passing a burning candle to each person, who speaks about something important that has happened in the previous month, and groups that start with coffee and cake. Some groups form as a branch of the local synagogue, some have no affiliation, some are geared to a particular age-group, some purposely try to be cross-generational. Activities can focus on a Jewish holiday happening that month, a guest speaker, someone's experience or a creative activity.[97]

Many of the early groups incorporated a ritual element, often focusing on the moon as a specifically female symbol. Sheila Dorfman, who founded the Pinner group, recalled that 'in the early days quite a few groups used to light a tealight in a bowl of water, to represent the moon . . . all of the groups tend to have some sort of food ritual, either they have a food relating to the month or they have moon-shaped food, or something to do with food which becomes quite a ritual in their group.' She recalled that Rosh Hodesh groups were even founded at some Jewish schools, spurring an interesting reaction from the boys:

When we had [a Rosh Hodesh group] at Sinai [school], two of the boys tried to gatecrash in girls' PE skirts, because they felt very very excluded, and I found that fascinating because they didn't realize at all how girls feel excluded from their leyning clubs and their 'Anim zemirot' clubs and everything else that *they're* allowed to do, but once we did something just for the girls, they felt excluded.

The highlight of the Rosh Hodesh movement was the two weekend events (*shabatonim*) organized in Bournemouth in 1991 and 1992, which not only included intense programmes of study and discussion, but also women-only sabbath services at which women chanted from a Torah scroll. For almost all the women, this was the first time they had ever handled a Torah scroll, and many of them found the experience both liberating and deeply emotional. Dr Alice Shalvi spoke at both events, and Dr Deborah Weissman, an American-born Orthodox feminist educator from Jerusalem, was invited to speak at the second by Sharon Jastrow. These events are still recalled with excitement and awe by those who were involved. Shortly afterwards one of the women organized a women-only service as a batmitzvah celebration for her

closed down in the early 2000s, and the money donated to women's charities. More recently, the charity entrepreneur Dame Hilary Blume purchased a Torah scroll that can be used by groups of women or partnership *minyanim*.

[97] Berkovic, *Under My Hat*, 178.

daughter, at which Katherine Marks had her first, rather overwhelming, experience of being called up to the Torah:

I was very nervous, and I realized that I'd been going to shul—that classic moment —all my life, and by that time was well established as a Jewish educator, and I didn't know what to do. Of course I knew the words, but I didn't know where to touch the *sefer* [scroll], I was terribly nervous, and had to be helped a little bit. And this was videoed, and people watched the video afterwards, I also saw it, and people were laughing, I mean in a nice way, with me, but they said I looked wide-eyed with nerves and shock, and I felt it was just such an absolutely weird and peculiar thing to do. It was wonderful, but not at the time, you know, afterwards I was so glad I did it, and I'm still glad I did it.

The shock of transformation from a spectator, unaware of technical details of ritual because of the absence of the possibility of personal involvement, to an active participant, who suddenly realizes that ritual involves previously invisible skills, is perhaps the central experience of Orthodox women who seek greater participation in core Jewish rituals.

The publication of the Preston Report in 1994 intensified the feeling that at last Orthodox women had found their voice, but within a few years many of the initiatives that had been inspired by the Rosh Hodesh movement petered out, apparently as a result of rabbinic and lay opposition and most Orthodox women's reluctance to defy rabbinic authority and to risk the very real discomfort attendant upon undertaking new ritual practice. The nature of the Rosh Hodesh groups themselves gradually changed; some faded away, while others became more general in tone and less concerned with women's issues, losing their explicitly feminist character. Sheila Dorfman noted:

The Pinner group has undergone several metamorphoses; it started off as a straight Rosh Hodesh group, then it kind of died, then it was relaunched, and then we relaunched it as a sort of more fun group called Calendar Girls, and that had its own lifespan, and died . . . The people who ran Calendar Girls didn't want intensive Jewish education, they wanted the fun bit of Judaism, and we showed some Jewish films, and we had strawberry teas, and so it was a lot more cultural and social than intensive education, but with a Jewish heart and a Jewish theme. And that was great because it brought in women who *never* come to shul.

Ultimately a feminist agenda of radical cultural change was swamped by a nervous retreat to 'fun' and conformity to community expectations. Rosh Hodesh groups still exist, often associated with synagogues, but they have lost both their ritual and their radical character, as well as their cross-communal nature. Several of the women who founded and participated in the early groups have left Orthodoxy, or have lost interest in religious participation, often as a result of feeling that their efforts had borne no fruit. Asked whether she thought her activities during the heyday of the Rosh Hodesh movement had left any legacy, Linda Stone felt that they had had no real effect:

Everybody told me [that] I made a big difference, 'you've done this and that', but actually I just think it shows how impenetrable it is . . . I think it's because women are disenfranchised within Orthodoxy—if you have always got to ask permission from a man before anything can change, why shouldn't they say no? . . . I don't think there's any progress within Orthodoxy, I haven't seen any.[98]

Current Rosh Hodesh groups tend to follow the format of a talk on a topic of general or Jewish interest, followed by refreshments. A group founded in Edgware in 2009 by a graduate of the Bradfield Women Educators programme, for instance, met in private homes, either on the sabbath nearest Rosh Hodesh or midweek, and attracted about twenty women, both younger and middle-aged, with speakers from the group and outside. Talks included 'a couple of Jewish book reviews; medical talks with a Jewish component; Lilith plus ghosts, etc., Hanukah, and a talk on "Honour your Father and Mother: How about Foster Parents?"'.[99] If the meeting was not on the sabbath, each attendee contributed £1 for charity,[100] and each meeting ended with time for refreshments and informal conversation. After a few years, however, the group ceased to meet.

Ironically, the concept of Rosh Hodesh groups for women has been adapted and recoded—indeed tamed—by the Orthodox establishment and the haredi world. At Mill Hill United Synagogue, the rabbi organized a women's group bearing this name, to whom he lectured on subjects he considered appropriate.[101] A haredi 'Rosh Hodesh Society', part of a Habad-Lubavitch outreach programme, is described as 'a sisterhood dedicated to inspiring and empowering Jewish women through monthly cultural learning experiences', but turns out to be a series of seven self-help lectures on 'kabbalistic insights for taking charge of your life'. At Kinloss (Finchley) United Synagogue, a 2013 event entitled 'Lunar: A Monthly Learning Event for Kinloss Women', explicitly scheduled for Rosh Hodesh, was actually an educational event about Purim, with lectures by the synagogue's female community educator and a rabbi.

The Rosh Hodesh movement in Britain was started and embraced by non-haredi women who had been brought up in traditional households, but

---

[98] Stone no longer considers herself Orthodox or religious. Of the other three women involved in the Rosh Hodesh movement whom I interviewed, one belongs to the Masorti movement and two remain within Orthodoxy, though frustrated with the lack of change.

[99] Diane Sheer, telephone conversation, 2 Dec. 2010.

[100] Money cannot be handled on the sabbath.   [101] Linda Stone, interview.

wanted greater participation in Jewish ritual and worship, more Jewish knowledge, and greater spiritual satisfaction. It was explicitly feminist, drawing on Jewish models from the USA and including elements of both consciousness-raising and action, which made it deeply threatening to the rabbinic establishment and indeed to many Orthodox men; one of my interviewees curtailed her activities as a result of her husband's disapproval and unease with her very public profile and perception as a 'difficult woman', and other women noted that they were perceived as radical and threatening. The fact that non-Orthodox women participated was also a source of alarm for the Orthodox establishment, which has generally ignored (and sometimes demonized) non-Orthodox denominations. Many traditionalist women found the movement's activities threatening to their own sense of identity, since they so clearly aimed at restructuring Jewish women's traditional roles and the wider community. These women often countered the activists' proposals by insisting on the maintenance of 'authentic', traditional roles for women.[102] Ultimately, this attempt to reshape the role of Orthodox women foundered on resistance from traditionalist laymen and women, and largely haredi rabbinic authority. It has left little obvious legacy (though two of the women's *tefilah* groups it inspired have survived), but it is of considerable significance as an example of the wider feminist movement's influence on the Orthodox world. It illustrates the possibilities for creative religious action and agency by women, and serves as an example of the way in which such action and agency in Orthodoxy are vulnerable to resistance, condemnation, and subversion by the male establishment, supported by traditionalist women who see such initiatives as a threat to their own ethnic/identity-based religious role. While it had little or no impact on haredi women, the Rosh Hodesh movement pointed up the differences between Modern Orthodox women, who were involved in it, and traditionalists, who generally were not, or who changed their stance as a result of participating.

Having examined several rituals that create separate sacred spaces for women, where their voices can be heard and their concerns highlighted, including their desire for increased spiritual engagement, I now turn to communal rituals and practices that are designed to nurture, support, and assist the community as a whole.

---

[102] The discourse on 'authenticity' is often deployed against non-Orthodoxy and initiatives to change women's roles within Orthodoxy.

Nurturing the Community

Berakhah Parties

A very different type of women's communal ritual has developed in the last decade. *Berakhah* ('blessing') parties, also known, particularly in Israel, as 'amen parties' (Hebrew: *se'udot amen*), seem to have first appeared in Israel in the early twenty-first century, but as they are so new, only one academic study of them has yet been carried out.[103] They apparently started as children's educational events, designed to teach the blessings for different types of food, and they still exist in this form alongside the women's version. Another predecessor seems to be the Sephardi custom of men reciting blessings over different types of food on the sabbath, often as part of the third sabbath meal (*se'udah shelishit*) held at the synagogue after *minḥah* (afternoon service).[104] At some point, groups of women began to assemble in order to say the formal blessings over five types of food, responding to each other's blessing with a fervent 'amen', and each blessing became associated with a particular *segulah* (e.g. the blessing over baked goods was linked to livelihood). From Israel the practice spread to the United States.

The *berakhah* party that takes place on a regular basis in London was introduced by three women, one of whom is Israeli;[105] individuals have also held them in their own homes, on a one-off basis or more regularly, publicizing the event among friends or in community newsletters and email lists. Most British Jews are unfamiliar with the practice,[106] but knowledge of it is gradually spreading, as it is in both Israel and the United States.[107]

[103] See the excellent article by Neriya-Ben Shahar, '"At 'Amen Meals' It's Me and God"', which records features that are both parallel to and significantly different from the British version. In particular, Israeli 'amen meals' are women-only events, with no rabbi present, and are characterized by a higher level of emotional community. There are now professional 'amen meals' organizers in Israel, where the practice has become popular among non-religious as well as religious women.

[104] I am indebted to Rabbi Dr Raphael Zarum for this information. Other influences, such as the kabbalistic *seder* for the minor festival of Tu Bishvat, when foods of different types are eaten in a particular, symbolic, order, may also have shaped its development.

[105] Rabbi Mordechai Locardo, interview.

[106] Neither of the two women I interviewed from the hasidic community had heard of them; nor had most of the United Synagogue women I talked to. Of five rabbis to whom I spoke, only the rabbi from the synagogue where the *berakhah* party was held knew of this practice, describing it as 'a semi-institution—it's not an old custom' (Rabbi Locardo, interview).

[107] A brief survey of Orthodox women's websites, such as Imamother, revealed that the concept was still unfamiliar to many American Jewish women in 2004 and even later, and there were frequent requests to explain the term. 'Seudat Amen', an article written to describe a *berakhah* party at a girls' seminary in Israel in 2008, noted: 'Having never heard of a *Seudat Amen*, most girls wore confused looks on their faces as they entered the classroom.'

History

One of the few written sources that discuss the ritual's origins is a work of popular piety, *Just One Word: Amen*, by Esther Stern, published in 2005.[108] It consists of anecdotes and stories that highlight the spiritual power of responding 'amen' to prayers and blessings, a concept that can be traced to rabbinic sources.[109] The book goes well beyond the classical sources, however, in assigning a miraculous effect to the enthusiastic utterance of 'amen'.[110] The book's last section deals with 'brachos parties' and provides an origin story. According to this, Rabbi Avraham Kessler, author of a book on the importance of saying 'amen', gathered twenty boys in his home on a sabbath afternoon and led them through the sequence of blessings over the five food types.[111] In a 2007 article, Shoshana Chen locates Rabbi Kessler in Benei Berak in the 1970s and claims that this original party was in response to the deaths of two children in the building where he lived.[112] At this stage there seems to have been no link to *segulot*. Stern's book describes how a young woman called Gitti witnessed this party and decided to transfer it to a girls' summer camp in Benei Berak, and how those present spontaneously linked *segulot* to each blessing.[113] A 2015 study on this phenomenon by Rivka Neriya-Ben Shahar, and Shoshana Chen's 2007 article 'The Amen Chorus', however, name a Tovi Tzeitlin Baron as responsible, rather than Gitti, and Chen mentions two other women who encouraged others to imitate the practice: Sarah Meisels and Esther Stern, the author of the *Amen* book. Another article, also written in 2007,[114] traces the practice to the death of Rebbetsin Sarah Meisels's daughter, Alte Nechama Wachsman, in an accident in 2001; in response to the tragedy, Rebbetsin Meisels, with the approval of Rabbi Chaim Kanievsky of Benei Berak, formed a group of women who met early in the morning to respond 'amen' to each other's recital of the dawn blessings (*birkhot ha-shaḥar*),[115] a variant of the ritual that has not become as popular as the 'party' version.[116] It is interesting that in this case, as with the Stanmore *tefilah* group,

[108] See also Chen, 'The Amen Chorus'.

[109] Two talmudic statements note that the letters of *amen* stand for *el melekh ne'eman*, 'God, faithful king' (BT *Shab.* 119b, *San.* 111a); another talmudic statement records that 'Resh Lakish said: He who answers "amen" with all his strength, they open the gates of paradise for him' (BT *Shab.* 119b). Compare a different evaluation of the importance of saying 'amen' in BT *Ber.* 53b: 'He who says the blessing is more quickly [rewarded] than he who answers "amen".'

[110] For more miracle stories about the power of 'amen', see Mansour, 'The Importance of Saying Amen'. [111] Stern, *Just One Word*, 176–8. [112] Chen, 'The Amen Chorus'.

[113] Stern, *Just One Word*, 178–81. [114] G. Hammer, 'The Amen Phenomenon'.

[115] The dawn blessings form the first section of *shaḥarit*, morning prayers; see *Authorised Daily Prayer Book*, 16–24.

[116] This is not surprising, since it would necessitate women leaving their homes and congregating early in the morning, just when they would be getting children ready for school.

there are several origin stories; as in that case, some seek to stress the involvement of a respected rabbi (which would automatically give the practice an
approved basis), while others emphasize the purely spiritual motives of the
women involved in starting the practice, thus deflecting possible accusations
of feminist influence.

The London *berakhah* party was initiated by three women, one of them
Israeli, who, after conducting a few parties in their own homes, went with a
dozen other women to the rabbi of the local Sephardi synagogue and asked
him whether they could hold the ritual in the synagogue; they also invited him
to speak at it. He was happy to accommodate them, and the parties began to
be held in the synagogue in about 2006, continuing at the same location ever
since.[117]

Description

The *berakhah* party, held in Hendon, takes place in the women's section of a
Sephardi synagogue, generally on Rosh Hodesh or the nearest convenient
day.[118] Long trestle tables are arranged in a U shape, covered with tablecloths
protected by clear plastic sheets, on which stand paper plates, small plastic
cups containing grape juice, paper napkins, bowls of crisps, plates of fruit,
vegetables, cake, and sweets, and bottles of fruit juice and fizzy drinks. At the
top of the U stands a small table and a pair of green armchairs, reserved for
the rabbis, and another table bears covered bowls of dough, which some participants have brought in order to perform the commandment of separating
challah (colloquially referred to as 'taking challah').[119] The Israeli organizer,
Esti, and a few volunteers are responsible for the preparations. Although the
party is advertised to start at 8 p.m., the women drift in slowly, and things only
get going after forty minutes. On a low bookcase lie paper sheets, headed in
Hebrew with 'Partners', 'Healing', 'Livelihood', 'Children';[120] those who want
the rabbi to pray for particular individuals who need help in these areas write
down their Hebrew names.

Eventually the women settle at the tables; they range from teenagers to
women in their sixties, and are of varying degrees of religious observance.[121]
Numbers vary between thirty-five and fifty, and the group seems to be com-

---

[117] Rabbi Locardo, interview.

[118] I attended some seven *berakhah* parties at this synagogue, starting on 7 Oct. 2010. I also
went to a small one held in a private house in Edgware, which seems to be a spin-off of the
Hendon one; eight people were present, and the homeowner, a Sephardi rabbi, conducted the
proceedings.   [119] See Ch. 1 n. 16.

[120] Respectively *zivug, refuah, parnasah, yeladim*, the first four of the *segulot* associated with
the blessings.

[121] Several women wore wigs, and others covered their hair with hats or kerchiefs, but there
were also several older women with uncovered hair, and occasionally some who wore trousers,

posed of roughly equal numbers of Sephardi and Ashkenazi women.[122] Many are Israeli. Friends often sit together, and the entire evening proceeds against a background of conversation in Hebrew and English, texting, and mobile phone calls; when the noise gets too loud, the organizer stands up and reminds the women, 'Ladies! We want to hear the *berakhot!*' The atmosphere is relaxed and informal, and women often interrupt the rabbi's mini-sermons with comments, corrections, and questions, as well as frequent exclamations of wonder and pious ejaculations at the culmination of miracle stories.

There are five 'rounds' of blessings, with an occasional extra one at the end. The ritual starts with the synagogue's rabbi (or the organizer if he is not present) making the *mezonot* blessing over baked goods, followed by all the women, each of whom in turn picks up a biscuit and recites the blessing, answered with an enthusiastic 'amen' by all the other women. Each round can take fifteen or more minutes, with delays as latecomers arrive and catch up on their blessings. The second round is the blessing over wine, the third that over tree fruit, the fourth over vegetables and fruit that grows on smaller plants, and the fifth the 'all-purpose' *shehakol* blessing, recited over anything not covered by the previous blessings (in this context, usually sweets). Sometimes an extra round of blessings, recited before smelling aromatic plants, is added. The organizer usually reminds the women of the associated *segulah* for each blessing at the beginning of the round. The blessings are correlated with *segulot* as shown in Table 5.[123]

Most women recite the blessings quietly and quickly, but now and then a woman stands up and announces that she is reciting the blessing to benefit a particular person (or list of people), particularly during the round for healing; sometimes she will add an extempore prayer for the safety of all Israeli soldiers or the Jewish people. The other women respond to these personal interjections with even more enthusiastic amens. The rabbi ends each round by reciting a prayer in Hebrew that emphasizes the associated *segulah.*

Between rounds, the rabbi or a guest speaker delivers a short talk;[124] it

forbidden for women in haredi circles and discouraged in synagogue contexts in the non-haredi community.

[122] Sephardim customarily recite the phrase *barukh hu uvarukh shemo* ('blessed is he, and blessed is his name') in response to the first part of a blessing, and also recite a version of the *shehakol* blessing that differs from the Ashkenazi formula (*nihyah* instead of *nihyeh*), enabling me to estimate relative numbers.

[123] Every blessing starts with the formula: 'Blessed are you, Lord, our God, king of the universe'; Table 5 contains the final words of each blessing.

[124] I only heard one female guest speaker, whose talk was unusual in that she cited precise sources, spoke from prepared notes, and had clearly structured her talk with care. All other speakers (except for a visiting rabbi from Argentina) were local rabbis who spoke off the cuff. The synagogue rabbi organizes the speakers.

Table 5 Material and spiritual benefits (*segulot*) associated with blessings recited before eating different foods

Blessing	Translation	Recited before eating	Associated benefit
Boré minei mezonot	Creator of varieties of nourishment	Baked goods	Livelihood (*parnasah*)
Boré peri hagefen	Creator of the fruit of the vine	Wine	Finding a spouse (*zivug*)
Boré peri ha'ets	Creator of the fruit of the tree	Tree fruit	Fertility (*yeladim*)
Boré peri ha'adamah	Creator of the fruit of the earth	Vegetables, fruit that grows on bushes, etc.	Healing (*refuah*)
Shehakol nihyeh bidvaro	By whose word everything came into being	Fish, meat, milk, dairy products, etc.—anything not covered by other blessings	Any petition

Note: The blessings are listed in the order specified by halakhah when one is eating several different types of food. A further blessing, *boré atsei vesamim* (Creator of fragrant trees), is occasionally recited at *berakhah* parties over fragrant plants or shrubs, with the associated benefit of the elevation of the soul (*ilui neshamah*) of a deceased person.

often refers to the weekly Torah portion or the next festival, and is inspirational in character. Miracle stories of cures or of apparent setbacks that end in unexpected rescues or opportunities to perform a commandment are frequent, and often elicit gasps of wonder or cries of *barukh hashem!* ('Blessed be God!') from the women. Current affairs are also woven in, particularly anything to do with Israel. Common themes include the power of blessings to bring protection and 'pierce the heavens', the power of prayer, and the need to acknowledge everyday miracles, as well as the superiority and spiritual nature of the Jewish people. Instances of improvement in the health of those prayed for are frequently reported by the rabbi or the women, and are attributed to the effect of the parties.

The rabbi often leaves for other duties before the end of the party (which can last three hours) or arrives late; his presence is not essential, though in his absence the women do not recite the prayer at the end of each round.[125] Nor are they particularly interested in reciting the final blessing over food at the end of the evening, and many leave without doing so.[126] A range of optional

[125] The rabbi told me that there would be no problem with the women reciting these prayers; perhaps they do not know them or do not know where to find them.
[126] Halakhically speaking, it is mandatory to recite a final blessing (*berakhah aharonah*) after consuming any food. Since this blessing has no associated *segulah*, many of the women who do not regularly recite blessings over food may regard it as unimportant; it is also much

activities may be performed between blessing rounds during the party: these include the ritual of separating challah, performed by a few women, who often recite a list of names of those in whose merit they are performing this commandment; the recital of the 'Nishmat' prayer;[127] a telephone call to a former attendee suffering from cancer, to allow her to join in the recital of blessings; a telephone call to the Tomb of Benjamin in Israel in order to receive a blessing;[128] or an opportunity to donate money, either to an institution represented by a guest speaker or to individuals who enter and request money.[129]

Significance for the Women

The *berakhah* party serves many purposes, both religious and social. Many women come every month, while others attend occasionally; since no study or preparation is involved, it attracts a wide range of women, who feel comfortable in this relaxed, convivial atmosphere, as well as having a sense of spiritual empowerment and practical achievement. Many of the women believe that the parties help others in palpable and physical ways. The advertisement for the parties on the local Jewish email list claims, 'We have seen many *yeshuot* [miracles] from these events and hope to hear many more.' One young woman told me that 'the rabbi just got a message to say someone got good test results', and attributed this directly to the party. On another occasion, it was announced that a cancer victim who had been a regular attendee had just eaten a meal for the first time in two weeks and showed signs of improvement; the women were very excited and two jumped to their feet to announce that they had performed additional pious acts on her behalf. There was a very

longer than the other blessings, thus requiring more knowledge and possibly a prayer book to provide the text. The rabbi certainly thought they should be saying it, when asked why so few women recited it.

[127] 'Nishmat' forms part of the sabbath morning service. The prayer is regarded by Sephardim as having special powers: Rabbi Locardo told me that 'it confers an extra soul' on the sabbath and that women had 'taken on' the practice of reciting it publicly. One *berakhah* party attendee told me, '"Nishmat" is to say thank you, whenever anything happens, or if somebody has a car accident, God forbid, and they've come out of it, or they've had a fire in the house, or they've lost their home, or they had a big trial. So you make a *se'udat mitsvah*, *hoda'ah* [ceremonial meal, for thanksgiving], thanking Hashem, so they always say "Nishmat"' (Menucha Mizrahi, interview).

[128] Presumably a rabbi at the tomb issued the blessing; a mobile phone was held up by Rabbi Locardo and a long, incomprehensible speech in Hebrew poured out, to which the women eagerly responded with cries of 'amen'. Printed forms were also distributed on which attendees could write requests (and fill in direct debit details for donations); these were collected to be taken to the tomb.

[129] At the first *berakhah* party I attended, a woman entered halfway through and spoke to the rabbi; he told the attendees that she was ill and had an autistic son, and urged them to help her. The women responded with overwhelming generosity (see below).

real sense of achievement among the participants. In addition, just as in the Stanmore *tefilah* group, the party provides an opportunity for women to serve as the agents of prayer for friends and family in need; this was apparent when they listed the names of those for whom they were praying, or offered more general prayers for the welfare of the Jewish people before reciting a blessing. In a world where women's voices are not heard in synagogue, the *berakhah* party provides a sacred space and time in which they are the main players, powerful and prominent. The women were very conscious of the existence of practices and opportunities for wielding such spiritual power, and the organizer and others often told them about similar events which they could attend: challah parties in private homes were advertised, for instance, with one described by the organizer as 'very powerful'.

The rabbi who acted as 'host' was aware of this:

Experience is so powerful. A *shiur* or class is passive and people feel intimidated. When all you have to do is to say a blessing, it's not intimidating. It's very empowering, it helps women's self-esteem; they leave feeling elated and special, having made a difference. . . . The women feel very holy, it works . . . It's most important that a woman can feel on top of the world by reciting a blessing, everybody can do it, plus it has educational value, they learn the correct blessings, it's didactic.[130]

The women clearly preferred to exercise such spiritual power themselves rather than delegate it, as shown by their eagerness to give money to a woman who entered to ask for donations. Seizing this opportunity to give directly to someone who needed it,[131] they crammed a few plastic cups full of £20 notes and coins, with almost every woman making a contribution. In contrast, when a visiting rabbi asked for donations to support his study institution for married men (*kolel*) and passed out direct debit forms to fill in, few women availed themselves of the opportunity, in spite of the organizer's announcement that 'They get all the *yeshuot* in the world! Put your name and they will pray for you!' A similarly half-hearted response was made to the appeal for donations for the Tomb of Benjamin.

In addition, the party is an enjoyable social occasion, at which friends can chat and enjoy each other's company, while simultaneously 'doing good'. One middle-aged woman of Tunisian origin confided to me that she was 'not religious' but liked being around religious people, and since she lived on her own, the party provided a good social opportunity: 'Yesterday I went to the theatre, tomorrow it's shul, this evening there's this.' She also took the

---

[130]   Rabbi Locardo, interview.
[131]   Not only is the giving of charity a commandment, but it is widely regarded as a powerful protective practice: 'Charity preserves from death' (Prov. 10: 2).

opportunity to fill in the form for prayers to be sent to the Tomb of Benjamin, adding a request for 'a good husband' and good health.

The *berakhah* party is an exception to the usual exclusion of women's communal religious activities from the synagogue. In contrast to the Stanmore group, it is not frowned upon by the religious authorities, but is incorporated into sacred space, with the synagogue rabbi, the representative of those authorities, present and playing a central role. It is significant that it takes place in a Sephardi synagogue, which is not controlled by the London Beth Din, and in a context of conscious Sephardi self-definition in relation to the larger Ashkenazi community. Many Sephardim feel slighted and despised by Ashkenazim,[132] and one form of response is to present the position of Sephardi women as better than that of Ashkenazi women.[133]

While *berakhah* parties in Israel and America have developed as women-only rituals, the London examples are very clearly dominated and validated by the presence of rabbis. Though this gives gravitas and an official character to the ritual, it also means that the women are not perceived as running an all-female event in the sacred space of the synagogue, thus reducing potential male opposition.[134]

The fact that the ritual itself is completely new, with no precedent, might have been expected to raise some suspicion or even condemnation in the Orthodox community, where innovation is downplayed in favour of conformity with tradition, and is sometimes used as a reason to denigrate activities.[135] Two factors account for this absence of suspicion: first, the ritual itself is made up of familiar and core practices (blessings over food), and second, it is not a practice which men have the slightest interest in reproducing—indeed, they regard it as somewhat childish. When I asked the rabbi why men would not hold *berakhah* parties, he observed:

They don't have the time, or the patience—it seems too trivial. It's a unique way for women to express their Judaism and see it as a vehicle for a relationship with the

[132] 'I think that people do still think that Sephardis don't know anything, and that we're not as learned as Ashkenazis, we're not as *frum* as Ashkenazis, and I take great umbrage, and my answer to that is, "While your ancestors were still peasants in Poland, mine were advising kings and princes in Spain."' Flora Rendberg, interview.

[133] Rabbi Locardo took care to let me (an Ashkenazi) know that Sephardi women are permitted to recite *birkat hagomel* (see above, n. 57) in synagogue, 'unlike Ashkenazi women'. In fact, some Ashkenazi women do recite the blessing in synagogue.

[134] Rabbi Locardo told me there had been no opposition; it was unlikely that anyone would object to a practice approved of and led by a respected rabbi.

[135] Cf. the London Beth Din's justification of its refusal to let a batmitzvah girl read from the Torah: 'Our mothers, grandmothers and great-grandmothers . . . were never called up to the Torah'. See the section on batmitzvah in Ch. 3.

Creator . . . for men, it's the ritual, halakhah. For women, the message conveyed by a *berakhah* is like that of a Gemara [Talmud] class for men; because women are not obliged [to undertake Torah study] and don't express themselves through Torah study, Torah commentary becomes the mitzvah. So the mitzvah becomes Torah; the Torah commentary becomes energized—whereas for men 'action' and 'commentary' are separate. What's the point of a *berakhah* unless it makes you think about relationship [with God]? Men are not able to do this. They look at the halakhah rather than at the meaning . . . According to kabbalah, learning is part of the mitzvah —this doesn't apply to every man. But that is all women do—it is not an arbitrary act. Men are only conscious of time and duty.[136]

While not entirely coherent, this comment follows a recent line of Orthodox apologetic that denigrates men's traditional activities (men are 'only conscious of time and duty') while exalting the inner, essentialist spirituality of women; unsurprisingly it stops short of applying this notion in practice, and of drawing the potential conclusion that women should therefore be in charge of their own spiritual lives and activities, and indeed should actually provide leadership and models for men. In spite of this apologetic claim, the observation that men have no interest in *berakhah* parties is confirmed by the behaviour of the men present at the parties. The rabbis who attended as speakers took no further part in the proceedings; while they did recite blessings before they ate (as they would have in any case), they did not answer 'amen' to the women's blessings, and spent the time taken up by the blessing rounds studying sacred books, texting, and talking to each other. Through the closed windows in the wall separating the women's section from the main synagogue, a dozen or so men were visible throughout the entire party, studying in small groups or on their own. It was clear to everyone that the 'trivial' *berakhah* party is for women only. The ritual can thus be seen as non-threatening, even if held in the synagogue; it simply does not compete with the central male activities of Torah study and formal prayer.

Interestingly, this male dissociation from *berakhah* parties leads to divergent understandings of the event by men and women. While the rabbi described it as an occasion for empowering women and making them 'feel holy', he also saw it as an opportunity to teach them the correct blessings. He denied any 'magic' component, offering an elaborate kabbalistic explanation of the effect of the ritual: the performance of commandments, such as reciting blessings or giving charity, leads to and expresses the repentance (*teshuvah*) of the individual, which in return is rewarded by the accumulation of merit; this enables prayer to be answered.

In contrast, the women see the ritual in a much more functional way, as a

---

[136] Rabbi Locardo, interview.

'powerful' activity that achieves tangible results through the intervention of angels, or by semi-magical means. The organizer told me that the power of the word 'amen' is immense, and that it is more important to say 'amen' to a blessing than to say the blessing itself; she also noted that 'when we say "amen", all the angels say it too'. Another attendee told me that 'A *malakh* [angel] is created for every "amen" you answer. A *malakh* that protects you and protects the person who made the *berakhah*.'[137] Just before some women took challah, the organizer announced that this was 'a very good time to make *kavanot* [prayer intentions]',[138] and another woman added that 'whatever somebody wants to wish they can wish', even if not taking challah themselves, because 'we are all part of *am yisra'el* [the Jewish people]'.[139] It was also notable that when a visiting rabbi solicited donations, he made no claims that this would have tangible results—it was a woman who remarked that his *kolel* 'gets all the *yeshuot* in the world', and another woman who observed that those who gave more than £5 would get all the benefits of the *kolel*'s prayers. On two occasions male speakers attempted to play down the thaumaturgic qualities of the ritual by observing that sincere prayer has to precede trust in the efficacy of *segulot*, and that rituals to remove the evil eye are only needed by those who have no trust in God; but this did not impress the women, in contrast to the miracle stories, which they greeted with exclamations of wonder and appreciation.

Tehilim Groups, Challah Parties, and Ahavat Yisra'el Groups

I turn now to a group of women's communal rituals that resemble the *berakhah* party in their goals and, in the case of the first two, techniques. Reciting the book of Psalms (*Sefer tehilim*) has been considered a pious activity for centuries. Many men and women recite the entire book once a week, or even once a day, often on behalf of friends or acquaintances with health or other problems. Psalm recitation is considered particularly appropriate for women, especially in haredi circles, since they do not (or are not thought to) share men's obligation to recite the three daily prayer services, or to study Torah, another source of merit. In recent years, however, a new practice has developed of women gathering to say psalms together, often dividing the book up between those present in order to complete the entire book during the session. These

[137] Menucha Mizrahi, interview.
[138] The term *kavanot* comes from the kabbalistic tradition, in which it is used in the sense of intentions in prayer for the unification and 'well-being' of the divine spheres, or *sefirot*. The women do not seem to be using the term in this sense, however, but in the sense of intending to pray on behalf of other people experiencing difficulties.
[139] The use of the word 'wish' rather than 'pray' also suggests a mechanical or magical view of the ritual's efficacy.

gatherings are usually preceded or followed by listing the names of those individuals on whose behalf the recitation is being performed; the categories of finding a livelihood, finding a marriage partner, having children, and regaining health used at the *berakhah* parties are often mentioned on these occasions too. Occasionally a *tehilim* group may be convened as a one-off event for a specific purpose, such as the one advertised in September 2012 on the EdgwareK email list: 'We are trying to organize a tehillim group for next shabbos [sabbath], which is also Rachel Imainu's [the matriarch Rachel's] yahrzeit, so the whole sefer tehillim can be said for those in need of shidduchim [matches].' There are also regular groups that meet weekly or monthly.

The group I attended in a private home in Golders Green started in 2008 in response to a particular individual's illness, and now meets once a month, on or near Rosh Hodesh. It consisted of seven haredi women, ranging in age from the twenties to the seventies.[140] All wore wigs and dark clothes. We sat around the dining table, covered with a flowery plastic cloth and surrounded by tall bookshelves housing a substantial library of classic religious texts and a large collection of family photographs. After some relaxed conversation as newcomers took off their coats, we got down to business. Each woman took a few sky-blue pamphlets from a heap on the table; these contained the book of Psalms, divided into twenty-four parts (one per booklet), produced by Aneinu ('Answer Us'),[141] an American haredi organization founded in 1999 and dedicated to encouraging Jewish women to hold communal recitations of psalms. Our hostess, Zelda Ehrlich, a rabbi's wife and librarian in her seventies, read a long prayer printed at the beginning of each booklet, and we then started reciting our individual booklets simultaneously, whispering the words rapidly under our breath. The pace seemed very fast, as I had only just reached my second booklet by the time my neighbour had completed all hers and reached for one from my pile. I finished fifth (there was a very faint flavour of a race, and clearly one was not meant to linger with devotion over every word), and waited silently with the others till the last two women completed their booklets. Zelda then recited the standard 'Mi sheberakh' prayer, asking for God's blessings on particular people; when she reached the point at which personal names are inserted, she picked up a long list of names and read them out. Each woman then kissed the booklet she was holding, and returned it to the pile before leaving; the whole recitation had taken little more than half an hour. In contrast to the rather chaotic and strongly social atmosphere at *berakhah* parties, the mood here was down to earth, focused, and business-like; the only amens uttered were said quietly at the end of the 'Mi sheberakh' prayer.

[140] I attended on 3 Mar. 2011.   [141] See the Aneinu website, <http://www.aneinu.com/>.

In contrast to the quiet, devotional atmosphere of the *tehilim* group, challah parties tend to be highly sociable. In 2012 I attended one at a private home in Edgware. It was organized by Bracha Abelman, a young, devout Modern Orthodox mother, who had read about challah parties in *Binah*, an American haredi women's magazine widely available in Britain. She originally decided to hold a challah party after the death of a young mother which had had a profound effect on the Modern Orthodox community in north-west London, both 'as a memorial and as a response'. A group of women studied the laws of taking challah during the thirty-day mourning period (*sheloshim*), and met on the thirtieth day for the actual event. They then decided to hold it every month, on or near Rosh Hodesh.[142]

When I arrived, carrying a large plastic bowl containing a packet of flour as instructed, several women were already in the spacious kitchen, unpacking their bowls and flour onto a long line of tables pushed together and covered with plastic sheets. Bottles of olive oil, salt containers, packets of dried yeast, and water jugs were arranged along the centre of the tables. More women crowded in, until there were about twenty, all talking at once. It was clear that many had not attended before, and that several had never actually made bread. Bracha had printed out a recipe for challah (which signifies both 'dough' and the braided loaves made for the sabbath), which also carried basic rules for the ritual of taking challah, including the appropriate blessing. She had some trouble making herself heard over the noise of women enquiring about the next step in the process, asking for ingredients to be passed, laughing at the mess they were making, and chatting to each other, but patiently explained, advised, and assisted, until everyone had produced a large mass of bread dough. At this point she managed to get everyone to be quiet as they kneaded their dough, and gave a homiletic explanation of the commandment, linking each ingredient with a desirable trait: 'Flour represents the energy we need for serving God . . . salt, like criticism, is painful and can sting the hearer, so should come in small doses . . . Jewish kings are anointed with olive oil. Anointing the bread for our royal table reminds us of the honour due to our friends, family, and ourselves.'

A certain amount of confusion ensued when she explained that, since none of us was making enough dough to require the taking of challah, we would have to 'combine' our dough in pairs to enable one of each pair to perform the commandment, though we could separate it afterwards and retain our own dough, to be baked at home. Bracha patiently sorted out the pairs and helped those taking challah to do it correctly and say the blessing, to which everyone responded 'amen'. Some women preceded their blessing by

---

[142] Bracha Abelman, telephone conversation, 15 Nov. 2011.

mentioning the Hebrew name of a friend or acquaintance seeking a marriage partner or suffering from illness, and 'dedicating' the merit conferred by fulfilling the commandment for their benefit. The event ended with the women braiding loaves, once again talking and asking for advice, before taking them home to bake in preparation for the sabbath.[143]

The third type of activity, the *ahavat yisra'el* group, seems to have been introduced to Britain in July 2012, when the Jewish Women's Project for Ahavas Yisrael, founded in America in 2008, was presented at a Tishah Be'av programme run by Orah, a haredi organization for women's education. The project is run from an American haredi website,[144] which provides material to be downloaded and used in discussion groups; its aim is to help women 'Learn, discuss and interact with others to learn about the tremendous mitzvah of Ahavas Yisrael—loving your fellow Jew—thereby accruing tremendous merit for Klal Yisroel [the Jewish people]'. A group for post-seminary girls in Golders Green started advertising in September 2012, and the group I visited was started in October 2012 by Deborah Greenbaum, a young married woman, who had heard about the project in a class.

About eight young women usually attend the group, which meets every month in Deborah's house, though on the occasion I visited there was only one other woman, an unmarried friend of Deborah's in her twenties. We sat in the living room, with the shelves of religious classics and long lines of family photographs typical of Orthodox homes; a book entitled *Stages of Spiritual Growth* was lying on a chair. Deborah had moved from a traditionalist upbringing towards a haredi lifestyle; she had also persuaded her parents, who live in the same house, to move from Ilford, an area with a declining traditionalist population and next to no haredim, to Edgware, which has a growing haredi community, and to adopt a more observant lifestyle. Her mother, who joined the session in the middle, wore a head covering, but her grandmother, who also lives there, did not. After bringing refreshments, Deborah handed out printed lesson sheets she had downloaded from the Ahavas Yisrael website, and read the week's lesson script aloud. We discussed the previous week's 'stretch'—a challenge 'to smile at everyone and greet them first' (neither woman could remember how she had done on this), before reading a moralistic story based on the concept of *ona'at devarim* (injuring someone by means of words), used here to indicate the need for sensitivity to others: a woman had asked to help at an engagement party but had been told there was no

[143] For an account and analysis of an Israeli challah party, in which the ritual was explicitly linked to the Temple, with the women acting as priests, see El-Or, 'A Temple in Your Kitchen'.

[144] See the Ahavas Yisrael website, <ayproject.com>. It records sixteen groups in Britain, eight of which are in London, in haredi or partly haredi areas, seven in Manchester, and one in Gateshead. Over 200 groups are listed for the USA and about twenty-five for Israel.

need. Later she phoned the organizer and explained to her how hurt she had been by her exclusion. The script underlined the moral that one should 'refrain from causing pain to another Jew', and identified the character fault presented here as 'a desire to control, and a lack of clarity in communicating'. As instructed by the script, we discussed the topic for a while, and then moved on to the next discussion topic: 'When we have the urge to be nasty, it's a sign we are suffering: is this true?', followed by another gentle, meandering, and rather directionless discussion. At one point Deborah observed that 'We should all be asking, "Am I being an *eved hashem* [servant of God] right now?"' and that this kind of issue 'is deeper than mitzvot'. After we ran out of things to say, Deborah ended the session by reading out next week's 'stretch': 'Count to ten and think what the person is really saying to you before lashing out.' The general tone of the session was that of a slightly self-conscious but very earnest self-help group, with emphasis on developing positive ethical traits.

All three groups are examples of a new trend in haredi women's religious activity. All are designed to accumulate merit on behalf of others in order to promote their welfare, in line with the central role of nurturing and protecting the family and the community assigned to women in haredi culture. It is also significant that these three groups were inspired by American haredi models or organized using material from American haredi websites of a type that has proliferated in recent years (in spite of bans on using the Internet imposed by right-wing haredi rabbis).[145] Many of these websites and the practices they promote are closely linked to non-Jewish self-help literature and movements in their emphasis on introspective analysis and improvement of one's character traits.[146] Both websites mentioned here, as well as articles about such practices in *Binah*, record the fact that these practices were initiated by women, but all these sources take great pains to emphasize that they are under rabbinic supervision and have full rabbinic approval. Women's initiatives may be praiseworthy, but in the haredi world they have to be validated by male rabbinic authority.

Like the *berakhah* party, these pietistic activities encourage women to focus on other people and their relationships with them, as well as to shape an ideal self that is self-sacrificing, considerate, and modest. They revolve around the idea of accumulating merit (*zekhut*), spiritual 'capital' that can be donated for the welfare of others rather than used for oneself.[147] A similar concept can be

---

[145] Portnoy, 'Haredim and the Internet'.

[146] Haredi 'self-help' classes specifically aimed at women are often advertised on EdgwareK. They closely resemble the techniques of producing a pious self described by Mahmood in *Politics of Piety*.

[147] The idea of *zekhut* as spiritual capital is deeply rooted in Judaism, as in the concept of *zekhut avot*, the 'merit of the ancestors', or of the biblical patriarchs, which can be mobilized on

seen in other recent pietistic practices pursued by women, such as '*leshon hara* [gossip] watches', in which women undertake to refrain from any hurtful talk or gossip for periods of several hours, thereby earning merit; or mutual prayer watches, in which childless couples undertake to pray for other couples in the same situation.[148]

Gemaḥs

A *gemaḥ* (acronym of *gemilut ḥasadim*, 'the granting of kindnesses') is a free loan society. Common in eastern Europe before the Second World War, they exist in most large Jewish communities, particularly in haredi circles, though non-haredim also run *gemaḥs*. Modern *gemaḥs* often lend items, such as wedding dresses or medical equipment, rather than making monetary loans. The EdgwareK community email list ran advertisements for about fifty *gemaḥs* between November 2010 and May 2013, only one of which offered traditional interest-free loans. The items available for loan range from clothing, baby equipment, and breast pumps to mezuzahs, balloons, folding chairs, children's Purim costumes, and bread for those who have discovered that they have run out of it after the shops close. I called about twenty-five of the telephone numbers provided, and spoke to the founders or managers of thirteen *gemaḥs*.

Nine of them had been founded and were run by women; three had been founded by married couples, and one by a man, reinforcing the claim of those to whom I talked that 'most *gemaḥs* are run by women'. Nine had been established in memory of a relation, a friend, or a neighbour, with equal numbers of men and women being commemorated, several of whom 'had no family' to remember them. The smallest consisted of a satnav device that a man lent out in memory of his father, while the largest, the Family World Clothing Gemach, was founded by two haredi women over thirty years ago; with the help of ten volunteers they supply clothes, shoes, wigs, and bed linen and other household items to anyone who needs them—'we don't ask questions'. The founder to whom I spoke regarded the enterprise as a practical expression of *ḥesed*, and felt it was supported by divine providence. She emphasized that the *gemaḥ* was organized with particular care to avoid embarrassing or shaming others—a central Jewish value; individual appointments at the ware-

behalf of the Jewish people. The idea that *zekhut* may be accumulated on someone else's behalf rather than for one's own benefit receives a particularly strong emphasis in recent haredi women's practices, parallel to the emphasis on women as enablers of husbands and children.

[148] This is not totally selfless, since there is a rabbinic dictum that those who pray for others who are in need will have their own needs fulfilled; see BT *BK* 92a. I am indebted to Ian Gamse for this reference.

house were scheduled for recipients so they would not bump into acquaintances.

Other women shared this view of the foundation and maintenance of a *gemaḥ* as a religious activity: a young woman who had set up a *gemaḥ* for Israeli sim cards with her husband, with help from her sisters, spoke of it as 'a way to do *ḥesed*', and another, South African woman, who had founded a baby and toddler equipment *gemaḥ*, 'felt that if we have things we should give them . . . my religion is a strong sense of community'.[149] The desire to perpetuate the memory of a dead relative or friend, or to 'elevate their soul', is often central: the founder of a *gemaḥ* for breast pumps and sterilisers named it after her maternal grandmother 'in her merit', and another woman had joined her two sisters in founding a *gemaḥ* for 'wedding *shtick*' (props for wedding entertainments) after their father died, '*le'ilui neshamah* [for the elevation of his soul]; we couldn't go to weddings,[150] and we wanted to bring some happiness to other people'.

As with women's involvement in welfare organizations, their founding of and extensive participation in *gemaḥ*s tend to go unnoticed as an aspect of their religious lives, but it undoubtedly plays a central role in women's desire to live in conformity with Jewish values and models.

New Developments: Sharing the Sacred with Men

Recently, a new trend has emerged within the British Orthodox community: the co-operation of men and women in creating sacred space or rituals that can be shared, at least to some extent. Once again drawing on precedents from America and Israel, small groups, predominantly of highly educated professionals in their thirties and forties from the Modern Orthodox sector of the community, have begun to hold services known as partnership *minyanim*, in which women lead non-obligatory parts of the service, as well as reading the Torah and *haftarah* and being called up to recite the Torah blessings. Women also give sermons at these services,[151] and recite Kaddish if they are mourners. The much less spectacular (and generally unremarked) practice of celebrating the birth of a daughter with some type of *simḥat bat* ceremony, which is becoming more common among the Modern Orthodox, is part of the same trend.

---

[149] She emphasized that 'community' included both Jews and non-Jews.

[150] Attendance at joyous or recreational events is forbidden in the year after a parent's death.

[151] As opposed to the United Synagogue practice of allowing batmitzvah girls (though not other women) to give a sermon only after the conclusion of the formal service.

Partnership *Minyanim*

The first partnership *minyan*, Shirah Hadashah, was founded in Jerusalem in 2002. Others have followed, with about twenty-eight groups in Israel, the USA, Canada, and Australia by 2011, and at least forty-six worldwide by 2018, thirty-three of which are in the USA.[152] Practice varies somewhat between the different groups, but common features usually include a *meḥitsah* that runs down the middle of the prayer space, so that men and women pray side by side, rather than with the women at the back; women leading non-obligatory parts of the prayers and participating in reading the Torah and *haftarah*;[153] and both women and men giving sermons. Most of those involved are Modern Orthodox and religiously observant, and are often highly educated in both secular and Jewish terms; it is notable that five groups exist close to major universities in the Boston and Cambridge area in Massachusetts, for example.

In the first decade of the twenty-first century, several British Orthodox women returned from holidays in Israel with accounts of having attended and enjoyed Shirah Hadashah, but they do not seem to have taken any steps to initiate anything similar at home until 2009, when a group of a few dozen people in north-west London, mostly young families with school-age children and parents who work in elite professions, decided to hold partnership services in private houses on Friday nights.[154] In practice this was not very different from a standard service, since the only non-obligatory part of the prayers is *kabalat shabat*, a sequence of psalms and the sixteenth-century kabbalistic hymn 'Lekhah dodi', most of which are sung by the entire community; this was duly led by a woman. A short *devar torah* was also presented by a woman, with a man leading the main part of the service. About fifty people, with a slight predominance of women, attended these services, held on a more or less monthly basis for about a year and a half. The atmosphere was joyful and enthusiastic, with sermons of high quality, often given by prominent educators. The services differed from standard synagogue prayers in the spirited

---

[152] See Fishman, foreword to Sztokman, *The Men's Section*, p. ix, on numbers in 2011; for a survey of partnership *minyanim* in Israel, the USA, Canada, and the UK in 2013, see Borschel-Dan, 'Orthodox, Separate—And Almost Equal'; for 2018, see 'Partnership Minyan Locations' on the JOFA website, which lists 33 groups in the USA, 5 in Israel, 5 in the UK, 2 in Australia, and 1 in Canada.

[153] Different parts of the liturgy carry different levels of obligation; since women are halakhically considered to have a lower level of obligation than men in certain central prayers, they cannot discharge men's obligations by leading such prayers. In partnership *minyan* practice, women generally lead *birkhot hashaḥar* (dawn blessings) and *pesukei dezimra* (a sequence of psalms), the first two sections of the morning liturgy, as well as leading the Torah service and sometimes the concluding prayers; men lead the central Shema and Amidah sections.

[154] I took part in four or five of these.

singing and the presence of women, since very few women attend standard synagogues on a Friday night.

There was some discussion about trying a sabbath morning service, which would have been much more complicated, as it necessitated the borrowing of a Torah scroll and the training of women to read it, but at this point several individuals, both men and women, became nervous, and the plan was never carried out. The principal issue of concern was that 'someone' would 'find out' that a particular person had attended, and that their children might have difficulty in being accepted at Jewish schools; for a couple of people who held prominent positions in Jewish education, there were concerns that the authorities in charge of their institutions would not approve, or that institutional funders might withdraw support if they learned of their participation. The social price of failure to conform was very apparent, for both men and women.[155] Shortly after this, the services gradually came to an end, apparently because of these fears and the lack of a strong organizer.

Not all participants were content to return to the previous state of affairs, however, and two years later some of them organized a partnership morning service on a Rosh Hodesh that fell on a Sunday,[156] immediately preceding the launch of the British branch of the Jewish Orthodox Feminist Association (JOFA) on 9 June 2013. Over a hundred people turned up, with some having to be turned away for lack of space, and two groups subsequently formed to organize services: one in Borehamwood, a commuter town just north of London,[157] and the other in north-west London. In addition to the regular services, the Borehamwood group organized a series of well-attended lectures on related halakhic issues (such as the status of the prohibition on men hearing women sing[158]), and also set up an elaborate website and an email newsletter.[159] Several of the women involved had already been active in the women's Megillah group in Borehamwood, and the experience of attending the first partnership *minyan* in June 2013 served as a catalyst for action for those frustrated with the status quo. One of the founders, Miriam Lorie, identified three main factors in the founding of the group: women's sense of

---

[155] It seems unlikely that any such social sanctions, particularly in the case of schools, could have been imposed, but the fear of them is very significant, testifying to participants' perceptions. The issues of job security and loss of institutional funding seem to be more real.

[156] The Rosh Hodesh service includes Torah reading, which makes it ideal for a partnership *minyan*: women can take part in the Torah reading, but unlike on the sabbath, travel by car is permitted, thus enabling people who live further than walking distance to attend the service.

[157] Rocker, 'Women to Lead Prayers'.   [158] On this halakhic question see above, Ch. 3, n. 29.

[159] The group later renamed itself 'Kehillat Nashira'; see their website, which includes podcasts of the lecture series and links to online articles on the subject of partnership *minyanim*, as well as details of future services.

'disenfranchisement' in Judaism, especially in contrast with their equal status in most other areas of their lives; men's and women's desire for more 'spiritual' worship; and men's and women's need for a context in which they could 'bring their whole intellectual life' to Judaism.[160] The original four core organizers gathered support at an initial meeting, at which about twenty people turned up. Subsequently, however, some felt it 'was a step too far', or were unable to participate due to the opposition of their husbands or their employment within mainstream community organizations, where they felt that affiliation with such a controversial group might be problematic. Aware that issues of boundaries and authority were very important for those who wanted to participate but lacked confidence that such services were halakhically approved, the group contacted Rabbi Daniel Sperber (b.1940), a British-born Israeli academic who has supported greater involvement for Orthodox women in religious ritual,[161] to act as their rabbinic consultant (a role he has also taken on for two other partnership *minyanim* in the UK). In addition, they deliberately refrained from introducing novel prayers or rituals, wanting it 'to feel as traditional as possible'.

By mid-2015 three new groups had been founded in Golders Green, Hendon, and Finchley, with attendance ranging from about fifty to a hundred, as well as a group in Hampstead that mostly held Friday night services.[162] Another group started services in West Hampstead in June 2018. The services are proving increasingly popular for the celebration of batmitzvah, with the girl reading part of the *parashah* or the *haftarah*, and plenty of active roles available for both male and female relatives.

I attended the first sabbath morning service in Borehamwood on 14 December 2013. It was held in a local events hall, which proved much too small for the 120 or so people who turned up, and several had to stand just outside the door, or squeeze in and sit on the floor. A children's service was organized in another room. Most participants were young—not surprisingly for a community with a high number of young families, seeking cheaper housing than that available in north-west London—and all were Modern Orthodox or traditionalist. The *meḥitsah* divided the space longitudinally, so that men and women were side by side, rather than women being behind the men, as would be more usual in other Orthodox contexts. Unusually for an Orthodox service, most women turned up at the beginning, and there was a

---

[160] Interview, Miriam Lorie, 8 Aug. 2016.

[161] See e.g. his 'Congregational Dignity and Human Dignity'.

[162] The main factor preventing them from holding regular Saturday morning services was the lack of women who had Torah-reading skills and could lead prayers. For an account of their second morning service, in Nov. 2017, see Freud-Kandel and Paris, 'Partners in Prayer'.

real sense of excitement. The preliminary sections of the service were led by a woman, a young journalist and mother who sang loudly and confidently, and subsequent sections were led by men. During the Torah reading, four women read from the Torah—it was noticeable that the standard of their reading was sometimes higher than that of the male readers—and I read the *haftarah*. At the end, the liturgical poem 'Anim zemirot' was led by two little girls. There was very little talking, and both men and women threw themselves into the singing with energy; after the service a participant noted that 'the passion of the congregation lifted my prayer', and another described it as a 'lively, uplifting, and spiritual experience'.[163] After the end of the sabbath, about twenty participants turned up for a social and educational event in a private home, featuring a talk by one of the leaders of the Jerusalem Shirah Hadashah community, as well as devotional singing, refreshments, and a chance to socialize.

Services are now held about once a month (after a brief experiment with a service once every three weeks, which proved 'too much work'). Several participants originally came 'just to watch', and gradually extended their participation and learned new skills, such as reading the Torah and leading services, as they grew in confidence. Older women who are called up to the Torah for the first time often remark that this is the first time they have ever seen the inside of a Torah scroll close up, and are often deeply moved by the experience. Miriam Lorie observed that 'there's no going back' for most people once they have attended a partnership *minyan*, and that they often become more aware of issues regarding women's seating, participation, and exclusion in standard services and more inclined to point out such shortcomings to the rabbi or other authorities. As with the women's *tefilah* groups, many participants appreciate the more spiritual and focused atmosphere of the partnership *minyan* services, especially in comparison with standard United Synagogue services, in which many men and women talk all the way through. By 2018, three batmitzvahs and one barmitzvah had taken place at the Borehamwood partnership *minyan*, and services had been held on Simhat Torah and other festivals, including a 'mixed' reading (by men and women) of the Megillah on Purim. The other partnership groups have also hosted batmitzvahs and barmitzvahs, and conducted services for Shavuot, Tishah Be'av, and other occasions in addition to sabbath services.

At the time of writing, it is too early to predict whether partnership *minyanim* will continue to flourish or even spread.[164] Initially, there were some

---

[163] These remarks tally closely with observations by Elana Sztokman in *The Men's Section*, her study of men who attend partnership *minyanim*, many of whom were seeking a more deeply spiritual experience in prayer than that provided by standard synagogues.

[164] As of 2019, the Borehamwood group is continuing to attract plenty of worshippers, numbering thirty to fifty on a Saturday morning; they have also held a very successful Simhat

rumbles of opposition from the Orthodox establishment: in December 2013 the new chief rabbi announced that such services could not be held on United Synagogue premises, but he stopped short of declaring them forbidden.[165] In 2016 two individuals associated with partnership *minyanim* were banned from leading prayers and teaching in Borehamwood United Synagogue by Rabbi Chaim Kanterowitz, the local rabbi, though this does not seem to have discouraged regular attendees from participating in the partnership services. The episode sparked off a full-scale controversy in the *Jewish Chronicle*,[166] which only died down when Rabbi Kanterowitz retracted his ban on partnership *minyan* attendees teaching in the synagogue (though he upheld the ban on them leading communal prayers on the High Holidays). However, the existence of partnership *minyanim* has undoubtedly moved the goalposts in terms of women's participation, stimulating some rabbis to provide 'something for the women'. As noted above, some rabbis have turned to the older women's *tefilah* group model to counteract the attraction of partnership *minyanim*. In addition, a handful of United synagogues have experimented with women-only Friday night services and Simhat Torah *hakafot*,[167] and in June 2018 Kinloss United Synagogue held a women-only Friday night service for a batmitzvah, with the girl leading those prayers for which a male quorum is not required.[168] Previously marginal and somewhat controversial women's activities, such as the Borehamwood women's Megillah reading, have now become completely mainstream.

If the *minyanim* continue, it will be instructive to see whether they develop along the lines described by Elana Sztokman in her analysis of similar groups

Torah morning service, with a *ḥatan torah* and a *kalat bereshit* (see the section on Simhat Torah in Ch. 3), and about eighty participants; the other groups appear to be maintaining their numbers and frequency of services, except for the one in Hendon, which suspended activity in 2019 due to difficulties in attracting the required quorum of ten men (though there were plenty of women).

[165] Much fiercer opposition was encountered in France, where in June 2017 a group of women who read from the Torah in a sabbath service in Marseilles were threatened and insulted on social media and via email; see 'Women Torah Readers'.

[166] See Rocker, '"Excluded" for Running Partnership Minyanim'; id., 'United Synagogue Rabbi Defends Restrictions'; Lorie, 'Partnership Minyanim'; and the correspondence pages of the *Jewish Chronicle*, November and December 2016.

[167] Hampstead Garden Suburb Synagogue (commonly known as Norrice Lea, the street on which it stands) held its first Friday night, women-led *kabalat shabat* service on 1 Dec. 2017, though the women then joined the men for the rest of the evening service.

[168] Although two synagogues in Borehamwood introduced women's *kabalat shabat* services shortly after the start of the local partnership *minyan*, they have struggled to survive. Ironically, at the beginning most of the women who attended the *kabalat shabat* service at Borehamwood United Synagogue were partnership *minyan* participants who felt they should support these initiatives.

in Israel, the USA, Canada, and Australia. With the exception of *simḥat bat* ceremonies, this is the first attempt in Britain by Orthodox men and women to co-operate in creating a sacred space and a form of ritual that enables women's participation, perhaps marking the beginning of a fundamental shift in Orthodox perceptions of gender, at least in some sections of the community.

Simḥat Bat Ceremonies

Though much more low-profile than partnership *minyanim*, *simḥat bat* ceremonies marking a girl's birth also provide a rare example of a ritual shared by men and women. Historical studies reveal the existence of such ceremonies,[169] sometimes held only among women in earlier periods, but in Britain they are recent, except for the *zeved bat* ('gift of a daughter') and *fada* ceremonies held by the Sephardi community:

I was taken to shul when I was a month old, by my mother and father, and I had what we call a *fada*, where I was brought in and named at a special ceremony in front of the ark on Sunday, and my sister brought me in on a cushion.[170]

The trend towards marking a daughter's birth has grown considerably in the last three or four decades, particularly in America and Israel, and these foreign models have probably influenced developments in Britain. *Simḥat bat* is particularly popular among the Modern Orthodox, less usual among traditionalists, and unknown in the haredi community. In October 2003 the chief rabbi, Jonathan Sacks, composed a *simḥat bat* ceremony for his granddaughter, partly based on the traditional Sephardi *zeved bat* ceremony.[171] This text was circulated and used by others, and was incorporated into the new edition of the United Synagogue prayer book, published in December 2006, at the chief rabbi's insistence.[172] It has since been used by many families; in late 2013 it was even used in a ceremony held in Finchley United Synagogue, led by a rabbi. Others prefer to design their own ceremony, which often incorporates elements such as readings about female biblical figures, a *devar torah* given by a parent or a friend, refreshments, and an explanation of the baby's names.[173] Because *simḥat bat* is a new, unofficial ceremony, with no fixed form or halakhic rules, women often play a prominent role—reading texts or

[169] The Ashkenazi Hollekreisch (a naming ritual for baby girls) and Sephardi *zeved bat* are examples. See Ch. 6.

[170] Flora Rendberg, interview. No other interviewees mentioned any birth-connected ceremony, either for themselves or for their daughters. [171] Eve Sacks, email, 27 Jan. 2014.

[172] Elkan Levy and Simon Gould, both involved in producing the prayer book, confirmed this in personal conversation, 11 Feb. 2014.

[173] Among Ashkenazim in Britain, it is customary to give children both an 'English' and a

giving a speech—in stark contrast to traditional *berit milah* (circumcision) ceremonies, in which the only female role is for a female friend of the family to
carry in the baby and hand him to a man,[174] who takes him to the father. At a
berit, the mother plays no role at all; she usually sits anxiously in another
room while the baby is socialized into the male world by men; at a *simḥat bat*,
in contrast, she often gives the *devar torah* or speaks about the baby's name.

The *simḥat bat* is a unique example of a non-traditional, female-focused
ceremony in which women play a role alongside men, and which seems to be
accepted by the traditionalists and Modern Orthodox alike, with no opposition—in contrast to partnership *minyanim*. Once again we see that new ceremonies with no halakhic implications and no intrusion upon male ritual
ground arouse little resistance, particularly if they are initiated or explicitly
approved by rabbinic authorities,[175] in contrast to women's participation in
the performance of traditional rituals that are perceived as constitutive of
masculinity, as in the case of the partnership *minyanim*.

Consideration of these non-official communal rituals provides further support for the threefold division of Orthodox women into haredi, Modern
Orthodox, and traditionalist groups. In the ritual practices examined above,
the key element is that of male initiation or approval of the practice. If it is initiated or approved by a rabbi, as with *berakhah* parties, problematic elements
of innovation or location in the sacred space of a synagogue can be ignored.
This is the type of communal ritual initiated and promoted by haredi women.
If women initiate and carry through a practice in the face of rabbinic disapproval, however, the innovative elements are precisely those that are cited as
preventing its approval. The only women unhappy enough with the current
state of affairs to run this risk are some of the Modern Orthodox. Traditionalist women tend to accept the status quo, especially those whose attachment
to Orthodoxy is ethnic rather than religious or 'spiritual'; for them the existing rituals and roles are definitive of their identity, and any change to them
is likely to be viewed as a threat. This accounts for the opposition to initiatives such as women's prayer services or partnership *minyanim* frequently
expressed by non-observant women.

'Jewish' name, the latter usually replicating the Hebrew or Yiddish name of a deceased relative.
Sephardim often name children after living relatives.

[174] The woman is called a *kvaterin*, and usually the man she hands the baby over to is her
husband (the *kvater*); this honour is often given to childless couples. See Ch. 6.

[175] The ceremony's authorship by the chief rabbi and its inclusion in the Orthodox prayer
book provided it with official backing, neutralizing wariness about such a major innovation.

In addition, the more a practice replicates a traditionally male activity, such as communal performance of liturgy or Torah reading, the less likely it is to be approved, since it is perceived as threatening gender roles and invading exclusively male territory. Since public ritual is constitutive of Orthodox masculinity, women's performance of it has implications that go far beyond the halakhic issues. Women's activity in setting up and running *gemaḥ*s is thus unproblematic, as these have no ritual or gendered character, but women's Megillah readings and *tefilah* groups, in contrast, are contested. Though some haredi women do attend women's Megillah readings, no such readings have been set up by them, and I do not know of any haredi women who have attended the more controversial *tefilah* groups; surprisingly, one or two have ventured to attend partnership *minyan* services.

Both these principles—the importance of male initiation or approval of a practice, and its resemblance to traditionally male activities—are illustrated in the history of the Stanmore Women's Tefillah Group. Although it was originally set up either on the local rabbi's initiative or with his support, the London Beth Din, a higher source of rabbinic authority, deemed it transgressive and took active steps to discourage and control it.[176] As noted in Chapter 3, in most Orthodox communities, women's absence from synagogue is not generally remarked upon. However, the concept of women attending and running a service that parallels the standard one is immediately seen by the authorities as a challenge, and as potentially subversive; hence the insistence of the London Beth Din, when the women's service was finally allowed to take place in the synagogue, that the group's name be changed to 'The Women's Learning Experience', to avoid the implication that they were praying or holding a ritual comparable to what was going on in the synagogue sanctuary.

In the haredi sector, women who promote new practices such as *tehilim* groups and *ahavat yisra'el* groups feel that they must obtain rabbinic approval. Even though many of these practices aid the construction of a pious and ethical self, as described by Saba Mahmood, the aims and nature of this pious ideal are controlled by the male hierarchy, so that women's agency is largely exercised around and within the constraints imposed by men and male-determined ideals of pious women (a point underemphasized by Mahmood). In spite of this, however, women's different interpretations and understandings of their activity can undermine established relations of power, even unintentionally, as in the case of *berakhah* parties. These new rituals parallel the feminist concept

[176] They also intervened in 2014 to prevent the Torah scroll being carried by a woman through the women's section at Golders Green United Synagogue in sabbath morning services, even though they acknowledged that there was no halakhic bar to this, and the synagogue's rabbi had introduced the practice in response to requests from women. The reason given was that the practice was not according to 'the *minhag* [custom] of the synagogue'.

of 'women's spaces', encouraging and enabling women's autonomy,[177] although this, along with the participants' sense of power and control of events, goes unnoticed by male authorities, who might well be disturbed by these aspects and by the thaumaturgic interpretations of the ritual given by some attendees.

Traditionalist women generally shun or even oppose innovations in women's ritual roles, unless male authorities approve them: many of them strongly oppose women's prayer services and partnership *minyanim*, while they often attend events such as *berakhah* and challah parties, which run no risk of being categorized as inauthentic and hence threatening their Jewish identity. They do not initiate new rituals and generally display little interest in reaching new spiritual heights or creating a pious self; their main interest in attending communal rituals appears to be social, reinforcing their sense of Jewish identity and community belonging.

Having examined the different ways in which these three types of Orthodox women relate to both completely new rituals and female performance of existing rituals, we can consider some wider implications of the significance and contestation of ritual activity. In *Ritual Theory, Ritual Practice* (1992), Catherine Bell describes ritualization as 'first and foremost a strategy for the construction of certain types of power relationships effective within particular social organizations'.[178] She builds upon Michel Foucault's characterization of power as 'a mode of action' that seeks 'to structure the possible field of action of others',[179] and on his observation that 'power is exercised over free subjects and only so far as they are free'. This leads her to note that 'The deployment of ritualization, consciously or unconsciously, is the deployment of a particular construction of power relationships, a particular relationship of domination, consent, and resistance.'[180] In contrast to earlier theorists, such as Steven Lukes and Abner Cohen, who view power in terms of sovereignty and strategies of control, Foucault's more diffuse account of power, not as founded on coercion but as essentially embodied in a web of relationships, provides a better understanding of this dimension of ritual. However, Bell would advance beyond Foucault's conception of power relationships as inevitably containing an element of resistance, a 'means of escape or possible flight',[181] to modulate this dichotomous view (power–resistance) with a more nuanced approach that examines the interplay and intensity of elements such as consent, empowerment, appropriation, negotiation, resistance, and coercion that continuously shape every ritual. She argues for a more contextual-

---

[177] McFadden, 'Why Women's Spaces Are Critical'.
[178] *Ritual Theory, Ritual Practice*, 197.
[179] Ibid. 200, quoting Foucault, 'The Subject and Power'.
[180] Ibid. 206.   [181] Ibid. 201, quoting Foucault, 'The Subject and Power'.

ized analysis of ritual: 'Ritual acts must be understood within a semantic framework whereby the significance of an action is dependent upon its place and relationship within a context of all other ways of acting: what it echoes, what it inverts, what it alludes to, what it denies.'[182]

Such a set of complex power relationships is evident in the standard services held in Orthodox synagogues in London; equally, the establishment of women-only versions of these services, whether *tefilah* groups or Megillah readings, produces an alternative set of relationships. (Yet another set of such relationships is created by the completely new rituals of the *berakhah* and challah parties.) When women's rituals are viewed in these terms, it is not surprising that those whose power is expressed in existing rituals find the women-only versions disturbing, undesirable, and potentially divisive. The presence of women, as a sector of the community, in the ladies' gallery in an Orthodox synagogue is consequently recoded as an essential part of the standard ritual, with accusations that those who attend women's services are 'dividing the community'. This explains why the Orthodox establishment finds it impossible to tolerate the absence of women involved in a 'rival' ritual, in spite of not noticing their absence in other contexts. Individual attendance is not the issue here: as noted above, Orthodox women do not arrive at the beginning of the service and frequently leave before the end, and their absence is not generally remarked upon. However, when women themselves run a service that parallels the standard, male-led one, this is seen as challenging and potentially undermining the status quo.

A vivid example of 'a particular relationship of domination, consent, and resistance', as postulated by Bell, is illustrated here. On the other side of this relationship, the women involved in the *tefilah* groups are aware of the authorities' perception of their activities. In response they stress their desire for spiritual fulfilment (an unimpeachable aim) and their readiness to comply with the Beth Din's demands that they omit use of the central symbol of a standard service—the Torah scroll—and the prayers that may only be said by a *minyan*, which synecdochically symbolizes the community. Far from desiring to seize power or to reverse the gender relationships embodied in Orthodox ritual,[183]

---

[182] Ibid. 226.

[183] Their opponents often accused them of 'wanting to be like men', and labelled them as 'feminists' (not a positive word in the Orthodox community), although very few of the women involved would have identified themselves as feminists. See letters to the editor, *Jewish Chronicle*, cited above, n. 25. For a perceptive analysis of the antagonism to feminism in Modern Orthodoxy in spite of its enthusiastic integration of other aspects of Western liberalism, such as its ethical principles, see Hartman, *Feminism Encounters Traditional Judaism*, ch. 1, and for a more positive Modern Orthodox response, see Harris, *Faith without Fear*, ch. 2.

they use every opportunity to obtain rabbinic approval, and decline to 'opt out' of the Orthodox community, often to their own disadvantage.[184]

The differences between the rituals described in this chapter, as well as their differing receptions, can indeed be seen in terms of what the new rituals 'echo . . . invert . . . allude to . . . and den[y]'. When women's prayer services echo standard, male-led services but invert the gender of the leaders, denying men's exclusive power to lead and represent the entire community, they become troubling and illicit; when *berakhah* parties allude to a minor, non-obligatory ritual such as a Tu Bishvat *seder*, and echo traditional ideas of women's nurturing role, they are perceived by men as harmless and unthreatening—though it is noticeable that women describe them as 'powerful'. Indeed, when the wider context changes, as with the introduction of the highly threatening partnership *minyanim*, which assert much more balanced (though not egalitarian) gender roles, the previously dangerous women's gatherings may be re-evaluated as a protective measure that can be employed to ward off the greater danger and may therefore be recategorized as acceptable, as has happened in some United synagogues from 2015 onwards.

---

[184] Though exit has its own price; see Reitman, 'On Exit', where she speaks of the 'socio-psychological' obstacles facing those who consider leaving minority communities: 'fear of ostracism by family, friends, associates and community . . . the loss of moral support and the sense of belonging and rootedness derived from community . . . change and the unknown . . . obstacles which stem from the fact that cultural membership can be pervasively defining of one's sense of self' (p. 195).

FIVE

THE VIEW FROM THE KITCHEN: WOMEN'S 'OFFICIAL' LIFE IN THE FAMILY

It's the woman who keeps things going, I mean if the woman doesn't want to keep kosher there's *no way in the world* the house will be kosher . . . I think the woman's role is *very* important, I think it's even more important than the man's role, because it's the wife who does the things that ensure continuity.

FLORA RENDBERG, interview

A FTER having examined women's activity in the communal, public sphere, I now turn to their life at home and as individuals. Orthodox Judaism is firmly rooted in the world of everyday action: several central commandments and their halakhic elaboration include activities such as the preparation and consumption of food, the observance of the weekly sabbath and numerous festivals, dress, education, and the recital of blessings before and after eating and in other daily contexts. The home is explicitly designated as a sacred sphere, to a greater extent than in Christian and general British culture. The sociologist Nancy Ammerman, in her survey of everyday religion in *Sacred Stories, Spiritual Tribes*, feels obliged to urge the study of all aspects of daily life, not just formal religious affiliation and religious institutions, in order to find 'the presence of religion in society', and pleads with scholars to 'put away the biases about "real religion" that have often characterized scientific attempts at explanation'.[1] Such study is a natural and essential part of investigating Orthodox Jews.

Since Orthodox Judaism has always defined women's role as primarily domestic, it is essential to look with fresh eyes at this 'official' sphere of women's religious lives in order to compare reality with the ideal, and to discover how women understand their role as Jewish women and the place of domestic activity within that role. I will start by considering a standard, male-authored description on the website of Habad:

In a Jewish household, the wife and mother is called in Hebrew *akeret habayit*. This means literally the 'mainstay' of the home.[2] It is she who largely determines the

---

[1] *Sacred Stories*, 5.

[2] The phrase comes from Ps. 113: 9: 'He gives the barren woman [*akeret*] a home, making her

character and atmosphere of the entire home . . . She has been entrusted with, and is completely in charge of, the *kashrut* of the foods and beverages that come into her kitchen and appear on the dining table.[3] She has been given the privilege of ushering in the holy Shabbat by lighting the candles on Friday . . . Thus she actually and symbolically brightens up her home with peace and harmony and with the light of Torah and mitzvot. It is largely in her merits that G-d bestows the blessing of true happiness on her husband and children and the entire household.

In addition to such mitzvot as candle-lighting, separating challoh [challah] from the dough, and others which the Torah entrusted primarily to Jewish daughters, there are matters which, in the natural order of things, lie in the woman's domain . . . This refers to the observance of Taharat Hamishpachah,[4] which by its very nature lies in the hands of the Jewish woman. The husband is required to encourage and facilitate this mutual observance; certainly not hinder it in any way, G-d forbid. But the main responsibility—and privilege—is the wife's.[5]

This somewhat idealized rabbinic picture focuses on the traditional three 'women's mitzvot', though they do not encapsulate the entire range of women's domestic role: in the interviews, the religious activities of which women spoke included preserving family traditions, making and serving food for the sabbath and festivals, hosting guests, cleaning for Passover, visiting the cemetery, praying, and educating their children. Though most married (and some unmarried) women light sabbath and festival candles, they usually talked about this in the context of sabbath preparations; very few mentioned the observance of menstrual purity laws or going to the *mikveh* (ritual bath), partly because of the private nature of these practices and partly because many United Synagogue women do not observe these rituals; and many women do not make their own challot, since challah is easily available in Jewish bakeries.

Though the Habad source quoted above presents women as central, powerful figures, 'largely determin[ing] the character and atmosphere of the entire home', it ignores the fact that women do not usually lead or perform most of the home-based rituals, such as reciting the blessings over wine and bread on the sabbath,[6] reciting Havdalah at the end of the sabbath, reciting the blessing over the search for *hamets* on the night before Passover,[7] leading the Pass-

the joyous mother of children.' A midrashic interpretation links the root of the word *akeret* with *ikar*, 'principle' or 'main part' (hence 'mainstay'), rather than with *akarah*, 'barren woman'; see *Bereshit rabah* 71: 2.

[3] In practice, the kashrut of the food the housewife buys is guaranteed by a complex system of predominantly male supervision of food manufacturers; in addition, any question regarding kashrut is meant to be referred to a rabbi.

[4] See Ch. 1, n. 17.   [5] Dubov, 'What Is the Role of the Woman in Judaism?'

[6] Even in exclusively female households, women will often ask a male guest to recite these blessings, and only perform these rituals themselves if no men are present.

[7] *Hamets*, 'leavened food', is forbidden on Passover. After intensive cleaning (see below), a

over Seder, and so on, all of which are conventionally performed by men, even though women have an equal obligation to perform these rituals (with the possible exception of Havdalah[8]). The only exception to this lack of ritual performance is the lighting of sabbath candles, though it is not reserved for women: it is halakhically incumbent upon the household, rather than the individual, and is performed by men in the absence of a woman. Sabbath and festival candle-lighting has been associated with women from rabbinic times, but this may originally have had to do more with the fact that men are supposed to be in synagogue at candle-lighting time than with a recognition of women's ritual role within the home. Only in some Modern Orthodox families have women and men renegotiated the performance of these home rituals, as documented below.

The conception, nurturing, and education of children are often seen as central to the Jewish woman's role, even though no formal commandments are entailed: both procreation and education are halakhically incumbent on Jewish men, but not on Jewish women. Nevertheless, both men and women see these as central concerns, and women often compromise on their own religious needs or desires for the sake of their children—whether in attending synagogues where they feel alienated but their children can enjoy a friendly children's service; in refraining from controversial practices or conforming to religious standards with which they do not identify in order to get their children into a particular Jewish school; or in missing educational opportunities, women's services, or religious events in order to be present at a child's activity.

It seems clear that it is not halakhah alone that determines what women do and do not do in the domestic context. Family tradition is often much more important in women's accounts, as well as their perception that they are responsible for the continuity of Jewish tradition and affiliation to the Jewish community; another crucial factor is the social pressures exerted by that community.

The Sabbath

Most interviewees spoke of the sabbath (shabat) as central to their lives, religious practice, and Jewish identity. Even in the past, when many Jewish

ritual search for ḥamets is conducted the night before Passover, customarily by candlelight, and preceded by a blessing; in one common variant of this, families 'hide' ten pieces of ḥamets to be found during the search.

[8] Some authorities permit women to make Havdalah (e.g. Karo, Shulḥan arukh, 'Oraḥ ḥayim', 296: 8), while others recommend that they hear a man recite it (e.g. Moses Isserles ad loc.; Israel Me'ir Hakohen, Mishnah berurah, 297: 35), though they permit women to recite it if no man is present.

parents could not afford to take off time from work for the sabbath, women marked it as sacred time, often by preparing special food. Katherine Marks remembers that when she was growing up in a strongly Jewish but not very observant family,

Friday night was Friday night. Friday night we lit the candles, always on time, whenever that was. We didn't make Kiddush, we didn't *bentsh* [say grace], but my mum would make chicken and also she would do *cholent* for *shabat* lunch, and my mum had her own [practices]—you know there was no washing or ironing on *shabat*, it was a different day for her, although she would be quite happy to watch TV or write things or break some of the *halakhot* [laws],[9] but the day was conceptually different.

This pattern continues today, with space made for *shabat* at differing levels of observance:

Friday night we don't [go to synagogue]—George doesn't go, and we do have the TV on, we've got it on a timer switch. We'll change the channel, but not turn it on and off, that's our line in the sand. We've got the lights on a time switch. In the winter we'll eat at 6, in the summer we eat [later], when George's come home and checked his emails and whatever—the computer doesn't get switched on on *shabat*. And then we have dinner and we watch a bit of TV. And on *shabat* morning we'll go to synagogue most weeks.[10]

Watching television on the sabbath, even if on a time switch and thus not technically violating sabbath laws prohibiting the operation of electrical appliances, would be viewed as inappropriate in mainstream Orthodox thought, while changing channels would be forbidden. Nevertheless, even those who do not conform to Orthodox standards of practice clearly maintain a strong sense of the sanctity and special nature of the sabbath.

Many women organize their week around the sabbath: 'My week revolves round making Friday night dinner', said Belinda Cohen, and several other women were intensely conscious of its approach. When asked how she thought of her 'Jewish week', Flora Rendberg immediately responded, 'What I might do on Sunday, if I was running low, would be my *shabat* salads . . . I do make special salads which we only have on *shabat*, and there are three of those.'

Sabbath preparations take on their own ritual quality for some women, like Belinda Cohen:

On Friday afternoons I'm winding down my week. I have a ritual: I do the cooking in the morning, I usually go to the hairdresser . . . I come home, the table's set, I get

---

[9] These practices would not be acceptable in an Orthodox reading of halakhah.

[10] Flora Rendberg, interview.

everything ready, and I sort of feel I'm closing down until *shabat*. I make a few phone calls to see how people are, catch up, and then there's a sort of quiet lull. I don't tend to do very much on a Friday afternoon, it's quite unusual if I do, maybe visit someone if they're not well, but mostly I'm just waiting for *shabat*.

The creation of personal rituals extends into the sabbath itself, as Katherine Marks described:

I really do light *shabat* candles on time, that's important to me. I like the idea that I'm going in the rhythm of the sun setting or whatever, and I will make enormous efforts to make sure that I'm home, and that's not such a small thing. It's got to be a different day for me, so I will put away the kettle, not because it's *muktseh* so much halakhically,[11] but just because that's part of my private ritual to put it away and then to get it out *motsa'ei shabat*.[12] I'm almost going *beyond* what I have to do there, but I do clear the kitchen of all appliances, not because I think I'm going to use them, but just because it will *remind* me that it will be *shabat*. Also, non-halakhic things like I don't bake, except I do bake on a Friday if I can, so that there is some fresh homemade something for *shabat* breakfast, because again *shabat* breakfast is a different meal . . . I won't wear trousers on *shabat*, it wouldn't feel right. Now, what's that? That's not halakhic, that's not even metahalakhic, that's not even anything, but there are ways that I will remind myself that it's *shabat*.

Women often expressed a deep attachment to lighting sabbath candles, as did Shirley Daniels, who reflected on the sense of continuity with the biblical and more recent past that the ritual gave her: 'Sarah Imenu [the biblical matriarch Sarah] lit candles for *shabat* . . . we still do the same thing today, like my grandmother's grandmother's grandmother's grandmother's grandmother, we all did it, *erev shabat*, two of them, at that time.' However, not all women light candles; as we have seen earlier, in many families it is only the mother who performs the ritual.[13]

Sabbath observance was also one of the markers by which women measured their own religious position in comparison with that of their parents, and by means of which they expressed changes in their religious lives and identity. Several women spoke of an early desire to engage more deeply with *shabat* than their parents had; Katherine Marks 'created a home which was *shomer shabat* [sabbath observant]' when she married, and so did Miriam Rothman:

[We] three daughters kept *shabat* more than Mum and Dad did, so for example very quickly we didn't want to drive on *shabat*, or phone or anything like that,

---

[11] *Muktseh*: a halakhic term referring to objects that cannot be used on the sabbath and therefore may not be handled.

[12] Lit. 'the goings out of the sabbath': Saturday night after the end of the sabbath.

[13] See Sheyna Marcus's remarks on candle-lighting in Ch. 3 above.

even though my parents still would if they were invited to a family barmitzvah or whatever in London, they would drive. But we decided very quickly that we wouldn't, and they were very supportive of that despite the ribbing, especially from my mother's family, who were *very very* traditional, but very suspicious of over-enthusiastic religiosity.

A more recent, though less widespread, change can be seen in the gradual shift in some Modern Orthodox families to women performing some or all of the domestic sabbath rituals hitherto reserved for men, often alternating with their husbands. In several homes women now recite the blessing over the sabbath challot, particularly if they have baked them themselves, or they will take turns in reciting Kiddush, or, more rarely, Havdalah. This is not something that they had seen their mothers do, but rather is the result of a family's decision to alter traditional practice while respecting halakhah in order to give women a greater ritual role. For women like Keturah Allweiss, this is linked with a desire to provide their children with positive models of active, engaged women:

Usually on a Friday night I make Kiddush somehow, because we just ended up with that . . . and we encourage our children each to make Kiddush; it takes a long time on a Friday night, especially as now obviously the boys do it because they're older, but now Rachel's actually saying it along with me . . . Rachel's 6, and Margalit's 3. So Margalit always says *bore peri hagafen* [the final blessing of Kiddush], but Rachel, she started to say Kiddush with me. And sometimes we give them their own challot, but always the same for the girls and the boys. And if we have three women and only two men, [my husband]'s always the one to say, '*Nu*, are you going to do a women's *mezuman*?'[14] And I sometimes do and I sometimes don't, because if I have a woman who really would just wince at the thought of it, it's not worth [it]. I don't want to make people in my home feel uncomfortable, so I have to find that balance.

Most traditionalist women are unaware that women may perform such rituals according to halakhah. In contrast, haredi women actively expressed a lack of interest in performing rituals that they regarded as properly per-formed by men, even if they knew that halakhically they could perform them themselves; this may be in reaction partly to 'outsider' and feminist criti-cism of traditional Jewish women's roles, and partly to a perception of women's performance of these rituals as an aggressive 'feminist statement'. Kate Mosko-

---

[14]　*Mezuman* is the term for a halakhically defined group of three individuals who have eaten together and who must add an introductory paragraph to the standard Grace after Meals. A wide range of halakhic opinions exists on whether three women eating together may or should con-stitute a *mezuman* group: see 'Zimun—Party of Three: III. Women and Zimun' on the Chabura-Net website. In terms of current British practice, traditionalist and haredi women do not form a women's *mezuman* in the presence of men (and generally not even when only women are present); a few Modern Orthodox families do so.

vitz reacted defensively to my question about how she saw the role of Jewish women:

I just can't think of anything that [my husband] does that I'm glad to do . . . well, when he's not around I can make Kiddush but I'm *very much* happier to give it over to one of my sons, which of course they would do, it would be a son doing it, but if they're not there I would do it. I wouldn't make Havdalah though.

Women's performance or non-performance of such home rituals has become something of a shibboleth in the Jewish community: their participation instantly marks a family as Modern Orthodox and actively seeking change in women's roles. Like Keturah Allweiss, I often experience this tension between accommodating traditionalist guests and upholding my own liberal halakhic position at sabbath meals; the conflicting pulls of community expectations and individual conviction are epitomized in this balancing act. The sabbath is a beloved source of spiritual and physical rest and recharging for Orthodox Jews, but it also provides both new opportunities for women to expand their ritual roles and sources of communal tension.

Food and Kashrut

The women I interviewed often discussed food in relation to the sabbath, emphasizing the central role that sabbath meals, particularly Friday night dinner, play in uniting and maintaining the family. Many families actively seek guests for sabbath and festival meals, especially those who live alone, the elderly, and travellers.[15] The elaborate network of reciprocal (and non-reciprocal) invitations to sabbath and festival meals is another dimension of the creation and maintenance of community networks, embodied in women's activity. Women prize and regularly make traditional family recipes,[16] especially those associated with particular festivals, thus acting as guardians of family continuity. For Flora Rendberg, festivals (and even fasts) were principally defined by the 'correct' food:

I still make on festivals the same things that my mother would make, so for Rosh Hashanah we have the soup of seven vegetables, which we must have on Rosh Hashanah otherwise it isn't Rosh Hashanah. It has chickpeas and all different root vegetables in it. And we'll have couscous on the first day of Rosh Hashanah, also, and on Shavuot we have couscous, that's a tradition also . . . I'm very particular: to

---

[15] Rebbetsins in particular are expected to host guests, whom their husbands often bring back from synagogue with no prior notice, and regard this as a central religious duty.

[16] Some insisted on giving me detailed recipes during interviews; in the same vein, Martha Hubert ended her *Jewish Women's Handbook* with five pages of family recipes.

start Tishah Be'av we must have split pea soup and hard-boiled eggs, and I make boiled potatoes, and we always break the fast on fried fish and grilled pepper and tomato salad.[17]

A food-related commandment performed principally by women is that of giving *mishlo'ah manot* at Purim. Though it is equally incumbent on men and women, in practice it is usually women who prepare and package the food, with men often serving as delivery boys. Although the halakhic minimum for correct performance of this commandment is to give two types of food to one individual, women from across the entire Orthodox spectrum often give large and elaborate food gifts to dozens of friends, frequently including home-made specialities. There is sometimes a perceptible air of competition, and the judging of reciprocal gifts is a fine art; food and its distribution form one of the arenas in which women compete for social and religious status. Some families deliberately avoid this temptation by giving the minimum food gift to one friend, and then distributing cards to other friends that record a donation made to a food charity on behalf of the recipient.

In many communities, especially haredi and young Modern Orthodox ones, women from the synagogue will organize ad hoc rotas for the supply of food to newly bereaved families, or to couples who have just had a baby, usually for a week but longer if needed. This practice is significant to women on several levels: it is a practical form of community-building, embodying women's perception of their role as maintaining and nourishing families and communities; it is also an important part of the practical mitzvah of *ḥesed*, in which they are deeply involved, as well as part of the mitzvah of comforting mourners; and it is a source of merit.

In the complex and multifaceted process of food preparation as a religious activity, London Orthodox women closely resemble the elderly Sephardi women of Jerusalem studied by Susan Sered, who,

as feeders of the hungry and the link between the generations, tie together the Jewish people, connecting the future with the past, the stranger with the friend, the rich with the poor, the biological kin with kin of a more mythical nature . . . the giving itself is a sacred act, one that makes them holy, puts them into closer contact with divinity.[18]

For London women too, 'Food is central to the women's understanding of sacred time',[19] and, just as for the Jerusalem women, feeding family, friends, and strangers has a deep spiritual significance. Sarah Segal, a young hasidic mother, noted:

---

[17] Flora attached extra importance to food as a way of preserving her specific Gibraltarian identity within a larger Jewish identity.   [18] Sered, *Women as Ritual Experts*, 93.   [19] Ibid. 95.

For example if I would squeeze out a carrot for a drink [for my son], it's not that I'm just giving him a drink but I'm also giving [it to] somebody who's going to be doing something spiritual with that carrot juice inside him, so everything has that added dimension to it, because you know it's for a higher purpose really . . . not that I think about that enough, but that's the thinking beneath everything.

However, unlike the elderly Sephardi women, and indeed their own grandmothers, London women are less confident and empowered in their kashrut practices. While Sered's informants told her that 'they never need to ask a rabbi questions involving kashrut; they already know everything that they need to know',[20] most women in London are far more dependent on male-administered and controlled systems of kashrut supervision, organized by the London Beth Din, the Sephardi Kashrut Authority, the Federation Kashrut Authority, and the UOHC's Kedassia authority, and on the decisions and standards of rabbis. Classes on kashrut, initiated and taught by rabbis, are frequently run by United synagogues and educational institutions nowadays, whereas in the past women learnt kashrut rules from their mothers. Several different standards of kashrut are operative in the community, from haredi insistence on rabbinic supervision of all prepared (and some raw) food products (such as milk, sugar, and eggs[21]), through Modern Orthodox and traditionalist reliance on the standards prescribed by the United Synagogue's food guide (which permits unsupervised milk and several other unsupervised products),[22] to a variety of personal interpretations among less observant traditionalists that include maintaining basic kosher standards at home but eating non-kosher food outside the house. The question of who will eat in whose house can become a major social issue, and women are very aware of this:

I shop for general groceries in supermarkets, but what I call *Jewish* bits and pieces I buy only in Jewish shops, kosher shops. And I don't buy anything that is not kosher or supervised in terms of like cheese or things like that; you know, people might say, 'It's OK, it's vegetarian', I don't, so I hope I can have the rabbi into my home if he would come.[23]

Standards have become increasingly strict in recent decades, with foods that were often not considered problematic earlier now being subject to regulation.[24] One woman told me, 'there was no such thing as "kosher cheese" when I was growing up—we just ate ordinary cheese', and others echoed this.

---

[20] Ibid. 89.

[21] Since bloodspots in eggs render them unkosher, many haredi women now buy only 'candled' eggs, which have been checked for bloodspots.

[22] The *Really Jewish Food Guide*, produced annually by the London Beth Din Kashrut Division.

[23] Belinda Cohen, interview.

[24] For instance, Martha Hubert's *Jewish Woman's Handbook* includes a mention of 'Flora

Several women remembered their parents' kashrut standards as considerably more lenient than their own, as did Katherine Marks:

My parents kept kosher in the home, but ate out,[25] very occasionally would eat *treyf* [non-kosher] out, but be very upset to do it in front of me. Occasionally on holiday there were sort of crises that I can remember.

'Keeping kosher' is a major feature of Jewish identity, and, along with sabbath observance, is one of the main areas in which people mark changes in their level of religiosity. Miriam Rothman noted:

I remember very clearly turning round to Mum at some point and saying, 'Why don't we keep kosher? I want to keep kosher at home.' My father grew up kosher at home, with separate meat and milk and the rest of it, my mother hadn't, but very quickly they thought, 'Let's seize the moment.' It was something that I think they felt was right for them, and also because they wanted to *seize* that enthusiasm for Judaism and Jewish culture that we were starting to evince, and so with quite extraordinary alacrity they became kosher.

In this case, the parents became more observant thanks to the influence of their daughter, principally because of their desire to strengthen her Jewish identity rather than out of 'religious' conviction that this was commanded by God.

In another aspect of the intertwined nature of kashrut and Jewish identity, as different segments of the British Jewish community become more concerned with claiming their 'authenticity' (and denying that of other groups), kashrut increasingly becomes an arena where these claims are played out, with strictness of observance often equated with the 'authentic', and social pressure sometimes forcing women to alter their mimetically learned practices. Not every woman is concerned about this, however, and there are still those, like Flora Rendberg, who place their family tradition above rabbinic authority. When I asked her whether she would consult anyone on questions of kashrut, she replied:

No. I do what my mother brought me up to do, and in those days one didn't look at the packets of biscuits, and there weren't kosher biscuits, and one bought normal biscuits. Obviously now one buys kosher biscuits because one can. For example, Christmas time I will buy the stuff from the Spanish shop that we always had at

margarine', an unsupervised product that was presumably acceptable in 1975, when the booklet was published. It has been obliterated with a black felt pen in all the copies that I have seen.

[25] 'Eating out' in Anglo-Jewish parlance refers to eating in an unsupervised restaurant, whether it is vegetarian or serves non-kosher food such as pork and shellfish.

Christmas time, and they do it with olive oil, they do some with olive oil and some with lard, so I know which ones are which, and so I just buy them. I'm certainly not going to ask the rabbi and I'm not going to give them to him if he were to come round!

Lesley Sandman was troubled by the increasing involvement of the rabbinic establishment in matters that had traditionally been entrusted to women:

[The rabbis] don't trust women. I really feel that they give over to women things far too reluctantly. There's too much of the 'better you shouldn't, dearie' kind of phenomenon in Jewish life. Yes, it's much more convenient that all of our meat is kashered,[26] but that came because they were worried. When I was first married in this country, you had to kasher your own meat. End of story. And now it doesn't go out of the butcher's shop without being kashered. How many of the young girls know how to kasher meat, how to kasher liver, and how to tell if it is or it isn't? There are so many safeguards because 'well, they might not do it right'.

The partial loss of women's autonomy and the reduction in their religious roles entailed by the expansion of rabbinic authority in this field was also noted, a little wistfully, by Shirley Daniels:

Even today, when I buy a chicken from the butcher and I stick it in my oven, I feel like I'm cheating. I feel like really there should be some process in between that I ought to be doing, and I do have a memory of my mother kashering, but you know my children will never have that. They'll never know what kashering was.

This sense of loss of autonomy and of part of women's traditional role may contribute to the increasing popularity of baking one's own challot, a practice that has spread in recent years. As noted in Chapter 4, the taking of challah during baking has recently become associated with acquiring merit to be used on others' behalf; in addition, influences from the wider, non-Jewish community have also had an effect. In a context where the middle classes value organic, 'natural', and homemade food, the traditional Jewish association of women with feeding and nurturing their families and communities receives strong social reinforcement, so that baking one's own challot becomes a highly symbolic activity, indicating a woman's commitment to traditional ideals, active acceptance of her maternal and nurturing role, and ability to acquire spiritual power. Following the usual pattern of women's accommodation to rabbinically imposed limitations, little criticism is heard of the rabbis' curtailment of traditional women's activities in the realm of

[26] While all meat must be slaughtered by a qualified *shoḥet* (slaughterer), the process of removing blood from the meat by salting and rinsing it, known as 'kashering', may be performed by anybody familiar with the process. Liver is kashered by being broiled.

kashrut,[27] but instead women expand their activity by developing new practices or reviving and adapting older ones that have declined, such as challah-
baking. Challot are now baked as part of batmitzvah celebrations and healing rituals, and are promoted in women's classes: in July 2014 the Edgware
branch of N'shei Chabad, a Lubavitch women's organization, ran three classes
based on the three 'women's mitzvot', collectively (and significantly) entitled
'Powerhouse'.[28] The class concerned with challah-baking, which promised
that women would make challah and 'learn its secrets', was entitled 'The
Power behind the Dough'. Larger communal organizations have also promoted communal challah-baking as a celebration of women's traditional role.
From about 2012 onwards, several United synagogues have organized annual
communal 'challah bakes', open to men and women, as a way of promoting sabbath awareness and building a sense of community. Far more women
than men attend these events.[29] Through this and other food-associated rituals, such as the *berakhah* parties discussed in Chapter 4, women celebrate
and reassert their central role in the family and the community, and their
desire to gain both spiritual power and closeness to God through preparing
and serving food, often with support and encouragement from community
institutions.

Passover

A particularly important time in relation to food and its ritualization is
Passover, which involves complicated and time-consuming preparations.
No leavened food (*hamets*) may be consumed or owned during the eight-day
festival; special pots, pans, crockery, and cutlery must be used, and the entire
house, especially the kitchen, must be cleaned to ensure that not the tiniest
crumb of *hamets* remains. Most Orthodox women, including many who are
not particularly concerned about kashrut during the rest of the year, are seized
by an overpowering urge to clean the entire house, even in areas where it is
unlikely that *hamets* is present, and many go to extreme lengths in preparing
for the festival—covering stoves, worktops, and walls with aluminium foil,
cleaning out wardrobes, and repainting the kitchen.[30] This has little to do

[27] Lesley Sandman and Shirley Daniels were the only women who talked about this.
[28] EdgwareK email list, 20 July 2014. The session on family purity was entitled 'Channelling
the Power', and that on lighting sabbath candles 'Lighthouse'.
[29] See Rocker, 'Thousands Join in Challah Bake', who notes that 'more than 3,000 women —
and a few men' attended a huge bake held in 2014 at a football stadium. See the United Synagogue website for details of several of these events.
[30] The phenomenon exists in America and Israel too. See Rotem, 'The Festival of Freedom?';
Fader, *Mitzvah Girls*, 26; and also Sered, *Women as Ritual Experts*, 81, who notes that the inten-

with halakhah: every year, before the festival, rabbis give lectures on Passover preparation that seek to distinguish between what is halakhically necessary and some of the more extreme precautions that women take, in response to the extraordinary level of fervour that women display. The classes are not addressed to men, even if they assist with Passover preparation, as it is (rightly) assumed that in most houses it is the women who insist on the stringencies. In spite of these rabbis' attempts to lift some of the heavy burden of preparation from women, many are determined to follow the standards they have set themselves or inherited from their own mothers, rather than follow the advice of a rabbi, whose experience in the kitchen they perceive to be less than their own. In a halakhah class I attended in the early 2000s, I witnessed a traditionalist woman who described a non-halakhic Passover practice that she followed to the teacher, a Modern Orthodox rabbi; when he very gently observed that it ran counter to accepted practice and suggested an alternative, she refused to accept his explanation. Given the completely uncritical acceptance of rabbis' pronouncements common in most of the Orthodox community, this behaviour was very unusual.

Some pressure to add stringencies to existing customs may come from sources such as the glossy haredi family magazines *Mishpachah* and *Binah*, produced in the USA but available in Britain. A recent edition of a haredi teenage magazine entitled *Aim!* included an article listing twelve stringent customs (*ḥumrot*) for Passover, including not using any cutlery that has been dropped on the floor during the festival, not eating anywhere outside one's home, and peeling all fruits and vegetables.[31] The article presented these practices in a positive light, citing a renowned kabbalist (R. Isaac Luria, 1534–72) as the source for the claim that 'being careful not to have the smallest amount of *chametz* will help you stay away from *aveiros* [sins] all year'.

Sered notes that her elderly Sephardi informants saw the weeks of cleaning as a deeply spiritual process, and sensed 'God's presence helping them carry out their Passover preparations', which included sorting through all the rice to be used on the festival seven times, grain by grain. She concluded that 'Passover laws of cleaning and food preparation give spiritual meaning and legitimization to their everyday, female activities', and 'make sacred women's entire profane domain: the domain of sinks, buckets, mops, and rags'.[32] None of the women to whom I talked felt this way about Passover preparations, about which they often spoke with a very real sense of dread and worry; Flora Rendberg even spoke of the festival as 'the P word', jokingly equating it with

sity of Passover cleaning is 'one of the most important measures of a pious woman', and that 'Jewish women have made a cult of Passover cleaning'.

[31] *Aim!* (9 Nisan 2014).   [32] Sered, *Women as Ritual Experts*, 83.

something obscene or too terrible to be named. Katherine Marks had witnessed her mother's ambivalent feelings about the festival:

I know she found Pesach an *enormous* hardship, and I remember her, as we all do, saying, 'What am I doing this for?' at one point, when she was sweeping out a cupboard in the middle of the night or whatever, 'What am I doing this for?', and we've all asked that, but I always felt for *her*, she really didn't like it or even believe in it or really see much value in it, so she *really* was asking that question, but having said that it would absolutely not occur to her not to do it.

The simultaneous dread of the weeks of hard physical labour and the insistence on doing things the way they have always been done or adding even more precautions are very common, regardless of age: 'I don't particularly enjoy the build-up to Pesach, but most women don't', said Sheyna Marcus. Other women complained that the preparations wore them out, so that they were too exhausted to enjoy the Seder on the first night of Passover. The only woman who spoke positively of preparing for the festival, Stella James, was recalling the excitement of childhood:

But when I was little I *adored* Seder, I adored all the preparation. Both of my parents were working in their own family business—and *I* was the one, when it was time to start changing everything over, and getting the crockery, I was the one that used to do it, and I remember one year when we were about to start, I just got the whole lot out and did virtually all of it, before my mother was even ready to start, because I was just so excited by the whole thing, I just loved it.

Like Simhat Torah, Passover is a time of tension and resentment for many Orthodox women, perhaps in this instance because, in spite of their hard work in preparation, the running of the Seder ceremony, the high point of the festival, is very often completely in the hands of men, especially in haredi and traditionalist families. In many Modern Orthodox families women now recite parts of the Hagadah, the text of the Seder ceremony, and make their own contributions to the traditional discussion and explication. These are often the families in which men participate in food and Passover preparations on a more egalitarian basis, perhaps reducing the sense of resentment and dread of the work beforehand. In a few instances new feminist rituals, such as the introduction of Miriam's Cup to match the traditional Elijah's Cup,[33] have been adopted or at least tried, as in Stella James's family:

---

[33] Miriam's Cup is a new ritual developed in the USA in the late 1980s; see Levy, 'The Orange on the Seder Plate and Miriam's Cup'. The biblical figure of Miriam is associated with water, and the presence of 'her' cup at the Seder symbolizes the redemptive role of Israelite women during the Exodus.

I did start a few years ago introducing things like Miriam's Cup of water, and all sorts of slightly feminine type of things, and now I lead Grace after Meals at our Seder, and I'd *never* have been allowed to do such a thing, even if I'd been able to, which I wouldn't have been, when my grandfather was alive, he wouldn't have liked that at all. But as it happens, some of these things have kind of gone by the board now, because they're too new, and they haven't stuck; Miriam's Cup hasn't stuck actually.

In a traditionalist family, innovative practices can never fulfil the function of confirming and reinforcing identity, since they have no link with the past. However, the desire to reclaim Jewish women as part of Jewish history and continuity can move even someone as devoted to preserving her family customs as Flora Rendberg, who thought it was important to make women visible in the Seder:

If I find something that I think is meaningful, for example Miriam's Cup on Pesach, which I'm a big fan of—of things that *show* where women have played a part—and I think it's really important, particularly in Orthodox circles, to promulgate that. Because I think a lot of the time we're taught—certainly I was taught—you know, Abraham, Isaac, Jacob, Moses, Joseph, Aaron. We're not *really* taught about what *women* did and how important their role is.

While haredi women generally accept their preparatory role at Passover as another opportunity to serve their family and enable them to perform mitzvot—a necessary component of the process of moulding a pious self—many women in the non-haredi sector seem to be tired of this auxiliary role, and some are seeking more active participation in the 'rewarding' aspects of Passover.

Mikveh and 'Family Purity'

Having explored women's experience of the sabbath and food preparation, areas associated with the first two of the three 'women's mitzvot', I now turn to an investigation of how they experience and understand the third area, that of the regulations governing sexual activity known as the 'family purity' system (*taharat hamishpaḥah*). Though details of the halakhic rules and rituals are easily accessible,[34] this is obviously a very personal and intimate subject for women, and has traditionally been included in the feminine ideal of *tseni'ut* (modesty), which eschews open discussion of sexual matters. Hardly any women mentioned the subject, and my principal source of information was an interview with Shirley Daniels, a young mother who has worked as a

---

[34] See Wasserfall (ed.), *Women and Water*; Kaplan, *Waters of Eden*.

mikveh (ritual bath) attendant for several years and who gives *kalah* classes, training sessions for brides-to-be. She was very open, and freely discussed both positive and negative experiences of the system.

While all married haredi women, and probably most Modern Orthodox women, visit the *mikveh* and observe the halakhic regulations, a surprisingly high proportion of Ashkenazi traditionalist women do not, or only go before their wedding. One woman noted:

When I got married we went to the *mikveh* during the day and we took my mum's best friend and my best friend, and we had chocolates afterwards. Because it's a big deal. I've not ever been since. It's not something that [my husband] wanted me to do and I've never felt that I wanted to do it.[35]

Other women also mentioned that their mothers had never been to the *mikveh*, and this seems to have been very common among Ashkenazi traditionalist women for several decades. United Synagogue rabbis do not even seem to have expected women to go:

I was married in the early 1980s and although we had a United Synagogue wedding ceremony, there was no expectation that I should go to the *mikveh* beforehand. The rabbi did spend a long time explaining to us how the *mikveh* was built but did not express any spiritual benefits of the process of immersing [oneself] in the *mikveh*. It seemed unattractive and irrelevant to our lives at the time.[36]

Sephardi women are far more likely to observe *taharat hamishpaḥah*, according to Shirley Daniels:

From the Spanish and Portuguese community, so the Sephardi community, it tends to be that 90% and above brides go to the *mikveh* before they get married, irrespective of their background and religious knowledge and Jewish practice, because culturally that's what they do. And in the United Synagogue the percentages were historically much lower, and they've worked very hard, to the point where in the last year they've got between 95 and 100%, depending on the month, attendance of brides. They've made a massive department in the United Synagogue to enable that to happen. So I think that if you look at Anglo-Jewry as a whole, you're getting 95% plus of brides per year going to *mikveh* before marriage . . . but [after marriage] the community who are not that observant, where it's still a question mark as to 'Will I', I think the Sephardi community have a higher uptake because knowledge and religious practice don't go hand in hand, whereas in the Ashkenazi community knowledge and practice are more equal to one another.

---

[35] Since the subject is so private I have omitted the pseudonyms used to identify interviewees in this section as an extra measure to ensure anonymity.

[36] Bloch and Bloch, 'Mother and Daughter Reflect'.

Since these practices are of biblical origin and are as important as sabbath and kashrut observance in halakhic terms, I would suggest that the low rates of performance among Ashkenazi traditionalist women are the result of the strongly assimilationist trend in Anglo-Jewry during the early twentieth century, when many traditional practices were viewed as primitive and barbaric and were discouraged or abandoned. The poor physical state of many *mikvaot* and old-fashioned, insensitive *kalah* teachers probably reinforced this. Shirley observed very different attitudes to the practice among Sephardi and Ashkenazi women, unrelated to their level of religious observance in other areas:

The Central London *mikveh*, which is based in Maida Vale, has a huge corps of regular [Sephardi] attenders who turn up in boots and jeans and low-cut tops, not covering their hair, not going to kosher restaurants, maybe not even keeping a kosher home at all either, but keeping *taharat hamishpaḥah*, not just doing a *mikveh*, but actually saying the Sephardi *tefilot* [prayers] during the month coming to the *mikveh*, saying additional *tehilim* [psalms], doing the *bedikahs*,[37] making sure that their preparation is completely *kasher*, and finding it a very wonderful spiritual experience.

While halakhic regulations shape every stage of the ritual, there is also room for family custom and individual preferences, often with symbolic value:

So standard Ashkenazi custom is to do either two dips (with no family history),[38] one dip, *berakhah*,[39] another dip; if there's a family custom to do three dips, it would be dip, *berakhah*, two dips, and then for Sephardim, more will do three than two [dips], and often seven. I've seen it split different ways, I've seen it be a dip, a *berakhah*, and six more dips; I've seen it be three dips, a *berakhah*, and four more dips, and there are interesting people who come with thirteen, fifteen, or eighteen [dips]. [Some] people say *pesukim* [biblical verses] in between each dip; [there are] people who recite certain *tehilim* [psalms] before and certain *tehilim* afterwards. I think the majority of people go, dip, come out . . . The seven for Sephardim—seven is a very spiritual, deep, heavy number, I suppose that thirteen is as well,[40] and eighteen for *ḥai*,[41] there are connotations with these numbers, but seven is very mystical, and I think of seven days of the week, seven times around the *ḥatan*,[42] you

---

[37] Literally 'checks', halakhically prescribed internal examinations to ensure that menstrual bleeding has completely ceased for seven days before *mikveh* immersion.

[38] i.e. no special tradition from one's family.

[39] A formal blessing is recited during immersion, between 'dips'.

[40] The number 13 is associated with the number of God's attributes.

[41] The numerical value (gematria) of *ḥai* ('life') is 18; charity is often given in multiples of 18.

[42] Many Ashkenazi brides follow the custom of walking seven times around the groom under the bridal canopy, a practice associated with protection.

know, and I do think that there's something beautiful about that for Sephardim that I know; they talk about it that way.[43]

Some women find visiting the *mikveh* stressful and uninspiring, particularly if they have not been taught about the spiritual dimensions of the practice. The inadequate and insensitive character of many *kalah* classes was noted in the 1994 Preston Report; women commented that 'The attitude that, unless a woman can keep the commandment in every particular—she is negating the whole process is a damaging approach.'[44] The same report recorded complaints that *mikvaot* were often 'dirty and dilapidated', with 'prying and unsympathetic attendants', and that women were not consulted in the planning process for building new *mikvaot*.[45] In a few cases, women's compliance with the 'family purity' system has been encouraged by the use of threats; the Preston Report noted an instance where literature given to future brides included '"a veiled threat of cervical cancer" if the laws of family purity were not followed',[46] and in a north-west London synagogue, a respected rabbi asserted in a sabbath sermon that women who do not observe this commandment run the risk of giving birth to mentally deficient or criminal children, prompting a Modern Orthodox midwife to stand up in the ladies' gallery and shout, 'That's not true!'[47]

Both the physical standards of *mikvaot* and the sensitivity of the *kalah* teachers seem to have improved in the last two decades, possibly as a result of the Preston Report: luxurious new *mikvaot* have been built, some old ones have been revamped, and the United Synagogue now runs a 'Marriage Enhancement Programme' with trained *kalah* teachers as well as individual male teachers for grooms.[48] Other problems cannot be so easily dealt with. For some haredi women, for instance, their lifelong education in the importance of *tseni'ut* can make going to the *mikveh* a traumatic experience:

[There was] a young bride who's been married for a few years and hasn't had any children yet and wasn't taught properly, and I just retaught her. [She] was brought up in the *frum* community, and this concept of being *tsanua* [modest] was imbued in every area of her life, and then [she was] shoved to go to Golders Green *mikveh*, where it's basically a communal waiting room,[49] and she just freaked out about it

---

[43]   Shirley Daniels, interview.

[44]   Preston, Goodkin, and Citron, *Women in the Jewish Community*, 43.

[45]   Ibid. 44.   [46]   Ibid.   [47]   Reported to me by the midwife.

[48]   See 'Marriage Enhancement Programme' on the United Synagogue website.

[49]   While the actual immersion is performed with only the attendant present, after preparation in an individual bathroom with a door that opens directly to the *mikveh* room, many *mikveh* buildings have a communal waiting room where a dozen or more women may sit while waiting for a bathroom to be free. Most women chat in the waiting room with no sign of awkwardness,

and felt *so* uncomfortable, really worried and upset about knowing that it was coming up to her time to go, because of that experience of it, not necessarily the *mikveh*, but just the discrepancy between being *tsanua* and everyone knowing your business. And her attitude was, 'My biggest fear would be that I'm going to see my *mother*, and that she'd know where we're at.' That was sad. Sad because it doesn't have to be like that. So obviously I taught her, and I told her about three other *mikvehs*, where you don't have any communal waiting, and it really really helped.[50]

Shirley also reported that 'there are people in the community who have issues, whether it be a phobia or a fear . . . [or] they feel that it's a barbaric custom, or they feel that it's completely improper'. A young Modern Orthodox woman who was fully committed to the observance of this commandment noted that there were times when it became very difficult for her:

There have been times when *mikveh* hasn't been easy. Due to having been in hospital, I had a line in my arm and of course I managed to get my period while I was in hospital. And because I had this line in my arm I ended up being in *nidah* [ritually impure] for three months. I had no use of my right side, I couldn't get dressed, so to then be in *nidah* was also really doubly traumatic, because I couldn't help myself, I needed assistance and [my husband] couldn't do that for me at all,[51] and I *really hated* God, I *hated* rabbis, and I *hated* religion, religious practice, for putting another stumbling block before me from my recovery. I was *really* angry about it, and I found it very difficult to be apart. But then once it was out and I could go to *mikveh*, it felt wonderful.

In spite of her frustration at the time, she still experienced the practice as something deeply spiritual:

There are other times when I'm euphoric that I have this mitzvah in my life that allows me to have this connection in my life to Hakadosh Barukh Hu [God],[52] and other times it's about the practicalities, can I be together with my husband, can we pass things to each other . . . Yes, it's difficult with young children to do the preparation and get out of the house and find the time when it's all busy busy, but if I didn't have it I'd be really sad.

but for someone from a haredi background like this bride, it would be a deeply embarrassing experience.

[50] Shirley Daniels, interview.

[51] Full observance of *taharat mishpahah* precludes any physical contact or passing of objects between husband and wife while she is in a state of *nidah*. One new bride confided to me that she found these restrictions almost impossible to bear, though she had no problem with actually going to the *mikveh*.

[52] Heb. 'The Holy One, blessed be He', a common name for God derived from rabbinic literature.

From her experience as a *mikveh* attendant, Shirley felt that most women enjoyed visiting the *mikveh* and found it both a pleasant and a spiritual experience:

People love the time it gives them to be on their own, to come away from the rigours of daily life, the demands of email and telephone and constant communication. They enter the *mikveh* [building], they turn whatever they've got on, off, put it on pause and silent, and they step away from their life, and they sink into a bathtub, and they relax, and they go through their preparation working towards a moment of connection with Hashem [God] and water . . . I see people coming out of the water and crying, especially brides, who didn't know it was going to be like that . . . I try to educate the girls, when they're at the bridal level, that they're in the middle of doing a mitzvah when they're in the water, and that they should take a moment to stop, to pause. Yes, you've done your quantity [of dips], so you've got your preparation, your thinking process over, you've done your dips and the counting is over, but you're still in the water. Take a moment—it's like standing under the *ḥupah* [bridal canopy] still, you're surrounded by the Shekhinah [Divine Presence] of Hashem and therefore you've got the opportunity to connect, and to try and do that, open up your heart and your soul and ask for the things you want, give thanks for the things that you have, and show that level of appreciation and communication.

Shirley speaks of an opportunity both for personal time and space and for communication with the Divine, which can transform a set of physical practices mandated by halakhah into an intensely female, embodied ritual that ushers a woman into the presence of God. While not all women experience *mikveh* and its associated practices in this way, it is clear that for many Orthodox women it provides a unique, and uniquely female, dimension of spirituality that they treasure.

Modesty

Modesty (*tseni'ut*), a central Jewish value encountered above in the discussion of *mikveh*, is a non-gendered concept that applies to all behaviour: dress, speech, deportment, lifestyle, and social relationships. However, as currently used in much of the Orthodox community, it is generally restricted to women's dress and behaviour, and is often spoken of as though it is only relevant to women, who are regarded as responsible for ensuring that men are not aroused by them. In haredi communities throughout the world, calamities and accidents are often blamed by prominent rabbis on women's lack of *tseni'ut*, to which many haredi women respond by urging each other to don longer skirts, thicker stockings, and tops with higher necklines in order to prevent cancer, missile attacks on Israel, and road accidents.[53] Standards are constantly getting stricter: haredi publications will not carry pictures of women (however they are dressed), a modesty hotline has been set up in Stamford Hill for the reporting of 'breaches of decency',[54] and there is a steady stream of new literature designed to teach women what they may and may not wear.[55] Modesty has become the defining feature of the haredi woman—'Tzenius is as integral to the woman as Torah and Talmud study is to the man'[56]—while also being deployed by some haredi men to control women and use them as scapegoats, particularly in Israel.[57]

Traditionalist and most Modern Orthodox women disregard most of this haredi modesty discourse, and wear what they deem to be suitable for the social context. Trousers, however, are a particularly sensitive issue, and women often define their own level of observance (or that of someone else) by noting whether they do or do not wear trousers; it would be a major faux pas to wear them to synagogue or to a religious event.[58] Traditionalist and older Modern Orthodox married women usually wear hats to synagogue, but do not cover their hair elsewhere; more observant, generally younger Modern Orthodox women may wear a scarf or hat. Wigs are most commonly worn by haredi women, though some Modern Orthodox women may wear them, particularly if they work in a non-Jewish environment and do not wish to stand out. As in all Jewish communities, the social significance of women's hair covering (or the lack of it) is complex.[59]

For most interviewees, modesty was not an issue: the 'ground rules' on dress for each part of the community are obvious to all, and few women deliberately break them. Even haredi women did not refer to the current rabbinic discourse on modesty, much less express interest in or acceptance of it. However, the importance of modesty as a behavioural ideal, as well as a code

[53] For recent extreme instances of *tseni'ut* enforcement in the haredi world and haredi claims of the damage done by lack of observance of modesty rules, see an anonymous online post from a woman in Crown Heights: 'Tznius Campaign Gone Too Far'. See also El-Or, *Educated and Ignorant*, 193–200, for a discussion of the modesty discourse among Israeli haredim.

[54] Rocker, 'Modesty Hotline Launched by London Rabbis'.

[55] e.g. Falk, *Modesty: An Adornment for Life*, which displays an almost obsessive level of interest in the covering of women's bodies. For a recent 'checklist' of modest behaviour for women circulated in Stamford Hill, including practices such as affixing rubber to shoe heels in order to avoid making a noise when one walks, and speaking quietly in the street, especially around religious men, see the scanned flyer 'Kabbalos in Tznius' on the Failed Messiah website.

[56] Osgood, 'After Years of Delay'.

[57] See Shoshan, 'Obsession with Modesty Killing Us', for a haredi woman's protest.

[58] Note Katherine Marks's comment above, or the assertion of a United Synagogue woman visiting Bushey cemetery: 'I am dressed in trousers and will not visit [my parents'] grave' (Francis, Kellaher, and Neophtou, *The Secret Cemetery*, 110).

[59] See Carrel, 'Hasidic Women's Head Coverings'.

of dress, was explored in some depth by a young, single interviewee who defined herself as 'between haredi and Modern Orthodox'. In spite of all the rabbinic focus on a narrowly defined concept of *tseni'ut* and on the disastrous consequences of neglecting the (male-determined) rules, Sheyna Marcus understood modesty as part of the ideal of Jewish womanhood to which she aspired, and defined it as part of her personal spiritual self-formation and refinement:[60]

In the morning [on the sabbath] I'm quite *makpid* [strict] on getting to shul quite early. I don't like to get there at the same time as the men for a couple of reasons, one for *tsnius* reasons, to be the one woman amongst thirty men may not be the right thing to do, and also, second reason is because I don't want to really . . . embarrass men—let's say some members of my family may not be so good at time-keeping, and it looks bad on them if their woman—their female person in their family—gets to shul before them. I think that looks bad on them especially since there's no *ḥiyuv* [obligation] for a woman to be in shul, however nice it might be. I like to be in shul within ten minutes of its start.

In addition to her concern that she might arrive simultaneously with the men, thus perhaps encountering them inappropriately in the entrance hall before she reached the women's section,[61] Sheyna takes great pains to avoid 'embarrassing' her male relations by arriving before them, which might imply criticism either by herself or by other, male observers. She does so even at the risk of arriving later than she would personally prefer. Such delicacy of feeling would probably not be reciprocated by the men, who would be unaware of her presence once she is sitting in the women's section, but it exemplifies the agency she exerts in forming herself in accordance with Jewish ideals, which stress the seriousness of embarrassing others.[62] Her understanding of *tseni'ut* in relation to dress revealed a similar ethical, rather than mechanical, interpretation of this ideal:

One of the only things actually that I don't think I ever find too much of a bind is *tsnius*. I find that quite easy. And I'm quite strict on myself. I'm not Rav [Rabbi] Falk,[63] I don't go quite as far as that, I feel that you need to use your initiative a bit, and you shouldn't need to be told about bending down and your neckline perhaps being shown. You should know on your own what's too tight, you should know on your own what colours might be too promiscuous, you should know on your own

---

[60] Cf. Mahmood, *Politics of Piety*. See also El-Or, *Educated and Ignorant*, 177–9, on the personal, though socially contextualized, construction of modesty.

[61] The inappropriateness would be because she would be the only woman there and thus unavoidably conspicuous.

[62] The Talmud compares embarrassing a person in public to murder; see BT *BM* 58a–59b.

[63] The author of the work on women's modesty mentioned above, n. 55.

which hairstyles are not [suitable]—not just neck, elbow, knee, what *tsnius* is really about . . . If *tsnius* is about, in some way, being inconspicuous, then my personality is generally I don't enjoy being the centre of attention, so that it's not difficult for me to do that . . . I think that people need to be true to themselves, and they also need to use their own initiative and their own feeling—yeah, there are guidelines, but it's about you rather than about rules.

By internalizing this central religious value and developing her own responsibility for embodying and interpreting it in her daily life, Sheyna sidesteps the strident male discourse on women's modesty, and recreates the practice as her own, serving as her own authority and displaying agency in her choice to interpret the associated restrictions and train herself to observe them. As has been noted in the discussion of other women's practices, from *berakhah* parties to food preparation, women often understand and perform elements of their religious lives in ways that are quite different from how male religious authorities (not to speak of non-Jewish observers) understand them.[64]

Visiting the Dead

As guardians of the home, women are viewed as particularly responsible for maintaining family links, and this continues after the death of loved ones. Though both men and women visit family graves, women in particular maintain a relationship with deceased members of the family, especially their mothers, consulting them about problems or reporting family news to them when they stand at the tomb. It is customary to visit family graves either in the month of Elul[65] or between Rosh Hashanah and Yom Kippur. A survey carried out at Bushey, a large United Synagogue cemetery north of London, on the Sunday before Yom Kippur 1996 recorded 2,859 visitors, of whom women formed 50.2%.[66] Visitors aged 45–65 were the largest group (40%), while those aged 65 and older constituted about 31%. In contrast, a comparative survey carried out on an ordinary Thursday in October 1996 listed only 262 visitors, of whom 52% were women. These figures suggest that though women are commonly perceived as the main link between the living and the dead members of the family, actual practice does not bear this out.

While numbers of men and women were more or less equal, however, interviews conducted with visitors revealed different emphases in men's and women's visits. Women spoke more often of coming to the cemetery in order to communicate with the dead:

[64] Cf. the current discourse on Muslim women and the *hijab*; see Tarlo, *Visibly Muslim*.

[65] The month before Rosh Hashanah, a time of preparation for the major festivals.

[66] This information and the quotations below appear in Francis, Kellaher, and Neophtou, *The Secret Cemetery*.

When there is anything momentous in the family, I come: births, marriage, an upset. It is a mark of respect to go there, it is making an effort on her behalf. It is easy to have a conversation [with the deceased] at home; I do not have to be dressed, I do not have to put on make-up. The cemetery requires special effort; it is not en route to anywhere. It is an offering, an effort to go.[67]

  I have things on my mind and I want to talk to my mother and to ask her help . . . I come for her guidance, to get outside help . . . and I ask her to sort it out. I'll ask her to give me a sign—like breaking a good plate. Even if it's not related, I make it so that it is. I feel better when I talk to her; she's the only one I might talk to about this.[68]

There were both men and women who came to inform the dead about births, marriages, and deaths, and two women who were thinking of re-marrying told the interviewers that they had come to tell their dead spouses, and hoped to receive approval at their mothers' graves.[69] In addition, several women spoke of carrying on regular conversation with their dead mothers at home.[70] Others felt the connection particularly strongly when engaged in religious rituals: 'On lighting the Friday night candles, I welcome the light and all the people I knew who have passed on—I expect them to be there . . . I need their approval. The fact that they're dead is not important to me.'[71]

The same picture emerged from my interviews: the women listed cemetery visits as 'part of their Jewish year'. Flora Rendberg visits several cemeteries, including both relatives and community members in her rounds, in a combination of conversation and prayer:

I go on my father's—we call it *naḥalah*, not *yahrzeit*[72]—I go on my father's *naḥalah*, and I go on Lag Ba'omer,[73] which are a week apart, so that's very exciting, and I go before Rosh Hashanah. I don't go any other time . . . So I've done Hoop Lane, I've got a stone-setting at 4 in Bushey, in between that I'm going to Edgwarebury Lane,[74] that's our other cemetery . . . When I go to Hoop Lane, if I go for a stone-setting or whatever I always go to my dad and my uncle and my dad's best friend, and as it happens, on the way to my dad there's a *whole load* of people from [my synagogue], so I have to say hello to them as I go by . . . Sometimes I have a chat, I don't talk to my dad all that much . . . So I take the prayer book with me, and usually I'll say the

---

[67] Francis, Kellaher, and Neophtou, *The Secret Cemetery*, 92.   [68] Ibid. 151.
[69] Ibid.   [70] Ibid. 90–1.   [71] Ibid. 90.
[72] Anniversary of death. *Yahrzeit* (Yid.) is the Ashkenazi term, *naḥalah* (Heb.) the Sephardi one.
[73] The thirty-third day of counting the *omer*, a sequence of forty-nine days, each counted with a blessing, from Passover to Shavuot.
[74] Hoop Lane cemetery in Golders Green serves the Reform and Spanish and Portuguese (Orthodox) communities; Edgwarebury cemetery serves the Reform, Liberal, Masorti, and Spanish and Portuguese communities.

prayer for visiting the cemetery, and sometimes I'll say Kaddish, to myself,[75] but today the page I happened to open it up was at *hashkavah*,[76] so I thought that's obviously the page that I'm supposed to read today. I'm not that fussed to go with the rabbi and him say *hashkavah* for me. If I want to say it I can say it myself.

When the authors of the cemetery survey asked Rabbi Ivan Binstock, a leading judge of the London Beth Din, to comment on the purpose and nature of Jewish cemetery visits, he gave a very different view, telling them that 'reflection on life values in presence of the dead' is based on 'the religious tenet that the worthy lives of bereaved survivors—inspired and influenced by the teachings and proper deeds of their deceased parents—can confer an enhanced spiritual status upon the souls of the departed'. He explained that, 'according to this belief, the living can redeem the dead, their activities enabling the passage of the soul to a higher realm'. While the rabbi saw cemetery visits as a source of merit for the dead, as they are virtuous deeds performed by their descendants, the women I interviewed understood them as a prolongation of their pre-existing relationship with relations and friends; they initiated communication with the dead in order to receive the help, advice, and approval of their beloved family members. In this instance too, women's understanding of their religious activities differed markedly from that of the rabbinic elite.

Prayer and Relationship with God

The British Jewish community as a whole does not often engage in formal theological thought, and though in recent years several Jewish scholars such as Tamar Ross, Melissa Raphael, Judith Plaskow, and Rachel Adler have written widely on feminist Jewish theology,[77] none of my interviewees mentioned this literature or spoke of related issues, such as the problem of the male language used to describe God in classical Jewish texts. Very few of my interviewees have heard of these ideas or of the theologians involved, so, since

[75] According to halakhah, Kaddish may only be recited in the presence of a male *minyan*, so this is a non-halakhic individual practice that accords well with other situations in which Flora preferred her own judgement to seeking rabbinic permission or authority (see the section on kashrut above).

[76] The Sephardi memorial prayer. Texts for female and male versions can be found on the Jewish Funeral Guide website.

[77] See Adler, *Engendering Judaism*; Plaskow, *Standing Again at Sinai*; Raphael, *The Female Face of God in Auschwitz* and 'The Impact of Gender'; and Ross, *Expanding the Palace of Torah*. Ross is Orthodox, while the other three authors are not. Raphael has also made the salient point that, apart from Tamar Ross, Orthodox Jewish feminist theologians have restricted their area of interest to halakhah rather than treating purely theological issues.

I was interested in exploring their own understandings of their religious lives, I did not introduce questions on these topics.

Many Jewish women are shy about discussing belief, spirituality, and personal philosophy, especially with a stranger, or may never have spent time examining their beliefs or constructing a coherent belief system; if questioned, they are often embarrassed at their uncertainty or the inconsistent nature of what they believe. This made it hard to ask women direct questions about such issues, but the subject did emerge in less obvious ways. As a Jewish studies teacher I am often asked theological or philosophical questions by women who lead an unimpeachable Orthodox lifestyle but preface their questions with apologetic disclaimers such as 'Of course I'm a terrible *apikoros* [heretic], but I wondered whether . . .' or 'I'm afraid this is a really stupid question, but do we believe . . .'. I have drawn on this material as well as on interviews in the discussion that follows.

About half of the interviewees, including all the haredi women, said that they prayed on a daily basis, usually at home rather than in synagogue. Not all of them, however, felt secure in their faith or their relationship with God. Bernice Susser, who did not pray except in synagogue (where prayer 'very rarely touched' her), had experienced several tragedies in her life, and explained how this had affected her: 'my own personal faith peaks and troughs, but I'm very profoundly Jewish all the way through, and it's very much part of my essence'. Suffering was also cited by Flora Rendberg as a factor in her relationship to the Divine: 'I have had quite a crisis of faith, because of all that happened with my friend's family, and then [several relations] having breast cancer', but, like Bernice, she felt that this did not affect either her religious practice or her sense of Jewishness: 'It's very hard, but I suppose I don't know what's the most important thing—I suppose keeping the traditions going, keeping everything going . . . and being part of something that's different, that's not what everybody else does. It must be important if it's different and it's been different for so many years.'

Flora did not see a crisis of faith as a reason to stop praying: 'I always say 'Modeh ani' when I get up,[78] and I always say Shema just before I fall asleep . . . I don't tend to say *berakhot* during the day.'[79] Some women, like Beatrice Levi, a traditionalist member of the United Synagogue, adopted a particular prayer practice rather than reciting the formal services from the prayer book, even though she too was ambivalent about 'religion':

A woman at school told me I have to say 'Asher yatsar',[80] so I say that when I can

[78] A brief prayer upon waking; see *Authorised Daily Prayer Book*, 4.
[79] The blessings before and after eating or drinking.
[80] The blessing after using the lavatory. See *Authorised Daily Prayer Book*, 12–13.

remember, when I've been to the toilet. But I have to be honest—I feel like I'm probably the furthest away from religion that I've ever been in my life now, from feeling any closeness to religion. I actually feel quite disconnected, apart from the fact that I'm actually working at a religious school. Basically I can do the ritual, and I know everything, because I've been taught, and I know how to do everything, but I don't really feel it.

Her feelings were echoed by other traditionalist women. Even women who did pray regularly and had no doubts about their basic faith acknowledged that prayer is not always easy: Sheyna Marcus noted that 'you can have high points and you can have times when it says nothing to you and you can't be bothered'. Sarah Segal, from the Satmar hasidic community, after emphasizing that prayer was very important to her, explained that it was

not just from the *sidur*, though, it can be just by talking as well. I strongly believe in having an honest relationship with God, very honest. Sometimes it's difficult but, once I feel I can't pray, I just can't say it, I just don't feel in a place to pray, but praying is a big part . . . whenever something goes wrong, or I need something, I need a bit extra, or thanking . . . I think it's very meaningful for women particularly.

Several women felt the need to incorporate prayer into their daily routine in a regular way, making individual choices of what to say from the prayer book. Katherine Marks, like several other women, described the way in which she links parts of the formal prayers to her own life:

I always felt that it was just second best doing it at home, but I also decided that it was better for me to daven at home than to go to shul and actually come out really feeling upset, depressed, alienated . . . I don't particularly feel obligated to do everything, so I do edited highlights that mean things to me . . . Not a week goes by when I'm not teaching a class or preparing a class, so [Torah study] is very much in my consciousness, and I really really like that . . . *la'asok bedivrei torah* is a very very important *berakhah* for me[81] . . . the idea of being immersed and of that being part of my life is very very important. I think it's become very important because I've not been able to find fulfilment in so many other aspects of Judaism, which have just not worked for me.

When frustrated by the communal aspect of Judaism, especially its limitations on women's participation, Katherine finds consolation and meaning in private prayer. Others, like Shirley Daniels, spoke of the uplifting and intensifying effect music had on their experience of prayer, transporting them to a level beyond that of mere words:

[81]   One of the three morning blessings over Torah study; this one refers to God's command to 'be busy with' or 'immerse oneself in' words of Torah.

I still remember a Yom Kippur service . . . and the *ḥazan* [cantor] from Israel was just phenomenal, the best *ḥazan* I've ever heard. It wasn't like *ḥazanut*,[82] it was just so powerful and emotional, and that tune was used over *again* and *again* and *again*, and I can't help but feel, when somebody else uses that in the *tefilah*, that I've been opened up and connect with the *tefilot* [prayers] on a different level; it's an emotional and spiritual level maybe, I don't know, but it's not about the *words*, it's about the feeling.

Her words were echoed by Miriam Rothman, who explained what she found attractive in the Grassroots services she had helped to organize:

It was unapologetic about being spiritually involving, uplifting, there was no shame or embarrassment about being *really involved* and uplifted by the davening and the singing, and it was that transportive quality of music and of davening which I hadn't really had since I'd been in Israel.

Several United Synagogue members spoke with frustration of the dull and alienating experience of prayer in their synagogues, and many spoke yearn-ingly of the rare sensation of being swept up in prayer, which they often described as 'spirituality', or 'a spiritual atmosphere', and which the women who founded and ran the Stanmore Women's Tefillah Group saw as the aim of their services. The deep desire for spiritual growth and connection to the Divine, expressed by many of the Stanmore women, was described by Sheila Dorfman, along with a simultaneous fear of its transformative possibilities:

If I could change my religious life I think I would want to learn and practise reli-gious meditation, and really find that space in myself that really wants to connect with God. And I think it's quite threatening and it's quite challenging and that's probably why I don't do it, there's no reason why I couldn't do it, it's just a very difficult place to go. There's a book called *Praying with Fire*,[83] and they gave away a little booklet of it a couple of Rosh Hashanahs ago as a sort of taster, and I started reading it, it's one of these five-minutes-a-day things, and I couldn't continue because I found it too threatening. It was wonderful but it would take me to a dif-ferent place and I'm not sure that I'm ready to go there, but I would like to be in a place that I *would* like to go there.

Many traditionalist and some Modern Orthodox women are insecure and feel lost in this dimension of their religious lives, longing to deepen their faith and develop a meaningful spiritual life, but unsure how to go about it, and doubtful that their religious leaders can provide direction. They are uncertain

---

[82]   The cantorial style of prayer, sometimes very florid and elaborate.

[83]   This was probably Heshy Kleinman, *Praying with Fire* (Brooklyn, NY, 2006), which offers a '5-minute lesson a day'.

as to what they think about much of the 'official' belief system, as defined in Maimonides' 'Thirteen Principles',[84] for example, and about issues such as the afterlife or the effectiveness of prayer. In particular, they have trouble reconciling Western rational and scientific patterns of thought and traditional Jewish ideas. Haredi women like Kate Moskovitz were prepared to sacrifice Western thought ('logic') if it posed a threat to traditional Jewish ideas:

When I think of it *logically*, these things are nuts, right? When I think of it logically, if you put *logic* into this thing, then it doesn't make sense. You wouldn't believe in anything. That's why I don't like scientists in a way, they're trying to make it [logical] —I can't get this science thing—because once you start trying to make it into logic it's like chalk and cheese, because there's no logic in the way Hakadosh Barukh Hu [God] works, it's not logical at all, it's just something we don't understand.

As a result of this choice to privilege traditional Jewish thought over Western ideas, the most confident (though not necessarily the most sophisticated) articulation of belief and theological ideas came from haredi women, such as Menucha Mizrahi:

It is very important to understand that *everything we do*, it's not coincidence . . . There's a tsunami, there's a hurricane, Hurricane Katrina . . . This is Hashem telling us that we're doing things, I'm telling you, I see things that happen, they want to make these gay marriages in New York, and they made this, you know, 'Oh it's legal and it's now going to be this.' The next week came a thunderstorm and in New York, it was like the basements were flooded. I'm not saying that they deserve it, don't misunderstand me, non-Jewish people are just as good,[85] we're all created equally in the eyes of God, but Hashem feels He wants to show, 'I've got the upper hand, I'm Hashem.' I see it all the time.

Both Menucha and Kate articulated the theology of 'accumulated merit' that can be won by means of pietistic practices and good deeds, and then 'redeemed' on behalf of those in need (or redirected by God to benefit someone), in combination with an innovative interpretation of the creation and role of angels:

If you do a mitzvah to some degree, it might not show itself for you here and now, but it's held in abeyance or something, or could benefit another person 50 million miles away, and in the other way, if somebody does something which is terrible or bad, it might not affect them particularly there, but it could affect another Jewish person . . . It doesn't mean that the person doing the good gets necessarily the

---

[84] See his commentary on Mishnah *San.* 10. For contemporary and later criticism of this list, see Shapiro, *The Limits of Orthodox Theology.*

[85] Though she also told me several stories designed to prove the innate moral and behavioural superiority of Jews.

reward, it could be something good happens, and because of that, that's affecting something that we have no idea about; that's the whole idea of what Hakadosh Barukh Hu's got out there for us, we have *no* idea of what's going on . . . Some people say you do a mitzvah and an angel appears, and if you do something bad, your accusing angel appears, and that's what we're told; we don't understand any of it, but it's much bigger than we know.[86]

A *malakh* [angel] is created for every 'amen' you answer. A *malakh* that protects you and protects the person who made the *berakhah*. Unbelievable![87]

This 'theology of angels and merit' seems to be characteristic of haredi women; it is notable that rabbis rarely advance it. In contrast, non-haredi women are reluctant to pronounce on such issues, preferring to focus on personal spirituality while often struggling to find some synthesis between the Western ideas they have imbibed from the wider society and their education on the one hand, and the world of Jewish thought on the other, in which they often have had little education.

Orthodox polemic often claims that Jewish women who seek fulfilment outside the domestic arena are misguided and lost, influenced by feminist propaganda that encourages them to 'ape men' and lose sight of their God-given roles; at the other end of the polemical spectrum, some radical feminists assert that all marriage is inherently oppressive and that women who aspire to build and nurture a family are victims of false consciousness and self-deceit. Most Orthodox women see their domestic role in very different, more nuanced, and complex terms, viewing it as central to their identity and to Jewish continuity, but not as the only sphere in which they should be active religiously. Many of them, particularly the Modern Orthodox, have indeed internalized feminist arguments and seek to extend their religious lives outside the boundaries of the home, and to take a more active religious role within it, but they all share the conviction that the creation of a Jewish home and the raising of children to be good human beings and faithful Jews is a task of vital importance.[88] Haredi women, who rarely express opposition to haredi ideology, see their role in preparing the essential infrastructure for the observance of sabbath and festivals, running a kosher kitchen, maintaining social networks, and nurturing children, the elderly, and needy community members as the heart of Jewish practice and the basis of Jewish spirituality. Non-haredi women, while often frustrated and impatient with inequalities and lack of opportunities in both the public and the domestic spheres, still see

[86] Kate Moskovitz, interview.   [87] Menucha Mizrachi, interview.
[88] This attitude could be viewed as an expression of 'maternalist feminism', 'a form of feminism that focuses on improving the condition of women as mothers', as defined in Walby, *The Future of Feminism*, 16.

their domestic roles as central, and as providing opportunities for the service of God.

As we have seen in this chapter, while there are perceptible differences between the practices, beliefs, and attitudes of traditionalist, Modern Orthodox, and haredi women in the domestic sphere, they are united in their understanding of the home as a sacred Jewish space. Whether preparing food for the sabbath, listening to their children recite the Shema at bedtime, or immersing themselves in a *mikveh*, women show remarkable creativity in investing the most mundane activities with a spiritual dimension, often applying innovative interpretations of their actions that owe little or nothing to male and rabbinic understandings.

SIX

RED THREADS AND AMULETS: WOMEN'S 'UNOFFICIAL' LIFE IN THE FAMILY

I don't do any things like this . . . But I've grown up with loads of them. A lot of them are halakhah, a lot of them are customs, and they're all mixed together.

SARAH SEGAL, interview

THE LEAST VISIBLE aspect of Jewish women's life is the individual customs or practices they perform in a domestic or everyday context, many learnt from female relatives, and the part these play in their religious lives. This is a difficult set of phenomena to investigate: individual practices are often so automatic that women do not reflect on them—one hasidic interviewee remarked that 'they are integral to our lives but we don't really think about them'.[1] In some cases they receive so little attention from rabbis or in popular Jewish literature that women themselves discount or denigrate them as 'superstitions',[2] even as they practise them. In contrast, men's customs, particularly those connected to the areas of Torah study and prayer, are often recognized as *minhagim*, official customs practised by particular communities and individuals, and are frequently enshrined or discussed in halakhic literature. Even though largely undocumented, however, customs, beliefs, and practices of the types revealed in my survey form a rich source of data as they constitute the close texture of women's religious lives, giving expression to their own conception of their role as Jewish women and colouring the everyday with Jewish consciousness. In addition, they reflect changing trends of religiosity and concepts of women's religious role, and provide an opportunity for women to express and think about their relationships to their family, their community, and the Divine.

---

[1] Hannah Zeved, phone conversation, 9 July 2013.
[2] I have avoided the word 'superstitions' in my analysis since it is highly subjective, carries denigratory overtones, and cannot be defined satisfactorily. Even though some of my interviewees did use the term, it is no longer acceptable in anthropological usage.

Questioning the Community: Limitations and Caveats

Many of these practices are previously unrecorded and rarely discussed, and occupy an ambivalent position in Jewish culture; women do not often bring them up spontaneously for discussion, which makes them all the more important as a hitherto untapped source of data. After coming across several examples in casual conversation, I developed a questionnaire to elicit more information on how widespread these practices were, and to what extent they were currently observed as opposed to being family folklore, invoked in memories of older relatives but not actually performed.[3] Given the differing interpretations and attitudes of respondents, the small size of the sample (100 women), and the practical complications encountered, as described below, I must emphasize that the data derived from the questionnaire can only serve as a qualitative guide to this aspect of women's religious lives rather than a definitive quantitative survey.

Most earlier studies of such practices have been folkloristic in character,[4] often recording the existence of customs in a particular community, but giving little idea of the period at which these customs were practised, little if any information about the number of individuals who actually observed a particular custom (as opposed to having heard of it), and few if any details about how customs were transmitted. Speculation on the origin of customs, rather than investigation of their meaning for those who practise them or variation in attitudes towards them, has been the focus of these works. A more sophisticated analysis is offered by Judy Baumel-Schwartz, who investigated the transmission,[5] and in some cases invention, of customs on Orthodox women's English-language Internet forums, concluding that they provide a means of maintaining social boundaries, promoting social cohesion, and legitimating existing hierarchies. She also noted that haredi women tended to stress the importance of 'blind faith' in accepting and performing such customs, while Modern Orthodox women were far more ready to analyse their origins and examine relevant Jewish texts in order to evaluate and critique the customs' relevance in the modern world.

---

[3] Appendix IV presents basic data about the respondents to the questionnaire, while Appendix III presents a full list of the customs documented, with bibliographical annotations.

[4] While there are several folkloristic studies of Jewish customs, many of which mention some women's practices, they tend to deal with communities before the Second World War, or else describe customs without any chronological or geographical context. See e.g. Brav, 'The Evil Eye'; Dundes, *The Evil Eye*; Klein, *A Time To Be Born*; Moss and Cappannari, 'Mal'occhio'; Patai, *On Jewish Folklore*; Pomeroy, '"From the Cradle to the Grave"'; Sabar, 'Childbirth and Magic'; Sperber, *The Jewish Life Cycle*. I know of no earlier study of these customs in the British Jewish community.

[5] Baumel-Schwartz, '"It is Our Custom from *Der alter Heim*"'. I am indebted to Dr Miri Freud-Kandel for this reference.

My conversations with questionnaire respondents often revealed major differences in reactions to these practices, such as that between the amusement occasioned by getting a little girl to hold the Havdalah candle at the hoped-for height of her future husband[6] and the outrage of a grandmother at her granddaughter's 'stepping over' her brother as he sat on the floor, which is thought to discourage growth and to be only remediable by 'unstepping' in the opposite direction. Both of these practices are very common (39% of respondents observed the Havdalah candle custom, with another 36% aware of it; and 22% observed the 'stepping' custom, with another 29% aware of it), but one is regarded as an endearing though not very serious practice, omission of which carries no consequences, while transgressing the other is often understood as a very real threat to health.

My initial list, of some sixty customs, was developed by asking participants at a lecture I gave at the Limmud conference in December 2009 whether they knew of any practices of this kind. I was almost overwhelmed by the rapid and detailed response, which yielded about eighty customs.[7] The questionnaire was based on these. Respondents were encouraged to add practices that did not appear on the list, with the result that by August 2012 it had expanded to over 200 customs, the majority of which are linked to women. To give some idea of whether these practices are changing over time (and if so, how), respondents were classed in six age groups,[8] and there was also a question on the birthplace of grandparents, so that the influence of origin or of Ashkenazi/ Sephardi identity on custom performance could be assessed. Respondents were asked whether they practised the custom themselves, had family members who practised it, or had only heard about it, so that it would be possible to distinguish actual practice from mere knowledge about customs—a distinction often overlooked in previous discussions of this type of material.

Since the questionnaire had expanded over time, in summer 2013 I contacted as many respondents who had filled in the earlier version as possible, and asked them to fill in the new version in order to chart their responses to customs that had not been in the original list. This was done by a combination of phoning some respondents and by emailing or giving updated versions of the questionnaire, or in some cases a list of supplementary questions, to

---

[6] Havdalah, literally 'separation', is the ceremony that ends the sabbath, marking its separation from the working week; blessings are said over wine, fragrant spices, and a candle with two wicks, often held by the youngest girl present.

[7] Several men present were very surprised by accounts of these customs. Some commented audibly to their wives, 'I never knew you did that!', though a few men did contribute items, often linked to their mothers or grandmothers.

[8] These were: 18–30, 31–40, 41–50, 51–60, 61–70, and over 71.

others.[9] Notably, some respondents who filled in the new, expanded, question-naire gave different answers to those they had recorded on the earlier version —for instance 'I do this' in place of an earlier 'I've never heard of this' or vice versa—thus underlining the impressionistic nature of the survey.[10] In addi-tion, the phone conversations often became 'mini-interviews', with a chance for the women to express their feelings about certain customs and to describe where they had learned them, variations in their personal practice over time, and their general perception of the significance of this type of practice.

The questionnaire is divided into rough categories that group the customs by goal or context. The categories are as follows: 'to avoid the evil eye or for good luck', 'to find a marriage partner', 'to get pregnant', 'during pregnancy', 'birth', 'protection of babies and small children', 'first menstruation, 'medical and curative practices', 'death and funerals', and 'miscellaneous customs'. Many in the last category are associated with the sabbath and festivals, and are not unique to women. Some practices appeared in several categories (such as checking *mezuzot*, which was done to ward off the evil eye or to cure sickness and solve other problems). Space was provided for comments, and respon-dents were encouraged to write down their understanding of the practices, and where they had learned about them; about a quarter of the respondents availed themselves of this opportunity.

Women thoroughly enjoyed filling in the questionnaires, often laughing at some of the customs or remembering relatives to whom they had been impor-tant; they were keenly interested and often greeted a familiar custom like an old friend, discussing it with a warmth and intimacy that did not often appear when they talked about their experiences in synagogue or in more formal contexts. However, I cannot be sure that all the answers reflect actual prac-tice; in some instances, women may have denied knowledge of a custom they practise but which they fear would be regarded with ridicule. A notable in-stance was the custom of a mother slapping a daughter when she gets her first period. A mother and daughter who answered this gave contradictory replies: the daughter noted that her mother had indeed slapped her, and the mother recorded that she had never heard of this custom. While such disparate responses cast doubt on the actual performance of this custom, they may well reveal changing attitudes: perhaps a practice once seen as standard now appears unacceptable in the light of changing attitudes to hitting children?

[9] About twenty-five women could not be reached; some questionnaires had been completed anonymously, while other respondents had not provided contact details.

[10] This might be because they had recently started to practise this custom. It should also be noted that when respondents said they had heard of a custom of which they had been unaware in their first set of answers, this could be because they had heard of it from the questionnaire itself!

In general, the sample seems fairly representative of the London Jewish community in terms of origin, age, and proportions of Ashkenazim and Sephardim.[11] Unsurprisingly, most respondents (78%) were born in the United Kingdom (62% in London). Another 5% were born in South Africa, 4% in Israel, 10% elsewhere,[12] and three respondents did not record their birthplace. The most common birthplace of respondents' grandparents is the United Kingdom, at 27%, though if the constituent countries of eastern Europe are combined,[13] this group easily takes precedence, totalling 45%. The next largest grouping is Germany and Austria, at 8%, with the rest (17%) scattered among nineteen countries,[14] with the birthplace of the remaining 3% either unknown or unrecorded. The age distribution closely matched that of the community, and about 5% of the respondents were Sephardi (with another 4% of mixed Ashkenazi–Sephardi heritage, as determined by the birthplaces of their grandparents), which is close to the proportion of Sephardim in the UK Jewish community, estimated at 3%. The overall picture corresponds with what is generally known of the Anglo-Jewish community, most of whom have lived in Britain for at least two generations, and most of whose ancestors came from eastern Europe.

Definitions and Status of Practices

Orthodox Jews observe many customs, both in communal and in domestic life, that are not explicitly prescribed by halakhah, ranging from widely accepted and uncontroversial practices (for instance the Ashkenazi custom of eating cheesecake and dairy foods on Shavuot) to little-known and occasionally theologically problematic ones (such as licking a child's forehead or eyelids to protect it from the evil eye[15]). I was particularly interested in researching customs that are or have been important to women but do not usually appear in modern practical guides to Jewish observance (whether written or orally taught), and my first challenge was to find a descriptive term to explain what I was looking for. In an attempt to keep such terms as neutral as possible, I generally used 'folk custom' or 'folk practice', or gave a few examples of such customs. In spite of the difficulty of finding an appropriate term, all the interviewees immediately recognized what I was talking about, though several of them responded, 'Oh, you mean *superstitions*'. Though many of the practices

---

[11] See Appendix IV for background data on respondents.   [12] See Appendix IV for details.
[13] Including Belarus, Czechoslovakia, Latvia, Lithuania, Poland, Romania, Russia, 'Russia/Poland', Slovakia, and Ukraine.   [14] See Appendix IV for details.
[15] In my survey, only 4% of the 100 respondents had heard of this custom; none practised it themselves, but they remembered mothers or grandmothers who had.

can be traced back either to pre-war Europe or to the medieval or rabbinic periods,[16] some appeared to be of recent or non-Jewish origin, such as baking a cake
during labour in order to help childless friends conceive.[17]

The question of the halakhic status and correct nomenclature of these
practices frequently arose with respondents from the haredi and Modern
Orthodox sectors, or among those with a higher level of Jewish education.
These women often objected to the inclusion of a practice they regarded as
normative or obligatory, and which they generally practised themselves, in a
list that included other practices, which they generally did *not* practise and
which they regarded as 'superstitions' or 'just customs'. Even when I pointed
out that the list was composed of customs that women had chosen to tell me
about, without any formal parameters for inclusion, they would often protest, 'But there are sources for this one! It's halakhic!'—frequently in connection with a practice that another respondent might dismiss as a 'ridiculous
superstition'.

As an illustration, we can consider the range of responses to the questionnaire entry 'not counting children', included in the category 'to avoid the evil
eye', which was practised by 9% of respondents, with another 58% having
heard of it. One woman wrote that it applied 'to grandchildren', five other
women noted that it applied 'to all living people', three wrote that it applied 'to
every Jew'. One woman described it as 'an ultra-Orthodox custom', and another two thought it was a Lubavitch custom. Only two women described it as
a halakhic obligation, one of them a young Modern Orthodox woman and the
other a haredi, non-hasidic woman in her sixties:

LTG: I know you're not keen on counting children.

KATE MOSKOVITZ: Well, you can't count people anyway, even if you count them
for a *minyan* you don't count them one two three, no, you don't.

LTG: What's the reason you do it? Because people have different reasons.

KM: But look, that comes from the Torah, that's a Torah-based thing, half a
shekel, *ḥetsi shekel*, that's what it comes from, everyone gives a *ḥetsi shekel*
and then you count the *shekalim*. So that's the basis of that, isn't it?

LTG: So you'd feel you do it because it's a Torah thing, not an evil eye thing.

KM: Yes, that one I think so.[18]

---

[16] For instance the use of red thread for fertility or protection; see Teman, 'The Red String'.

[17] I found no Jewish references to this practice; perhaps it was adapted from a similar custom
of baking a 'groaning' or 'kimbly' cake during labour to sustain the mother, which, though
described on several birth-related websites as of ancient (possibly Cornish) origin, seems to have
first been mentioned in a 2010 novel, *The Birth House*, by Ami McKay.

[18] Kate Moskovitz, interview.

Mrs Moskovitz (and one other survey respondent) linked the custom to the Torah commandment of a half-shekel tax associated with the divinely mandated census of adult Israelite males, in Exodus 30: 12: 'When you take the count of the Israelites, their number, every man must give a ransom for himself to the Lord when you count them so that there will be no plague.' Expanding this warning to apply in all situations and times, and to all Israelites, some rabbinic interpreters derived a universal prohibition on counting Jews from this verse. The Talmud records: 'Rabbi Eleazar said: Whosoever counts Israel transgresses a [biblical] prohibition.'[19] King David's attempted census of Israel,[20] which was followed by a plague, was adduced as proof of the terrible consequences of such counting. The commentator Rashi (1040–1105) gave a rationale: 'The evil eye controls something which is counted', and the prohibition was codified by some medieval and early modern halakhic authorities.[21] The issue still comes up in connection with censuses, both in Israel and elsewhere. Similar fears about counting people (or animals) are known from many cultures; they are often associated with the belief that the evil eye or some other malign force will be able to harm individuals who have been counted.[22]

However, if we examine how respondents to the questionnaire regarded this custom, it is remarkable that, notwithstanding the long halakhic tradition discussing this issue, only two women classed it as a 'halakhic' practice, while several others explicitly stated that they thought it was an 'ultra-Orthodox' or 'Lubavitch' (i.e. hasidic) custom, and 33% had never heard of it. Some respondents described it as a 'superstition'. Thus, in spite of its undoubted halakhic codification, 91% of the Orthodox respondents, including over thirty observant Modern Orthodox and haredi women, did not regard this custom as mandatory or as important enough to be included in their own practice.

In the light of this variation in understanding of the halakhic and rational status of this custom, how is it to be defined? Should we use its internal (emic) definition by part of the male rabbinic elite,[23] and shared by two women respondents, as halakhically based and mandatory? Should we use the understanding, equally internal to the Jewish community and held by other respondents, that it is a hasidic or haredi custom? Or another internal interpretation,

---

[19] BT *Yoma* 22b.   [20] 2 Sam. 24: 10–15.
[21] Including R. Hai Gaon (d.1083) and R. Avraham Gombiner (d.1683), *Magen avraham*, 156: 2. For a review of the halakhic literature on this topic, see Golinkin, 'Does Jewish Law Permit Taking a Census?'
[22] e.g. Opie and Tatem, *Dictionary*, 101–2; Murgoci, 'The Evil Eye in Roumania'.
[23] Rabbis who regard the custom as mandatory whenever Jews might be counted are mostly haredi, while many Modern Orthodox rabbis argue that it does not apply to most situations, including censuses.

which views this as an optional or even superstitious custom? Or should we apply an external (etic), rationalist or academic definition as a common apotropaic belief, paralleled in many non-Jewish cultures?

In the light of this multiple set of world-views and understandings of the phenomena under investigation, my omission of precise definitions from the questionnaire was deliberate; I did not want to impose any external classification system, since this would tell me little about the importance of such customs in women's religious lives. Instead I attempted to establish what women themselves regarded as practices worthy of note, and whether this in turn revealed any internal systems or principles of classification.

The questionnaire data revealed the existence of several, sometimes contradictory, definitions and classifications that varied in accordance with the complex intertwining of personal and familial identity, religious outlook (*hashkafah*), Jewish educational level, and emotional factors. In addition, many of the customs, especially those associated with women (such as the pregnancy- and birth-related practices), do not appear in halakhic literature or in traditional compilations of customs (*sifrei minhagim*), and are thus easy to describe as superstitions or as unimportant by those who do not practise them. One United Synagogue rabbi to whom I showed the questionnaire dismissed all the practices recorded there succinctly: 'My opinion would be, in one word, rubbish. Absolute rubbish.' Here we can observe the exercise of power in the definition of practices as being outside or inside the halakhic framework. In halakhic terms, practices may be categorized as biblical commandments (*mitsvot de'oraita*), rabbinic commandments (*mitsvot derabanan*), rabbinic decrees (*takanot*), customs (*minhagim*), erroneous customs (*minhagei ta'ut*), or even 'superstitions' or 'magic' (related, though not identical, terms in Hebrew would be *darkhei ha'emori*, literally 'ways of the Amorites', and *kishuf*, 'magic' or 'witchcraft').[24] Interestingly, a word that has recently become very popular in the haredi sector in Israel and elsewhere in describing many of these practices, particularly newly coined ones, is *segulah* (pl. *segulot*), a non-halakhic term that carries positive overtones of 'blessing', 'charm', and 'remedy'.[25]

Only one or two of my haredi respondents or interviewees used the word *segulah*, however. Very few women (and by no means all men) have

---

[24] For full definitions of these halakhic terms, see Elon, *Jewish Law*.

[25] In some instances, extant non-halakhic 'folk' practices are being redefined as *segulot*. A case in point is the custom of an unmarried girl holding the Havdalah candle at the height she would like her husband to be (mentioned above). Although most respondents regarded this as a gentle tease, some websites that list *segulot* for getting married have included it: see 'A Segulah to Get Married' on Rivki Silver's blog, *Life in the Married Lane*, and a list of *segulot* on the Shidduch Center website.

the necessary knowledge to apply the halakhic system and its definitions to the customs they learn from their families; most derive their knowledge and personal practice from their relatives, friends, and communities. In general, they do not perform certain customs because of their secure halakhic basis, but because they have grown up watching their mothers perform them, because they associate them with a beloved grandmother, or even because a friend or a teacher has recommended them as being powerful *segulot* that will help them achieve a goal, such as finding someone to marry, having a child, or healing a sick friend.[26] The distinction between this mimetic attitude and a predominantly text-based, halakhic one has been described by Haym Soloveitchik: 'A mimetic tradition mirrors rather than discriminates. Without criteria by which to evaluate practice, it cannot generally distinguish between central and peripheral, or even between religious demands and folkways.'[27]

This is precisely what the questionnaire responses reveal: an organic and non-hierarchical attitude to a wide variety of practices of different halakhic status and origin that is not based on halakhic texts. Unlike the male elite, the majority of respondents are uninterested in the origins and halakhic significance of what they do, but are passionately invested in the emotional and personal resonances of these practices—their associations with family, their familiarity, the sense of security and identity that they provide, and their efficacy in achieving goals of personal, familial, and community flourishing.

Testing Stereotypes and Assumptions

As I collected the questionnaires, I became aware of a stereotype, held by many respondents, to the effect that Sephardim are generally more 'superstitious' and would be likely to observe far more customs of this type than Ashkenazim. This does not seem to be borne out by the evidence: of the thirty 'high performers'—women who practised twenty-five or more of the customs listed—the top seven were all Ashkenazi, and only one Sephardi appeared in the group. Conversely, the woman who ranked eighth lowest in the number of customs performed (two) was born in Baghdad, of pure Iraqi origin. The presence in the 'high performers' group of all four respondents of mixed Sephardi–Ashkenazi ancestry and of three Ashkenazi women married to

---

[26] This trend seems likely to become stronger as new *segulot* are circulated on websites, community email lists, and social media sites.

[27] Soloveitchik, 'Rupture and Reconstruction', and also Friedman, 'The Lost *Kiddush* Cup'. Both these essays focus on the loss of organic, mimetic transmission of tradition among men; my research indicates that the process has been slower among women, precisely because they are less exposed to halakhic literature.

Table 6 Sources of knowledge for women's customs, grouped by generation and gender of source

Source of knowledge	Number of responses recorded
Learned from an older generation	
Mother, mother-in-law, grandmother	153
Father, father-in-law, grandfather	25
Aunt, great-aunt	17
'Mother's family', 'parents', 'grandparents'	15
Uncle	1
Total	**211**
Learned from own generation	
Husband	21
Sister, sister-in-law	7
Female in-laws, non-specific	6
Brother, 'brother-in-law's family'	3
Total	**37**
Learned from a younger generation	
Daughter, daughter-in-law	22
Son	10
Granddaughter	2
Total	**34**

Sephardim probably reflects their access to two traditions, and the higher total number of customs that would thus be available to them, rather than any Sephardi proclivity to practise folk customs.

Another assumption was supported by the results, however: that women learn most customs of this type from female relatives, particularly older ones. Although I encouraged respondents to note in the 'Comments' space on the questionnaire where or from whom they had learned particular customs, few actually did this,[28] but of the 282 relevant responses, the majority indicated that they had learned from older women (see Table 6).

The fact that daughters, daughters-in-law, sons, and even granddaughters appear as the sources of customs is significant; I suggest that this is the result

[28] Aware that asking respondents to answer 209 questions, in addition to providing details about their background, was quite demanding, I decided to make the 'Comments' section optional rather than risk discouraging respondents from filling in the questionnaire. Women often told me that their mothers or grandmothers had performed several of these customs, even when they did not write this on the questionnaire.

both of increased levels of Jewish education in recent decades and of the *ba'al teshuvah* phenomenon, in which younger members of the community develop an intense commitment to religious observance, sometimes to their parents' dismay. This process has been a feature of Jewish communities worldwide since the 1970s, and has been documented elsewhere, particularly in the American context,[29] but its relevance here is in the higher levels of Jewish education and enthusiasm for Jewish practice among those who become observant, and who sometimes suggest or even demand changes in practice at home. This often involves higher levels of kashrut and sabbath observance, but may also include the adoption of pietistic practices.[30] Most of the responses indicating a daughter as the source of a custom came from one United Synagogue woman in her sixties whose daughter had become much more observant, strongly influencing her mother's knowledge and level of practice.

Who Practises These Customs?

Returning to the group of thirty women who practise more than twenty-five customs, it was apparent that most (nine) of the haredi respondents are included, as well as all seven rabbis' wives who completed the questionnaire. Rather surprisingly, one haredi woman appears in the 'low performers' group of thirty-nine women who practise fewer than ten of the listed customs, but this may be because she came from a non-observant, traditionalist background before joining the Lubavitch hasidim in her twenties. The non-haredi women in the 'high performers' group are from the more observant, consciously Modern Orthodox end of the spectrum, and their presence in the group along with haredi women indicates that, rather than being marginal 'superstitions', as often supposed, many of these practices form an integral part of the life of the most Jewishly educated and religiously observant respondents; as noted above, several practices are discussed and approved in classic halakhic texts.

The highest number of customs practised by an individual is eighty-three, but only eight women practise more than fifty customs. Given that there were over 200 customs on the questionnaire, this emphasizes the fact that these customs do not form any type of 'set', but rather depend on family tradition

---

[29]   See e.g. Benor, *Becoming Frum*; Davidman, *Tradition in a Rootless World*; Heilman, *Sliding to the Right*; Kaufman, *Rachel's Daughters*; Mock-Degen, *Dynamics of Becoming Orthodox* (a unique study of Dutch Jewish women).

[30]   See Friedman, 'The Lost *Kiddush* Cup', 185 for a discussion of the similar influence of yeshiva students on their parents' practice in the 1950s and 1960s.

and education; even those women who have a high performance rate may not even have heard of other common customs. This is further confirmed by the fact that several of the thirty-nine women in the 'low performers' group are religiously observant, so the practice of these customs is not necessarily linked to either the performance or the lack of performance of mainstream, obligatory religious practices, such as observing dietary laws or the sabbath. Additional support for the importance of the family in transmitting these customs comes from the fact that the two converts among the respondents reported moderate and low levels of performance, at sixteen and five customs respectively, and from the fact that two sisters in their twenties, from an observant Modern Orthodox family, showed very similar patterns of performance (seven and eight customs respectively).

Another factor that shapes women's performance of and knowledge about these customs is life experience: it seems self-explanatory that an unmarried, observant United Synagogue woman in her late fifties appears near the bottom of the 'low performers' group, since she would not have had the chance to perform any of the large number of customs associated with marriage, pregnancy, and birth.

What Customs Are Practised?

The questionnaire was organized into categories based on the purpose or context of the customs (see Table 7).

Table 7 Number of distinct customs reported within categories of customs on the questionnaire, in declining order

Category	Number of distinct customs reported within category
To avoid the evil eye or for good luck	26
Death and funerals	25
To find a marriage partner and marriage-related customs	19
During pregnancy	17
To get pregnant	16
Protection of babies and small children	16
Medical and curative practices	15
Birth	9
First menstruation	3
Subtotal	146
Miscellaneous other customs	45
Total	**191**

Table 8 Customs most commonly performed, by age group (%)

Custom	All age groups N = 100	18–30 n = 14	31–40 n = 17	41–50 n = 15	51–60 n = 25	61–70 n = 19[a]	71+ n =10
Washing hands ritually after visiting a cemetery[b]	82	60	100	93	85	79	50
Putting honey, not salt, on challah during the High Holiday period to symbolize the wish for a 'sweet year'	73	80	80	92	65	72	33
Leaving the synagogue during the Yizkor memorial prayer if one's parents are still alive[c]	57	90	60	58	40	65	17
Covering mirrors in a house where mourning customs are being observed for the *shivah* period	51	18	38	42	61	88	44
Baking round rather than elongated challah during the High Holiday period	50	45	57	64	39	50	44
Eating chicken soup to cure illness	49	36	62	64	39	44	44
Not revealing a boy's name before his circumcision	45	9	44	71	52	50	22
Not having the foot of the bed face the door[d]	41	20	71	54	32	44	20
Bride and groom not meeting for some days before the wedding	41	9	76	57	35	44	11
Not stepping on graves	39	27	47	47	32	56	20
Holding Havdalah candle at the height one wants one's future husband to be	39	47	71	40	32	28	10
Putting money in a new purse given as a present[e]	34	8	18	40	52	53	11
Reciting psalms to invoke divine help in healing the sick	33	40	55	27	32	23	0
Saying *tfu tfu tfu* or *po po po* against the evil eye	32	20	18	54	32	28	50
Checking *mezuzot* if troubled by the evil eye	32	22	27	36	31	35	60
Drinking from the goblet used for *sheva berakhot* in order to find a marriage partner[f]	32	33	71	40	16	28	0
Taking a fragment from the plate broken at a betrothal ceremony in order to find a marriage partner[g]	31	47	41	34	16	34	20
Chewing on something if someone mends your clothes while you are wearing them[h]	28	7	18	20	32	50	40
Being *kvater/in* at a circumcision in order to get pregnant[i]	27	23	71	36	10	18	0
Not making any preparations before a birth	27	13	35	33	24	34	20

Table 8 *(cont.)*

Custom	All age groups N = 100	18–30 n = 14	31–40 n = 17	41–50 n = 15	51–60 n = 25	61–70 n = 19[a]	71+ n =10
Not mending your own clothes while wearing them[j]	25	8	18	21	26	47	22
Pregnant women not attending funerals	25	7	30	28	30	36	0
Bride praying under wedding canopy for unmarried friends	25	27	65	33	8	17	0
Giving charity before lighting sabbath candles	25	9	31	29	26	38	0

Note: The customs are presented in order of popularity among all age groups considered together. Highlighting indicates the age group in which each custom is the most popular.

[a] One respondent, who had not specified her age, was assigned to the 61–70 age group on the basis of my personal knowledge.

[b] This (non-gendered) custom is prescribed in several halakhic works, starting with Karo, *Shulḥan arukh*, 'Oraḥ ḥayim' 4: 18. One probable reason for its widespread performance is its public nature; people attending funerals copy others performing the ritual.

[c] Yizkor is the memorial service for the dead held on major festivals. Though the (non-gendered) practice of leaving the synagogue during Yizkor if both one's parents are alive is a *minhag* (custom) rather than a halakhic obligation, feelings run high on the matter; several Modern Orthodox rabbis have encouraged everyone to remain in place for the service (see n. 40 below), while many haredi rabbis insist that if someone already practises this custom they should not change it. See Jakobovits, *Dear Chief Rabbi*, 103. Several respondents felt that they might unintentionally cause their parents harm if they remained in synagogue for this ritual.

[d] Since 'they carry out the dead feet first'. See Opie and Tatem, *Dictionary*, 15–16. This seems to be non-Jewish in origin, though now widely practised among Jews.

[e] A widespread non-Jewish custom; see Opie and Tatem, *Dictionary*, 188–9.

[f] *Sheva berakhot*, lit. 'seven blessings'. The seven blessings recited at the wedding ceremony are repeated for the whole of the following week at festive meals held in celebration of the young couple if a *minyan* is present.

[g] Betrothal (Heb. *tena'im*, 'conditions') is a non-obligatory ceremony in which two sets of parents agree the terms for their children's marriage. It developed among Ashkenazim in the eleventh–twelfth centuries, but had declined by the twentieth century, being performed only in hasidic communities, until a recent rise in its popularity, apparently as a Jewish version of a secular engagement party. After the *tena'im* document is signed, the two mothers break a plate, often giving the fragments to unmarried girls as a *segulah* for marriage. See Sperber, *Jewish Life Cycle*, 151–7, which also mentions a custom of giving the fragments to unmarried men for this reason (p. 153).

[h] Since 'it resembles sewing shrouds on the dead'; a person who is chewing something cannot be dead.

[i] See Ch. 4 above, section on *simḥat bat* and n. 174, and Klein, *A Time to Be Born*, 183.

[j] A variant of the custom of chewing on something if someone is mending clothes while the other person is wearing them. I listed it separately since it appeared independently of the other variant.

The first six categories are gender-linked, covering women's life-cycle events from first menstruation to marriage, pregnancy, birth, and (culturally assigned) childcare. The next three are not gendered categories, although some of the specific practices they include are gender-linked, such as women not attending funerals or not going to a *shivah* when pregnant. A few of the 'miscellaneous' customs are similarly gendered, such as a husband preparing the sabbath candles for his wife to light,[31] or a woman eating a sweet as she leaves the *mikveh*.[32] Several others are associated with the sabbath and festivals, such as the custom of having round loaves for the blessing over bread at sabbath and festival meals, rather than the usual plaited ones, between Rosh Hashanah and Shemini Atseret (or Sukkot). Others are pietistic practices to ensure the efficacy of prayers, such as praying at the Western Wall for forty days, or 'rules' associated with avoiding bad fortune, such as 'Return borrowed pins or you will quarrel with the lender.'[33]

Of the list of roughly 200 customs, twenty-five were not actually practised by any of the respondents; these included two specific to men,[34] as well as practices from earlier times that have died out.[35] Several would be viewed as irrational in the wider, non-Jewish community, and were often described by respondents as 'superstitions', making it less likely that anyone would admit to practising them.[36] In Table 8 I have listed the twenty-four most common customs, practised by at least 25% of respondents.

The table shows the percentage of those who actually perform the custom within each age group; thus, 60% of respondents aged 18–30 wash their hands after going to a funeral, 100% of respondents aged 31–40 do so, and so on, with 82% of all the age groups combined observing this custom.

The most common category here (eight customs) is that of death-linked customs, most of which are designed to avoid contact with the dead or are

[31] 22% of respondents observe this; the usual explanation is that it gives the husband a share in the commandment of lighting sabbath candles.

[32] 6% of respondents do this, but 90% had never heard of the practice. Respondents explained that this 'ensures a sweet week'.

[33] Nobody actually did this, but 8% of respondents had heard of it. Thanks to the decline in home sewing, this seems to be a custom that is dying out, like others associated with domestic technologies.

[34] Immersion in the *mikveh* of the Ari (the kabbalist Isaac Luria, 1534–72), in order to ensure proper repentance before death, and being called up for the honour of dressing the Torah scroll after a public reading (*gelilah*), in order to get married.

[35] e.g. the Hollekreisch, a naming ritual for baby girls, common in German-speaking areas from medieval times to the twentieth century. See J. Hammer, 'Holle's Cry', and Baumgarten, *Mothers and Children*, 93–9.

[36] e.g. the avoidance of pictures of birds (thought to bring death or bad luck), or tying a red string around the waist of a pregnant woman to protect her unborn child. Some of these are paralleled in non-Jewish cultures and may have been derived from them.

associated with mourning and funerals. Another five practices are intended to ward off the evil eye or other malign forces, with another two designed to prevent illness. Four are *segulot* for marriage, and there is one *segulah* to promote conception. Though very few are intrinsically gendered, most of them reflect traditional women's concerns such as marriage, childbearing and childrearing, and the protection of the family from evil forces, illness, and death. Respondents recorded no *segulot* at all connected with Torah learning, though these exist among men,[37] and only about ten customs associated with good fortune appeared in the survey, most of which were general in purpose rather than specific.[38] Three practices might be described as pietistic—performing an accepted and praiseworthy religious action in order to accrue merit, either for the performer or for someone in need.[39] One practice (putting money in a gift purse) is not of Jewish origin, a phenomenon that I will examine later.

Age as a Factor in the Knowledge and Performance of Customs

Differing patterns of performance and knowledge between different age groups offer evidence of change in women's customs over time, and an opportunity to consider what factors lie behind this. Surprisingly, the oldest women know far fewer customs than younger ones (see Table 9).

The 18–30 age group is the second least knowledgeable about customs. This pattern is also visible when age distribution is compared to the performance (as opposed to the knowledge) of customs. Women aged 31–40 constitute almost a third of the 'high performers' group (the thirty women who practise more than twenty-five customs), in line with high performance rates for 30–50-year-olds revealed elsewhere in the analysis (see Table 10).

Table 10 also reveals that only one woman in the 18–30 age category and two among those over 70 belong to the 'high performers' group, which reinforces the trend observed above that the oldest and youngest women know

[37] See BT *Hor.* 13b for lists of practices that make one forget one's Torah learning and adversely affect study, and of practices that reverse forgetfulness. Current male practices of this type include not walking between two women, and not eating the end of the challah.

[38] The principal exception was the custom of *shlisl-khale* (Yid. 'key challah'), baking a key into challah or baking challah in the shape of a key for the sabbath following Passover, which is a *segulah* for 'good *parnasah*' (livelihood). 10% of respondents practised this custom; another 21% had heard of it. It was first mentioned by R. Abraham Joshua Heschel, the Apter Rebbe (1748–1825), in *Ohev yisra'el*. Debate rages on Internet forums about its authenticity and origins; see Alfassa, 'Origins', for a denunciation of it as a recent practice of Christian origin, and Brill, 'Schlissel Challah', for a meditation on its recent revival in American Orthodox circles.

[39] Saying psalms for the sick; a bride praying under the wedding canopy for her unmarried friends; and giving charity before lighting sabbath candles.

Table 9 Respondents' knowledge of the 191 customs recorded on the questionnaire, by age group

Age group	No. of customs unfamiliar to respondents
18–30	40
31–40	14
41–50	22
51–60	14
61–70	21
71+	85

Table 10 'High performers' of customs, by age group

Age group	'High performers'	
	No.	%
18–30	1	3
31–40	9	30
41–50	7	23
51–60	5	17
61–70	6	20
71+	2	7
Total	30	100

Note: 'High performers' are women who practise twenty-five or more of the customs listed on the questionnaire. Percentages have been rounded.

Table 11 'Low performers' of customs, by age group

Age group	'Low performers'	
	No.	%
18–30	9	23
31–40	2	5
41–50	5	13
51–60	10	26
61–70	7	18
71+	6	15
Total	39	100

Note: 'Low performers' are women who practise ten or fewer of the customs listed on the questionnaire. Percentages have been rounded.

Table 12 'High' and 'low' performers within each age group

Age group	Total respondents	'High performers'		'Low performers'	
	n	n	%	n	%
18–30	14	1	7	9	64
31–40	17	9	52	2	12
41–50	15	7	47	5	33
51–60	25	5	20	10	40
61–70	19[a]	6	33	7	37
71+	10	2	20	6	60
Total	100	30	—	39	—

Note: For a definition of 'high' and 'low' performers, see Tables 10 and 11. Percentages have been rounded.

[a] One respondent, who had not specified her age, was assigned to the 61–70 age group on the basis of my personal knowledge.

and perform the fewest customs. The age distribution for the 'low performers' group (who practise fewer than ten customs) roughly reverses this pattern, with the youngest and oldest groups together accounting for almost 40% of the group (see Table 11).

The same pattern emerges if we compare percentages of 'high' and 'low' performers *within* the age categories (see Table 12). Thus, 64% of women in the youngest group can be classified as 'low' performers, with only 7% of that group in the 'high' performer category, and so on. As with our earlier tables, this too shows that it is the youngest and oldest women in the survey who are the least likely to practise these customs. It is not immediately obvious that this correlates directly with their lower level of knowledge about customs, though this might be one factor among several others. For instance, in the case of the youngest, low performance of some customs might be partly due to the fact that some of them have not yet married or had children, and are therefore under-represented in the categories associated with pregnancy, birth, and small children. Another factor, in their low performance of death-related customs, might be the greater likelihood that their parents and siblings are still alive, giving them less exposure to customs associated with death and funerals. This hypothesis would not account for the low rate of performance of the oldest women, however, who could be expected to have experienced most life cycle events. When we look at the types of custom practised by these two age groups, however, rather than at the flat rates of knowledge and performance of all customs, the similarity between them recedes (see Tables 13 and 14).

Table 13 Customs most popular among 18–30-year-olds (N = 14)

Custom	% practising
Leaving the synagogue during the Yizkor memorial prayer if one's parents are still alive	90
Putting honey, not salt, on challah during the High Holiday period to symbolizethe wish for a 'sweet year'	80
Washing hands ritually after visiting a cemetery	60
Holding Havdalah candle at the height one wants one's future husband to be	47
Taking a fragment from the plate broken at a betrothal ceremony in order to find a marriage partner	47
Baking round rather than elongated challah during the High Holiday period	45
Reciting psalms to invoke divine help in healing the sick	40
Responding with particular devotion (*kavanah*) to the Kaddish to enhance the success of personal petitionary prayers	38
Eating chicken soup to cure illness	36
Drinking from the goblet used for *sheva berakhot* in order to find a marriage partner	33

Note: Customs are defined as popular if performed by at least 30% of the age group. They are presented here in declining order of popularity.

In Table 13, the most common custom is that of leaving the Yizkor memorial service if one's parents are alive; in comparison, only 17% of women over
71 practised this custom. This may be due to older women interpreting the
survey question as relating to their current practice rather than including
what they used to do when their own parents were alive.[40] Unsurprisingly,
three of the customs most popular among 18–30-year-olds are *segulot* for
finding a husband (or ensuring one of the right height), a major concern
for younger Jewish women given the strong social expectations of universal

[40] Alternatively it might reflect the influence of the strenuous (and controversial) efforts of
some United Synagogue rabbis in the 1980s to discourage the practice, which they regarded as
superstitious: '[In 1980] I introduced a Yizkor memorial booklet, [with] meditations for
departed members of the family . . . and I included a prayer that I composed for the health and
well-being of one's parents, because I strongly recommended that people should not leave the
shul, they should stay in, and that the original reason for leaving the shul was the *eina bisha* [evil
eye] . . . the *satan* [adversary] says, "Oh, you want to stay in for Yizkor? With pleasure, I'll go along
with it and give you a reason." And I strongly opposed that sort of mentality . . . There were
always some who left shul, but a high proportion of people did change their perception, thank
goodness, and they stayed in and recited the prayer . . . I remember the late Rabbi Bernstein
strongly disagreeing with me, and instructing his people to leave the shul.' Rabbi Jeffrey Cohen,
interview.

Table 14 Customs most popular among women aged 71 and over (N = 10)

Custom	% practising
Checking *mezuzot* if troubled by the evil eye	60
Washing hands ritually after visiting a cemetery	50
Saying *tfu tfu tfu* or *po po po* against the evil eye	50
Covering mirrors in a house where mourning customs are being observed for the *shivah* period	44
Baking round rather than elongated challah during the High Holiday period	44
Eating chicken soup to cure illness	44
Chewing on something if someone mends your clothes while you are wearing them	40
Not giving knives as a present (unless recipient makes a token payment)[a]	40
Bride throwing her bouquet to unmarried friends	34
Putting honey, not salt, on challah during the High Holiday period to symbolize the wish for a 'sweet year'	33
Bringing salt, oil, flour, candles, and sugar into a new home[b]	33
Not stepping over someone sitting on the floor, and 'unstepping' if you do	30
Tying red thread on things against the evil eye	30
Using salt against the evil eye[c]	30

Note: Customs are defined as popular if performed by at least 30% of the age group. They are presented here in declining order of popularity.

[a] Of non-Jewish origin; see Opie and Tatem, *Dictionary*, 217–18. Such a gift would 'cut the friendship'.

[b] A rarer variant was hiding these materials in a new house before the owners moved in, so the house and its inhabitants will never lack food, light, etc.; also known outside the Jewish world; see Opie and Tatem, *Dictionary*, 204–5.

[c] One woman in her fifties reported that her mother used to pin a small bag of salt tied with a blue ribbon to her underwear. Other informants reported that parents or grandparents threw salt 'over their shoulder', a common non-Jewish custom, so several traditions, not all Jewish, seem to be represented here. See Opie and Tatem, *Dictionary*, 339, and Sperber, *Jewish Customs* (Heb.), vol. viii, ch. 9, for the use of salt against demons.

marriage throughout the Jewish community. If this table is compared with the one documenting the most popular customs among women over 71, some sharp contrasts can be seen (see Table 14).

Only four of these customs appear in the 18–30s table above.[41] Protection against the evil eye emerges as a major concern for older women, in contrast

[41] Two customs associated with challah between Rosh Hashanah and Shemini Atseret, washing hands after a cemetery visit, and the 'medicinal' use of chicken soup, all of which are very common.

Table 15 Knowledge of customs against the evil eye versus performance in the 18–30 and 71+ age groups

Custom	18–30 (n = 14)		71+ (n = 10)	
	Custom known but not performed (%)	Custom performed (%)	Custom known but not performed (%)	Custom performed (%)
Checking *mezuzot*	60	20	0	50
Saying *tfu tfu tfu* or *po po po*	67	20	40	50
Tying red thread on things	80	20	20	30
Using salt	40	7	10	30

to the 18–30-year-olds, who seem less concerned about this (except in their very high performance rate for leaving Yizkor if their parents are living, though this may be understood by them as demonstrating respect for parents rather than avoiding the evil eye). The importance of concerns about the evil eye for the oldest women in contrast to their lesser importance for the youngest women is highlighted when we compare the rate of actual performance of customs designed to repel the evil eye to mere knowledge about such customs (see Table 15).

A far higher rate of older women who know about these customs actually perform them (from over half to all of them), in contrast to the youngest women, of whom only a seventh to a quarter of those who know about these customs practise them. This difference between the oldest and the youngest generation holds true across the entire range of customs, with the youngest women consistently knowing about more customs but performing fewer of them, in contrast to the oldest women, who know of far fewer customs but perform more of them. At first sight this seems counter-intuitive: surely older women would be more familiar with traditional practices and know more customs than much younger women? However, this evidence reinforces other data from my research, which point to a profound change in the nature of women's religious lives and support Soloveitchik's hypothesis of the replacement of a mimetic system of education and socialization by a text- and institution-based one. To throw more light on this, let us return to the comparison of the most popular customs (in terms of performance) among the 18–30 and over-71 groups.[42]

Two of the most popular customs among women aged 71 and over are of non-Jewish origin (not giving knives as a gift, and the bride throwing her bouquet to unmarried friends),[43] in contrast to the absence of customs of

[42] See Tables 13 and 14.
[43] As opposed to customs *paralleled* in non-Jewish societies, such as using salt to ward off evil, or the use of red in apotropaic rituals.

Table 16 Popularity of customs of non-Jewish origin, by age group (%)

Custom	All age groups (N = 100)	18–30 (n = 14)	31–40 (n = 17)	41–50 (n = 15)	51–60 (n = 25)	61–70 (n = 19[a])	71+ (n = 10)
Putting money in a new purse given as a present	34	8	18	40	52	53	11
Not giving knives as a present	23	11	13	21	32	28	40
Touching wood	20	20	7	29	32	7	17
Bride throwing her bouquet to unmarried friends	12	0	0	8	11	29	33
Using a cotton pad soaked in wine or tea to cure styes	5	0	12	14	4	0	34
Rubbing a gold ring around the eye to cure styes	4	0	6	7	4	6	0
Curing warts with raw meat or tied string	4	0	0	7	9	6	0
Avoiding green	3	0	0	0	8	0	10

Note: The customs are presented in order of popularity among all age groups considered together. Highlighting indicates the age group in which each custom is the most popular.

[a] One respondent, who had not specified her age, was assigned to the 61–70 age group on the basis of my personal knowledge.

non-Jewish origin among the 18–30 group's top ten customs. If we examine the eight customs on the questionnaire that are definitely of non-Jewish origin,[44] and compare the performance rates in the different age groups, it is clear that they are more often practised by older than by younger women (see Table 16).

Although several respondents described touching wood and the bride's throwing of the bouquet as 'non-Jewish' or 'Christian' customs, a fifth of all the women surveyed actually did touch wood, with a third of women aged 41–60 and 17% of the oldest group practising this custom. Again, this might seem counter-intuitive, but again it points to a difference in the nature of older and younger women's religious lives. Very few of the women aged 71

[44] There may be others that I have not securely identified as being non-Jewish in origin. In addition, it is difficult to know how to categorize an old custom that was probably originally not Jewish but is now widely accepted as Jewish. For example, not placing a bed with its foot facing a door, though widely observed (41% of respondents), is not mentioned in any Jewish source or context. The customs I define here as non-Jewish are those of which I can find no mention in any Jewish context, those which respondents often categorize as non-Jewish, and those which are amply documented in non-Jewish contexts.

Table 17 Popularity of customs of pietistic origin, by age group (%)

Custom	All age groups N = 100	18–30 n = 14	31–40 n = 17	41–50 n = 15	51–60 n = 25	61–70 n = 19[a]	71+ n = 10
Reciting psalms to invoke divine help in healing the sick	33	40	55	27	32	23	0
Bride praying under wedding canopy for unmarried friends	25	27	65	33	8	17	0
Giving charity before lighting sabbath candles	25	9	31	29	26	38	0
Responding with particular devotion (*kavanah*) to the Kaddish to enhance the success of personal petitionary prayers[b]	24	38	35	36	8	18	22
Giving charity to invoke divine mercy to protect another person	22	0	33	35	11	39	0
Inserting one's 'personal verse' in the 'Elokai netsor' prayer[c]	20	23	41	36	8	12	0
Taking challah to invoke divine mercy for the sick	17	10	33	43	5	0	0
Reciting the prayer of the Shelah[d]	17	0	13	38	12	23	0
Taking on an extra mitzvah to invoke divine mercy for the sick	16	9	26	29	13	12	0

Note: The customs are presented in order of popularity among all age groups considered together. Highlighting indicates the age group in which each custom is the most popular.

[a] One respondent, who had not specified her age, was assigned to the 61–70 age group on the basis of my personal knowledge.

[b] While the idea that one should recite prayers with devotion goes back to the Mishnah, saying certain phrases with 'extra' *kavanah* in order to attain one's desire seems to be a recent practice.

[c] After reciting the last paragraph ('Elokai netsor') of the Amidah prayer, one adds a biblical verse that begins and ends with the letters that begin and end one's Hebrew name. For the seventeenth-century origin of this custom, intended to preclude forgetting one's name when facing divine judgement after death, see Golinkin, 'Why Do Some Jews Recite a Special Verse?'

[d] A prayer composed by the kabbalist R. Isaiah Horowitz (the Shelah, c.1565–1630) for the welfare of one's children, recited on the eve of Rosh Hodesh Sivan. It is currently being popularized on Orthodox blogs, websites, and email lists.

and over went to Jewish schools, and in many cases their Jewish education (usually at cheder or at home) was disrupted by their evacuation during the Second World War. In contrast, by 2011 about half of all Jewish children aged 4–18 attended Jewish schools.[45]

Increasing numbers of Orthodox Jewish girls now spend a 'gap year' before university (or, in haredi circles, before marriage) studying at seminaries in Israel or Gateshead, in parallel with the more established practice of

[45] See the section on 'Women and Jewish Education' in Ch. 3. The proportion of Orthodox children attending Jewish schools is considerably higher.

Table 17 (cont.)

Custom	All age groups N = 100	18–30 n = 14	31–40 n = 17	41–50 n = 15	51–60 n = 25	61–70 n = 19[a]	71+ n = 10
Reciting psalms to invoke divine help in finding a marriage partner	15	13	24	20	16	6	10
Reciting psalms/prayers to invoke divine help in getting pregnant	13	0	14	40	0	0	0
Reciting special prayers during pregnancy	5	0	0	13	4	12	0
Baking challah and giving it away in order to get pregnant	4	7	0	7	8	0	0
Reciting 'Shir hama'alot' during labour[e]	3	0	7	7	0	0	0
Reciting Perek shirah for forty days in order to get married[f]	3	8	0	7	4	0	0
Praying during labour for childless friends	2	0	6	0	4	0	0
Reciting the Song of Songs every Friday night in order to get married[g]	2	8	0	0	0	6	0
Giving double tithes in order to increase one's wealth	1	0	0	0	5	0	0
Praying for forty consecutive days at the Western Wall to attain one's desire[h]	0	0	0	0	0	0	0

[e] There are fifteen psalms (120–34) that begin with the words *Shir hama'alot*; the respondents did not specify which one should be recited, but may have meant Ps. 126, the best-known.

[f] *Perek shirah* is an ancient compilation of biblical quotations listing the praises of God recited by all elements of creation. The *Jewish Encyclopedia* (1906) notes that it is rarely recited, 'except by very pious Israelites', but in recent years it has become popular among women as a way of arousing God's mercy.

[g] The Song of Songs is recited every Friday afternoon at synagogue by Sephardi men and every Friday night by hasidim. Its recitation by women as a talisman for finding a marriage partner seems to be recent.

[h] This is also of recent origin; R. Yosef Shelomoh Elyashiv (1910–2012), a leading haredi rabbi, says it has no basis in halakhah or tradition. See 'Interesting Psak from Rav Elyashiv'.

sending boys to yeshiva to study.[46] As a result, younger Jewish women have a far higher level of formal Jewish education than their grandmothers and mothers, which often trumps mimetically learned and family-based customs; these may seem incorrect, suspect, or simply worthless in the light of greater text-based knowledge. Stories abound of girls 'coming back from sem' and criticizing Jewish practice at home, or persuading their parents to adopt more stringent forms of kashrut and sabbath observance. Traditional practices

[46] This began to be popular in the 1970s, and is now considered obligatory in observant circles, both haredi and non-haredi.

Table 18 Knowledge of the ten most popular pietistic customs versus performance in the 18–30 and 71+ age groups

Custom	All age groups (N = 100)	18–30 (n = 14)		71+ (n = 10)	
		Performed (%)	Known but not performed (%)	Performed (%)	Known but not performed (%)
Reciting psalms to invoke divine help in healing the sick	33	40	47	0	10
Bride praying under wedding canopy for unmarried friends	25	27	47	0	0
Giving charity before lighting sabbath candles	25	9	36	0	33
Responding with particular devotion (kavanah) to the Kaddish to enhance the success of personal petitionary prayers	24	38	31	22	11
Giving charity to invoke divine mercy to protect another person	22	0	45	0	0
Inserting one's 'personal verse' in the 'Elokai netsor' prayer	20	23	15	0	0
Taking challah to invoke divine mercy for the sick	17	10	20	0	17
Reciting the prayer of the Shelah	17	0	0	0	0
Taking on an extra mitzvah to invoke divine mercy for the sick	16	9	64	10	0
Reciting psalms to invoke divine help in finding a marriage partner	15	13	60	10	0

Note: The customs are presented in order of popularity among all age groups considered together.

associated with warding off the evil eye, though several are recorded in the Talmud and in medieval sources, can seem superstitious and embarrassing in the light of modernity, while newly minted pietistic practices are often learnt at 'sem', either from teachers or from peers, or from the Internet. This is borne out by analysis of the pietistic customs recorded in the questionnaire, several of which are of recent origin,[47] by age group (see Table 17).

Very few of these customs are performed by the oldest women; the highest rates of performance are among those aged 31–50, followed by the 18–30 group.[48] Older women's ignorance of these customs is clearly demonstrated by a comparison of their rates of performance and their knowledge of such customs with those among 18–30-year-olds, in relation to the top ten pietistic customs (see Table 18).

The older women have simply never heard of many of these customs, in contrast to both the youngest women and those aged 31–50, more of whom have attended a Jewish school and been to a seminary, or use the Internet, which is now a major source of *segulot* both old and newly minted.

Origins and Development

To what extent do the customs collected in the questionnaire reflect what is known of women's practices in earlier periods? This is very difficult to assess, since so little was written about what women did, and what was recorded was documented by men. In addition, the definition of halakhah and *minhag* and their interrelationship in the medieval period constitutes a major area of academic debate, which cannot be summarized here, though for convenience we may cite Israel Ta-Shma's definition of *minhag* as 'any religious action that has halakhic or quasi-halakhic status in the rabbinic sources but no talmudic source'.[49] This, however, would apply only to some of the customs recorded by the survey and is not a very useful concept in the context of the present analysis. The medieval and early modern manuals of customs (*sifrei minhagim*) or

[47] Sometimes the practice itself is mainstream or ancient, but has recently been repurposed as a pietistic custom: thus taking challah to accumulate merit for a sick person, in order to aid their recovery, is a new twist on the biblical commandment to take challah when baking bread, regarded as a major 'women's mitzvah' since rabbinic times, but not performed to benefit others.

[48] The two pietistic customs which show the highest rates of performance by women aged 61–70 are ancient (giving charity before lighting sabbath candles, and giving charity to protect someone); those of recent origin are completely unknown to the older women.

[49] Ta-Shma, *Early Franco-German Ritual and Custom* (Heb.), 21; my translation. For further discussion of the relationship of *minhag* and halakhah, see ibid., esp. 16–41, 49–73, and Ta-Shma, *Ritual, Custom, and Reality in Franco-Germany 1100–1350* (Heb.), esp. chs. 1 and 5. See also Zimmer, *Society and Its Customs* (Heb.), 10.

books of recommended practices (*sifrei hanhagut*) rarely mention women, and when they do, they record practices that the male elite thought women should be observing rather than documenting what women were actually doing.[50] As noted by Ta-Shma,[51] many of these manuals, which became popular in the thirteenth century, were written by individuals who had served great religious leaders and wished to record their practices, especially in the synagogue; it is thus not surprising that women are rarely mentioned. The pietistic practices that other sources recommend to their (male) readers include frequent fasting, extreme humility, confession of sins, care to pronounce every word of the obligatory prayers with proper intent (*kavanah*), not looking at women, wearing two sets of *tefilin*, and an intensification of avoidance of menstruating women[52]—few of which would apply to women, and none of which (with the exception of reciting certain liturgical responses with extra devotion in order to obtain one's desire) have parallels in the material gathered in the questionnaires.

Other premodern sources include halakhic codes and responsa, and books explaining the meaning of customs, which also generally present men's religious lives as the norm, with only occasional mentions of women's practices.[53] In her analysis of the representation of women in *Sefer ḥasidim*, a pietistic work of the twelfth–thirteenth centuries, Judith Baskin observes: 'We cannot find women's voices in *Sefer Hasidim* . . . we cannot know what any individual woman thought or felt, though occasionally we may know how they acted. Rather, we are left with one male elite's perceptions of a wide range of females and female behaviours, both approved and disapproved.'[54] Exceptions to the male-authored and male-dominated sources are provided by the books of *tkhines*, women's Yiddish prayers, which uniquely preserve information about women's understanding of various practices and about their spiritual lives. However, they only mention these practices indirectly unless

[50] e.g. Isaac of Tyrnau's *Sefer minhagim*, written in the late fourteenth century and first printed in 1566. It starts with chapters on the three daily prayer services, festivals and fasts of the Jewish liturgical year, and life-cycle rituals; apart from weddings, women have little role in most of the practices described, which focus on synagogue rituals and formal prayer.

[51] *Ritual, Custom, and Reality in Franco-Germany 1100–1350* (Heb.), 110–11.

[52] This list is derived from Kanarfogel, 'Peering through the Lattices', ch. 1.

[53] For instance, an examination of the fifty-four customs in the section on funerals and mourning in Sperling, *Sefer ta'amei haminhagim*, published in 1890, revealed only two that were paralleled in the survey, plus an additional twenty-four (non-gendered) customs that are widely practised (such as mourners not wearing leather shoes, or placing a stone on a grave when visiting it) but were not mentioned by the respondents, either because they thought they were obvious or because they were unaware of them. Only one custom from Sperling's work is specifically associated with women—the recitation of a special *kinah* (elegy)—but this no longer seems to be practised.   [54] 'From Separation to Displacement', 2.

there is a *tkhine* associated with them.[55] As a result of the near-invisibility of women in most of these sources, our knowledge of their practices and religious lives in the past is patchy at best (as indeed is our knowledge of current women's practice).[56] Information about regional variation is almost non-existent, and the lives of premodern Sephardi women in particular are poorly documented, except in folkloristic studies, which, as noted above, generally omit the social context of the customs described.[57]

However, some practices recorded in my survey, including some non-gendered examples, can be traced back to the Talmud, or even the Bible. These include not counting Jews (discussed above), the use of red string for protection,[58] wearing amulets,[59] eating mandrake root to aid conception,[60] wearing an *even tekumah* against miscarriage,[61] and the belief that treading on toenail cuttings causes miscarriage.[62] Others are documented in medieval and nineteenth-century sources, such as checking *mezuzot* in cases of illness or misfortune,[63] spitting to ward off demons or the evil eye,[64] or changing the

---

[55] Some later *tkhines* were written by men. For a superb analysis of premodern Jewish women's spirituality as revealed by analysis of *tkhines*, see Weissler, *Voices of the Matriarchs*. Since they are principally prayers, however, they do not often refer to non-verbal customs of the type discussed here.

[56] For recent works on medieval Jewish women, see Baskin (ed.), *Jewish Women in Historical Perspective*; Goldin, *Jewish Women in Europe in the Middle Ages*; Grossman, *Pious and Rebellious*; and Kaplan and Moore (eds.), *Gender and Jewish History*. For the history of women's Torah education, see Zolty, *'And All Your Children Shall Be Learned'*. For an edition, translation, and introduction to a popular Yiddish guide to the 'women's mitzvot', R. Benjamin Slonik's *Seyder mitsvos noshim* (Kraków, 1577), together with a discussion of its social context, see Fram, *My Dear Daughter*.

[57] e.g. Sabar, 'Childbirth and Magic'. See also Sered, *Women as Ritual Experts*, 127–31, for Kurdish Jewish women, and a bibliography of studies of oriental Jewish women's religious lives (pp. 166–9).   [58] See Teman, 'The Red String', for biblical and post-biblical sources.

[59] Trachtenberg, *Jewish Magic and Superstition*, ch. 10. See also Schrire, *Hebrew Magic Amulets*. Of the questionnaire respondents, 17% said they wear amulets, while another 41% were aware of the custom.

[60] See Gen. 30: 14–17. No respondent actually practised this, though 11% had heard of it. Only two women described it as a modern custom; three identified it as a biblical practice.

[61] A special stone; see BT *Shab.* 66b and Klein, *A Time To Be Born*, 92. Only 2% of respondents had done this; another 3% had heard of the practice or had a family member who had done it.

[62] BT *Nid.* 17b, *MK* 18a. This was not included in the questionnaire, but several women mentioned it after the survey was finished.

[63] Sperber, *Jewish Customs* (Heb.), vol. viii, ch. 8. Checking *mezuzot* is very common, and appeared five times on the questionnaire in the following contexts: evil eye (31%); infertility (9%); ill health (17%); seeking a marriage partner (2%); and 'for any problem' (21%).

[64] Trachtenberg, *Jewish Magic and Superstition*, 159; 7% of respondents did this, 61% knew of it.

name of a sick person.[65] The sources cited above also preserve information about customs that are no longer practised, such as the early modern Ashkenazi women's practice of measuring graves with wicks that they then used to make candles for the synagogue on Yom Kippur,[66] or a nineteenth-century practice of aiding a difficult delivery by giving the mother water drawn from seven wells.[67] Present practice is often quite different from that of the past; some changes are linked to technological and material change (since candles are no longer made at home, it is not surprising that candle-making rituals have disappeared), but other disappearances and innovations are more difficult to explain. The questionnaire data reveal that practice is constantly changing, as noted above, with the assimilation of non-Jewish customs (a process operative in the past as well), the gradual abandonment of practices that seem 'superstitious' to women with a good secular education, and the introduction of new, often pietistic customs, especially among the young. Unlike most of the other customs recorded, the pietistic practices introduce a new element of prayer- or text-linked verbal techniques, as opposed to the action- and object-centred nature of many earlier customs.[68] As well as reflecting the higher level of text-based education among younger women, this may also reflect a desire to engage in practices formerly associated with male forms of piety.

One interesting feature of women's practice is that the purpose of a custom is sometimes realigned or extended to fit contemporary or personal needs.[69] Elly Teman has documented the birth of a new Israeli application of the ancient custom of tying red thread or string on people and objects,[70] which seems to have originated as a protective device and symbolic maintainer of boundaries.[71] In the 1930s, the practice acquired connotations of promoting fertility: women visited Rachel's Tomb near Bethlehem and purchased red thread that had been wrapped around the tomb to help them conceive. Teman

[65] Trachtenberg, *Jewish Magic and Superstition*, 204–5; 8% of respondents had done this, 16% had a family member who had done it, and 52% had heard of it.

[66] Weissler, *Voices of the Matriarchs*, 133–46, notes that this custom may go back at least to the eleventh century.   [67] Sperling, *Sefer ta'amei haminhagim*.

[68] Apart from the *tkhines* of the early modern period, some of which are still used in hasidic circles, though none of my informants mentioned them.

[69] See, for instance, the new interpretation of holding a Havdalah candle, discussed above, n. 25.

[70] This practice appeared in four contexts in my survey: worn against the evil eye (19% performed this, with another 60% aware of the custom); sewn into a wedding dress (8% performed, 18% aware); worn around the waist when pregnant (no performers, 9% aware); and attached to children's clothes or beds (8% performed, 28% aware). All seemed to be seen as protective in nature; no respondents mentioned this practice in the context of fertility.

[71] Teman, 'The Red String'.

found that from the 1980s onwards, Israeli women had transformed the custom into a new protective ritual, tying red thread around their soldier sons' hands at their passing-out parade, thus adapting an ancient practice in response to the stress experienced in a period of repeated conflict and terrorist attacks.

In one unusual case among my interviewees, a fertility custom seems to have been repurposed as a charm for promoting marriage: Sheyna Marcus, a single woman in her twenties under considerable pressure to get married, reported that her father had given her the amputated foreskin from her nephew's circumcision, explaining that her sister-in-law had said that burying it was a *segulah* for getting married![72] The original custom, common among the Jews of North Africa and Turkey, was to swallow the foreskin to promote conception, especially of a son, but presumably this was toned down to suit modern sensibilities.[73] Another instance, typifying the current enthusiasm, especially in the haredi sector, for new *segulot* and pietistic practices, is the commandment of separating challah, described in Chapter 4, which in recent years has taken on a new significance as a *segulah* or source of merit that can be 'stored' and used for others' benefit—in itself an idea that seems to be relatively recent. Classical Jewish thought includes the idea of *zekhut avot*, the protective merit of the patriarchs,[74] but the concept of earning merit by the performance of meritorious deeds and *segulot*, which can then be used as a spiritual equivalent of financial capital and 'donated' to other people, seems to be strongly associated with the recent proliferation of pietistic practices.

The Question of Magic

Looking at the customs recorded in the questionnaire, one may wonder whether some, at least, of these practices should be categorized as magical. Some are definitely not mainstream and could perhaps be described as magical: examples include *blay gisn*, the practice of detecting and removing the influence of the evil eye by pouring molten lead into a glass of water,[75] and biting off the stalk end of an *etrog* in order to conceive a male child.[76] Here we

[72] She decided that she would comply, 'to keep her [sister-in-law] happy, and I appreciate the thought, even if it is a bit gross. It can't hurt to be involved in a mitzvah, *segulah* or not.' For the 'it can't hurt' response, see below.

[73] Raphael Patai, 'Folk Customs and Charms Relating to Birth' (Heb.), *Talpiyot*, 6 (1953), 1–2, cited in Sperber, *The Jewish Life Cycle*, 15–16. Several rabbis have forbidden the practice, e.g. R. Ya'akov Mosheh Toledano (1880–1960), in his *Sefer yam hagadol*.

[74] See Ch. 4 n. 147 above.   [75] 4% of respondents had done this; another 11% knew of it.

[76] 1% had done this; another 14% knew of it. An *etrog* is a citrus fruit, used as part of the ritual of Sukkot.

come up against the long-running anthropological debate about the definition of, boundary between, and relationship of the terms 'magic' and 'religion', and the role of rationality in both categories, as well as the relationship
between these concepts and that of 'science'.[77]

Starting with E. E. Evans-Pritchard (1902–73), the ideal of a definition of
magic that conforms to a culture's own understanding has often been urged,
which would aim to understand practices in terms of the categories and
values of the culture under consideration. Though it is somewhat doubtful
that a completely accurate definition and interpretation of such practices
that matched the culture's own definitions could actually be achieved by
anthropologists (whose field of study is in itself an irredeemably 'external' and
Western project), it is undeniable that elucidating the internal understandings of cultural phenomena is essential. Scholars of ancient magic and religion seem to be more realistic about this ideal, partly because of the difficulty
of reconstructing an 'internal' view for ancient societies, given the fragmen-
tary evidence.[78] When we consider Jewish practices, formulating a satisfactory
definition internal to Judaism is somewhat complicated by the fact that there
is no single Jewish definition of magic, or even any agreement as to where
the boundary between permitted and forbidden practices lies—a phenomenon equally familiar in modern Western culture, as Gideon Bohak observes:
'A quick glance at the relevant literature will reveal that scholars and lay-
persons alike can hardly agree on what we mean by "magic", that is, on the
emic definition of this term within our own [modern Western] culture.'[79]
Since my interest lies in women's understandings and practice of these
customs, which often reveal tensions between Jewish and non-Jewish definitions of magic,[80] as well as between different Jewish definitions, I propose
to use a fairly generalized 'external' or etic definition alongside a range of
'internal' or emic definitions, and to examine the relationship between these
various definitions as reflected in women's discussions of these practices.

For present purposes I use a 'common-sense' definition of magic as widely
understood in the non-academic Western world: magic consists of practices
and beliefs that imply 'a more active control of the environment than simply
requesting the deity to intercede',[81] and which are often of an 'irrational'

[77] See Tambiah, *Magic, Science, and Religion*, ch. 1, for the history of the debate.

[78] Both Bohak (*Ancient Jewish Magic*, 4) and Hoffman ('Fiat magia', 190) argue that etic and
emic approaches should be used simultaneously. See also Harari, *Early Jewish Magic* (Heb.).

[79] *Ancient Jewish Magic*, 4.

[80] For instance in the interpretation of affixing a *mezuzah*: what might seem to be a divinely
ordained commandment to an observant Orthodox woman might be classed as a classic
apotropaic magical practice by an academic rationalist.

[81] Luhrmann, *Persuasions of the Witch's Craft*, 170.

nature and ignore scientific concepts of causality. In addition, magic often involves rituals, verbal formulae, and the manipulation of objects. In contrast to this definition lies the shifting and negotiable field of intra-Jewish attitudes to and definitions of magic, the origins of which are masterfully portrayed by Bohak in his *Ancient Jewish Magic*. He notes that 'not only is the Hebrew Bible far from systematically outlawing all forms of magic, it even lays the foundations for the development of some specifically Jewish magical technology',[82] opening the way for the rabbis of the Mishnah and Talmud to find plenty of exceptions to their blanket ban on magical practices (*keshafim*): magic could be used in healing, to counter magic, and for social control, and they had no qualms about the use of amulets or the study of magic.[83] Rabbinic literature contains many examples of rabbis using magic themselves, sometimes to counter magicians but occasionally to destroy or control their enemies. Bohak emphasizes that magic

was not some socially deviant set of practices and beliefs condemned by heresiologists and punished by the authorities, nor was it a set of silly superstitions practiced solely by the ignorant masses. Rather, it was a technology mastered by many specialists and lay persons and accepted, and even utilized, by the religious establishment itself.[84]

Later attempts, such as that made by Maimonides (1138–1204), to delegitimize magical practices and brand them as idolatrous or as *darkhei ha'emori*, 'ways of the Amorites'—a loose category applied by the talmudic rabbis to practices of which they did not approve[85]—did not meet with unqualified success. Maimonides' strictures against magic and the magical performance and interpretation of the commandments form part of his wider battle against mystical, proto-kabbalistic trends in the Judaism of his time, which provided the necessary conceptual basis for the acceptance of magic. Ultimately his reform campaign did not succeed, and the essentialist, kabbalistic world-view largely prevailed, and has been normalized in the haredi world.[86] In the nineteenth and twentieth centuries anti-magic attitudes made considerable headway in Jewish communities that were more open to their host societies in the West, where post-Enlightenment conceptions of rationality and of the authority of science held sway. These conceptions, however, failed to make much

---

[82] *Ancient Jewish Magic*, 67.   [83] Ibid., ch. 6.   [84] Ibid. 428.

[85] For a discussion of this category, see ibid. 382–5. Not all the practices listed as belonging to it (e.g. in BT *Shab.* 6–7) would fall into the etic, 'common-sense' category of magic used here, but it is interesting to note that one of the practices specified is that of tying red thread onto people or things—a custom familiar to 80% of the survey sample.

[86] See Kellner, *Maimonides' Confrontation with Mysticism*, and the review by Diamond, 'Maimonides contra Kabbalah'.

impression in those communities that remained untouched by the Enlightenment or that chose to react against it, such as the traditional communities of eastern Europe, and ultimately the haredi world.

Given this background of solid support and precedents for Jewish magic in classical and central Jewish texts, it is perhaps not surprising that magical or quasi-magical activity (using our 'commonsense' definition) is not only tolerated but quite common in the British Orthodox Jewish community, particularly in the haredi sector, nor that it is often not regarded as magical by its practitioners. Compared with much rabbinic or medieval Jewish magic, the practices of the women who responded to my questionnaire were quite low-key: I found no trace of any aggressive or erotic magical practices at all. Most were apotropaic or protective in nature, with a focus on promoting marriage, fertility, easy childbirth, health, and general welfare—all of which are non-controversial aims central to most Jewish women's understanding of their roles. A conspicuous departure from classical Jewish magical techniques was the sparse amount of written and verbal activity among these women: classical Jewish magic focuses upon the recitation of spells and formulae (sometimes involving biblical verses) and the writing of amulets and other magical documents. In contrast, only twenty-nine customs from my survey involved recited or written words in any form (whether magical or not), and these fall into three groups:

GROUP 1

- Pray in one's own words (under the marriage canopy for others to marry; during labour, for others to have children; at the grave of Rabbi Yonatan ben Uziel in order to find a mate;[87] for forty days at the Western Wall to obtain one's desire)

- Recite biblical or classical texts (Psalms, Song of Songs, *Perek shirah*, to get married; when pregnant; during labour; to heal sickness; to obtain one's desire; recite one's verse in the 'Elokai netsor' prayer[88])

- Recite the liturgy or *tkhines* (recite *tkhines* to get pregnant; say 'amen' and *yehe shemeh raba mevorakh* from the liturgy with devotion to obtain one's desire)

- Recite 'special prayers' (unspecified) during pregnancy

GROUP 2

- Wear an amulet (both adults and children)

[87] At Amuka, in the Galilee; see Sasson, 'From Unknown Saint to State Site'.
[88] See Golinkin, 'Why Do Some Jews Recite a Special Verse?'

- Place the name of a sick person under the circumcision pillow
- Place a prayer book or 'holy book' under the pillow during pregnancy[89]
- Place a copy of the book *No'am elimelekh* under the pillow during labour
- Check *mezuzot* for errors (against the evil eye; in case of illness; in case of infertility; to get married; for any problem)
- Check parents' *ketubah* (marriage contract) for errors if experiencing difficulty in getting married[90]

GROUP 3

- Boys come to the house to recite the Shema and/or psalms in the week before a baby's circumcision
- Study the Zohar and/or sing songs in the house the night before a circumcision
- Receive a blessing from a 'holy rabbi' to get pregnant
- Read *maftir*[91] on Yom Kippur for prosperity in the coming year
- Say the 'Atah horeta' verses[92] on Simhat Torah for prosperity in the coming year

When we examine these practices, it becomes apparent that the majority of texts or words to be recited are either prayers from the standard liturgy or *tkhines*, biblical or classical texts, or personal prayers on behalf of oneself or others. No magical texts appear at all in the first group. The second group reveals the use of written material as amulets or in an amuletic manner, approximating more closely to classic Jewish magical techniques. However, the women only use, and do not produce, the texts involved (nor do they even

[89] The 'holy book' may be *Sefer razi'el hamalakh* (Book of the Angel Razi'el), a medieval kabbalistic book of spells and incantations, often used for protecting pregnant women. In a message on the EdgwareK email list in November 2011, a woman asked to borrow a copy of this and of *No'am elimelekh*, 'for a few weeks', clearly for this purpose. (The request actually named the book as *Sefer razi'el hamelekh*, literally 'Book of King Razi'el'—an interesting example of the lack of classical Jewish literacy among women.) *No'am elimelekh* is a hasidic Torah commentary by R. Elimelekh of Lyzhansk; on its magical properties see *No'am elimelekh*, ed. Nigal, i. 13. I am indebted to Professor Ada Rapoport-Albert for this reference.

[90] I have found no other reference to this belief, though there seems to be a (modern) kabbalistic belief that mistakes in a *ketubah* can cause childlessness; see Hirsch, 'N.Y. Kabbalist Combs Ketubot for Mistakes'.

[91] The 'additional' Torah reading; the man honoured with this also reads the *haftarah*, the prophetic portion.

[92] A series of biblical verses recited when the Torah scrolls are taken out of the Ark before the *hakafot* (circuits), during which men carry and dance with the scrolls.

read them), and, except for the amulets (of unspecified character) and possibly *Sefer razi'el hamalakh*, a classic magical text, all the texts used are non-
magical in nature: the prayer book, a hasidic Torah commentary, *mezuzot*,[93]
a slip of paper with an individual's name, and the *ketubah*. The checking
of *mezuzot* and the parents' *ketubah* reflects the principle that written words
have power in and of themselves (which could be externally defined as a magical belief). This is strongly supported by classical Jewish sources that view
Hebrew as 'the language of creation' and immensely powerful.[94] Although
Maimonides, who has a non-essentialist view of Hebrew, might argue about
this,[95] it would be difficult to classify it as a magical belief from a traditional
Jewish perspective. The third group includes customs associated with men,
from a 'holy rabbi' giving a blessing to promote conception to male performance of festival liturgy that promotes prosperity.[96] They cannot be classified as
women's practices even though they were reported by women.

Women's Understandings of Customs and Practices

Though several practices recorded in the survey could definitely be classed as
magical in terms of a 'common-sense' definition, as we saw at the beginning
of this chapter, Jewish women think about the wide range of customs reported
in much more diverse and nuanced ways than merely as 'magical' or 'non-
magical'. Their attitudes include complete, uncritical trust in the practices'
efficacy and belief in their authenticity; the reinterpretation of some practices
in psychological or spiritual terms; the imposition of a sharp division between
'halakhic' or meritorious practices and 'superstitious' or even harmful ones;
uncertainty about their effectiveness, leading to performance as a kind of
insurance policy; and acceptance of the 'common-sense' view of these practices as magical and superstitious. I examine these responses in more detail
below.

   Many of the respondents most committed to these customs came from the
haredi sector, and would occasionally demonstrate the authentic nature of the

---

[93]   Though *mezuzot* can be regarded as magical according to both etic and emic definitions,
they are primarily viewed as biblical commandments. Maimonides fulminated against the
treatment of *mezuzot* as magical charms; for a discussion of his attitude to 'magic' and his part
in the cultural battles over this question, see Ravitzky, '"The Ravings of Amulet Writers"'.

[94]   e.g. in *Sefer yetsirah* (of early though uncertain date) and in the thought of Judah Halevi
(*c*.1075–1141), for which see Kellner, *Maimonides' Confrontation with Mysticism*, 155–8. The idea
is also common in kabbalistic tradition.

[95]   Kellner, *Maimonides' Confrontation with Mysticism*, 159–78.

[96]   Women would be barred from reading *maftir* or reciting the 'Atah horeta' verses in almost
every Orthodox synagogue.

practices by telling me miracle stories about the successes they had brought. We may take as an example Menucha Mizrahi, a grandmother from a hasidic family and married to a Sephardi rabbi, who performed more customs (83) than any other respondent and was utterly convinced of their efficacy. Telling me about her weekly baking of challah as part of a group of forty women who do this in the merit of the sick, she reported: 'We get back stories—a woman had stage 4 cancer. They gave her three months to live. It's wiped out the cancer.'[97] She was very reluctant to suggest any boundary between permitted and forbidden or magical practices and did not characterize any of the customs on the questionnaire as unacceptable. Both she and her family members had consulted Rebbetsin Aidel Miller, an Israeli specialist in the *blay gisn* anti-evil eye technique who advertises in and periodically visits both the UK and the USA. For Menucha, the effectiveness and permissibility of the practice was guaranteed by the fact that Rebbetsin Miller has letters of approval from famous rabbis, and she treasured some special leaves given to her as a protective charm by the rebbetsin. Such practices structure and give meaning to her religious life: she spends a lot of time performing them on behalf of people who are sick, have no job, are infertile, or are having difficulty finding a marriage partner. She estimated that she was praying for about 150 people every day, as well as visiting the tomb of the Shotzer Rebbe[98] in Enfield every Friday, where she lights two candles for the ascent of his soul, and extra candles for the people for whom she is praying. In addition, she takes part in a group project to help people find marriage partners: she has taken responsibility for praying for two individuals, as well as learning the laws concerning gossip (*leshon hara*) and participating in round-the-clock '*leshon hara* watches',[99] in which people sign up to refrain from any gossip for a set period, in order to accumulate merit on others' behalf. As mentioned above, she also bakes challah every week and gives it to needy families or the elderly, to accumulate merit for sick people. For Menucha, performing these practices and involving herself in her synagogue's ladies' guild embody the essence of her mission as a Jewish woman—to help and nurture others—and she was very conscious of this as a special and holy role for women, with biblical models:

[97] This and the following quotations come from an interview with Menucha Mizrahi.

[98] R. Shulem Moshkovitz (d.1958), a Romanian hasidic rebbe whose grave has become a place of pilgrimage.

[99] Other women mentioned this practice to me; it appears to be recent in origin, and is popular both in haredi circles and among observant Modern Orthodox women. The popularization of two books on the laws of gossip, *Ḥafets ḥayim* and *Shemirat halashon*, by R. Israel Me'ir Hakohen (1838–1933), both available in English translation, probably underlies this.

Through the prayers of the women, *nashim tsidkaniyot* [righteous women], like the women in Mitsrayim [Egypt], who got us [redeemed from slavery], if you believe I think it does help, you know, and how many people we've seen who didn't have *zivugim hagunim* [good marriages], didn't have *shidukhim* [marriage partners], and thank God! I'm not saying that one particular thing works, but everything put together, [like] baking challah with forty women.

In contrast, Sarah Segal, another hasidic woman, expressed religious reservations about such customs and the *do ut des* attitude they imply, while avoiding any condemnation of women who do practise such things:

I'm not a custom person actually. I *do* do things, I do lots of the customs that I was born into, those *minhagim* and things like that, but, if say, for example, I had an issue about something, I'd rather look at it and see what the issue is about, I'll take it apart rather than say, 'OK I'm going to now do this and this and this'. I don't run for *segulot* so much . . . I do think it's got a lot of meaning, and I think they're good things to do, but I don't like to sort of barter with God, that's the way I like to see it . . . I see it as a bit immature, to be honest, I feel it's like a little bit immature, because God doesn't just want actions, He wants the heart.[100]

Nevertheless, she did perform thirty customs from the questionnaire, particularly those relating to protection during pregnancy and the avoidance of death. She differed from Menucha's somewhat mechanical approach (action X produces result Y) in giving spiritual and theological meanings to several customs, occasionally linking them:

Change of name, that's very meaningful. Your name is everything, your name is your whole being, it's your whole persona. If you change your name you change your *mazel* [fortune] . . . There's a name that we call each other as friends, the way people know you, then there's a name that you call yourself, that's how you know yourself, and there's a name that God calls you, and there's a name that your parents call you. And the goal of life is to make all those four names meet—that's why people say the *pasuk* [verse] of their name in Shemoneh-Esrei,[101] because you can't come up to the next world and say, 'You know my name is Sarah Segal', there's no surnames there, but if you know your *pasuk* then you might recognize the potential of what you could have been. It's quite awesome, so many people don't fulfil their potential while they're here, so when they come up to the next world there's a shock, like 'I could have been *that*', but if you say your *pasuk* at least you'll recognize, because then the Hebrew name is the potential. So that's what we *hope* we can arrive at, the potential that God had in mind for us.

[100] Sarah Segal, interview.
[101] An alternative name for the Amidah prayer, which ends with the paragraph 'Elokai netsor', where the 'name verse' is inserted.

Sarah starts with the well-known idea that a person's Hebrew name embodies that person's essence,[102] and that changes in the name bring about changes in one's life and fortune (hence the common custom of changing the name of someone who falls ill). However, she then links this custom and its underlying concept to the practice of reciting a biblical verse whose first and last letters match those of one's name, and gives this her own interpretation: each individual possesses four names that reflect aspects of his or her identity—social, personal, familial, and divine—and which should ideally be united in order for the individual to achieve his or her true potential, as known to God and apparent in the afterlife. Recitation of the verse enables one to acquire knowledge of this potential and work towards it. Perhaps taking the original idea behind the practice—that post-mortem knowledge of one's name, for which the verse recitation is a *segulah*, can save one from the pains of hell—as a starting point, Sarah reinterprets it as a way of intensifying spiritual progress towards perfection.[103] She applies the same process of resignification to the practice of hiding pregnancy:

I think hiding pregnancy [is important]. I've only had one child but because modesty is such an important part of the Jewish religion, and anything that's hidden has just got more blessing . . . I mean not hiding pregnancy as in if you're pregnant you're going to be seen, but in the early stages of it . . . anything that's hidden from the eyes, obviously you've got more power to grow, that's a very strong and meaningful concept that I like.

Hiding pregnancy is usually interpreted (both in etic and emic terms) as protecting the mother and unborn child from the evil eye and other negative influences, but Sarah reconceptualizes the practice as linked to the central value of modesty and to more general concepts of promoting growth and blessing. A few other women—not only from the haredi sector—also reinterpreted the significance of traditional customs, seeing them as opportunities for spiritual growth. Miriam Rothman, a strongly feminist, young Modern Orthodox woman from a mixed Ashkenazi–Sephardi background, saw spiritual value in her Egyptian grandmother's customs:[104]

All sorts of other things, about not overpraising children, about not mentioning somebody's eyes, or somebody's achievements, *ḥamsa ḥamsa*[105] . . . and it reflects a

---

[102] BT *Yoma* 83b.

[103] None of the other women who mentioned this custom provided any reason for it. I have no way of knowing whether Sarah built her novel interpretation on some knowledge of the original reason or whether she came up with it independently. See Golinkin, 'Why Do Some Jews Recite a Special Verse?' for the original rationale behind this practice.

[104] She performed twenty-nine of those on the questionnaire.

[105] *Ḥamsa* (Arabic: 'five') is the common Jewish name for an apotropaic hand-shaped

sort of humility and avoidance of hubris in the face of the universe, which is not understandable, and which you can't presume to fathom, and it's to remind you of your human littleness, and actually I think that's a very profound religious feeling that's important not to mock . . . so you may call it superstition but I think it reflects a very profound religious attitude.

Other women, particularly the more observant, were very careful to distinguish between correct or 'halakhic' customs, or ones for which there were sources, and practices that they regarded as 'superstitions', as we saw with Kate Moskovitz at the beginning of the chapter. Some women went further and characterized certain practices as potentially harmful. Sheila Dorfman, an observant United Synagogue member in her seventies,[106] felt very strongly:

The idea that you check your *mezuzah* if someone's ill I find very distasteful; I find it sick, absolutely sick. I hear these stories of people saying, 'Oh my husband went blind in one eye and they said we should check the *mezuzah*, and when we checked it the word for eye was damaged', and I think to myself, 'A God who makes somebody blind in one eye because the *mezuzah* had a mistake in the word for eye is not my God.'[107] . . . So superstition, when it comes to *that* level of superstition, can be very very damaging, and I think we have to guard against those.[108]

Sheila illustrates the conflicting attitudes and patterns of thought typical of non-haredi women who live simultaneously in a Western and a Jewish world and struggle daily to negotiate between their contradictory demands. As she herself realized, having grown up in and feeling part of Western secular culture influenced her attitude to these practices, several of which she had abandoned even though her family had practised them:

ornament worn as an amulet. It is common among both Jews and Muslims (who call it 'the hand of Fatima') in North Africa, and is very popular in Israel and elsewhere; 19% of respondents had one in the house. Here Miriam is imitating her grandmother's apotropaic use of the amulet's name, parallel to the Yiddish phrase *keyn ayn hore* ('no evil eye'; Heb. *beli ayin hara*).

[106]   She observed thirty-six customs from the questionnaire.

[107]   Cf. the causal links between *mezuzot* and health documented in Roland Littlewood's study of 'hasidic therapeutics of the divine' among the Lubavitch hasidim of Stamford Hill in his *Religion, Agency, Restitution*, ch. 5, esp. pp. 75–6, 101–2. The elaboration of the kabbalistic concepts analysed there clearly represents the views of the male elite; none of the women I interviewed, including the hasidic women, discussed sophisticated and systematic concepts of this type.

[108]   This and following quotations are from my interview with Sheila Dorfman. A young Sephardi woman who had just suffered a miscarriage told me that she wondered whether it had happened because of her failure to observe a *segulah* properly: a rabbi had told her to bake challot and give them away every Friday, but she had been busy on the Friday before the miscarriage and had put the challot in her freezer, intending to give them away after the sabbath. In such cases, it seems clear that certain practices can indeed have damaging psychological effects.

Some of the more silly things, which I felt were scientifically untenable, I sort of thought, that's just silly really. So I suppose things which I feel in the modern day and age don't have any scientific validity and don't have any purpose—I think I probably gave up on all of them, the red ribbon and the spitting and the throwing the salt over my shoulder, but not because I consciously oppose them, just because they're not who I am.

Though she did not mention feminism as an influence, feminist ideas were clearly an integral part of her world-view:

I think a lot of religion is *done to* women, and I think some of these things were dreamed up by men to keep women in their place, and in those instances I feel very strongly that they have to be put to bed and put in their place, and [we must say,] 'Yeah, well, that was fine 200 years ago but actually it's not who we are.'

On the other hand, she was reluctant to dismiss all practices that could not be rationalized:

I would never dismiss them out of hand, because there are things out there that we don't know about. I'm not at all cynical about aspects of religion which don't appeal to me; I think well OK, that's not for me but that doesn't mean it can't be right for other people, and it doesn't mean that I'm not wrong in dismissing them.

Sheila's efforts to find a balance between two world-views that contrasted sharply in their evaluation of these customs were echoed by several of the other non-haredi women to whom I talked. Reluctant to denigrate or mock customs that they associated both with beloved family members and with tradition, they were often ill at ease when discussing their beliefs about such practices, or would laugh it off with the words, 'Well, it can't hurt!',[109] admitting with embarrassment that they did still perform several of these customs as a sort of insurance policy, 'just in case'. These women are not quite sure what they should think, and receive contradictory messages from different spiritual leaders: haredi rabbis will assure them that these are holy and efficacious customs, while many non-haredi rabbis, like the Modern Orthodox rabbi referred to at the beginning of the chapter, will tell them that they are superstitions that have no place within Judaism.

Even women who did not hesitate to classify almost all the customs on the questionnaire as 'superstitions' shared this ambiguous reaction. Belinda Cohen, an observant United Synagogue member in her sixties, noted that 'Intellectually I think they're all nonsense', but when asked whether she had herself performed the rite of cutting the air with scissors in front of a child

---

[109] Neriya-Ben Shahar, '"At 'Amen Meals' It's Me and God"', 160, records this 'it can't hurt' response being used by Israeli secular women who attend 'amen meals'.

taking its first steps, she reluctantly admitted: 'We did, I'm ashamed to tell you because it's so ridiculous!'[110] Stella James, an observant United Synagogue woman in her fifties, asserted, 'For me it's all completely crackpot superstition, all the things that I've ticked [on the questionnaire]', but admitted a paradoxical emotional attachment, linked to her sense of family and identity:

It just takes me back, it's a memory of what it was like to be a little girl in my parents' home, and . . . I'm not anybody's little girl any more, 'cause I don't have parents, I'm the top of the tree, and I don't have siblings to share these things with . . . so when I hear those things it's lovely, it's nice, even though I think it's nonsense.

She also still observed one custom (placing beds so that their foot end does not face a door), and struggled to articulate why: 'That's the only thing I still do. It's not because I'm superstitious about it, it's just kind of—it's there, my husband's family obviously did that as well . . . We don't even think about it, you know, we just . . . don't.'

As noted above, Stella is very conscious of the difficulties involved in living in two worlds and doubtful about her identification as Orthodox, and this inner conflict plays out in her contradictory feelings about the practices and beliefs she learnt from her family, as well as in her intellectual engagement in Jewish studies.

The investigation of British Jewish women's customs and practices yielded a rich set of data. In spite of the small sample size and the qualitative nature of the information, it is possible to form a preliminary impression of the range and relative popularity of customs, as well as of the correlation (or lack of it) between knowledge about and performance of them. Analysis of the background of women who are 'high performers' has demonstrated that, far from being marginal, ignorant, or uneducated, they tend to be committed to greater religious observance, and typically belong to the haredi and Modern Orthodox groupings. In addition to disproving the stereotype that Sephardim are 'more superstitious' and confirming the assumption that most women learn these practices from older female relatives in a mimetic manner, the survey showed clear evidence of changing patterns of practice. There has been a decline in older practices, which are more likely to be identified as magical or superstitious by women operating partly within a Western worldview, whereas more pietistic practices have increased in number among

---

[110] She was the only person who had done this, though another 5% of respondents (including her daughter) had heard of the practice or had a family member who had done it.

young women with higher levels of formal Jewish education. Both newly religious women and younger, seminary-educated women typically use self-conscious techniques designed to form a pious self, similar to those described by Saba Mahmood, and these often include pietistic practices like those documented here. No ascetic practices were reported, and it seems unlikely that they would be regarded positively. Other factors that facilitate and shape change in women's religious lives include developing technology in the Western world, such as the replacement of domestic manufacture by industrial production, leading to the demise of customs associated with these technologies (such as candle-making or sewing), and the growing possibilities offered by the Internet in spreading knowledge and performance of recently invented or expanded customs.

In addition to advancing our knowledge of women's performance of and familiarity with traditional and newly minted customs, my investigation of women's understandings of and feelings about these practices has confirmed the hypothesis that there are three identifiable groups among British Orthodox women. Haredi women demonstrated a greater acceptance of and trust in the efficacy of these customs, in line with their general world-view, which prioritizes Jewish attitudes and values (defined largely by the male elite) over the Western, secular values of the surrounding non-Jewish culture. Even among some haredi women, however, and much more so among the Modern Orthodox, the conflict between the two world-views was palpable, and many of the women distinguished between 'authentic', halakhically based practices, of which they approved, and 'irrational superstitions' (defined in Western terms), which they either did not practise or, in some cases, roundly condemned. Modern Orthodox women were the most likely to assess the worth of family customs and abandon those they felt had no religious value, as well as being the most likely to adopt new practices that they regarded as promoting spirituality and a positive religious ethos. In contrast, traditionalist women harboured ambivalent feelings about many of the customs, valuing some as family and community traditions that contributed to their sense of identity and scorning others as incompatible with their fundamentally Western world-view, but often confessing to practising them as a form of insurance, on the grounds that 'it can't hurt'. Such inconsistencies are not restricted to women straddling Western and Jewish cultures.[111]

Traditionalist women in particular, though principally Western in their

---

[111] Cf. the modern London witches studied by T. M. Luhrmann, who live as part of a modern Western society while simultaneously believing in and practising witchcraft. See above, Ch. 2 n. 101, for her comment on the way in which people cope with operating within two belief systems at once.

education and thinking, are still inextricably linked to their Jewish identity, which often includes customs and practices for which they might struggle to find a rationale, but which they are committed to observing. Many of them commented that they 'never thought about these things', and were at a loss to explain why they practised them, but this does not mean that such practices were any less important to them; they help to create the intensely Jewish texture of daily life that underwrites and promotes a very real Jewish identity and sense of community, and they are often viewed as essential elements in 'being Jewish'.

Lastly, in terms of agency and creativity, these customs provide a fertile field for women to adapt and reinterpret existing practices, and to invent new ones that express their most urgent concerns and aims. As with some of the new communal rituals examined in Chapter 4, 'power' and 'strength' were often mentioned in connection with these customs, particularly by haredi women. Rather than constituting instances of resistance to male domination, such trends seem to express the interviewees' desire to embody the notion of equality between men and women within traditional Orthodoxy, which is promoted by Orthodox apologists as a response to feminism. Although this is a defensive tactic adopted by male Orthodox writers, haredi women seem to have taken such claims of gender equality literally, turning a blind eye to the very real inequalities of power and control in the Orthodox world while celebrating women's centrality within Judaism. While traditionalist women accept that they are marginalized in the religious sphere, but deal with it by a process of compartmentalization, and while many Modern Orthodox women resent their marginalization and work to change it, haredi women enthusiastically assured me that women and men had equal, if different, roles within Judaism. Sarah Segal noted:

I think that they're equal in worth, men or women, but I see their roles as different . . . The males are the foreign affairs ministers and the women are the interior ministers. So in effect the women actually effect the greatest changes in the home, and are much more dynamic internally, create much more, they can affect more by being in the background more, not because they have to be in the background but because that is the place where the greatest impact is made . . . If you compare it for example to a generator, the more powerful generators will be hidden, whereas the lights will be out on the street. So I would describe women as a very dynamic and powerful creation.

Haredi women thus indirectly accept much of the feminist message while reinterpreting it within a patriarchal framework. This reinterpretation includes the creation of new activities, both communal and individual, which give women their hidden, generator-like power, paradoxically implying that they are ultimately more powerful than men. New developments, such as the concept of 'bankable' merit earned by these rituals, which can be used on behalf of others, emphasize the way in which many haredi women, as well as some from the other groups, view the practice of rituals and customs as empowering them both to achieve new spiritual heights and to help others in their community, fulfilling their aims of nurturing and protecting others, which they see as the essence of women's role. Since there are already hundreds of popular customs whose origins are obscure, and no authoritative body to approve or disapprove them, women (and men) can freely adapt, elaborate, alter, or even invent new practices and *segulot*, which find a ready audience among pietistically minded Jews worldwide, whether by publication in Israeli 'segulah magazines',[112] websites devoted to *segulot*, local Orthodox email lists such as EdgwareK, and Orthodox women's blogs,[113] or via the numerous women's websites, such as Imamother, that cater to haredi and Modern Orthodox women.

Women's customs have thus proved a very fruitful field of research, revealing both change and continuity in women's practice, as well as instances of agency and theological and practical creativity, which can be compared and correlated with evidence from other spheres of women's religious lives.

[112] These are glossy advertising circulars that list telephone numbers that charge the caller for services such as having kabbalistic rabbis pray for oneself or members of one's family, and that also list *segulot* (some of them free).

[113] See Lieber, 'A Virtual *Veibershul*', for details of the lively and expanding world of Orthodox women's blogs, with over fifty such blogs identified by the author.

SEVEN

CONCLUSION

L IKE MOST Orthodox Jewish women in the diaspora, British Orthodox women inhabit a set of overlapping worlds, balancing between Western secular and Jewish religious values, male and female versions of Judaism, and majority British and minority Jewish identities. In their conformity and allegiance to the Jewish community, in their creativity in Jewish ritual and its interpretation, and in challenging or working around male-dominated structures to make spaces where their voices can be heard, these women demonstrate remarkable agency and adaptability in the face of numerous obstacles, as well as loyalty to their vision of their roles as nurturers and protectors of family and community.

As this study has shown, even within Orthodoxy there is considerable variation, both over time and across different groups. While earlier studies have often lumped all denominationally defined Orthodox Jewish women together, my observations suggest that three subgroups—haredi, Modern Orthodox, and traditionalist—exist, and that different patterns of belief, practice, and world-view characterize each group. This calls into question the methodology of categorization commonly used in sociological and anthropological studies of the 'Orthodox community' in general, since these groups are found among men as much as among women. This is particularly true in Britain, where the Jewish landscape differs significantly from that of the USA, as the majority of synagogue-affiliated British Jews belong to Orthodox synagogues, even if they are non-observant, and non-Orthodox Jews form a substantial minority 'rival', though the latter sector in turn is much larger than the non-Orthodox sector in Israel. The vast majority of the Orthodox in the UK, however, are firmly traditionalist in character, alongside a small (though growing) haredi community and an even smaller group of Modern Orthodox. With these basic differences in mind, it is not surprising that innovative trends in Anglo-Jewry (in both the haredi and the Modern Orthodox spheres) lag behind and often copy those in the American and Israeli communities, both of which play a vital role in introducing new ideas and practices. In terms of women's involvement, it is interesting to note that individual women from the American and Israeli Orthodox spheres (particularly the Modern Orthodox and *dati le'umi*), and British women who have spent significant periods of time in either country, form a disproportionately high percentage of those advocating change and greater participation for Orthodox women in the UK.

Although my research supports this new categorization of the UK Jewish community, it must also be recognized that there is significant overlap between the three groups, with increasing haredi influence in traditionalist Orthodoxy as haredi rabbis occupy many United Synagogue pulpits, and haredi teachers dominate Jewish studies in United Synagogue schools attended by non-haredi children. Since unprecedented numbers now attend these schools, pupils are exposed to largely haredi religious models and influences, and many identify Judaism with its haredi expression, whether or not they incorporate this into their own religious lives. This rightward drift is intensified by the increasingly common yeshiva or 'sem' year, spent by young British men and women in mostly haredi yeshivas and seminaries, in Israel or in Gateshead.

This 'slide to the right', as Samuel Heilman calls it, is a major factor in the current pattern of movement between Orthodox subgroups and across denominational boundaries. There is often a sense of disconnection between older, traditionalist women, who were brought up with a more relaxed, mimetic model of Jewish life and more receptivity to influences from the surrounding society (including feminist ideas), and younger women. The latter group is more polarized as some adopt a haredi lifestyle, others leave Orthodoxy (either for denominations to its left or by abandoning religious practice), and a declining number opt for the traditionalist centre. A few adopt a Modern Orthodox approach that strives to integrate Jewish and Western values. Together with the high haredi birth rate, this clearly has implications for the future character of Anglo-Jewry: the current process of polarization seems set to continue, with the traditionalist middle ground gradually fading away.

Haredi women generally adhere to well-defined ideologies that reject Western liberal influences, stress traditional Jewish gender roles and (increasing) gender separation, and valorize tradition (often including recently invented 'tradition') and rabbinic authority. These values have led them, more than the other two groups, to develop independent and novel women's rituals, particularly in the communal sphere, that promote pietistic practices as a means of healing the sick, combating infertility, solving economic problems, finding marriage partners, and protecting family and community. Though many of these rituals have little traditional basis, or combine traditional elements in innovative ways that distinguish them from men's practices—thus somewhat counter-intuitively constituting examples of the 'women's spaces' advocated by some feminists as encouraging women's autonomy—they are legitimated by rabbinic authorization, and have proved increasingly popular among haredi and traditionalist women alike, though they hold less appeal for the Modern Orthodox.

A novel theological approach has evolved in tandem, reworking older ideas about angels and the efficacy of sacred words in a quasi-magical direction that would be unlikely to receive rabbinic sanction, and of which rabbis seem to be unaware. The emphasis on gender segregation in the haredi world has led to mutually invisible and sometimes startlingly dissimilar male and female religious spheres, though in both individuals are expected to develop their personal spiritual lives and relationships with the Divine. In Israel and the USA, too, the emergence of a separate and innovative haredi women's religious culture can be observed.

In contrast, Modern Orthodox women have responded positively to Western feminist influences by seeking increased participation in standard rituals, both in all-female contexts, such as women's *tefilah* groups, and, more recently, in partnership *minyanim*, in which both men and women play active roles, as well as in ritual roles in the domestic context. These women typically draw on halakhic support or justification for women's involvement in standard rituals and public prayer, viewing traditional gender roles as largely dictated by sociological rather than halakhic considerations and thus open to a degree of change. They seek a compromise between shifting gender roles in Western culture and halakhic restrictions on women's ritual performance, rather than full egalitarianism. Modern Orthodox women are more likely to stress text-based education for women both as a sacred practice and as a route to greater equality, and to seek individual religious satisfaction and increased spirituality in greater participation in pre-existing ritual contexts rather than in newly invented ones. While by no means abandoning traditional conceptions of Jewish women's role in the home, they tend to expect both greater male participation in the non-ritual aspects of the domestic sphere and greater female participation in the ritual aspects of the public sphere. They view most rituals as open to both men and women, and often put this into practice in both domestic and public contexts. They show little or no interest in the quasi-magical rituals developed among haredi women, and are more likely than the latter to critique and discard family and community customs on the basis of Western rationalist world-views.

Modern Orthodox women are also the most vocal in expressing dissatisfaction with the current status of and opportunities for Orthodox women, and often actively seek change. The Anglo-Jewish 'women's renaissance' of the 1990s, based on Modern Orthodox ideas and practices in Israel and the USA (such as Rosh Hodesh groups and women's *tefilah* groups), was initiated and promoted by women from this sector, but encountered opposition from largely haredi religious authorities. Lacking halakhic competence and textual Jewish knowledge, as well as substantial male support, the women had few ways in which to defend their innovatory practices. In consequence, some of them moved 'leftwards', to the Masorti movement, abandoning the attempt to find a spiritual home in Orthodoxy. In the first two decades of the twenty-first century, however, a new impetus for change gathered strength among women in this sector, with increased opportunities for halakhic education (often viewed as the portal to power), enthusiasm for performing more of the domestic rituals traditionally carried out by men, a desire for new rituals that incorporate women's voices (as in the new *simhat bat* ceremonies and multiple new forms of batmitzvah), and increased participation in communal rituals, from Megillah readings to leading prayer. Although it is still too early to determine how this will influence women's religious lives, the high level of male support and co-operation it involves and the excitement generated among Modern Orthodox women are unprecedented. The most radical of these developments, the partnership *minyan* movement, seeks to introduce a more egalitarian attitude to sharing communal rituals. It seems to be more resilient than the radical Rosh Hodesh movement of the late 1980s and early 1990s, perhaps because of both the participation of men and the higher level of Jewish education characteristic of younger women. This recent trend may yet lead to wider changes in women's roles in United synagogues, though this is likely to be a slow and gradual process, and probably will not penetrate haredi circles.

Unlike haredi and Modern Orthodox women, traditionalist women often express uncertainty, doubt, or even indifference in matters of belief and personal spirituality, but avoid innovation in religious practice. They prefer the status quo, often reacting with disapproval to Modern Orthodox attempts to increase women's ritual participation, which they view as threatening their own identity. For a group whose members maintain Jewish customs and practices as the constitutive elements of their personal and communal identity, any change is liable to be regarded as an attack on that identity, unless authorized by traditional authority figures. It is noticeable that, while few traditionalist women would consider participating in Modern Orthodox initiatives such as women's *tefilah* groups or partnership *minyanim*, which lack official approval, several happily attend equally innovative haredi rituals such as *berakhah* parties, which enjoy rabbinic endorsement. Traditionalist women are often uninterested in halakhah as a guide to personal practice, and rely almost exclusively on mimetically transmitted family and community tradition. This undergirds their opposition to practices such as women making Kiddush in public, which, while halakhically permissible, is 'not done' in most Orthodox communities. While haredi women would probably cite the central value of modesty as justification for non-performance of these rituals, traditionalist women worry that acquiescence in (or worse, performance of) such rituals would endanger their own Orthodox identity in the eyes of others, perhaps labelling them as 'Reform'. With mimetic example as the basis of their religious praxis, most traditionalist women are not interested in improving their Jewish education by means of text-based study in the 'male' style. This makes them more open to the influence of haredi rabbis than Modern Orthodox women, who are more likely to have the halakhic knowledge with which to evaluate or challenge rabbinic directives concerning practice. Nevertheless, traditionalist and Modern Orthodox women will co-operate in some problematic areas of Jewish tradition, such as the lack of redress for Jewish women who want a divorce but whose husbands refuse to grant them one. Demonstrations demanding a solution to the *agunah* crisis unite the two groups in protesting an injustice that affects them equally.

This analysis of the importance of differing world-views for women's self-understanding and ritual performance raises some problems for Saba Mahmood's recent critique of feminist approaches to non-liberal religious women and her assertions of such women's agency in producing a 'pious self'. Indeed, as I noted at the outset, if applied to the Jewish world, her analysis would only fit the haredi group while failing to account for Modern Orthodox women, who struggle to reconcile Western liberal and traditional Jewish non-liberal world-views and to integrate both into their religious self-understanding and practice. Traditionalist women, whose religious identity is largely identical to their ethnic identity as members of a minority, and for whom a 'pious self' is far less important than a 'Jewish self', would equally be passed over by this account. In addition, Mahmood ignores much of the social and community dimension, which was of paramount importance to the women I studied and which profoundly influenced their practice.

While groundbreaking, Mahmood's work does not provide a satisfactory theoretical account of women from religious minorities in the West, who often strive to integrate the expectations of two cultures. Such women have not received much scholarly attention, but they constitute an important category that should be studied more intensively. This study has shown some of the ways in which Orthodox Jewish women attempt to achieve a practical and religiously valid balance, and comparison with future studies of women from other religious minorities should deepen our understanding of the strategies used, their level of success, and their implications for women's religious agency, building on Mahmood's analysis and enriching it. In addition, her account could be further developed by examining the ways in which non-liberal women work around and within patriarchal religious structures to achieve their goals (when these do not match those of the establishment), while fully supporting the existence and divine authority of the structures themselves; evidence of this emerged from my analysis of haredi women's ritual innovation and creativity.

The question of how Orthodox women themselves view their roles should similarly be approached with a more nuanced understanding. Much Orthodox apologetic discourse describes family and home as central but, crucially, does not grant women positions of power within the home. Even though it is described as their principal sphere of influence and power, it is hierarchically organized along gender lines, with men performing almost all domestic rituals. Nevertheless, most Orthodox women I encountered do regard their domestic role as central and essential to the preservation of the Jewish community, though they understand this differently from men (as did the women studied by Sered and Weissler). Many women believe that their role is actually more important than that of men; this may sometimes be a reaction to the perceived undervaluing of women and their activities, but for others, the ideals of promoting and protecting family, community, and continuity are far more central to their understanding and experience of Judaism than 'male' ideals of Torah study, halakhic observance, and prayer. My research has confirmed Sered's finding that women frequently 'sacralize the everyday' and sometimes develop their own theological interpretations of their activities, which tend to remain invisible to men—an aspect of Orthodox women's creativity rarely documented elsewhere.

Women preserve a surprisingly wide spectrum of traditional customs and beliefs, many tolerated rather than approved of or promoted by the religious establishment, and most linked to the protection of their families. They show remarkable commitment to continuing these practices, even when these are labelled as 'superstitions' or are devalued by some religious authorities. As we have seen, the nature of these customs is gradually changing, as those that clash with Western liberal and rational ideas decline, and others that conform to current, especially haredi, notions of piety rise. This seems to be the result of both an increasing if silent acceptance of Western liberalism (including elements of feminism) and of changing patterns of Jewish education, with earlier, mimetically based socialization in the home and family giving way to a more self-conscious, text-based education acquired in Jewish schools and seminaries.

Linked both to women's preservation of traditional customs and to their innovation in the ritual sphere is the question of the possibility and expression of creativity and agency among Orthodox women, who have often been viewed as passive victims of a patriarchal system. The wide variety of activities I have documented provides ample proof of women's creativity, while interviews revealed that most of them felt that they did possess agency, though Modern Orthodox women also voiced resentment at the limitations on their freedom and power to shape their religious lives imposed by the all-male religious establishment. However, when a particular form of creative practice is blocked, Modern Orthodox women often prove very resourceful in adapting to rabbinic restrictions in order to achieve at least some of their aims, whether by educating themselves in order to counter rabbinic opposition, accepting some limitations on their activities in order to make strategic gains, coming up with new practices and formats that bypass rabbinic opposition (as do haredi women), or reinterpreting traditional ideas and value judgements. Their agency is often shaped by the constraints of the system, but this makes it no less genuine, and often demands high levels of creativity precisely in order to adapt to the very real limitations on their religious activities.

It is possible that haredi women are also resentful of rabbinic authority, but if so, they do not voice it. In answer to the prevailing secular expectation of at least lip service to women's equality, haredi discourse has set up an ideal of 'different but equal', which both conceals and justifies the patriarchal distribution of power. Women who consciously strive to shape their lives according to haredi ideals create rituals in the 'hidden' women's space that differ from public male rituals and do not challenge them. New small-group activities, such as *berakhah* and challah parties, serve as community-building social occasions and extend women's nurturing and protective role by their focus on healing and social cohesion. By actively seeking rabbinic approval for these novel rituals and by avoiding male spaces such as synagogues, haredi women defuse potential tensions in advance.

In both Modern Orthodox and haredi groups, Catherine Bell's concept of rituals as 'a nexus of power relationships' can be usefully applied, as in both cases a complex pattern of male constraint and permission complemented by female innovation, acquiescence, negotiation, adaptation, and (occasional) subversion—rather than simple resistance—can be seen. Perhaps surprisingly, in the haredi sphere this process exists alongside women's desire to create pious selves—again, an overlapping area unexplored by Mahmood, who critiques the simplistic feminist binary opposition of 'dominance' and 'resistance' but does not analyse how women who fully subscribe to non-liberal systems work within them to achieve their aims, nor how those aims may have been influenced (even if unconsciously) by exposure to external, liberal factors. My research revealed that feminist thinking has shaped women's attitudes across the Orthodox spectrum, both as an unacknowledged influence and as a spur to counter-reaction, and it may well be a factor in the recent proliferation of haredi women's religious activities.

Creativity in theological areas, such as the beliefs held by many haredi women about angels and the efficacy of thaumaturgic rituals mentioned above, is far more subversive to rabbinic theological understandings, though this is not a conscious aim. Since these innovative beliefs are expressed, if at all, to other women rather than to rabbinic authority figures, who seem to be unaware of them, they do not constitute an overt threat to the establishment. Their development seems to be due to the increasing gender separation in haredi society and the rabbis' assumption that women interpret rituals and practices in the same way that they do. The overall effect of such beliefs is that haredi women feel very powerful and central in safeguarding their families and communities.

Traditionalist women are the least creative—unsurprisingly, since their Jewish identity relies on the maintenance of the status quo. Some, however, do join in new activities developed by haredi or Modern Orthodox women, as noted above, with a preference for the former type, as these are guaranteed by rabbinic approval. Those traditionalist women who feel a lack of personal agency in the religious sphere often 'compartmentalize', seeking personal satisfaction and agency elsewhere, in non-Jewish spheres such as work, or in 'less religious' Jewish spheres such as voluntary work and community administration. For some, the contrast between the level of agency they experience within the Orthodox community and the much higher level they enjoy in wider, non-Jewish society has led to a weakening of religious affiliation or practice, while others preserve the external communal indicators of Orthodox affiliation—maintaining a kosher kitchen, attending life-cycle and social events—while feeling a sense of alienation and loss. Since practice rather than belief serves as the yardstick of Orthodox affiliation, these women are 'invisible' misfits or dropouts from the Orthodox community.

In general, women's creativity and spiritual expression are always shaped by the constraints of the patriarchal system within which they operate, not only in the form of the rituals they create but also in terms of the goals to which they aspire. In addition to rabbinic and halakhic restrictions on their ability to innovate or extend their practice, Orthodox women also face social limitations and pressures; they want to remain in good standing within the Orthodox community, and will sacrifice personal spiritual aspirations to this end. As noted above, most women focus on protecting and nurturing their families and communities in their communal rituals—a goal in harmony with the traditional ideal of women's spiritual fulfilment in their role as wives and mothers. Personal satisfaction in participating in central Jewish rituals is often regarded as self-indulgent or the product of non-Jewish influences and, when employed as a justification for introducing ritual innovations, tends to be viewed with suspicion by rabbis.

Much of my research reveals the need for further investigation and new fields of enquiry. Further research on the partnership *minyanim* as they develop will be essential, and should shed light on the role played by changing patterns of Jewish education and influences from the wider society, which in turn could prove useful in studying the way in which influences from the host society shape change in religious minorities. My observation that women understand the significance and centrality of their domestic role in a different way from that in which men view this role goes some way towards answering Ardener's seminal question about how women's lives in male-dominated societies can be accurately represented,[1] but more research is needed to deepen knowledge of women's unique understandings and theological views, for instance in the realm of prayer. Further investigation could also gauge the extent of the differences between women's and men's theological views, especially in the haredi sphere, and test whether increased gender separation lies behind such developments. This too could be of significance in studies of theological uniformity or difference along gender lines in other faith communities. My study of women's customs, which has revealed the decline of traditional protective practices and the rise of pietistic *segulot*, suggests that changes in women's religious education shape even the most traditional and mimetically based areas of practice; comparable research among women of other faiths could illuminate the role played by changes in religious education in women's traditions generally.

Anglo-Jewry is facing unprecedented challenges: in addition to the long-term decline in United Synagogue membership, the rapid expansion of the haredi community and its influence, as well as the increasingly gender-egalitarian ideals of wider British society, are bringing 'women's issues' to the fore as the most visible touchstone of attitudes towards change in the Orthodox sphere. It remains to be seen whether the rabbinic leadership can offer a home within mainstream Orthodoxy for those women who want to increase their knowledge, participation, and spiritual development, while managing to avoid alienating traditionalists, or whether the current tendency to view haredi styles of piety and gender roles as desirable and normative will continue, giving further impetus to the process of polarization that is already apparent. Whatever rabbis decide, it is Orthodox women themselves who will play the largest part in determining their roles and position in the community, by their actions and reactions, and ultimately, by their creativity and agency.

[1]   See p. 13 above.

LIST OF INTERVIEWEES

THE RESEARCH for this study was conducted with the approval of the UCL Research Ethics Committee (project number 2578/001) and it adhered to the standards required by the committee. All interviewees who were recorded received an information sheet listing their rights, including that of withdrawing permission for quotation at any time, and all signed an informed consent form allowing the recorded material to be used. Some did not want to see transcripts of the interviews, while others did and marked sections that they did not want to be used, which were duly omitted. Interviews by phone were not recorded, nor were some short interviews on specific topics. All participants were given pseudonyms except for a few who were happy for their own names to be used; in one case a pseudonym was used even though permission to use the real name had been granted, as it might have led to the identification of other interviewees whose names had been disguised. In a few cases minor details of the interviewees have been altered to ensure anonymity.

LEONIE ADELMAN (pseud.) London-born divorcee in her late fifties, with no children. Grew up in an 'Adas' synagogue; joined the independent Yakar; now a United Synagogue member; traditionalist. *Interviewed by phone, 25 August 2013.*

KETURAH ALLWEISS (pseud.) Married mother of three in her late thirties, from a Modern Orthodox background, educated at a Jewish primary school, a non-Jewish secondary school, and university. Lived for two years in New York, where she got involved in a women's *tefilah* group. Set up a women's Megillah reading. United Synagogue member; Modern Orthodox. *Interview recorded 21 March 2012.*

BELINDA COHEN (pseud.) Married mother of three daughters in her late sixties, from an observant London family, educated in non-Jewish schools and cheder, and as a pharmacist. United Synagogue member; traditionalist. Mother of Beatrice Levi (see below). *Interview recorded 15 September 2010.*

RABBI DR JEFFREY COHEN   Retired rabbi of Stanmore and Canons Park United Synagogue. Married with four children. A central figure in the foundation of the Stanmore Women's Tefillah Group in 1992. Modern Orthodox. *Interview recorded 22 December 2011.*

SHIRLEY DANIELS (pseud.)   Mother of five in her mid-thirties, married to a Sephardi rabbi; brought up in a traditionalist London United Synagogue home; educated at Jewish primary school, cheder, Bnei Akiva, non-Jewish secondary school (with a year at Carmel College), university. Became much more observant after her mother's illness. Trained *mikveh* attendant. *Interview recorded 9 July 2012.*

CAROLINE DEUTSCH (pseud.)   Married mother of three, in her mid-forties; from a traditional background in south London. United Synagogue member; traditionalist. A leading member of community organizations; university-educated. *Interviewed 4 November 2013.*

SHEILA DORFMAN (pseud.)   Veteran Jewish studies teacher in her sixties, widowed and remarried, three daughters. Brought up in a small northern community in an observant family; educated in non-Jewish schools and cheder; MA in Jewish studies. United Synagogue member; Modern Orthodox. *Interview recorded 11 May 2011.*

KATYA FUCHS-MENDES (pseud.)   Married mother of two, in her mid-forties. From a very traditional family, members of a UOHC synagogue. United Synagogue member; Modern Orthodox. University-educated. Founder member of a partnership *minyan*. *Interviewed 7 August 2016.*

FIONA INMAN (pseud.)   Married, in her forties. United Synagogue member. Sister of Caroline Deutsch (see above); from a traditionalist south London background but has become more observant. University-educated. *Interviewed by phone 24 July 2013.*

STELLA JAMES (pseud.)   Married mother of two daughters, in her late fifties. From a traditional United Synagogue family in Ilford. Went to non-Jewish schools, cheder, Bnei Akiva, UCL, and trained as a lawyer. United Synagogue member; started a women's Megillah reading in her synagogue; traditionalist/Modern Orthodox. *Interview recorded 9 November 2010.*

SHARON JASTROW (pseud.)   Married mother of four, in her early sixties. Traditional background, from very small community; non-Jewish schools, cheder, music college, teacher training. Central figure in the Rosh Hodesh movement. Joined Masorti after marrying a non-religious man. *Interview recorded 22 November 2011.*

BRENDA JOHNS (pseud.)   Married mother of three, in her thirties; United Synagogue member; Modern Orthodox. Mixed background, North African mother and Ashkenazi father. University-educated. *Interviewed by phone and email correspondence, 2012–13.*

ARIELLA JULIAN (pseud.) Unmarried, in her forties. United Synagogue member. University-educated. *Interviewed by phone 10 October 2013.*

BEATRICE LEVI (pseud.) Married mother of two sons and one daughter, in her forties. From an observant United Synagogue family, educated at non-Jewish schools, cheder, and private Jewish lessons, plus university and teacher-training. United Synagogue member; traditionalist. Daughter of Belinda Cohen (above). *Interview recorded 15 September 2010.*

RABBI MORDECHAI LOCARDO (pseud.) In his sixties, of Iraqi origin. Haredi rabbi of a Sephardi synagogue. *Interviewed 1 August 2011.*

MIRIAM LORIE Married mother of two sons, in her thirties. From an observant United Synagogue family, educated at university and Pardes Institute of Jewish Studies, Jerusalem. Modern Orthodox; one of the founders of the Borehamwood Partnership Minyan. *Interviewed 8 August 2016.*

SHEYNA MARCUS (pseud.) Unmarried, in her late twenties, from a family she classified as 'between Modern Orthodox and haredi'. Educated at Jewish schools, seminary, and university. Attends a haredi synagogue. *Interview recorded 17 November 2011.*

KATHERINE MARKS (pseud.) Married with four children, in her fifties, from a traditional Ilford family. Educated at non-Jewish schools, cheder, Study Group, university, teacher training. United Synagogue member; Modern Orthodox. Leading Jewish educator. *Interview recorded 10 November 2011.*

MENUCHA MIZRAHI (pseud.) Mother of several children, in her sixties. Married to a Sephardi rabbi. American-born, from a hasidic background. Educated in Jewish schools, and as a special needs teacher; has an MA in Jewish studies. Haredi. *Interview recorded 28 January 2013.*

KATE MOSKOVITZ (pseud.) Mother of eight children, in her sixties. Married to a rabbi. From an observant family in a small provincial community. Educated at non-Jewish schools, cheder, and Bnei Akiva, and had secretarial training. Has lived in several provincial communities, where her husband was rabbi; she sometimes taught in cheder and batmitzvah girls. Haredi. *Interview recorded 3 January 2011.*

ALEXA NEVILLE Married with children, in her forties. From an observant United Synagogue family. Educated at non-Jewish schools, seminary, university. Organized two women's services at Cambridge in 1988. Modern Orthodox. Now lives in Israel. *Interviewed on Skype 6 January 2013.*

NICOLA PERLMAN (pseud.) Married with three children, in her sixties. United Synagogue member; Modern Orthodox/traditionalist. Educated at non-Jewish schools, cheder. One of the founders of the Stanmore Women's Tefillah Group. *Interview recorded 16 February 2011.*

FLORA RENDBERG (pseud.) Mother of one son, in her sixties. Sephardi, married to an Ashkenazi. From an observant London family from Gibraltar. Educated at a Jewish primary school, a non-Jewish secondary school, cheder, and *ulpan*. A mix of traditionalist and Modern Orthodox, belongs to a Sephardi synagogue. *Interviews recorded 26 and 31 July 2010.*

TANYA ROTH (pseud.) Married with adult children and grandchildren, in her sixties. From an observant family, with a higher than usual level of Jewish education. United Synagogue member; traditionalist/Modern Orthodox. *Interviewed by phone in 2016 and 2017.*

MIRIAM ROTHMAN (pseud.) Married with a young son, in her thirties. Grew up in a traditional family in a small provincial community, with an Ashkenazi father and a Sephardi mother. Educated at non-Jewish schools, cheder, a sixth-form Jewish study group, seminary, university; trained as a lawyer. Involved in running the Grassroots cross-denominational community. United Synagogue member; Modern Orthodox. *Interview recorded 18 November 2012.*

LESLEY SANDMAN (pseud.) Married with two daughters, in her sixties. From an observant family in New York. University-educated, M.Phil. in comparative Semitics. United Synagogue member; Modern Orthodox. *Interview recorded 21 November 2012.*

SARAH SEGAL (pseud.) Married to an American Satmar hasid, with one son, in her thirties. From a Satmar hasidic family in London. Educated at Jewish schools, seminary. Lives in Stamford Hill in the Satmar community. *Interview recorded 17 February 2011.*

LINDA STONE (pseud.) Married with three children, in her sixties. From a very observant family in a large provincial community. Educated in Jewish and non-Jewish schools, university. Was a United Synagogue member (her husband still is), attended Masorti services for some time but does not identify herself as religious any longer. Prominent figure in the Rosh Hodesh movement of the 1990s. *Interview recorded 25 July 2011.*

BERNICE SUSSER (pseud.) Married with two sons and a daughter, in her thirties. Secular schools, trained as a nurse. United Synagogue member; Modern Orthodox. *Interview recorded 29 January 2013.*

PERLE TAUBMAN (pseud.) Married with several children and grandchildren, in her late sixties. From a traditional family in a large provincial community, educated at non-Jewish schools and university. Became more religious after her marriage, and eventually joined Lubavitch with her husband. Lives in Stamford Hill. *Interviews recorded 17 February and 15 March 2011.*

DR TAMRA WRIGHT Married with two children. Director of Academic Studies at the London School of Jewish Studies; founder and director of the Susi Bradfield Women Educators Programme. Modern Orthodox. *Interviewed 18 October 2013.*

Consulted in person or by email, but not interviewed at length
(all pseudonyms)

BRACHA ABELMAN, young Modern Orthodox mother of three in her twenties.

GILL ARMSTRONG, United Synagogue member in her seventies.

HANNAH AUGSBERGER, young Modern Orthodox mother in her twenties.

ZELDA EHRLICH, haredi grandmother, originally from the Netherlands, in her seventies.

GWEN FISHMAN, traditionalist United Synagogue member, in her sixties.

DEBORAH GREENBAUM, young newly religious haredi woman in her twenties.

CHERIE JACKSON, ex-United Synagogue member, now Masorti, in her sixties.

LIORA LACHSMAN, unmarried woman in her forties, from a hasidic background, but university-educated and now an academic.

SHIRA LEMBERG, haredi mother in her fifties.

HANNAH ZEVED, haredi mother in her forties.

THE QUESTIONNAIRE:
A SAMPLE PAGE

Research for Ph.D. thesis, Lindsey Taylor-Guthartz, UCL
Contact details: [omitted]

I would be very grateful if you could fill out this questionnaire: it consists of a few questions about your background, and then a list of all sorts of Jewish customs, roughly ordered by the occasion with which they are linked.

Please tick the appropriate box ('I've heard of this' OR 'I do this/had this done to me' OR 'Someone in my family does this/did this') for each custom. If someone in your family practises a certain custom, please say who (e.g. 'mother', 'aunt'). Do feel free to add any comments in the box (or on the back of the sheet/margins if you need more room, but do please note which custom you're commenting on), and add any customs I've left out that you know about in the blank rows or at the end of the sections.

Thank you very much indeed,
Lindsey

Name and contact details

Age   ☐ 18–30   ☐ 31–40   ☐ 41–50   ☐ 51–60   ☐ 61–70   ☐ 70+
Place of birth

Grandparents' place of birth

Mother's mother

Mother's father

Father's mother

Father's father

Sample of Custom Checklist

Avoiding the Evil Eye or Ensuring Good Luck

Custom	I've heard of this	I do this/ had it done to me	Someone in my family does this/did this	Comment/ extra information
Spitting	☐	☐	☐	
Saying *tfu tfu tfu* or *po po po*	☐	☐	☐	
Using salt	☐	☐	☐	
Kissing a child three times and spitting between each kiss	☐	☐	☐	
Tying red thread on things	☐	☐	☐	

ANNOTATED LIST OF CUSTOMS FROM THE QUESTIONNAIRE

Abbreviations

Dictionary	Opie and Tatem, *A Dictionary of Superstitions*
MA	Evidence exists of this custom being practised in the medieval period
NJ	Custom documented in a non-Jewish context
Sperber	Sperber, *Jewish Customs* (Heb.)
Sperling	Sperling, *Sefer ta'amei haminhagim umekorei hadinim*

To avoid the evil eye or for good luck

Spitting	NJ; Trachtenberg, *Jewish Magic*, 159; *Dictionary*, 373
Saying *tfu tfu tfu* or *po po po* against the evil eye	
Using salt	MA, NJ; to ward off evil; *Dictionary*, 339; Sperber, vol. viii, ch. 9; Trachtenberg, *Jewish Magic*, 160
Kissing a child three times and spitting between each kiss	
Tying red thread on things	NJ; *Dictionary*, 326–7; Teman, 'The Red String'
Sewing red thread in wedding dress	Teman, 'The Red String'
Blay gisn (lead pouring)	NJ; German New Year fortune-telling custom; *Dictionary*, 228–9, for divining cause of illness, and future spouse
Spitting on fingertips	

Not praising children	NJ; *Dictionary*, 314–15
Avoiding pictures of birds	NJ; *Dictionary*, 25–6; Bebergal, 'Birds of Ill Omen'
Avoiding green	NJ; *Dictionary*, 181–2
Not counting children	NJ; see Ch. 6; *Dictionary*, 101–2
Using garlic	NJ; *Dictionary*, 172–3
Having a *ḥamsa* in the house	Sabar, 'From Sacred Symbol'
Bringing salt, oil, flour, candles, and sugar into a new home	Sperber, vol. viii, ch. 9
Variant. People (often the mother) hide things in house before new residents move in (e.g. salt, flour, oil)	MA, NJ; *Dictionary*, 204–5; Sperber, vol. viii, ch. 9; Trachtenberg, *Jewish Magic*, 161
Using a special stone to remove evil eye	From a Gibraltarean interviewee: the stone (perhaps from a holy tomb in Morocco) was used as part of a fumigatory rite to remove the evil eye from a house
Wearing an amulet (*kamea*)	NJ; Trachtenberg, *Jewish Magic*
Licking eyelids/forehead	NJ; *Dictionary*, 374
Putting money in a new purse given as a present	NJ; *Dictionary*, 188–9
Avoiding red	Moses Isserles on Joseph Karo, *Shulḥan arukh*, 'Yoreh de'ah' 178: 1; Shabetai Hakohen, *Siftei kohen*, 178: 3
Not counting money in your purse	
Not looking in people's eyes	
Not wearing gold	
Checking *mezuzot* if troubled by the evil eye	MA; Sperber, vol. viii, 96–124; sources quoted there include *Mekhilta* 'Pisḥa' 11, BT *Men.* 33*b*, JT *Pe'ah* 1: 1, 17*d*
Not giving knives as a present	NJ; said to 'cut the friendship'; antidote is to receive a small sum as 'payment'. *Dictionary*, 217–18

To find a marriage partner and marriage-related customs

Checking *mezuzot*	MA; Sperber, vol. viii, 96–124, and sources there including *Mekhilta* 'Pisḥa' 11, BT *Men.* 33b, JT *Pe'ah* 1: 1, 17d
Having a kiddush at synagogue if your parents didn't sponsor one for you when you were born	<http://lifeinthemarriedlane.com/2014 /02/03/a-segulah-to-get-married/> (accessed 23 June 2014); shown in Israeli TV series *Serugim*
Taking a fragment from the plate broken at a betrothal ceremony (*tena'im*)	Goldberg, *Jewish Passages*, 131; Nogg, 'Shtetl Engagement Custom'; Eisenstein, *Otsar dinim uminhagim*, 438 (no mention of *segulah*); Sperber, *The Jewish Life Cycle*, 153 (men); Sperber, vol. v, 58–61 (men)
Drinking from the goblet used for *sheva berakhot* at a wedding	
Bride praying under wedding canopy for unmarried friends	<http://lifeinthemarriedlane.com/2014 /02/03/a-segulah-to-get-married/> (accessed 23 June 2014)
Bride throwing her bouquet to unmarried friends	NJ; *Dictionary*, 41
Bride gives her own jewellery to unmarried friends at wedding to wear during *ḥupah*	<http://lifeinthemarriedlane.com/2014 /02/03/a-segulah-to-get-married/> (accessed 23 June 2014)
Man is given the honour of *gelilah* (rolling up the Torah scroll) in synagogue on Rosh Hashanah in order to get engaged	
Checking whether there's an error in one's parents' *ketubah*	<http://www.jweekly.com/article/full/ 5996/n-y-kabbalist-combs-ketubot-for-mistakes/> (accessed 2 July 2014)
Mother may not have gone to *mikveh*	This may be the reason why a woman cannot find a marriage partner
Reciting psalms (on one's own or in a group)	

Drinking from wine cup at a circumcision	
'Don't sit on a table or you'll get a stupid husband' (variation: at the corner of a table)	NJ; *Dictionary*, 390; won't get married
'Don't speak while eating or you'll get a stupid husband'	
Saying *Perek shirah* for forty days	Recent?
Reciting the Song of Songs every Friday night	Possibly based on Sephardi practice of men reciting it before Friday evening prayer?
Praying at the grave of Yonatan ben Uziel at Amuka, Israel	<http://torahideals.com/2009/06/18/the-mystical-power-of-amuka/> (accessed 12 May 2014); <http://www.jpost.com/Jewish-World/Judaism/Amuka-A-Legend-for-Lovers-315396> (accessed 12 May 2014)
Bride and groom not meeting for some days before the wedding	NJ; *Dictionary*, 40; only Ashkenazim
Not to try on the wedding ring before the wedding	Brings bad luck?

To get pregnant

Visiting holy tombs (e.g. Rachel's tomb)	Sasson, 'From Unknown Saint to State Site'
Eating fish at the wedding	Klein, *A Time To Be Born*, 6
Changing *mezuzot*	Sperber, vol. viii, 96–124
Baking challah weekly and giving it away	MA
Saying *tkhines* or special prayers	Weissler, *Voices of the Matriarchs*
Visiting a holy rabbi	Klein, *A Time To Be Born*, 22, and 225 n.
Sitting in the famous 'pregnancy' chair in Ashdod, Israel	One exists in the Ashkenazi Ari synagogue in Safed; on the Ashdod example, see <http://articles.sun-sentinel.com/1994-07-22/lifestyle/9407210277_1_chair-cashiers-menstrual-cycle>; Pinkney, *A Paranormal File*

Eating mandrake root	Biblical; NJ; Klein, *A Time To Be Born*, 31; *Dictionary*, 237
Wearing/carrying rubies and red stones to prevent miscarriage	MA; Klein, *A Time To Be Born*, 33, 93, 124, 228 n.; Pollack, *Jewish Folkways*, 135; Epstein, *Kitsur sheni luḥot haberit*; see current usage on <http://imamother.com/forum/viewtopic.php?p=3003908>; Sperling, 574; Rabenu Bahya ben Asher, comment on Exod. 28: 15
For a son: biting off the end of an *etrog*	Talmudic, MA; BT *Ket.* 61a; Klein, *A Time To Be Born*, 12, 82; Pollack, *Jewish Folkways*, 17; Weissler, *Voices of the Matriarchs*, 40; Sperling, 521
For a son: seeing the blood at a circumcision	
Wearing an amulet (*kamea*)	Klein, *A Time To Be Born*, 30
Drinking from wine cup at circumcision	
Being *kvater/in* at a circumcision	Klein, *A Time To Be Born*, 183
Putting the name of an ill person under the circumcision pillow	
Drinking tea of willow leaves; also carrying a willow leaf in one's purse	Klein, *A Time To Be Born*, 34–5
Immersing oneself in the *mikveh* after a woman in the ninth month of pregnancy or a woman going for the first time after giving birth	

During pregnancy

Wearing an apron	To protect the baby
Not looking at animals or ugly people on way home from the *mikveh* so as not to have a deformed child	MA, NJ; Klein, *A Time To Be Born*, 61; *Dictionary*, 317–18; Trachtenberg, *Jewish Magic*, 187
Holding a party in the fifth month and preparing baby clothes	Klein, *A Time To Be Born*, 70–1; Pomeroy, 'From the Cradle to the Grave', 64

Hiding pregnancy	Klein, *A Time To Be Born*, 70
Not making any preparations before a birth	NJ; *Dictionary*, 315
Going to the *mikveh* in the ninth month	Klein, *A Time To Be Born*, 76
Wearing a red string around waist	NJ; practised in Mexico, India, and elsewhere
Wearing a Torah binder around the waist (after an earlier miscarriage)	MA?; Klein, *A Time To Be Born*, 92
Putting siddur or holy book under one's pillow	Klein, *A Time To Be Born*, 93; *Sefer razi'el hamalakh*; Sabar, 'Childbirth and Magic', 674
Not telling people the due date	
Having someone good touch you as you leave the *mikveh*	
Husband is given the honour of *petiḥah* (opening the ark) in synagogue during the ninth month	Klein, *A Time To Be Born*, 122; Sperber, iii. 127
Taking challah in the ninth month	
Not wearing gold	
Wearing *even tekumah* against miscarriage	BT *Shab.* 66b; Klein, *A Time To Be Born*, 92; cf. *Dictionary*, 129 (eaglestone, which aids conception, pregnancy, birth)
Reciting special prayers	Klein, *A Time To Be Born*, 88–9; Weissler, *Voices of the Matriarchs*
Toenail cuttings may cause miscarriage	Talmud states that a woman who steps on nail cuttings will miscarry; BT *Nidah* 17a–b, MK 18a; Klein, *A Time To Be Born* 86; see <http://www.theyeshiva world.com/coffeeroom/topic/segulos> for extensive discussion of fingernail customs (accessed 14 Dec. 2014)

Birth

Baking a cake during labour to help others get pregnant	NJ?; see Ch. 6 n. 16
Opening drawers, cupboards, etc.	NJ; *Dictionary*, 27
Untying knots	Ancient; MA; Klein, *A Time To Be Born*, 122; *Dictionary*, 221
Praying during labour for childless friends	Modern?; Klein, *A Time To Be Born*, 125
If the baby is breach, checking all holy books are the right way up	
Not revealing a boy's name before his circumcision or until the father is called to the Torah in the synagogue	Cf. *Dictionary*, 278 (before christening)
Putting a copy of Elimelekh of Lyzhansk's *No'am elimelekh* under one's pillow for birth as instructed by one's rebbe	Klein, *A Time To Be Born*, 123, 150 (citing *Sefer razi'el hamalakh*)
Husband gets *petiḥah* of *Anim zemirot* on *Shabat Mevarkhin*	Klein, *A Time To Be Born*, 122
Reciting or listening to 'Shir hama'alot' (Ps. 126?) during labour	Klein, *A Time To Be Born*, 116, 123, 152

Protection of babies and small children

Placing an amulet (*kamea*) on or near the child	Klein, *A Time To Be Born*, 155
Not taking a baby out for first thirty days	
Not cutting baby's nails for first week / thirty days	NJ; *Dictionary*, 274 (for 1st year)
Inviting yeshiva boys in to sing psalms and say the Shema for the first week	Klein, *A Time To Be Born*, 171, 172
Waving a sword around the baby's room for the first week	Klein, *A Time To Be Born*, 153; Pomeroy, '"From the Cradle to the Grave"', 65; Sabar, 'Childbirth and Magic', 698

Studying the Zohar and/or singing songs the night before circumcision	Pollack, *Jewish Folkways*, 19 (*vakhnakht*); Trachtenberg, *Jewish Magic*, 157, 171; Pomeroy, '"From the Cradle to the Grave"', 65
Sephardi custom: welcoming a new girl on the thirtieth day	Klein, *A Time To Be Born*, 189 (*fados, hatas*)
Ashkenazi custom: welcoming a new girl with 'Hollekreish' ceremony	Klein, *A Time To Be Born*, 190; Baumgarten, *Mothers and Children*, 93–9; Hammer, 'Holle's Cry'
Tying red thread on the baby's cot or on its clothes	Teman, 'The Red String'
Cutting the air with scissors in front of the child's first steps	
Giving the child more than one name	Klein, *A Time To Be Born*, 200, 208–9; Leissner, 'Jewish Women's Naming Rites'
Selecting the child's name following kabbalistic calculation by one's rebbe	Klein, *A Time To Be Born*, 200; Leissner, 'Jewish Women's Naming Rites'
Placing the *mohel*'s knife under the baby's mattress on the night before circumcision to ward off Lilith	
Piercing a girl's ears in the first thirty days to enhance her eyesight	NJ; Klein, *A Time To Be Born*, 101; *Dictionary*, 176 (children and men)
Father visits *mikveh* on morning of circumcision	
Boys come to baby's house the night before circumcision	Klein, *A Time To Be Born*, 171, 172, 179–80, 181, 183; Pollack, *Jewish Folkways*, 19–20

First menstruation

Mother slaps daughter	Lithuanian? <http://ausis.gf.vu.lt/eka/customs/youth_ini.html>
Mother pulls daughter's ear	
Not touching cut flowers during period	

Medical and curative practices

Not stepping over someone sitting on the floor, and 'unstepping' if you do	NJ; *Dictionary*, 377
Reciting psalms (on one's own or in groups)	
Changing a person's Hebrew name	BT *RH* 16*b*; Karo, *Shulḥan arukh*, 'Yoreh de'ah' 335: 10 and Isserles' comment there; Trachtenberg, *Jewish Magic*, 204–5
Taking on an extra mitzvah	
Eating chicken soup to cure any illness	Klein, *A Time To Be Born*, 165
Checking *mezuzot*	Sperber, vol. viii, 96–124, and sources there, including *Mekhilta* 'Pisḥa' 11, BT *Men.* 33*b*, JT *Pe'ah* 1: 1, 17*d*
Lighting ten candles to keep evil spirits at bay	
Taking challah to invoke divine mercy for the sick	
For teething: hanging an animal tooth round the child's neck	Trachtenberg, *Jewish Magic*, 133
For measles or smallpox: throwing ten peas on the patient	
For eye styes: using a cotton pad soaked in wine or tea	
For eye styes: rubbing a gold ring around the eye	NJ; *Dictionary*, 175
For warts: rubbing raw meat on or tie string round with knots corresponding to warts and burying it in ground	NJ; *Dictionary*, 422–3
For jaundice: placing pigeons on the belly	NJ; Rosner, *Biomedical Ethics and Jewish Law*, 491–502; *Dictionary*, 308; *Talmudology* blog, 'Chullin 22b'

Death and funerals

Not pouring water 'backwards' as that's how it's poured on the dead	NJ; *Dictionary*, 314. A member of a burial society reported this is *not* how it is done for the dead.
Not wearing socks around the house	Mourners are halakhically required to avoid wearing (leather) shoes
Not sitting on the floor	Mourners are halakhically required to sit on the floor or low seats
Breaking the journey home after a funeral (e.g. going into a shop)	NJ; to ensure bad spirits do not follow one home from the cemetery. Trachtenberg, *Jewish Magic*, 179; *Dictionary*, 171; Sperling
Not having foot of bed face the door	NJ; some say because this is the way in which corpses are carried out. For extensive discussion, see <http://www.rabbiweisz.com/ask-the-rabbi/ask-the-rabbi-2/> (accessed 25 June 2013); see also *Dictionary*, 15–16
Chewing on something if someone mends your clothes while you are wearing them	Sperling, 571; NJ versions common on Internet
Not mending your clothes while wearing them	NJ; *Dictionary*, 87
Not cutting one's fingernails and toenails on the same day	Avraham Gumbiner, *Magen avraham*, 260; see <http://www.theyeshivaworld.com/coffeeroom/topic/segulos> for extensive discussion of fingernail customs (accessed 14 Dec. 2014)
Not serving cake without a doily	
Not eating boiled eggs	Eggs are traditionally given to mourners when they return from the funeral, as a symbol of the cycle of life
Not stepping on graves	NJ; *Dictionary*, 181; Ganzfried, *Kitsur shulḥan arukh*, 199: 14
If you sneeze when mentioning the dead you must pull your ears	

Not having arum lilies in the house	NJ; arum lilies are associated in Western culture with funerals. *Dictionary*, 443
Women not attending funerals	Kabbalistic? Also Muslim practice
Pregnant women not attending *shivah*	
Pregnant women not attending funerals	NJ; *Dictionary*, 181
People who have living parents do not go to a cemetery	This seems to contradict earlier practice; see Weissler, *Voices of the Matriarchs*
Not cutting one's nails on a Thursday	NJ; *Dictionary*, 275; see <http://www. theyeshivaworld.com/coffeeroom/topic /segulos> for extensive discussion of fingernail customs (accessed 14 Dec. 2014)
Not cutting one's nails in a fixed order	MA; Trachtenberg, *Jewish Magic*, 191; see <http://www.theyeshivaworld. com/coffeeroom/topic/segulos> for extensive discussion of fingernail customs (accessed 14 Dec. 2014)
Covering mirrors in a house where mourning customs are being observed for the *shivah* period	NJ; often interpreted as avoiding vanity in the presence of death; other interpretations note the association of mirrors with evil spirits; *Dictionary*, 250
Banging in nail to a *shivah* chair when someone gets up from *shivah* (i.e. finishes the seven-day mourning period)	Habad website: <http://www.chabad. org/library/article_cdo/aid/371151/ jewish/The-Last-Day-of-Shiva.htm> (accessed 24 June 2014)
No *hespedim* (eulogies)	One respondent: 'For fear that the *satan* will use them against the dead'
Leaving the synagogue during the Yizkor memorial prayer if one's parents are still alive	To avoid bringing misfortune on one's parents; Moss and Cappannari, *Mal'occhio*, 7
Washing hands ritually after visiting a cemetery	Originally a purity practice, later understood as removing evil spirits; Trachtenberg, *Jewish Magic*, 179; <http://www.thejc.com/judaism/rabbi-i-have-a-problem/69638/should-i-wash-my-hands-after-a-funeral>

Not wearing clothing that belonged to a dead person	NJ; *Dictionary*, 87; Sperber, *The Jewish Life Cycle*, 509–11 (shoes)

Miscellaneous other customs

'Sneeze on the truth'	NJ; many references on Internet, including <https://www.tonyhyland.com/sneezing-superstitions/>
Not drinking Havdalah wine or you'll grow a beard/get hair on your chest	Zivotofsky, 'Wine from Havdalah, Women and Beards'
Holding Havdalah candle at the height one wants one's future husband to be	Recently reinterpreted as a *segulah* for getting married—see <http://lifeinthe marriedlane.com/2014/02/03/a-segulah-to-get-married/> (accessed 23 June 2014)
Dipping your fingers in Havdalah liquid and touching your temples and pockets	To promote prosperity; Sperber, vol. iii, 134–5; *Pirkei derabi eli'ezer* (ch. 20); Karo, *Shulḥan arukh*, 296: 1: 'to wash one's face with the leftover wine to show how much we love the commandments'
Immersing oneself in the *mikveh* after a bride in order to receive a blessing	
Drinking nine sips of cold water before Yom Kippur	To make fasting easier? <http://bungalow-babe.blogspot.co.uk/2010/09/gift-of-yom-kippur-in-bed.html> (accessed 23 June 2014) (7 sips); <http://www.theyeshivaworld.com/coffeeroom/topic/tips-to-fast-easy> (accessed 23 June 2014)
Not eating the end of the challah	BT *Hor.* 13*b*: eating bread before it's baked leads to forgetting Torah; sometimes presented as a *segulah* to have male children
Praying for forty consecutive days at the Western Wall to attain one's desire	Recent; Rabbi Y. S. Elyashiv (d.2012) says it has no basis <http://lifeinisrael.blogspot.co.uk/2009/11/interesting-psak-form-rav-elyashiv-40.html> (accessed 24 June 2014)

Giving charity in memory of R. Meir Ba'al Hanes to find a lost object	BT *AZ* 18a–b; *Midrash talpiyot* and several later sources; see article by Joshua Waxman at <http://parsha. blogspot.co.uk/2007/11/rabbi-meir-baal-hanes-and-segulah-to.html> (accessed 12 Dec. 2014)
Baking a key in the challah or baking challah in a key shape for the first sabbath after Passover (*shlisl-khale*)	Seems to be first mentioned, as a segulah for prosperity, in 19th cent., by Abraham Joshua Heschel of Apt, *Ohev yisra'el*; see also Sperling, 249–50; for article claiming it is a pagan practice, see Alfassa, 'Origins'
Responding with particular devotion (*kavanah*) to the Kaddish to enhance the success of personal petitionary prayers	Cf. Kanarfogel, '*Peering through the Lattices*', 84, on the practice of Hasidei Ashkenaz for all prayers: 'reciting the liturgy slowly and accurately unlocks the esoteric meaning of the prayers'
Inserting one's 'personal verse' in the 'Elokai netsor' prayer	To bring good fortune? Perhaps from Isaiah Horowitz, *Shenei luḥot haberit*, as *segulah* on the day of judgement after death; *Sefer ben tsiyon*, Amsterdam, 1690: see the detailed discussion in the *On the Mainline* blog <http://onthemainline.blogspot.co.uk/2012/01/on-source-of-merit-of-reciting-verses.html> (accessed 6 July 2014)
Hanging flour, salt, and oil in the sukkah	To bring prosperity? Sperber, vol. viii, ch. 9, for use of salt against demons
Keeping a piece of Passover *afikoman* in the house from one year to the next	To prevent fires; mentioned in *Kav hayashar* and *Orḥat ḥayim*, see <http://zchusavos.blogspot.co.uk/2007/03/segulas-for-pesach.html> (accessed 23 June 2014)

Reciting the prayer of the Shelah (R. Isaiah Horowitz, *c.*1565–1630)	For the welfare of one's children; the prayer is to be recited on the eve of the New Moon of Sivan; currently being promoted on haredi websites, such as that of She'arim, a girl's seminary in Israel: <https://www.shearim.com/torah-online/tefilot/128-tefilla-of-the-shelah-hakadosh> (accessed 20 Aug. 2019); see Ch. 6, Table 18 for more information
Having itchy hands means you will give away money	NJ; *Dictionary*, 186
Having itchy feet means you will go somewhere new	NJ; *Dictionary*, 167
Giving charity before lighting sabbath candles	As well as being a commandment in its own right, 'Charity saves from death' (Prov. 10: 2)
One's husband should prepare the sabbath candles, so he is involved in the mitzvah	
Putting honey, not salt, on challah for the first year of marriage	Recent?
Lighting a sabbath candle for each member of one's family plus one extra to confuse the *satan*	Hasidic? One respondent said an extra candle should be lit on birthday cakes too
Leaving an undecorated patch of wall in one's home as *zekher laḥurban* (in memory of the Temple's destruction)	NJ; BT *BB* 60*b*; Karo, *Shulḥan arukh*, 'Oraḥ ḥayim', 560. Cf. *Dictionary*, 47, which gives rationale of leaving something unfinished to avoid replicating God's perfection
Baking round rather than elongated challah during the High Holiday period	

Putting honey, not salt, on challah during the High Holiday period to symbolize the wish for a 'sweet year'	Maharil, 'Hilkhot rosh hashanah' 7; Moses Isserles on Karo, *Shulḥan arukh*, 583:1, id., *Darkhei mosheh*, 3; Mordechai Yoffe, *Levush*, 583: 2; Shneur Zalman of Liadi, *Shulḥan arukh harav*, 1; Y. M. Epstein, *Arukh hashulḥan*, 2
Not eating *chrayn* (horseradish) or nuts between Rosh Hashanah and Shemini Atseret	Numerical value (*gematriya*) of the word *egoz* supposedly = *ḥet* ('sin'); Sperber, vol. iv, 42–59 (no nuts on Rosh Hashanah)
Men going to the *mikveh* of R. Isaac Luria in Safed so they won't die without repenting	
If doors, chimneys, or windows in a house are blocked up, one must leave a small hole to allow 'bad spirits' to flow in and out	
Eating a sweet as you leave the *mikveh* to have 'a sweet month'	
Not sewing on Saturday evening or you will sew all week	
Not leaving shoes upside down	One respondent: 'so as not to insult God'
Checking *mezuzot* for any problem	Sperber, vol. viii, 96–124 (MA), and sources there including *Mekhilta*, 'Pisḥa' 11, BT *Men.* 33*b*, JT *Pe'ah* 1: 1, 17*d*
Giving charity to invoke divine mercy to protect another person	See Kanarfogel, *Peering*, 84, on Hasidei Ashkenaz practice
Getting a blessing from a holy rabbi	
Touching wood	NJ; *Dictionary*, 449–50; very common
Being given the honour of opening the Torah ark during the *Ne'ilah* service of Yom Kippur for good fortune	
Reading *maftir* Yonah on Yom Kippur	
Saying 'Atah horeita' verses on Simhat Torah (night and day)	

Sweeping up or eating breadcrumbs to become rich	
Giving double tithes (20% of earnings) to charity to increase one's wealth	
Not counting *kneidlakh* (dumplings) as they are cooking or they will fall apart	
Entering and exiting buildings by the same door	NJ; *Dictionary*, 124
Returning borrowed pins to avoid quarrelling with the lender	NJ; *Dictionary*, 309–10
Bringing a present on first visit to a new house	NJ; *Dictionary*, 205
Not putting shoes on a table	NJ; *Dictionary*, 350
Not leaving water in a container/cup uncovered overnight	The Talmud says a bad spirit rests upon such water; BT *AZ* 30a and *Ḥul.* 9b; Karo, *Shulḥan arukh*, 'Yoreh de'ah' 116: 1; *Pitḥei teshuvah*, 'Yoreh de'ah' 116: 1, quoting Horowitz, *Shenei luḥot haberit*, that while uncovered drinks are halakhically permitted, it is advisable to refrain from drinking them; Ganzfried, *Kitsur shulḥan arukh*, 33: 5

BACKGROUND DATA ON RESPONDENTS

Table A.IV.1 Affiliation and age breakdown of respondents

Affiliation	Total number		Age group	n
Ashkenazi	89		18–30	14
Sephardi	5		31–40	17
			41–50	15
Mixed	4		51–60	25
Unknown	2		61–70	18
			71+	10
Total	100		Unstated	1[a]

[a] Assigned to the 61–70 group on the basis of personal knowledge.

Table A.IV.2 Place of birth of respondents

Place of birth	No. of respondents
Australia	2
Belgium	1
Canada	2
Gibraltar	1
Iraq	1
Israel	4
Netherlands	1
South Africa	5
United Kingdom	78
USA	1
Zimbabwe	1

Table A.IV.3 Countries accounting individually for less than 3% of respondents' grandparents (17% of sample)

Grandparents' country of birth	No. of grandparents	Percentage of all grandparents
Algeria	1	0.25
Australia	1	0.25
Belgium	3	0.75
Canada	2	0.50
Dutch East Indies	1	0.25
Egypt	2	0.50
France	3	0.75
Gibraltar	3	0.75
Greece	3	0.75
Hungary	11	2.75
Iran	1	0.25
Iraq	4	1.00
Israel/Palestine	2	0.50
Morocco	6	1.50
Netherlands	5	1.25
South Africa	8	2.00
Turkey	5	1.25
USA	7	1.75

GLOSSARY

'Adon olam' 'Lord of the world', concluding hymn of sabbath morning service

agunah (pl. *agunot*) 'chained woman', i.e. a wife who is unable to obtain a divorce from her recalcitrant or absent husband

ahavat yisra'el love of the Jewish people

aliyah (pl. *aliyot*) 'ascent', ritual of calling up an individual to recite blessings before and after the reading of a section of the weekly Torah portion

Amidah central prayer of eighteen blessings, recited three times daily

am yisra'el the Jewish people

aufruf the bridegroom's call-up to the Torah on the sabbath before his wedding

ba'al teshuvah (fem. *ba'alat teshuvah*; pl. *ba'alei/ba'alot teshuvah*) 'master of repentance'; newly religious man/woman

bat ḥayil 'daughter of valour', group ceremony marking girls' religious majority

beit din (Ashkenazi pronunciation: *beis din*, also *beth din*) rabbinic court

beli ayin hara 'no evil eye', an apotropaic expression

bentsh (Yid.) to recite the Grace after Meals

berakhah (pl. *berakhot*) blessing

berakhah aḥaronah 'final blessing', recited after eating or drinking

berit milah circumcision

bimah the central podium from which prayers are led and where the Torah is read

birkat hamazon Grace after Meals

birkhot hashaḥar 'dawn blessings', first part of the morning service

blay gisn (Yid.) the practice of detecting and removing the influence of the evil eye by pouring molten lead into water

challah (pl. **challot**) the braided loaves used for the sabbath, derived from the Hebrew word for dough, *ḥalah*

cheder classes in Hebrew and religious practice organized by synagogues for the children of their members on Sunday mornings and sometimes on weekdays after school

cholent (Yid.) traditional sabbath dish designed to cook slowly from Friday afternoon to Saturday lunchtime

darkhei ha'emori 'ways of the Amorite', magical practices

dati le'umi 'national religious' or religious Zionist, a subgroup of Israeli Orthodoxy

daven (Yid.) pray

dayan (pl. *dayanim*) judge in a rabbinic court (*beit din*)

derashah (pl. *derashot*) sermon

devar torah short sermon

eruv a halakhically defined construction linking private and public areas that permits Jews to carry objects and children in public areas on the sabbath

eshet ḥayil 'woman of valour', the opening words of a biblical poem praising women (Prov. 30: 10–31); by extension, a respected Jewish woman. Recently also used as the honorific title awarded to valued female members of the community on Simhat Torah

frum (Yid.) pious, strictly Orthodox

gelilah the rolling up of the Torah scroll after the Torah reading is completed

gemaḥ acronym of *gemilut ḥasadim*, 'the granting of kindnesses', i.e. loan association

grager (Yid.) rattle used on Purim during the Megillah reading

hafrashat ḥalah commandment to separate the first portion of dough when baking bread

haftarah weekly reading from the Prophets

ḥagim religious festivals

hakafah (pl. *hakafot*) circumambulations on **Simhat Torah**, during which all the synagogue's Torah scrolls are carried in procession, often with energetic dancing, around the prayer hall

halakhah Jewish law

ḥamets 'leaven', and by extension food that is not kosher for Passover

ḥamsa (Arab.) 'five', an apotropaic charm in the shape of a hand

haredi (pl. **haredim**) lit. 'trembling' (i.e. before God), the Hebrew term for 'ultra-Orthodox' or 'strictly Orthodox', used here in preference to both

Hashem 'the Name', a respectful euphemism employed to avoid everyday use of holy Hebrew names for God

hashkafah (pl. *hashkafot*) outlook or world-view

hashkamah early service, scheduled before the main synagogue prayers

hasid (pl. **hasidim**) 'pious one', adherent of a spiritually focused movement originating in eighteenth-century eastern Europe

ḥatan bridegroom

Havdalah 'separation', ceremony concluding the sabbath employing wine, spices, and a candle

ḥazan, ḥazanut cantor, cantorial music

ḥesed 'loving-kindness', welfare activity

hesped (pl. *hespedim*) eulogy

ḥumash a Torah in printed form, as opposed to the Sefer Torah, which is a scroll; the printed form makes it convenient for use in the home or synagogue. The term derives from the Hebrew for 'five' (*ḥamesh*), a reference to the Five Books of Moses (also known as the Pentateuch)

ḥupah wedding canopy

kabalat shabat Friday night sequence of prayers welcoming the sabbath

Kaddish mourner's prayer

kalah bride

kashering process of salting meat to remove blood in order to render it kosher; also the ritual cleansing of utensils that are not kosher

kashrut the laws and customs relating to kosher food

kavanah (pl. *kavanot*) 'intention'; either devotion and concentration in prayer or a specific intention made before reciting a blessing or prayer

Kedushah 'holiness', antiphonal doxology recited during the repetition of the Amidah prayer

ketubah marriage contract

kever grave

Kiddush 'sanctification'; recitation of the sabbath blessing over wine; by extension, snacks served following this ritual after the sabbath morning synagogue service

kishuf magic, witchcraft

kolel institution at which married men study Torah

kvater (masc.), *kvaterin* (fem.) (Yid.) at a circumcision ceremony, the man and woman who pass the baby from the mother to the *mohel* (circumciser)

le'ilui neshamah 'for the elevation of the soul'

leshon hara 'evil speech', gossip

leyn, leyning (Yid.) reading the Torah, *haftarah*, or **Megillah** in the traditional chant

ma'ariv evening service, recited daily

malakh angel

Megillah book of Esther, chanted on Purim

meḥitsah partition dividing men and women in the synagogue

menorah seven-branched candelabrum, one of the accessories in the Jerusalem Temple

mezuzah (pl. *mezuzot*) parchment bearing three biblical texts, affixed in a protective case to the right doorpost of a house or room, to fulfil a biblical commandment

mikveh (pl. *mikvaot*) ritual bath

minhag (pl. *minhagim*) custom

minhag ta'ut (pl. *minhagei ta'ut*) erroneous custom

minḥah afternoon service, recited daily

minyan (pl. *minyanim*) prayer quorum of ten adult men; also a group of people who meet for prayer services in a private home or a rented venue

mishlo'aḥ manot food gifts presented to friends on Purim

mitzvah (pl. mitzvot) commandment, meritorious act

'**Modeh ani**' 'I thank you', prayer said upon awakening

musaf additional service, recited on the sabbath and festivals

nidah menstrual impurity

'**Nishmat**' prayer recited as part of the sabbath morning service, and at other times as a *segulah*, particularly by Sephardim

omer sequence of 49 days, each counted with a blessing, from Passover to Shavuot

parashah (pl. *parashot/parashiyot*) weekly portion of the Torah read in synagogue

parnasah livelihood

partnership *minyan* new type of service in which women lead parts of the liturgy and read the Torah

pasuk (pl. *pesukim*) biblical verse

Pesach Passover

pesukei dezimrah 'verses of song', the second section of the morning service

Purim minor festival during which the **Megillah** (book of Esther) is ceremonially read and gifts of food (*mishlo'aḥ manot*) are presented to friends

rebbetsin (Yid.) rabbi's wife

Rosh Hashanah 'head of the year', New Year festival, lasting two days

Rosh Hodesh 'head of the month', New Moon, a minor festival traditionally associated with women

Seder ceremonial meal with accompanying liturgy celebrated on Passover Eve

sefer book or scroll

segulah charm, remedy, blessing

Shabat (also *shabes*) sabbath

shabaton communal sabbath programme with special events

Shavuot 'weeks', biblically prescribed festival to celebrate the beginning of the harvest, and later the giving of the Torah; the name refers to the seven weeks that pass between Passover and Shavuot

sheloshim 'thirty', mourning period during the first thirty days after a death

Shema central prayer, composed of Deut. 6: 4–9, 11: 13–21, and Num. 15: 37–41

Shemini Atseret closing festival of the autumn festive cycle

sheva berakhot 'seven blessings', the seven nights of festive gatherings after a wedding, at which a sequence of seven nuptial blessings is recited over wine

shiur traditional learning session

shivah 'seven', the first seven days of the mourning period

shul (Yid.) synagogue

simḥah 'joy', often used to refer to a life-cycle event such as a wedding

simḥat bat 'rejoicing in a daughter', ritual celebrating the birth of a girl

Simhat Torah Rejoicing in the Torah, festival celebrating the end and new beginning of the Torah-reading cycle

sukkah 'booth', a temporary structure in which Jews are commanded to reside during the festival of **Sukkot**

Sukkot Tabernacles, seven-day biblical festival celebrating the autumn harvest

taharat hamishpaḥah 'family purity', ritual purity system governing sexual relations

talit prayer shawl, with ritual fringes (*tsitsit*) attached to all four corners

tefilah (pl. *tefilot*) prayer

tefilin phylacteries; small leather boxes containing biblical texts written on parchment, worn on weekdays on the head and arm to fulfil a biblical commandment

tehilim psalms

tena'im 'conditions', non-obligatory ceremony in which two sets of parents agree to their children's marriage

Tishah Be'av Fast of the Ninth of Av, commemorating the destruction of the First and Second Temples

tkhines (Yid.) (from Heb. *teḥinah*, supplication), women's informal prayers, composed in Yiddish from the sixteenth century onwards

treyf (Yid.) non-kosher food

tsanua modest

tsedakah charity

tseni'ut modesty (Yid. *tsnius*)

tsitsit ritual fringes on four-cornered garments, worn in fulfilment of a biblical commandment

Tu Bishvat Fifteenth of Shevat, the new year of trees, when nature and its fruits are celebrated, often with a kabbalistic *seder* (a fruit-based ritual meal)

yahrzeit (Yid.) anniversary of the death of a close relative

yeshiva traditional institution for talmudic learning

yeshuot 'salvations', salvific events or miracles

Yizkor memorial service for the dead held on major festivals

Yom Kippur Day of Atonement, festival and fast day

zekhut merit; performing a commandment or a good deed in someone else's
zekhut means that one passes on the merit thus accrued to the other person

zeved bat traditional Sephardi celebration of the birth of a baby girl

zikhrono livrakhah 'May his memory be a blessing': a phrase used of the dead

BIBLIOGRAPHY

ABRAMSON, SARAH, DAVID GRAHAM, and JONATHAN BOYD, *Key Trends in the British Jewish Community: A Review of Data on Poverty, the Elderly, and Children* (London: Institute for Jewish Policy Research, 2011); available on the JPR website (accessed 25 July 2018).

ADELMAN, PENINA V., *Miriam's Well: Rituals for Jewish Women Around the Year*, 2nd edn. (New York: Biblio Press, 1990).

ADLER, RACHEL, *Engendering Judaism: An Inclusive Theology and Ethics* (Lincoln: University of Nebraska Press, 1998).

ALDERMAN, GEOFFREY, *Modern British Jewry* (Oxford: Clarendon Press, 1992).

—— '"Safe" Choice Is Probably the Last', *Jewish Chronicle* (24 Dec. 2012).

—— 'Yes, Bury the Absurd Eulogy Rule', *Jewish Chronicle* (21 Aug. 2008).

ALEXANDER, ELIZABETH SHANKS, *Gender and Timebound Commandments in Judaism* (Cambridge: Cambridge University Press, 2013).

ALFASSA, SHELOMO, 'Origins of the Non-Jewish Custom of "Shlissel Challah" (Key Bread): The Loaf of Idolatry?'; <http://www.mesora.org/Shlissel.html> (accessed 12 June 2014).

ALKALAI, REUVEN, *Complete Hebrew–English Dictionary* [Milon ivri–angli shalem] (Ramat Gan: Masada, n.d.).

AMMERMAN, NANCY, *Sacred Stories, Spiritual Tribes: Finding Religion in Everyday Life* (Oxford: Oxford University Press, 2013).

ARANOFF, SUSAN, and RIVKA HAUT, *The Wed-Locked Agunot: Orthodox Jewish Women Chained to Dead Marriages* (Jefferson, NC: McFarland and Co., 2015).

ARDENER, EDWIN, 'Belief and the Problem of Women', in Shirley Ardener (ed.), *Perceiving Women* (London: Malaly Press, 1975), 1–17.

Authorised Daily Prayer Book, with translation and commentary by Jonathan Sacks (London: Collins, 2007).

BASKIN, JUDITH R., 'From Separation to Displacement: The Problem of Women in *Sefer Hasidim*', *AJS Review*, 19/1 (1994), 1–18.

—— (ed.), *Jewish Women in Historical Perspective* (Detroit: Wayne State University Press, 1991).

BASS, CAROLINE, 'Women-Only Services Planned', *Jewish Chronicle* (6 Nov. 1992).

BAUMEL-SCHWARTZ, JUDY, '"It is Our Custom from *Der alter Heim*": The Role of Orthodox Jewish Women's Internet Forums in Reinventing and Transmitting Historical and Religious Tradition', *Journal of Jewish Identities*, 6/1 (Jan. 2013), 23–56.

BAUMGARTEN, ELISHEVA, *Mothers and Children: Jewish Family Life in Medieval Europe* (Princeton: University Press, 2004).

BEBERGAL, PETER, 'Birds of Ill Omen?', *Jewish Quarterly*, 53 (2006), 59–62.

BECHER, HARRIET, STANLEY WATERMAN, BARRY KOSMIN, and KATARINA THOMSON, *A Portrait of Jews in London and the South-East: A Community Study* (London: Institute for Jewish Policy Research, 2002); available on the JPR website (accessed 16 Oct. 2013).

BECHER, RONNIE, and BAT SHEVA MARCUS, 'Women's Tefillah Movement: How Orthodox Women Found a Halachic Way to be Involved in Services', Jewish Women's Archive website (accessed 18 Aug. 2014).

BELENKY, MARY, BLYTHE CLINCY, NANCY GOLDBERGER, and JILL TARULE, *Women's Ways of Knowing: The Development of Self and Voice and Mind* (New York: Basic Books, 1986).

BELL, CATHERINE, *Ritual Theory, Ritual Practice* (Oxford: Oxford University Press, 1992).

BENOR, SARAH BUNIN, *Becoming Frum: How Newcomers Learn the Language and Culture of Orthodox Judaism* (New Brunswick, NJ: Rutgers University Press, 2012).

'BEN YITZCHOK' (pseud.), 'A Courageous Stand', *Jewish Tribune* (1 Feb. 1993).

BERKOVIC, SALLY, *Under My Hat* (London: Joseph's Bookstore, 1997).

BERMANT, CHAIM, 'Time for Chief to be a Man about Women', *Jewish Chronicle* (20 Nov. 1992).

—— *Troubled Eden: An Anatomy of British Jewry* (London: Vallentine Mitchell, 1969).

BERRIN, SUSAN (ed.), *Celebrating the New Moon: A Rosh Chodesh Anthology* (Northvale, NJ: Jason Aronson, 1996).

BIALE, RACHEL, *Women and Jewish Law: The Essential Texts, Their History, and Their Relevance for Today* (New York: Schocken Books, 1984).

BLOCH, ANNA, and BRENDA BLOCH, 'Mother and Daughter Reflect on Their First Mikveh Experience' (18 July 2016); My Jewish Learning website (accessed 28 July 2016).

BLUTINGER, JEFFREY C., '"So-Called Orthodoxy": The History of an Unwanted Label', *Modern Judaism*, 27 (2007), 310–28.

BOHAK, GIDEON, *Ancient Jewish Magic: A History* (Cambridge: Cambridge University Press, 2008).

BORSCHEL-DAN, AMANDA, 'Orthodox, Separate—And Almost Equal', *The Times of Israel* (21 Nov. 2013; accessed 19 July 2018).

BOYARIN, DANIEL, *Carnal Israel: Reading Sex in Talmudic Culture* (Berkeley: University of California Press, 1993).

BRAV, AARON, 'The Evil Eye among the Hebrews', in Alan Dundes (ed.), *The Evil Eye: A Folklore Casebook* (New York: Garland Publishing, 1981), 44–54.

BREITOWITZ, IRVING A., *Between Civil and Religious Law: The Plight of the Agunah in American Society* (Westport, Conn.: Praeger, 1993).

BRILL, ALAN, 'Schlissel Challah, Bread Baking, and the Relief of Anxiety: An Update', *The Book of Doctrines and Opinions: Notes on Jewish Theology and Spirituality* blog (10 Apr. 2018; accessed 22 May 2018).

BRONNER, SIMON, and CASPAR BATTEGAY (eds.), *Connected Jews: Expressions of Community in Analogue and Digital Culture*, Jewish Cultural Studies 6 (London: Littman Library of Jewish Civilization, 2018).

BROOK, STEPHEN, *The Club: The Jews of Modern Britain* (London: Pan, 1990).

BROOTEN, BERNADETTE J., *Women Leaders in the Ancient Synagogue: Inscriptional Evidence and Background Issues* (Chico, Calif.: Scholars Press, 1982).

BROWN, ERICA S., 'The Bat Mitzvah in Jewish Law and Contemporary Practice', in Micah D. Halpern and Chana Safrai (eds.), *Jewish Legal Writings by Women* (Jerusalem: Urim Publications, 1998), 232–58.

BROWN, JEREMY, 'Chullin 22b: Yellow Pigeons, Folk Medicine, and Hepatitis', *Talmudology* blog (19 Dec. 2018; accessed 3 Sept. 2019).

CARREL, BARBARA GOLDMAN, 'Hasidic Women's Head Coverings: A Feminized System of Hasidic Distinction', in Linda B. Arthur (ed.), *Religion, Dress, and the Body* (Oxford: Berg, 1999), 163–79.

CHEN, SHOSHANA, 'The Amen Chorus', Ynet News website (2 Apr. 2007; accessed 25 Aug. 2011).

CLIFFORD, JAMES, and GEORGE MARCUS (eds.), *Writing Culture* (Berkeley: University of California Press, 1986).

COHEN, ANTHONY P., *The Symbolic Construction of Community* (London: Routledge, 1985).

COHEN, SHAYE J. D. 'Purity and Piety: The Separation of Menstruants from the Sancta', in Susan Grossman and Rivka Haut (eds.), *Daughters of the King: Women and the Synagogue* (Philadelphia: Jewish Publication Society, 1992), 103–13.

—— 'Purity, Piety, and Polemic: Medieval Rabbinic Denunciations of "Incorrect" Purification Practices', in id., *The Significance of Yavneh and Other Essays in Jewish Hellenism* (Tübingen: Mohr Siebeck, 2010), 416–34.

COUSINEAU, JENNIFER, 'The Domestication of Urban Jewish Space and the North-West London Eruv', in Simon J. Bronner (ed.), *Jews at Home: The Domestication of Identity*, Jewish Cultural Studies 2 (Oxford: Littman Library of Jewish Civilization, 2010), 43–74.

DAVIDMAN, LYNN, *Tradition in a Rootless World: Women Turn to Orthodox Judaism* (Oakland: University of California Press, 1993).

DAY, GRAHAM, *Community and Everyday Life* (London: Routledge, 2006).

DELLAPERGOLA, SERGIO, 'World Jewish Population, 2016', *American Jewish Year Book* (2016); available on the ResearchGate website (accessed 14 May 2018).

DIAMOND, JAMES A., 'Maimonides contra Kabbalah', review of Menachem Kellner, *Maimonides' Confrontation with Mysticism, Meorot*, 6 (2007), 1–11.

DUBOV, NISSAN DOVID, 'What Is the Role of the Woman in Judaism?'; chabad.org website (accessed 28 July 2016).

DUNDES, ALAN (ed.), *The Evil Eye: A Folklore Casebook* (New York: Garland Publishing, 1981).

EBNER, SARAH, 'Give Girls a Real Batmitzvah Experience', *Jewish Chronicle* (11 Jan. 2014).

EISENSTEIN, Y. D., *Otsar dinim uminhagim* (New York, 1917).

ELBOGEN, ISMAR, *Jewish Liturgy: A Comprehensive History*, trans. Raymond P. Scheindlin (Philadelphia: Jewish Publication Society, 1993).

ELEFF, ZEV, and MENACHEM BUTLER, 'How Bat Mitzvah Became Orthodox', Torah Musings website (accessed 24 Apr. 2019).

ELIMELEKH OF LYZHANSK, *No'am elimelekh*, ed. Gedaliah Nigal, 2 vols. (Jerusalem, 1978).

ELIOR, RACHEL, 'Like Sophia and Marcelle and Lizzie', in ead., *Dybbuks and Jewish Women in Social History, Mysticism, and Folklore* (Jerusalem: Urim Publications, 2008), 13–43.

ELON, MENAHEM, *Jewish Law: History, Sources, Principles*, trans. Bernard Auerbach and Melvin Sykes, 4 vols. (Philadelphia: Jewish Publication Society, 2003).

EL-OR, TAMAR, *Educated and Ignorant: Ultraorthodox Jewish Women and Their World*, trans. Haim Watzman (Boulder, Colo.: Lynne Rienner, 1994).

—— *Next Year I Will Know More: Literacy and Identity among Young Orthodox Women in Israel*, trans. Haim Watzman (Detroit: Wayne State University Press, 2002).

—— 'A Temple in Your Kitchen: Hafrashat Hallah—The Rebirth of a Forgotten Ritual as a Public Ceremony', in Ra'anan S. Boustan, Oren Kosansky, and Marina Rustow (eds.), *Jewish Studies at the Crossroads of Anthropology and History: Authority, Diaspora, and Tradition* (Philadelphia: University of Pennsylvania Press, 2011), 271–93.

ENDELMAN, TODD, *The Jews of Britain 1656–2000* (Berkeley: University of California Press, 2002).

—— *Radical Assimilation in English Jewish History, 1656–1945* (Bloomington: Indiana University Press, 1990).

FADER, AYALA, *Mitzvah Girls: Bringing Up the Next Generation of Hasidic Jews in Brooklyn* (Princeton: Princeton, NJ University Press, 2009).

FALK, PESACH ELIYAHU, *Modesty: An Adornment for Life* (Gateshead: Philipp Feldheim, 1998).

FEFFERMAN, DAN, *Rising Streams: Reform and Conservative Judaism in Israel*, Jewish People Policy Institute website (2018; accessed 15 July 2019).

FISHMAN, SYLVIA BARACK, Foreword in Elana Sztokman, *The Men's Section: Orthodox Jewish Men in an Egalitarian World* (Waltham, Mass.: Brandeis University Press, 2011), pp. ix–xvi.

FRAM, EDWARD, *My Dear Daughter: Rabbi Benjamin Slonik and the Education of Jewish Women in Sixteenth-Century Poland* (Cincinnati, Ohio: Hebrew Union College Press, 2007).

FRANCIS, DORIS, LEONIE KELLAHER, and GEORGINA NEOPHTOU, *The Secret Cemetery* (Oxford: Berg, 2005).

FREUD-KANDEL, MIRI, *Orthodox Judaism in Britain since 1913* (London: Vallentine Mitchell, 2006).

—— and BEVERLEY PARIS, 'Partners in Prayer: A Recipe for Success', *JOFA's Torch* blog (18 Nov. 2013), My Jewish Learning website (accessed 19 July 2018).

FRIEDMAN, MENACHEM, 'The Lost *Kiddush* Cup: Changes in Ashkenazic Ḥaredi Culture—A Tradition in Crisis', in Jack Wertheimer (ed.), *The Uses of Tradition: Jewish Continuity in the Modern Era* (New York: Jewish Theological Seminary of America, 1992), 175–86.

FRIMER, ARYEH A., 'Women's *Megilla* Reading', in Ora Wiskind-Elper (ed.), *Traditions and Celebrations for the Bat Mitzvah* (Jerusalem: Urim Publications, 2003), 281–304.

FUCHS, ILAN, *Jewish Women's Torah Study: Orthodox Religious Education and Modernity* (London: Routledge, 2014).

GILBEY, JULIAN, 'A Response to Rabbi Kimche's Essay: "Let's Be Honest About Limmud"', <https://www.d-and-j.net/jdg/Limmud/Limmud-response.pdf>.

GOLDBERG, HARVEY E., *Jewish Passages: Cycles of Jewish Life* (Berkeley: University of California Press, 2003).

GOLDIN, SIMHA, *Jewish Women in Europe in the Middle Ages: A Quiet Revolution* (Manchester: Manchester University Press, 2011).

GOLINKIN, DAVID, 'Does Jewish Law Permit Taking a Census?', *Responsa in a Moment*, 3/4 (Dec. 2008); available on the Schechter Institute website (accessed 2 Apr. 2014).

—— '"Kol B'ishah Ervah": Is It Really Forbidden for Jewish Men to Listen to Women Singing?', *Responsa in a Moment*, 6/2 (Nov. 2011), available on the Schechter Institute website (accessed 11 Aug. 2019).

—— 'The Participation of Jewish Women in Public Rituals and Torah Study 1845–2010', *Nashim*, 21 (2011), 46–66.

—— 'Why Do Some Jews Recite a Special Verse at the End of the Amidah?', *Responsa in a Moment*, 4/5 (Apr. 2010); available on the Schechter Institute website (accessed 6 July 2014).

GORSETMAN, CHAYA, and ELANA MARYLES SZTOKMAN, *Educating in the Divine Image: Gender Issues in Orthodox Jewish Day Schools* (Waltham, Mass.: Hadassah-Brandeis Institute, 2013).

GOSLINGA, GILLIAN, and GELYA FRANK, 'In the Shadows: Anthropological Encounters with Modernity', in Athena McLean and Annette Leibing (eds.), *The Shadow Side of Fieldwork: Exploring the Borders between Ethnography and Life* (Oxford: Blackwell, 2007), pp. xi–xviii.

GRAHAM, DAVID, *2011 Census Results (England and Wales): Initial Insights into Jewish Neighbourhoods* (London: Institute for Jewish Policy Research, Feb. 2013); available on the JPR website (accessed 25 July 2018).

—— *2011 Census Results (England and Wales): A Tale of Two Jewish Populations* (London: Institute for Jewish Policy Research, July 2013); available on the JPR website (accessed 25 July 2018).

—— *Britain's Israeli Diaspora: A Demographic Portrait* (London: Institute for Jewish Policy Research, 2015); available on the JPR website (accessed 25 July 2018).

GRAHAM, DAVID, *Secular or Religious? The Outlook of London's Jews* (London: Institute for Jewish Policy Research, 2003); available on the JPR website (accessed 25 July 2018).

——and JONATHAN BOYD, *Committed, Concerned, and Conciliatory: The Attitudes of Jews in Britain towards Israel* (London: Institute for Jewish Policy Research, 2010); available on the JPR website (accessed 6 Nov. 2018).

———— and DANIEL VULKAN, *2011 Census Results (England and Wales): Initial Insights about the UK Jewish Population* (London: Institute for Jewish Policy Research, 2012); available on the JPR website (accessed 25 July 2018).

GRENBY, JAY, 'St Albans Woman in Breakthrough United Synagogue Election', *Jewish Chronicle* (29 Apr. 2013).

GROSSMAN, AVRAHAM, *Pious and Rebellious: Jewish Women in Medieval Europe*, trans. Jonathan Chipman (Lebanon, NH: Brandeis University Press, 2004).

HALE, CHARLES R., 'In Praise of "Reckless Minds": Making a Case for Activist Anthropology', in L. Field and R. G. Fox (eds.), *Anthropology Put to Work* (Oxford: Berg, 2007), 103–27.

HAMMER, GAIL, 'The Amen Phenomenon', Jewish Action website (Summer 2007; accessed 25 Aug. 2011).

HAMMER, JILL, 'Holle's Cry: Unearthing a Birth Goddess in a German Jewish Naming Ceremony', *Nashim*, 9 (2005), 62–87.

HANDELMAN, SUSAN, 'Women and the Study of Torah in the Thought of the Lubavitcher Rebbe', in Micah D. Halpern and Chana Safrai (eds.), *Jewish Legal Writings by Women* (Jerusalem: Urim Publications, 1998), 143–78.

HARARI, YUVAL, *Early Jewish Magic: Research, Method, Sources* [Hakishuf hayehudi hakadum: meḥkar, shitah, mekorot] (Jerusalem: Yad Yitshak Ben-Tsevi, 2010).

HARRIS, MICHAEL J., *Faith without Fear: Unresolved Issues in Modern Orthodoxy* (London: Vallentine Mitchell, 2016).

HARTMAN, TOVA, *Feminism Encounters Traditional Judaism: Resistance and Accommodation* (Waltham, Mass.: Brandeis University Press, 2007).

HAUT, RIVKA, 'Women's Prayer Groups and the Orthodox Synagogue', in Susan Grossman and Rivka Haut (eds.), *Daughters of the King: Women and the Synagogue* (Philadelphia: Jewish Publication Society, 1992), 135–57.

HEELAS, PAUL, and LINDA WOODHEAD, *The Spiritual Revolution: Why Religion Is Giving Way to Spirituality* (Oxford: Blackwell, 2005).

HEILMAN, SAMUEL C., *Sliding to the Right: The Contest for the Future of American Jewish Orthodoxy* (Berkeley: University of California Press, 2006).

HESCHEL, ABRAHAM JOSHUA, *Ohev yisra'el* (Zhitomir, 1863).

HINDS, DIANA, 'Women-Only Worship Splits Orthodox Jews', *Independent* (26 Nov. 1992).

HIRSCH, RONA S., 'N.Y. Kabbalist Combs Ketubot for Mistakes', J. The Jewish News of Northern California website (13 June 1997; accessed 2 July 2014).

HOFFMAN, C. A., 'Fiat Magia', in Paul Mirecki and Marvin Meyer (eds.), *Magic and Ritual in the Ancient World* (Leiden: Brill, 2002), 179–94.

HUBERT, MARTHA, *A Jewish Woman's Handbook* (Blackpool [1975]).

HYMAN, PAULA, 'The Introduction of Bat Mitzvah in Conservative Judaism in Postwar America', *YIVO Annual of Jewish Social Science*, 19 (1990), 133–46.

INGE, ANABEL, *The Making of a Salafi Muslim Woman: Paths to Conversion* (Oxford: Oxford University Press, 2017).

Institute of Jewish Policy Research, *New Conceptions of Community* (London: JPR, 2010); available on the JPR website (accessed 23 Jan. 2014).

'Interesting Psak from Rav Elyashiv: 40 Days of Davening at the Kotel', *Life in Israel* blog (8 Nov. 2009; accessed 31 July 2016).

ISAAC OF TYRNAU, *Sefer minhagim* (Venice, 1566); available online at <http://www.seforimonline.org/seforimdb/pdf/72.pdf> (accessed 20 Aug. 2014).

ISRAEL ME'IR HAKOHEN, *Mishnah berurah*, 6 vols. (1884–1907; many edns.).

JACOBS, LOUIS, *Helping with Inquiries: An Autobiography* (London: Vallentine Mitchell, 1989).

JAKOBOVITS, IMMANUEL, *Dear Chief Rabbi: From the Correspondence of Chief Rabbi Immanuel Jakobovits on Matters of Jewish Law, Ethics and Contemporary Issues, 1980–1990* (New York: Ktav, 1995).

—— 'From the Chief Rabbi's Correspondence Files', *L'eylah*, 28 (Sept. 1989), 22.

Jewish Leadership Council, *Inspiring Women Leaders: Advancing Gender Equality in Jewish Communal Life* (London: JLC, 2012); available on the Jewish Leadership Council website (accessed 23 Jan. 2014).

Jewish Orthodox Feminist Alliance, *JOFA Journal*, 5/4 (Summer 2005).

JOSEPH, NORMA BAUMEL, 'Bat Mitzvah: Historical and Halakhic Aspects', *JOFA Journal* (Fall 2010), 4–5, 49.

KALMS, STANLEY, *United Synagogue Review: A Time for Change* (London: Stanley Kalms Foundation, 1996).

KANARFOGEL, EPHRAIM, *'Peering through the Lattices': Mystical, Magical, and Pietistic Dimensions in the Tosafist Period* (Detroit: Wayne State University Press, 2000).

KAPLAN, ARYEH, *Waters of Eden: The Mystery of the Mikveh* (New York: NCSY, 1993).

KAPLAN, MARION A., and DEBORAH DASH MOORE (eds.), *Gender and Jewish History* (Bloomington: Indiana University Press, 2011).

KAUFMAN, DEBRA, *Rachel's Daughters: Newly Orthodox Jewish Women* (New Brunswick, NJ: Rutgers University Press, 1991).

KELLNER, MENACHEM, *Maimonides' Confrontation with Mysticism* (Oxford: Littman Library of Jewish Civilization, 2006).

KERSHEN, ANNE J., and JONATHAN A. ROMAIN, *Tradition and Change: A History of Reform Judaism in Britain 1840–1995* (London: Vallentine Mitchell, 1995).

KIMCHE, ALAN, 'Let's Be Honest about Limmud' (18 Nov. 2013); the essay is no longer available at its original URL, but is quoted in full in Julian Gilbey, 'A Response to Rabbi Kimche's Essay: "Let's Be Honest About Limmud", <https://www.d-and-j.net/jdg/Limmud/Limmud-response.pdf>.

KLEIN, MICHELE, *A Time To Be Born: Customs and Folklore of Jewish Birth* (Philadelphia: Jewish Publication Society, 2000).

KNOX, HANNAH, 'Imitative Participation and the Politics of "Joining In": Paid Work as a Methodological Issue', *Anthropology Matters Journal*, 7/1 (2005), 1–9.

LAMM, MAURICE, *The Jewish Way in Death and Mourning* (New York: Jonathan David, 1979).

LANDES, DANIEL, 'The Reading of the Megilla on Purim Night', Elmad website (1 Feb. 1997; accessed 20 Aug. 2019).

LEE, SHARON, 'Women Await Halachic Ruling on Torah Use', *Jewish Chronicle* (7 Apr. 1995).

—— and DOREEN FINE, *Women's Tefilah Services: Some Personal Accounts by Women from the Stanmore Tefilah Group* ([London], 1994).

LE GUIN, URSULA K., 'Indian Uncles', in ead., *The Wave in the Mind: Talks and Essays on the Writer, the Reader, and the Imagination* (Boston, Mass.: Shambhala Publications, 2004), 10–19.

LEISSNER, OMI MORGENSTERN, 'Jewish Women's Naming Rites and the Rights of Jewish Women, *Nashim*, 4 (2001), 140–77.

LEVY, DAVID, 'The Orange on the Seder Plate and Miriam's Cup: Foregrounding Women at Your Seder'; Jewish Women's Archive website (accessed 21 July 2014).

LIEBER, ANDREA, 'A Virtual *Veibershul*: Blogging and the Blurring of Public and Private among Orthodox Jewish Women', *College English*, 72 (2010), 621–37.

LITTLEWOOD, ROLAND, *Religion, Agency, Restitution* (Oxford: Oxford University Press, 2001).

LORIE, MIRIAM, 'Partnership Minyanim, Banning, and Front Pages . . . Moving Forwards', *MiriamMuses* blog (17 Nov. 2016; accessed 26 June 2017).

LUHRMANN, T. M., *Persuasions of the Witch's Craft: Ritual Magic in Contemporary England* (Oxford: Blackwell, 1989).

McFADDEN, PATRICIA, 'Why Women's Spaces Are Critical to Feminist Autonomy', *Women in Action*, 1 (2001).

MAHMOOD, SABA, *Politics of Piety: The Islamic Revival and the Feminist Subject* (Princeton, NJ: Princeton University Press, 2005).

MALACH, GILAD, LEE CAHANER, and MAYA CHOSHEN, *Statistical Report on Ultra-Orthodox Society in Israel*, Israel Democracy Institute website (accessed 17 Jan. 2019).

MANSOUR, ELI, 'The Importance of Saying Amen', Pure Torah website (accessed 25 Aug. 2011).

MASHIAH, DONATELLA CASALE, *Vital Statistics of the UK Jewish Population: Births and Deaths* (London: Institute for Jewish Policy Research, 2018); available on the JPR website (accessed 25 July 2018).

—— and JONATHAN BOYD, *Synagogue Membership in the United Kingdom in 2016* (London: Institute for Jewish Policy Research, 2017); available on the JPR website (accessed 25 July 2018).

MAXTED, ANNA, 'Sacks Lends Support as Women's Service Thrives', *Jewish Chronicle* (14 May 1993).

MILLEN, ROCHELLE L., 'The Female Voice of Kaddish', in Micah D. Halpern and Chana Safrai (eds.), *Jewish Legal Writings by Women* (Jerusalem: Urim Publications, 1998), 179–201.

MILLER, STEPHEN, MARGARET HARRIS, and COLIN SHINDLER, *The Attitudes of British Jews towards Israel* (London: City University, 2015); available on the Yachad website (accessed 6 Nov. 2018).

——MARLENA SHMOOL, and ANTONY LERMAN, *Social and Political Attitudes of British Jews: Some Key Findings of the JPR Survey* (London: Institute for Jewish Policy Research, 1996); available on the JPR website (accessed 25 July 2018).

MOCK-DEGEN, MINNY E., *The Dynamics of Becoming Orthodox: Dutch Jewish Women Returning to Judaism and How Their Mothers Felt about It* (Amsterdam: Amphora Books, 2009).

MONCHI, VALERIE, 'Jerusalem Trio's Provocative Boost as the Yakar Centre Stages Pioneering Women's Seminar', *Jewish Chronicle* (5 May 1995).

——'"Overwhelming" Turnout at Pinner Women's Service', *Jewish Chronicle* (11 Feb. 1994).

——'Rebuke from Chief Rabbi Fails to Deter Women's Plan', *Jewish Chronicle* (18 Feb. 1994).

——'Women to Hold Second Service with Sefer Torah', *Jewish Chronicle* (5 Aug. 1994).

——and ANNA MAXTED, 'Women Make History amid Tears and Prayers', *Jewish Chronicle* (5 Mar. 1993).

MORRIS, BONNIE, 'Agents or Victims of Religious Ideology? Approaches to Locating Hasidic Women in Feminist Studies', in Janet S. Belcove-Shalin (ed.), *New World Hasidim: Ethnographic Studies of Hasidic Jews in America* (New York: State University of New York Press, 1995), 161–80.

——*Lubavitcher Women in America: Identity and Activism in the Postwar Era* (Albany, NY: State University of New York Press, 1998).

MOSS, LEONARD W., and STEPHEN C. CAPPANNARI, '*Mal'occhio, Ayin ha ra, Oculus Fascius, Judenblick*: The Evil Eye Hovers Above', in Clarence Maloney (ed.), *The Evil Eye* (New York: Columbia University Press, 1976), 1–15.

MURGOCI, A., 'The Evil Eye in Roumania', in Alan Dundes (ed.), *The Evil Eye: A Folklore Casebook* (New York: Garland Publishing, 1981), 124–9.

MYERHOFF, BARBARA, *Number Our Days* (New York: Touchstone, 1978).

NERIYA-BEN SHAHAR, RIVKA, '"At 'Amen Meals' It's Me and God": Religion and Gender: A New Jewish Women's Ritual', *Contemporary Jewry*, 5 (2015), 153–72.

Nishma Research, 'Starting a Conversation: A Pioneering Survey of Those Who Have Left the Orthodox Community: Summary Report', Nishma Research website (19 June 2016; accessed 22 June 2017).

NOGG, OZZIE, 'Shtetl Engagement Custom Makes Modern Comeback', *Jewish Journal* (10 Oct. 2008).

NUSBACHER, AILENE COHEN, 'Efforts at Change in a Traditional Denomination: The Case of Orthodox Women's Prayer Groups', *Nashim*, 2 (1999), 95–113.

—— 'Orthodox Jewish Women's Prayer Groups: Seeking a More Meaningful Religious Experience', *Le'eyla*, 49 (2000), 41–6.

OBEYESEKERE, GANETH, 'The Great Tradition and the Little in the Perspective of Sinhalese Buddhism', *Journal of Asian Studies*, 22 (1963), 139–53.

OHNUKI-TIERNEY, E., '"Native" Anthropologists', *American Ethnologist*, 11/3 (1984), 584–6.

OKELY, JUDITH, and HELEN CALLAWAY (eds.), *Anthropology and Autobiography* (London: Routledge, 1992).

OLIVER, CHARLOTTE, 'Ex-Charedi Women on How They Left the Fold', *Jewish Chronicle* (23 Dec. 2013).

OPIE, IONA, and MORIA TATEM, *A Dictionary of Superstitions* (Oxford: Oxford University Press, 1989).

ORTNER, SHELLEY, 'Ethnography among the Newark: The Class of '58 of Weequahic High School', *Michigan Quarterly Review*, 32/3 (1993), 411–29.

OSGOOD, KELSEY, 'After Years of Delay, Orthodox Women's EMT Corps Due to Launch in Brooklyn', Tablet website (27 May 2014; accessed 22 July 2014).

PATAI, RAPHAEL, *On Jewish Folklore* (Detroit: Wayne State University Press, 1983).

PATTON, MICHAEL QUINN, *Qualitative Research and Evaluation Methods* (Thousand Oaks, Calif.: Sage Publications, 2002).

Pew Research Center, 'Comparisons between Jews in Israel and the U.S.' (2016), Pew Research Center website (accessed 18 Jan. 2019).

—— *A Portrait of Jewish Americans* (2013), Pew Research Center website (accessed 18 Jan. 2019).

PINKNEY, JOHN, *A Paranormal File: An Australian Investigator's Casebook* (Richmond, Australia: Bonnier Publishing, 2000).

PLASKOW, JUDITH, *Standing Again at Sinai: Judaism from a Feminist Perspective* (New York: Harper, 1990).

POLLACK, HERMAN, *Jewish Folkways in Germanic Lands (1648–1806)* (Cambridge: Massachusetts Institute of Technology Press, 1971).

POMEROY, HILARY S., '"From the Cradle to the Grave": Life-Cycle Customs and Songs of the Sephardim', in Raphael Gatenio (ed.), *Judeo Espaniol: A Jewish Language in Search of its People* (Thessaloniki: Ets Ahaim Foundation, 2002), 63–74.

PORTNOY, EDWARD, 'Haredim and the Internet', Modiya Project, <https://modiya.nyu.edu/handle/1964/265> (accessed 9 Jan. 2014).

PRESTON, ROSALIND, *Connection, Continuity and Community: British Jewish Women Speak Out* (London: Board of Deputies of British Jews / Women's Review Task Force, 2009); available on the JPR website (accessed 28 Nov. 2019).

—— JUDY GOODKIN, and JUDITH CITRON, *Women in the Jewish Community: Review and Recommendations* [the Preston Report] (London: Women in the Community, 1994).

RAPHAEL, MELISSA, *The Female Face of God in Auschwitz: A Jewish Feminist Theology of the Holocaust* (London: Routledge, 2003).

—— 'The Impact of Gender on Jewish Religious Thought—Exemplar: Jewish Feminist Theology', Manchester Jewish Studies website (accessed 14 Nov. 2019).

RAPOPORT-ALBERT, ADA, *Women and the Messianic Heresy of Sabbatai Zevi 1666–1816* (Oxford: Littman Library of Jewish Civilization, 2011).

RAVITZKY, AVIEZER, '"The Ravings of Amulet Writers": Maimonides and his Disciples on Language, Nature, and Magic', in Ephraim Kanarfogel and Moshe Sokolow (eds.), *Between Rashi and Maimonides: Themes in Medieval Jewish Thought, Literature, and Exegesis* (New York: Yeshiva University Press, 2010), 93–130.

RAYNER, JOHN D., 'Women and Worship', *Jewish Chronicle* (19 Feb. 1993).

REDFIELD, ROBERT, *Peasant Society and Culture: An Anthropological Approach to Civilization* (Chicago: University of Chicago Press, 1956).

REGUER, SARA, 'Kaddish from the "Wrong" Side of the Mechitzah', in Susannah Heschel (ed.), *On Being a Jewish Feminist* (New York: Schocken, 1983), 177–81.

—— 'Women and the Synagogue in Medieval Cairo', in Susan Grossman and Rivka Haut (eds.), *Daughters of the King: Women and the Synagogue* (Philadelphia: Jewish Publication Society, 1992), 51–7.

REITMAN, OONAGH, 'On Exit', in Avigail Eisenberg and Jeff Spinner-Halev (eds.), *Minorities within Minorities: Equality, Rights, and Diversity* (Cambridge: Cambridge University Press, 2005), 189–208.

RIGAL, LAWRENCE, and ROSITA ROSENBERG, *Liberal Judaism: The First Hundred Years* (London: Union of Liberal and Progressive Synagogues, 2004).

ROCKER, SIMON, 'After Chairing Shuls, Women Could Soon Be US Trustees', *Jewish Chronicle* (14 Oct. 2013).

—— 'Beth Din: Why Women Are Not Called to Torah', *Jewish Chronicle* (26 Apr. 2012).

—— 'Chief Rabbi Mirvis Launches New Qualification for Female Educators', *Jewish Chronicle* (15 Feb. 2016).

—— '"Excluded" for Running Partnership Minyanim', *Jewish Chronicle* (17 Nov. 2016).

—— 'Expat and Excluded, Israelis in the UK', *Jewish Chronicle* (3 Apr. 2008).

—— 'How the Eruv Liberated Families on Shabbat', *Jewish Chronicle* (7 Feb. 2013).

—— 'Limmud Row Deepens after "Aberration" Slur', *Jewish Chronicle* (13 Nov. 2013).

—— 'London Synagogue Quits Strictly Orthodox Union over Halpern', *Jewish Chronicle* (2 Jan. 2013).

—— 'Modesty Hotline Launched by London Rabbis', *Jewish Chronicle* (2 May 2013).

—— 'Progress for Women at Federation Synagogues', *Jewish Chronicle* (9 May 2013).

—— 'Should Batmitzvah Girls Be Called to the Torah?', *Jewish Chronicle* (23 Jan. 2012).

—— 'Stanmore Women Meet in Shul at Last', *Jewish Chronicle* (16 Sept. 2011).

ROCKER, SIMON, 'Thousands Join in Challah Bake as Shabbat UK Gets Off to a Triumphant Start', *Jewish Chronicle* (24 Oct. 2014).

—— 'United Synagogue Rabbi Defends Restrictions on Partnership Minyan Leaders', *Jewish Chronicle* (18 Nov. 2016).

—— 'United Synagogue Says Yes to Women Leaders', *Jewish Chronicle* (6 Dec. 2012).

—— 'Where Have All the (US) Rabbis Gone?', *Jewish Chronicle* (10 Dec. 2015).

—— 'Why Can't My Girl Be Called to the Torah?', *Jewish Chronicle* (19 Jan. 2012).

—— 'Women to Lead Prayers at Partnership Minyan', *Jewish Chronicle* (2 Sept. 2013).

—— 'Women at Prayer Await Crowning Prize', *Jewish Chronicle* (27 Mar. 1998).

ROSNER, FRED, *Biomedical Ethics and Jewish Law* (Jersey City, NJ: Ktav, 2001).

ROSS, TAMAR, *Expanding the Palace of Torah: Orthodoxy and Feminism* (Waltham, Mass.: Brandeis University Press, 2004).

ROTEM, TAMAR, 'The Festival of Freedom? Not When You Have a House to Clean', *Haaretz* website (17 Apr. 2011; accessed 21 July 2014).

—— 'For Israelis Who Flee the Ultra-Orthodox Fold a Brave New World', *Haaretz* website (23 Jan. 2016; accessed 23 July 2018).

ROTHENBERG, RUTH, 'Stanmore Women Plan May Service', *Jewish Chronicle* (12 Mar. 1993).

ROTHSCHILD, SYLVIA, 'Undermining the Pillars that Support the Women's Gallery', in Sybil Sheridan (ed.), *Hear Our Voice: Women Rabbis Tell Their Stories* (London: SCM Press, 1994), 138–49.

ROY, OLIVIER, *Holy Ignorance: When Religion and Culture Part Ways* (Oxford: Oxford University Press, 2010).

RUBENSTEIN, JEFFREY L., *The Culture of the Babylonian Talmud* (Baltimore, Md.: Johns Hopkins University Press, 2005).

RUBIN, HERBERT J., and IRENE S. RUBIN, *Qualitative Interviewing: The Art of Hearing Data*, 2nd edn. (Thousand Oaks, Calif.: Sage Publications, 2005).

SABAR, SHALOM, 'Childbirth and Magic: Jewish Folklore and Material Change', in David Biale (ed.), *Cultures of the Jews: A New History* (New York: Random House, 2002), 671–722.

—— 'From Sacred Symbol to Key Ring: The Ḥamsa in Jewish and Israeli Societies', in Simon J. Bronner (ed.), *Jews at Home: The Domestication of Identity*, Jewish Cultural Studies 2 (Oxford: Littman Library of Jewish Civilization, 2010), 140–62.

SACKS, EVE, '"Ima shel Shabbat" and Other Gendered Moments in Jewish Preschool', *A Jewish Feminist*, blog (27 Nov. 2015; accessed 22 May 2018).

SACKS, JONATHAN, 'Women and Prayer', *New Moon* (Mar. 1993).

SALES, BEN, 'Why It's Easier to Ordain Orthodox Women in Israel than the US', *The Times of Israel* website (11 Oct. 2017; accessed 20 Aug. 2019).

SAMET, MOSHE, 'The Beginnings of Orthodoxy', *Modern Judaism*, 8 (1988), 249–69.

SASSON, AVI, 'From Unknown Saint to State Site: The Jewish Dimension in the Sanctification Process of Tombs in the State of Israel', in Marshall J. Breger, Yitshak Reiter, and Leonard Hammer (eds.), *Sacred Space in Israel and Palestine: Religion and Politics* (London: Routledge, 2012), 82–102.

SCHNEIDER, S. WEIDMAN, 'Jewish Women's Philanthropy. Part 1: Women's Giving to Jewish Organizations', *Lilith* (Winter 1992), 1–10.

SCHRIRE, THEODOR, *Hebrew Magic Amulets: Their Decipherment and Interpretation* (London: Routledge & Kegan Paul, 1966).

SERED, SUSAN STARR, *Women as Ritual Experts: The Religious Lives of Elderly Jewish Women in Jerusalem* (New York: Oxford University Press, 1992).

SHAPIRO, MARC, *The Limits of Orthodox Theology: Maimonides' Thirteen Principles Reappraised* (Oxford: Littman Library of Jewish Civilization, 2004).

SHERIDAN, SYBIL (ed.), *Hear Our Voice: Women Rabbis Tell Their Stories* (London: SCM Press, 1994).

SHOSHAN, ESTI, 'Obsession with Modesty Killing Us', *Ynet News* website (21 May 2013; accessed 28 July 2016).

SILBER, MICHAEL K., 'The Emergence of Ultra-Orthodoxy: The Invention of a Tradition', in Jack Wertheimer (ed.), *The Uses of Tradition: Jewish Continuity in the Modern Era* (New York: Jewish Theological Seminary of America, 1992), 23–83.

SIMMONDS, LINDSAY, 'Generating Piety: Agency and the Religious Subject', Ph.D. diss. (London School of Economics, 2020).

SLEE, NICOLA, 'Feminist Qualitative Research as Spiritual Practice: Reflections on the Process of Doing Qualitative Research', in Nicola Slee, Fran Porter, and Anne Phillips (eds.), *The Faith Lives of Women and Girls: Qualitative Research Perspectives* (London: Routledge, 2013), 13–24.

SOLOVEITCHIK, HAYM, 'Rupture and Reconstruction: The Transformation of Contemporary Orthodoxy', *Tradition*, 28/4 (Summer 1994), 64–131.

SOON KIM, C., 'Can an Anthropologist Go Home Again?', *American Anthropologist*, NS 89/4 (1987), 943–6.

SPERBER, DANIEL, 'Congregational Dignity and Human Dignity: Women and Public Torah Reading', in Chaim Trachtman (ed.), *Women and Men in Communal Prayer: Halakhic Perspectives* (New York: Jewish Orthodox Feminist Alliance, 2010), 27–205; available on the Edah website (accessed 27 Nov. 2019).

—— *Jewish Customs* [Minhagei yisra'el], 8 vols. (Jerusalem: Mosad Harav Kook, 1998–2007).

—— *The Jewish Life Cycle: Custom, Lore, and Iconography*, trans. Ed Levin (Ramat Gan: Bar-Ilan University Press, 2008).

SPERLING, AVRAHAM YITSHAK, *Sefer ta'amei haminhagim umekorei hadinim* (1890; Jerusalem, 1999).

STAETSKY, L. D., MARINA SHEPS, and JONATHAN BOYD, *Immigration from the United Kingdom to Israel* (London: Institute for Jewish Policy Research, 2013); available on the JPR website (accessed 6 Nov. 2018).

STAMPFER, SHAUL, 'Gender Differentation and the Education of Jewish Women', in id., *Families, Rabbis, and Education: Traditional Jewish Society in Nineteenth-Century Eastern Europe* (Oxford: Littman Library of Jewish Civilization, 2010), 167–89.

STEINBERG, BERNARD, 'Jewish Education in Great Britain during World War II', *Jewish Social Studies*, 29 (1967), 27–63.

STERN, ESTHER, *Just One Word: Amen* (Nanuet, NY: Feldheim, 2005).

SUSSER, BERNARD, *The History of the Willesden and Brondesbury Synagogue 1934–1994*, Jewishgen website (accessed 2 Oct. 2013).

SZTOKMAN, ELANA MARYLES, *The Men's Section: Orthodox Jewish Men in an Egalitarian World* (Waltham, Mass.: Brandeis University Press, 2011).

TAITZ, EMILY, 'Kol Ishah: The Voice of Women: Where Was It Heard in Medieval Europe?', *Conservative Judaism*, 38/3 (Spring 1986), 46–61.

—— 'Women's Voices, Women's Prayers: Women in the European Synagogues of the Middle Ages', in Susan Grossman and Rivka Haut (eds.), *Daughters of the King: Women and the Synagogue* (Philadelphia: Jewish Publication Society, 1992), 59–71.

TAMBIAH, STANLEY, *Magic, Science and Religion, and the Scope of Rationality*, Lewis Henry Morgan Lectures (Cambridge: Cambridge University Press, 1990).

TARLO, EMMA, *Visibly Muslim: Bodies of Faith* (Oxford: Berg, 2010).

TA-SHMA, ISRAEL M., *Early Franco-German Ritual and Custom* [Minhag ashkenaz hakadmon] (Jerusalem: Magnes Press, 1994).

—— *Ritual, Custom, and Reality in Franco-Germany, 1100–1350* [Halakhah, minhag umetsiyut be'ashkenaz 1100–1350] (Jerusalem: Magnes Press, 1996).

TEMAN, ELLY, 'The Red String: The Cultural History of a Jewish Folk Symbol', in Simon J. Bronner (ed.), *Jewishness: Expression, Identity, and Representation*, Jewish Cultural Studies 1 (Oxford: Littman Library of Jewish Civilization, 2008), 29–57.

TOLEDANO, YA'AKOV MOSHEH, *Sefer yam hagadol* (Cairo, 1931).

TRACHTENBERG, JOSHUA, *Jewish Magic and Superstition: A Study in Folk Religion* (New York: Behrman's Jewish Book House, 1939).

UMANSKY, ELLEN M., 'Spiritual Expressions: Jewish Women's Religious Lives in the United States in the Nineteenth and Twentieth Centuries', in Judith R. Baskin (ed.), *Jewish Women in Historical Perspective* (Detroit: Wayne State University Press), 265–88.

WACHMANN, DOREEN, 'Why Are Men So Scared to Let Women Hold Services in the Synagogue?', *Jewish Telegraph* (13 Nov. 1992).

WALBY, SYLVIA, *The Future of Feminism* (Cambridge: Polity, 2011).

WASSERFALL, RAHEL (ED.), *Women and Water: Menstruation in Jewish Life and Law* (Waltham, Mass.: Brandeis University Press, 1999).

WATERMAN, STANLEY, and BARRY KOSMIN, *British Jewry in the Eighties: A Statistical and Geographical Study* (London: Board of Deputies of British Jews, 1986).

Watson, Sophie, 'Symbolic Spaces of Difference: Contesting the Eruv in Barnet, London and Tenafly, New Jersey', *Environment and Planning D: Society and Space*, 23/4 (2005), 597–613.

Webber, Jonathan, 'Introduction', in id. (ed.), *Jewish Identities in the New Europe* (Oxford: Littman Library of Jewish Civilization, 1994), 1–32.

—— 'Modern Jewish Identities: The Ethnographic Complexities', *Journal of Jewish Studies*, 43 (1992), 246–67.

Weiss, Avraham, *Women at Prayer: A Halakhic Analysis of Women's Prayer Groups* (Hoboken, NJ: Ktav, 1990).

Weissler, Chava, *Voices of the Matriarchs: Listening to the Prayers of Early Modern Jewish Women* (Boston, Mass.: Beacon Press, 1998).

Wieseltier, Leon, *Kaddish* (London: Picador, 2000).

Winston, Hella, *Unchosen: The Hidden Lives of Hasidic Rebels* (Boston, Mass.: Beacon Press, 2006).

Wiskind-Elper, Ora (ed.), *Traditions and Ceremonies for the Bat Mitzvah* (Jerusalem: Urim Publications, 2003).

Wolfson, Judy, 'Fringe Festival', *New Moon* (Mar. 1993).

Wolowelsky, Joel B., 'Women and *Zimmun*', in Ora Wiskind-Elper (ed.), *Traditions and Celebrations for the Bat Mitzvah* (Jerusalem: Urim Publications, 2003), 256–68.

'Women Read Megilah', *Jewish Chronicle*, 24 Mar. 1995.

Zimmer, Eric (Yitshak), *Society and Its Customs: Studies in the History and Metamorphosis of Jewish Customs* [Olam keminhago noheg: perakim betoledot haminhagim, hilkhoteihem vegilguleihem] (Jerusalem: Zalman Shazar Centre, 1996).

Zivotofsky, Ari Z., 'Wine from Havdalah, Women and Beards', *Hakirah: The Flatbush Journal of Jewish Law and Thought*, 10 (2010), 175–87.

Zolty, Shoshana Pantel, *'And All Your Children Shall Be Learned': Women and the Study of Torah in Jewish Law and History* (Northvale, NJ: Jason Aronson, 1993).

INDEX